भारत

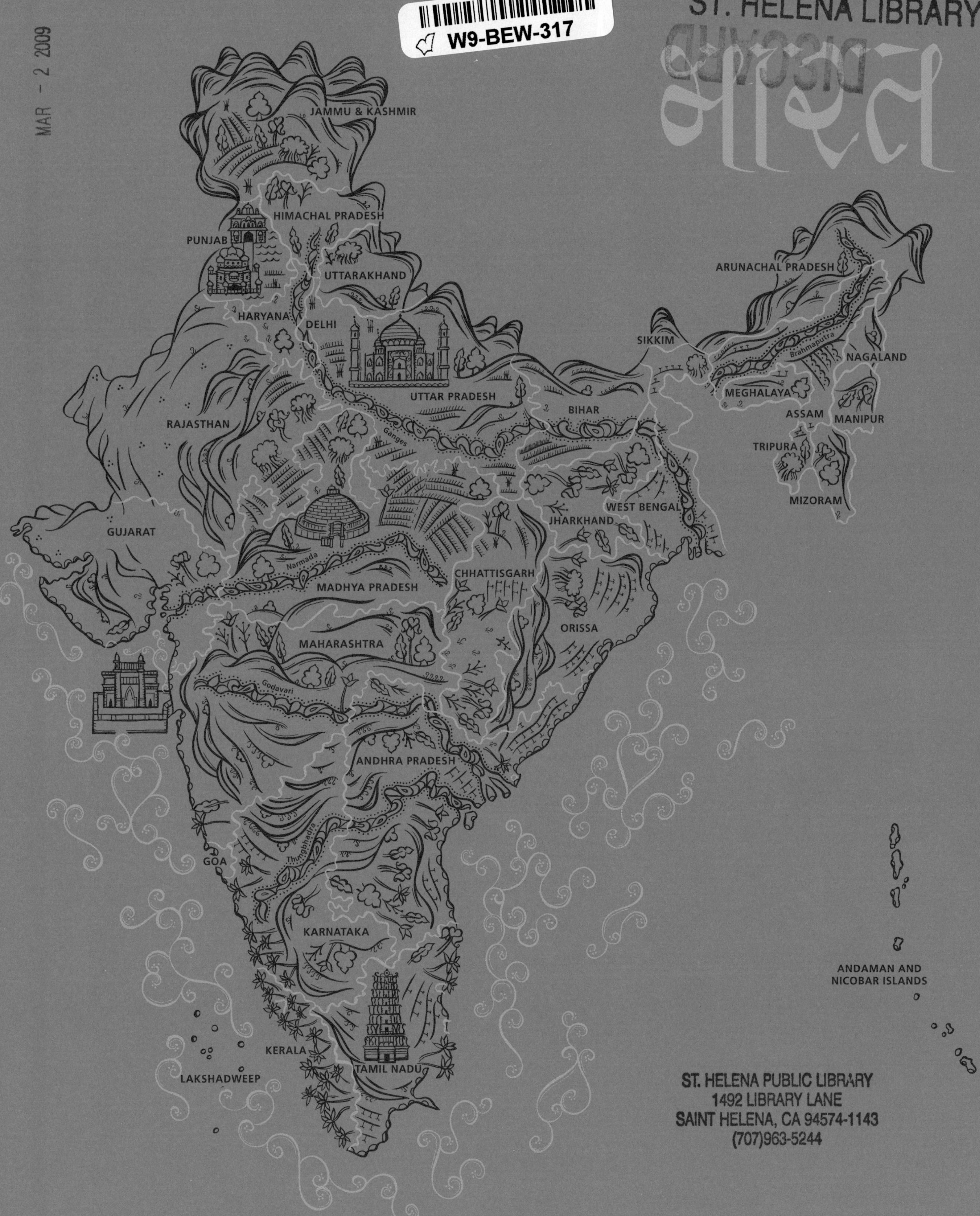
JAMMU & KASHMIR
HIMACHAL PRADESH
PUNJAB
UTTARAKHAND
HARYANA
DELHI
ARUNACHAL PRADESH
SIKKIM
Brahmaputra
NAGALAND
MEGHALAYA
ASSAM
MANIPUR
TRIPURA
MIZORAM
UTTAR PRADESH
BIHAR
RAJASTHAN
Ganges
WEST BENGAL
JHARKHAND
GUJARAT
Narmada
MADHYA PRADESH
CHHATTISGARH
ORISSA
MAHARASHTRA
Godavari
ANDHRA PRADESH
GOA
Tungbhadra
KARNATAKA
KERALA
TAMIL NADU
LAKSHADWEEP
ANDAMAN AND
NICOBAR ISLANDS

INDIA

भारत

INDIA

ABRAHAM ERALY | YASMIN KHAN | GEORGE MICHELL | MITALI SARAN

LONDON, NEW YORK, MELBOURNE,
MUNICH, AND DELHI

Senior editor Paula Regan
Project editors Sam Atkinson, Rohan Sinha, Sarah Tomley, Steve Setford
Assistant editor Manisha Thakkar
US editor Christine Heilman

Senior art editor Alison Shackleton
Project art editor Anna Hall
Designers Tannishtha Chakraborty, Elly King, Clare Shedden

Managing editor Debra Wolter
Managing art editor Karen Self
Art director Bryn Walls
Publisher Jonathan Metcalf

Production editor Phil Sergeant
Production controller Rita Sinha

Picture researcher Louise Thomas
Photography Gary Ombler and Christopher Pillitz
Additional photography Amit Pasricha and Deepak Aggarwal
Illustrations Cathy Brear and Phil Gamble
Researchers / interviewers Sudha Menon and Malavika Talukder

First American Edition, 2008

Published in the United States by
DK Publishing
375 Hudson Street
New York, New York 10014

08 09 10 11 10 9 8 7 6 5 4 3 2 1

ID077 – September 2008

Published in Great Britain by Dorling Kindersley Limited

A catalog record for this book is available from the Library of Congress

ISBN: 978-0-7566-3977-8 (PLC)
ISBN: 978-0-7566-4246-4 (PLCJ)

Color reproduction by Media Development & Printing Limited
Printed and bound in China by Leo Paper Products Ltd.

Discover more at
www.dk.com

CONTENTS

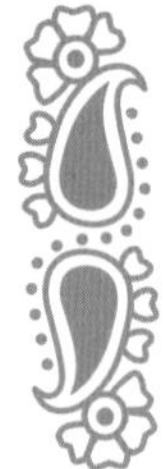

CULTURE THE SPIRIT OF INDIA

ARCHITECTURE BUILDING A NATION

TRAVEL EXPLORING INDIA

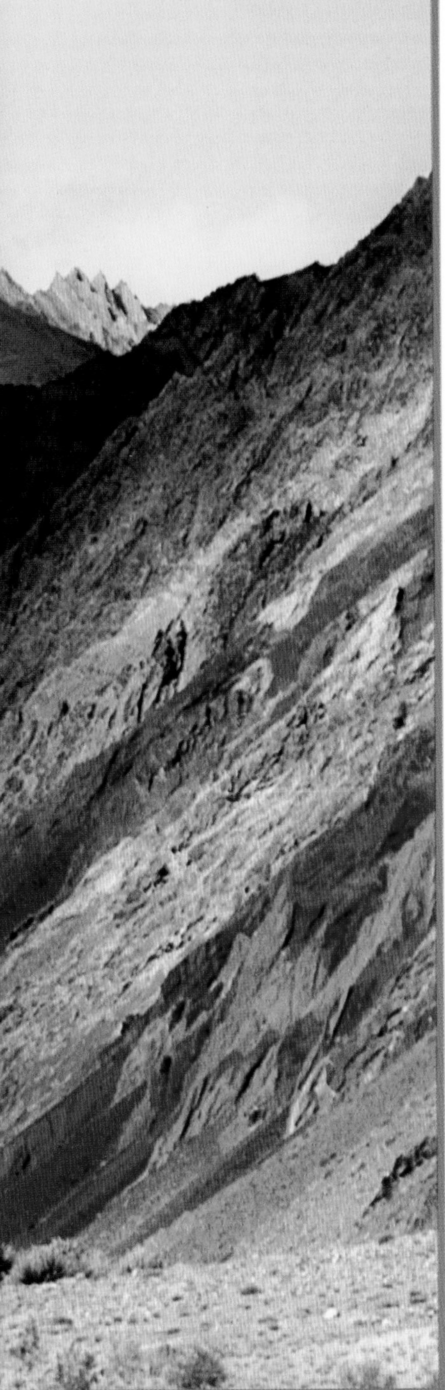

LANDSCAPE

INDIA'S HORIZONS

Stretching 1,960 miles (3,150 km) from north to south, India's vast territory includes some of the most varied terrain to be found in any one country. High mountains in the North give way to plains that are fed by some of the mightiest rivers in the world. The rich greenery and foothills of the central region contrast with the deserts and salt flats of the West, and the rocky belly of the Deccan Plateau in the South is edged by the green ridges of the hills known as the Ghats. Some of India's landscape is truly unique, such as the high-altitude desert of Ladakh in the North, or the immense tract of forest and saltwater that forms the Sundarbans estuary in West Bengal. Some of it is precious, like the forests that harbor tigers and other endangered species, and the wetlands that nurture rare bird life. Some of it is virginal, and some of it is marked forever by human presence. But the landscapes of India do have one thing in common: they are all extremely beautiful. This visual journey through the terrain of the country captures the many physical faces of the Indian subcontinent.

Extending along the northern edge of India from Jammu and Kashmir to Arunachal Pradesh, the Himalayas and their foothills comprise Earth's youngest and highest mountain range. This 1,550-mile- (2,500-km-) long barrier between the rest of India and the Tibetan Plateau includes varied terrain, from temperate forests and high-altitude deserts to icy peaks. India's northern mountains shelter fragile cultures and ecosystems, sustain fruit orchards, feed hydroelectric power, and draw travelers and adventurers with some of the world's most beautiful and exciting scenery.

NORTHERN MOUNTAINS

HIMALAYAS AND FOOTHILLS

KHALATSE, JAMMU AND KASHMIR

Winter snow patterns a field at Khalatse village, on the banks of the Suru River. Four-fifths of Ladakh's population lives in small settlements like this one, made largely self-sufficient by their remoteness.

Gautama Buddha first announced

enlightenment the Goal—

Nirvana—all desire trounced.

The Middle Way—the whole. "Buddha," Norman Davies

पर्वत

LIKIR GOMPA, JAMMU, AND KASHMIR
The 11th-century Buddhist gompa (monastery) overlooking Likir village is a very active center of worship, as the inhabitants of the Ladakh region are predominantly Buddhists of Tibetan ancestry.

Restless souls of trees hang over the desert

Like a mist

In a forest of an absence of trees

An absence of bird twitters

"Restless souls of Trees," Dilip Chitre (1938–)

पर्वत

NUBRA VALLEY, JAMMU AND KASHMIR

Beyond the high Khardung-La pass in Ladakh lies the fertile valley of the Nubra River. This small area contains a variety of landscapes, from sand dunes to wildflower fields and snowy mountain peaks.

Of soft cerulean colour was the sky, the sun had not yet risen o'er the scene,

the wild lark sang his morning hymn on the high, and heaven breathed sweetly o'er the foliage green. "Dust," Henry Derozio (1809–1831)

ZANSKAR VALLEY, JAMMU AND KASHMIR
Though inhabited, this remote valley is famously difficult to access. The Zanskar River Gorge is the only overland route, navigable by boat in summer, or on foot when the river freezes over in winter.

Bright tree! Bright branches! Tree that lives In the world's secret root, Scans sky, field and man, and gives

Devotion flower and fruit,   Of you I am a leaf: touch me with the sun: and I will laugh.   "A Leaf," P. Lal (1931–)

KULLU VALLEY, HIMACHAL PRADESH

This pristine, voluptuous glade is part of a heavily forested area known as the "Valley of the Gods." In the fast-developing hill state of Himachal Pradesh, conserving forest resources is a critical issue.

a shellburst of light greeted us
as fifty Indian peaks erupted
with snow and the spray-hangover
of icefalls and the blue of the distance

"Crossing Chorhoti," Keki N. Daruwalla (1937–)

पर्वत

MOUNT KANCHENJUNGA, SIKKIM

Mountains are the home of the gods in Indian tradition; the majestic spread of the Kanchenjunga massif in the Himalayas is said by many to look like the great destroyer, Shiva, propped up on his elbow.

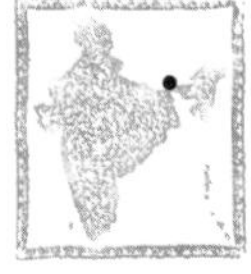

I hear a soft voice calling to me

Across the forests, beyond the skies.

In the heart of the Silence I seem to see

A Beauty that ever eludes these eyes.

"Voices," Harindranath Chattopadhyay (1898–1990)

पर्वत

TASHIDING SUSPENSION BRIDGE, SIKKIM
Building bridges, and even roads, can be a major feat of engineering in the craggy landscape of Sikkim, where the steep Himalayan foothills are as challenging as they are breathtaking.

In the shadow of the Himalayas lies a huge system of flood plains, watered by the Ganges and Brahmaputra rivers. These fertile river valleys—bounded in the north by the Himalayan foothills and in the south by the Vindhya mountain range—spread from Uttar Pradesh eastward to Bihar and West Bengal, and from Assam westward to the Bangladeshi coast. Most of the region endures hot summers and bitterly cold winters, while the humid east suffers occasional cyclones. Vast areas of cropland and settlement make this the breadbasket of India, and one of the most populated areas on Earth.

FERTILE VALLEYS

RIVERS AND PLAINS

RUDRASAGAR LAKE, TRIPURA
The Rudrasagar natural lake near Melaghar plays host to a variety of migratory birds every winter. Though landlocked, the hilly northeastern state of Tripura is home to many rivers and bodies of water.

When you meet the forest Your desires become the seasons Your smiles turn into brooks

Thorn and brush drag at your feet   And the hills stop you on your way.   "Coincidence," Jyotsna Das

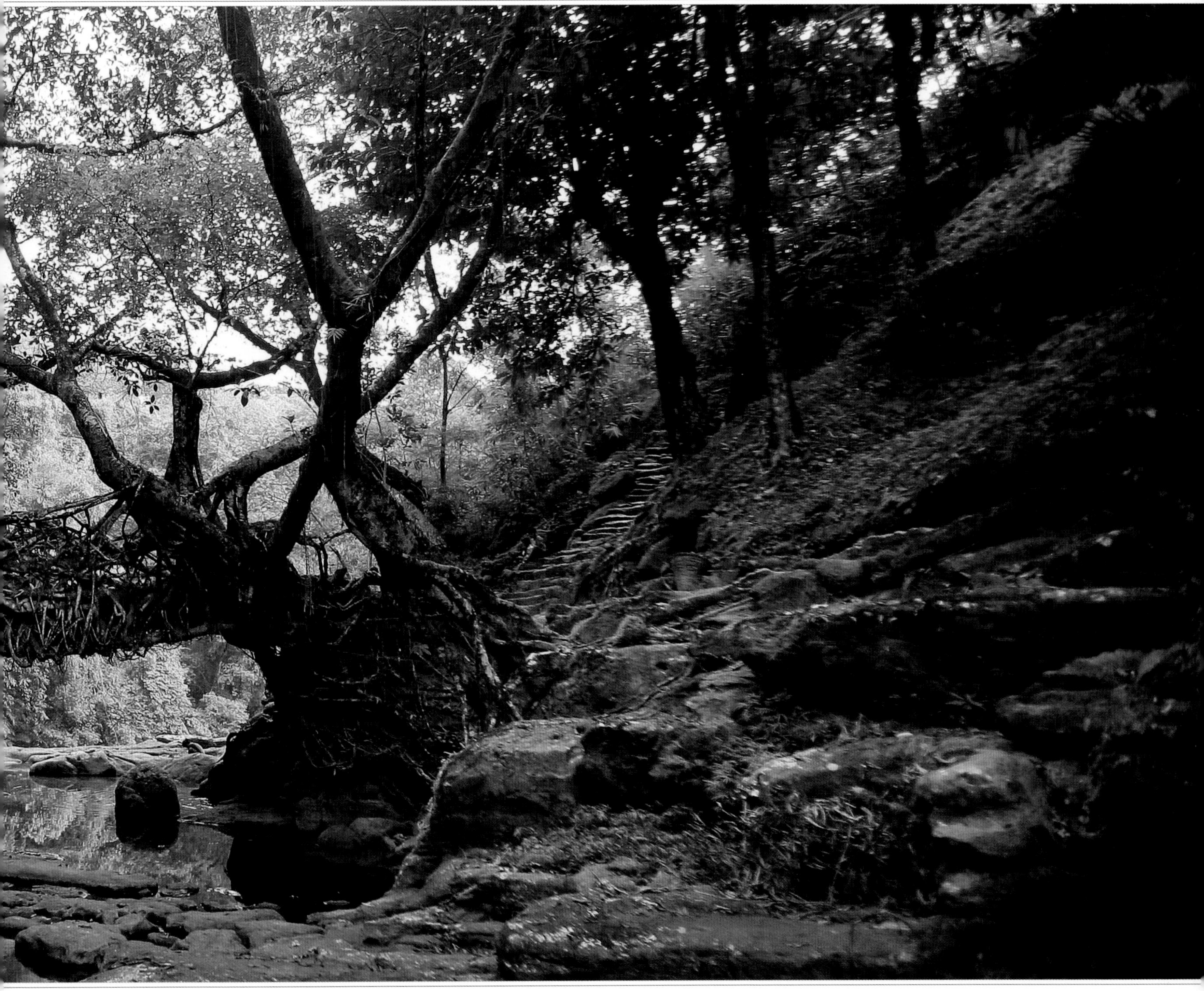

ROOT BRIDGE, KHASI HILLS, MEGHALAYA
Using a technique common throughout Northeast India, the people of the Khasi tribes bridge rivers by training and weaving the live roots of banyan trees. Bridges made this way will last for half a century.

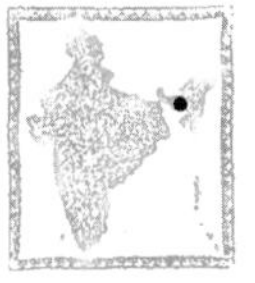

O waters! As you are the source of happiness, infuse strength into us, so that we have a great and beautiful vision. That essence of yours which is most auspicious, make us share it here, O you who are like loving mothers!

"Waters," Vedas

मैदान

MAJULI ISLAND, ASSAM

Villagers fish the waters of the sacred Brahmaputra at Majuli Island, the largest river island in South Asia. Formed centuries ago by shifts in the course of the river, Majuli has a population of 140,000 people.

Supposing you and I (connective, we) Were nothing more than two leaves of tea Being in hot water

Continuously Excessively Dispensably We'd solve the age-old problems easily. "Tea in the Universities," Adil Jussawalia (1940–)

TEA PLANTATION, ASSAM

The remote state of Assam in the far northeast is the heart of India's tea country, though the crop is also grown in West Bengal's Darjeeling district, and the Nilgiri Hills of Tamil Nadu and Kerala.

Life is a pilgrimage. The wise man does not rest by the roadside inns. He marches direct to the illimitable domain of eternal bliss, his ultimate destination.

Swami Sivananda (1887–1963)

मैदान

ALLAHABAD, UTTAR PRADESH

Millions of Hindu pilgrims camp during the six-week-long Ardh Kumbh Mela, the religious gathering that takes place every six years at the confluence of the Ganges, Yamuna, and Saraswati rivers.

Harness the plough, place the yokes, and in the prepared furrow here, sow the seed;

O Gods! May the ears of corn be full for us; let the ripe (grain) touch the sickle!

"For success in agriculture," *Vedas*

मैदान

FARM FIELDS, ORISSA
Around half the population of India still makes a living from agriculture. However, the resource-rich but relatively undeveloped coastal state of Orissa now also attracts industrial investment.

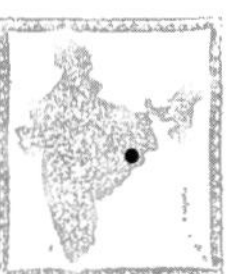

Much of western India, including Rajasthan and northern Gujarat, lies under the sand, scrub, rock, marshes, and loamy soil of the Thar Desert, the seventh-largest desert in the world. Only the Luni River waters this part of the country as it drains into to the Arabian Sea. The state of Rajasthan is on the international border with Pakistan, while Gujarat's famous salt flats in the Rann of Kutch lie on the Arabian sea. Beyond the arid zone, where only a little livestock and a few crops are raised, the farmlands of southern Gujarat flourish each year with the coming of the monsoon season.

THE ARID WEST

DESERTS, MARSHES, AND LAKES

PUSHKAR, RAJASTHAN
With its many temples, this small lakeside town is one of five sacred pilgrimage sites for devout Hindus. It also attracts thousands of visitors for its annual cattle fair, which is one of the largest in the world.

In a desert land, this pearl-studded city.

Peacocks perch on the brackets

and elephants roam on the walls.

Every balcony lace-embroidered in stone,

every window festooned

with the gashes of blunt swords.

"Jaisalmer, I," Ghulam Mohammed Sheikh (1937–)

मरुस्थल

JAISALMER, RAJASTHAN

Close to the border with Pakistan, "the Golden City" of Jaisalmer lies at the very heart of the Thar Desert. The skyline of this vibrant town is dominated by the ramparts of Jaisalmer Fort rising from the sands.

You've come where, if you were to drink, you'd forget what you held precious

and also what's trivial and not worth remembering: name, country, landscape, this memory, that anguish. "Lethe," Amit Chaudhuri (1962–)

JAL MAHAL ("WATER PALACE"), RAJASTHAN
Jaipur, the state capital of Rajasthan, is rich in royal architecture; this 18th-century structure in Man Sagar lake was built for duck-hunting parties. Like many heritage buildings, it is poised to become a hotel.

Out in the desert sands there roam
The lovely tribal girls
By night they hunt for lovers' hearts
They churn their pots by day
They fire their secret deadly darts
And many hearts they wound

"The Desert Girls," Khwaja Ghulam Farid (1844-1901)

मरुस्थल

THAR DESERT, RAJASTHAN
The inhospitable landscape of the Thar desert, which covers the western edge of Rajasthan, supports a wide variety of wildlife, as well as tribes such as the ecologically-minded Bishnois.

W R

We cross the bridge silently, without once

Looking back. At the railroad crossing.

We hear someone's heart beating loud.

Faraway. "Fugitive Poem," Vilas Sarang (1942–)

मरुस्थल

KATHIAWAR PENINSULA, GUJARAT
India's rail network is one of the most extensive in the world. In the western state of Gujarat, the railway connects the cities that dot the mainly flat and dry landscape of the Kathiawar Peninsula.

The roughly triangular block of ancient granite and basalt that constitutes the Deccan Plateau fills most of peninsular India, spreading over the states of Andhra Pradesh, Karnataka, Tamil Nadu, and Kerala. The rocky Deccan is rimmed on all sides by mountain ranges: the Vindhyas and Satpuras on the northern edge, and the Western and Eastern Ghats almost converging at the tip of the peninsula. The plateau is drained by numerous rivers, including the Godavari, the Tungabhadra, and the Kaveri, which depend on the monsoon for their water and tend to dry up in the summer.

SOUTHERN PLATEAU

THE DECCAN AND GHATS

MAHABALESHWAR, MAHARASHTRA

In the 19th century, this corner of western India was developed as a health resort. Today, its lush hills, fields of strawberries, and salubrious climate attract vacationers from all over the country.

The city was a lamp of time   It burned here in the storm of time

HAMPI, KARNATAKA
The Tungabhadra River curls through the UNESCO World Heritage site of Hampi. The village is home to the ruins of Vijayanagar, the capital of a South Indian empire from the 14th to the 16th century.

Brilliant, crouching, slouching, what escape through the green heart of the forest,
Gleaming eyes and mighty chest and soft soundless paws of grandeur and murder?

"The tiger and the deer," Aurobindo Ghosh (1872–1950)

पहाड़

LAKE PERIYAR, KERALA

A dawn cruise on the man-made reservoir at Periyar Wildlife Sanctuary in the Western Ghats is sometimes rewarded with the sight of wild elephants bathing. Dead tree stumps help to gauge the water level.

O Goatherds and you shepherds say　Which way has my darling gone?　I've goatherds here and goatherds there

I've shepherds on both sides of me Which way has my darling gone?

Kharia folksong

पहाड़

ERAVIKULAM NATIONAL PARK, KERALA
A herd of endangered Nilgiri tahr rests upon a ridge in a shola forest. Found at high altitudes in tropical South India, the trees of a shola forest can only survive in the valleys made by hills and rivers.

India has a 4,700-mile- (7,600-km-) long coastline, including its island territories. Some of the most beautiful palm-fringed sand beaches in the world lie on the west coast, along Goa and the Konkan Coast down to Kerala, and in the Lakshadweep islands in the Arabian Sea. The east, from Orissa down to the temple-dotted Coromandel Coast of Tamil Nadu, has rougher waters, but the Andaman and Nicobar Islands in the Bay of Bengal are known for their beauty, both above and below the waters. Thriving coastal cities include Mumbai in the west, Chennai in the south, and Kolkata in the east.

TROPICAL COASTS

CITIES, BEACHES, AND ISLANDS

MUMBAI, MAHARASHTRA

India's vibrant commercial capital, the city of Mumbai, is a blend of its Victorian heritage and the concrete towers and slums that house one of the largest and most dense populations on the planet.

Silence is round me, wideness ineffable;

White birds on the ocean—diving and wandering;

A soundless sea on a voiceless heaven,

Azure on azure, is mutely gazing.

"Ocean Oneness," Aurobindo Ghosh (1872–1950)

समुद्री तट

HAVELOCK, ANDAMAN AND NICOBAR ISLANDS
Besides their picture-perfect beauty, the Andaman Islands of the Indian Ocean also offer excellent waters for scuba diving and snorkeling. Havelock is one of 36 inhabited islands out of over 500.

A low temple keeps its god in the dark.

You lend a matchbox to the priest.

One by one the gods come to light.

Amused bronze. Smiling stone. Unsurprised.

"A Low Temple," Arun Kolatkar (1932–2004)

समुद्री तट

MAMALLAPURAM, TAMIL NADU
The 8th-century Shore Temple is one of a stunning collection of temples, cave sanctuaries, monuments, and art bequeathed by the ancient Pallava dynasty at the port of Mamallapuram on the Bay of Bengal.

The silent waters of the pond

Reflecting all the brightness of the air;

A shadowy bough of blossoms

Curving as the shoulders of a swan;

"Exchange," Amiya Chakravarty

समुद्री तट

CANSAULIM, GOA

The secluded beaches and villages of south Goa offer a contrast to the touristy shores farther north. The village of Cansaulim is surrounded by areas of stunning natural beauty, such as this lotus pond.

City of steel, gleaming bridges, cars flashing across glinting highways. Always the silence within the airconditioned cars.

lights flashing through the darkness   And the whole city blind and built of stone.   "My World," Anna Sujatha Modayil (1934–)

HOWRAH BRIDGE, WEST BENGAL

This busy cantilever bridge across the Hooghly River links Kolkata with New Howrah. Once India's capital, Kolkata remains an artistic, intellectual, and political center, and the commercial hub of East India.

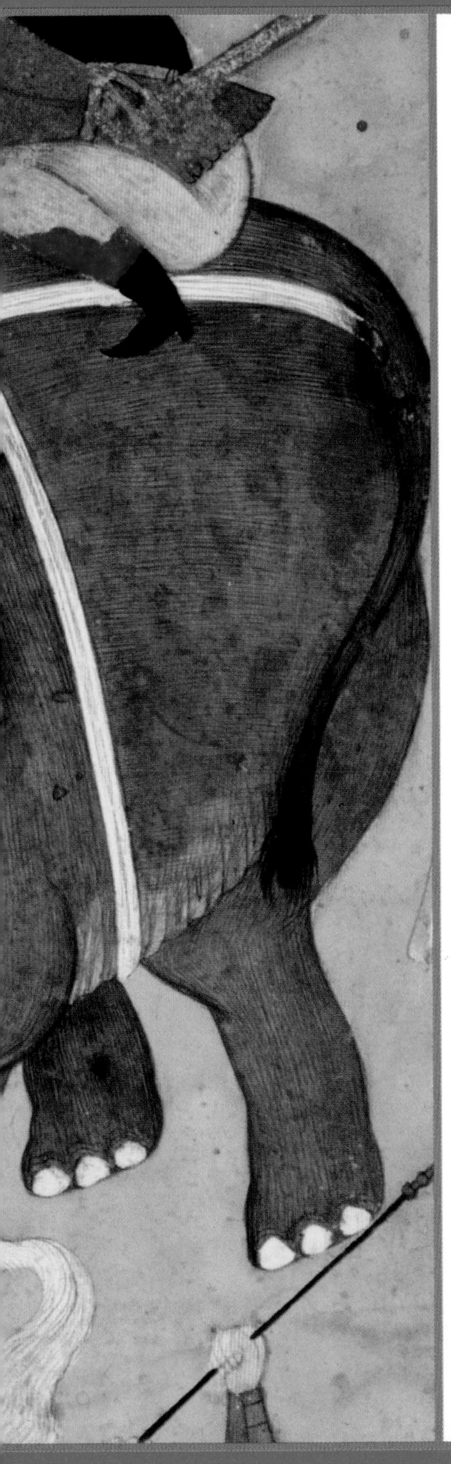

HISTORY

THE STORY OF INDIA

India's uniqueness lies in the fact that it is at once a young and an ancient nation, where the old and the new constantly jostle for space. Its recorded past goes back 5,000 years to the Indus Valley Civilization, believed to be the most sophisticated culture of its time. It was followed by the migration of the Aryans, who assimilated with the locals and evolved distinctive customs and traditions that still exist to this day. Over time, the subcontinent became a "melting pot" of cultures as it played host to invaders and conquerors, travelers and traders, including the Persians, Greeks, Scythians, and Huns. The Islamic influence, which reached its zenith with the Mughals, left a lasting impression on Indian society, architecture, arts, and culture. The seeds of modernity were planted by the British, who introduced Western values and institutions into the region during their 200-year rule. Today, after 60 years of independence, India is set to become a leading power in the world, fueled by new economic opportunities and a vibrant, secular democracy.

By the 7th millennium BCE, nomadic hunters in northwestern India began to farm, domesticate animals, and live in village settlements. Eventually, these people moved to the plains of the Indus River and established one of the greatest civilizations of the time, in which architecture and trade flourished. Over time, the inhabitants of the Indus Valley built well-planned cities and lived a refined urban life. However, the decline of the Indus civilization in the 2nd millennium BCE was hastened by the arrival of the nomadic Aryans from Central Asia, who conquered the Indus cities before taking to agriculture and settling in the Indo-Gangetic plains.

METALLURGY c. 4000 BCE
As humans in the Indian subcontinent began to take control of their environment, they created tools of copper and bronze, and later of iron, a major technological revolution that signaled the beginning of civilization.

MEHRGARH c. 7000–4000 BCE
The earliest Neolithic agricultural settlement in the Indian subcontinent, Mehrgarh lies on the Bolan River in modern-day Pakistan. Its inhabitants built mud-brick homes, cultivated wheat and barley, domesticated animals, and developed crafts.

Prehistoric tools
Simply designed metal tools were used for farming, hunting, and in battle.

THE PLOW
c. 3500 BCE
The adoption of the plow by the Indus Valley people signified great advances in farming methods.

SETTLEMENTS IN THE SOUTH c. 3000 BCE
Neolithic culture evolved later in south India independently of the north. There is evidence of settlements in Karnataka and Tamil Nadu from c. 3000 BCE.

TRADE c. 2500–1500 BCE
The Indus Valley cities had extensive trade contacts with the Middle East. Their main export was cotton cloth, but it is likely that they also traded in wood, ivory, and beads. Engraved Indus Valley seals have been found in Sumeria (present-day Iraq).

4000 3400 3100 2800 2500

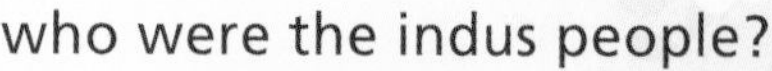

who were the indus people?

Archeological evidence suggests that the Indus people were a prosperous and contented group, who lived a settled life and enjoyed the pleasures of dance, music, and revelry. However, little is known of their origins. It is believed that they were a mix of Negritos and Australoids (descendants of the first hominids to enter India from Africa), as well as Mediterraneans (a Caucasoid subrace from West Asia), who may have introduced the initial civilizing impulse and the concept of agriculture. It is likely that the Mediterraneans formed the dominant class, while the others constituted the underclass. Their language is assumed to be a precursor to the languages still spoken in South India today.

Terra-cotta figurine
A figurine of an Indus Valley woman adorned with jewelry.

Seals from the Indus Valley

WRITING c. 2600 BCE
Over 3,000 Indus Valley inscriptions have been discovered. The majority are incised on seals, but a few are on seal impressions or engraved on artifacts. The script, which has yet to be deciphered, is logosyllabic in structure, containing both words and phonetic signs.

PREHISTORIC INDIA

THE FIRST SETTLEMENTS, 4000–700 BCE

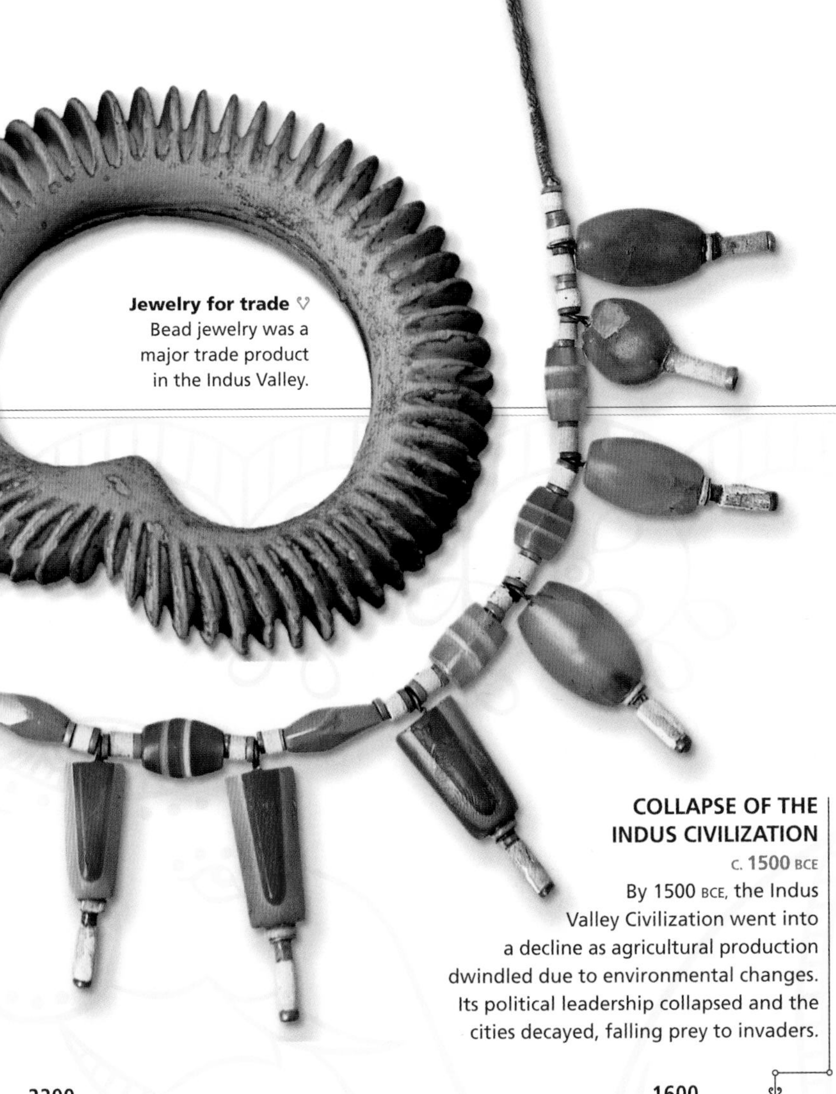

Jewelry for trade ▽ Bead jewelry was a major trade product in the Indus Valley.

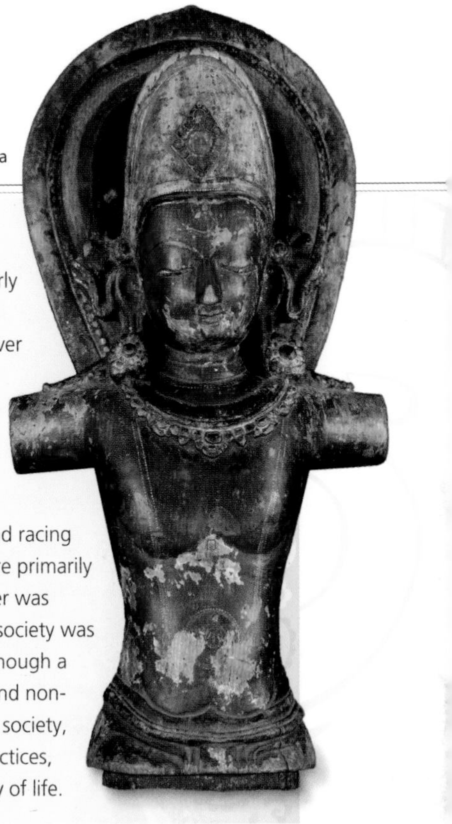

The Aryan god Indra

the early aryans

The only sources of information about the early Aryans are the four Vedas (*see pp.266–267*), India's oldest sacred texts, composed orally over several centuries before 800 BCE. Essentially liturgical works, they also describe the everyday life of the Aryans in some detail. According to the Vedas, the early Aryans were a fun-loving people who spent their days singing, dancing, gambling, drinking, and racing chariots. When they arrived in India, they were primarily nomadic tribes led by chieftains, whose power was dependent on the will of the tribesmen. The society was fundamentally classless and unstructured, although a social division did exist between the Aryans and non-Aryans. As they transformed into an agrarian society, the Aryans began to adopt new customs, practices, beliefs, and gods appropriate to their new way of life.

COLLAPSE OF THE INDUS CIVILIZATION c. 1500 BCE
By 1500 BCE, the Indus Valley Civilization went into a decline as agricultural production dwindled due to environmental changes. Its political leadership collapsed and the cities decayed, falling prey to invaders.

2200 1900 1600 1300 1000 700

ARRIVAL OF THE ARYANS c. 1500 BCE
Nomadic Aryan tribes from Central Asia migrated southward to India through the narrow passes of the Hindu Kush mountains around this time. They swept across the cities of the Indus Valley, hastening the end of a civilization already on the verge of collapse.

The Khyber Pass in the Hindu Kush mountains

A Painted Gray Ware bowl

PAINTED GRAY WARE c. 1200 BCE
Aryan settlements gradually spread from the Indus Valley to the upper plains of the Ganges. Evidence for this shift is the discovery of their Painted Gray Ware pottery all across the Gangetic region.

EXTENSIVE USE OF IRON c. 1000 BCE
By 1000 BCE, the Aryans began to make extensive use of implements made of iron, which was easily available in the region. These iron tools helped them to clear the thickly forested Gangetic plains.

IMPROVEMENTS IN FARMING c. 1000 BCE
After learning how to fertilize and irrigate fields, the Aryans gave up the slash-and-burn method of clearing land for farming, and instead cultivated the same fields year after year.

Priest-king
This Indus Valley sculpture is believed to depict a bearded priest-king dressed in a trefoil-patterned cloak, indicating a regal vestment.

City structure
The residential quarter of Mohenjo-daro was divided into neat rectangular blocks by broad, straight main streets.

indus valley cities

Mohenjo-Daro and Harappa, the "twin capitals" of the Indus Valley Civilization, were probably the world's first planned cities. Immense in size for their time, each covered about ⅔ sq mile (1.6 sq km) and probably housed a population of over 30,000. Although some 370 miles (600 km) apart along the Indus river system, both cities were built to virtually identical plans, suggesting a centralized state and local civic organization. Each city had a towering and heavily fortified citadel on the riverside, and a lower city—a residential quarter arranged on a grid pattern—located to the east of the citadel, and set slightly apart from it.

sanitation and hygiene

With elaborate, efficient civic amenities and sanitation systems, Mohenjo-Daro and Harappa were among the cleanest and most hygienic cities of the day. Sewage channels ran throughout each city, and household waste was conveyed through chutes into brick bins along the streets, from where it was regularly emptied by municipal workers. Personal hygiene, too, was important. Most houses had bathrooms, and the citadel was equipped with a pool, the Great Bath, most probably for ritual ablutions.

standards and regulations

A high degree of uniformity existed in the Indus Valley for centuries, from the layout of the cities to the dimensions of bricks, and from the design of pottery vessels and stamp-seals to the script. The discovery of sets of weights among excavated artifacts indicate that trade and industry were regulated by official weights and measures, and also by standardized production techniques. Who set these standards and how they were enforced is unknown. The Indus Valley government may have been a form of theocracy, comprising a small priestly class headed by a priest-king or a council of high priests.

Unusually, little evidence of religion has been found but the refined artifacts produced in the region—including finely worked gold jewelry, figurines made from terra-cotta, pottery, and bronze (*see p.258*); and seals—indicate that this was a highly advanced society.

Terra-cotta vase
This decorated vessel from Mohenjo-Daro, which was used to store grains, is a rare surviving piece from the period.

The whole conception shows a remarkable concern for sanitation and health without parallel . . . in the prehistoric past.

Historian Stuart Piggott on the sanitation arrangements in Indus cities

उद्धरण

Sewage system

The sewage from Mohenjo-daro's residential houses emptied into the sophisticated brick channels that ran along the center of the city's streets.

By the middle of the 1st millennium BCE, the Aryans had made the fertile Indo-Gangetic plains their homeland. The expansion of agriculture led to increased wealth, which in turn accelerated trade. Gradually, villages grew into territorial states and new urban centers appeared. Material prosperity turned the Aryans toward philosophical speculations—paving the way for new religious sects—and created a wealth that lured foreign invaders such as Darius I, who established Persian dominance over the western Indus Valley.

UPANISHADS c. 700 BCE
Philosophical inquiries, which began with the Vedas, culminated in the profound metaphysical speculations of the Upanishads. Composed by Aryan sages, the Upanishads replaced the Vedic concept of gods with the concept of *brahman*—the impersonal, changeless essence of the universe.

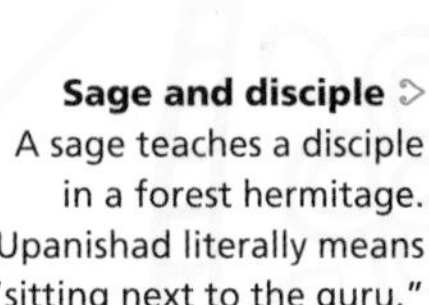

Sage and disciple
A sage teaches a disciple in a forest hermitage. Upanishad literally means "sitting next to the guru."

VALMIKI c. 600 BCE
The sage Valmiki is believed to have composed core sections of the *Ramayana* in the 6th century BCE. One of India's greatest epics, it recounts the life and times of the legendary Aryan king, Rama.

A battle scene from the *Ramayana*

NEW RELIGIONS c. 600 BCE
Flourishing agriculture and trade made Aryan lives much more secure than before. No longer preoccupied with physical survival, they began to explore the meaning of life and existence, which gave rise to new religious sects and systems.

700 660 620 580

680 640 600 560

Mathura
Modern-day a, which was one of the first Aryan urban centers.

the emergence of territorial states

The gradual transition of the Aryan economy from nomadic pastoralism to settled agriculture brought about several changes in society and government. Agricultural prosperity led to trade, and towns began to appear in large numbers in the Gangetic plains. As social and economic functions became specialized, the Aryans developed a rudimentary class system in which some sections of society enjoyed greater privileges. Politically, territorial states and hereditary monarchies replaced tribal governments headed by chieftains, while standing armies replaced tribal militias. Kings fought for territory instead of cattle—as tribal chieftains had once done—which led to the emergence of several large kingdoms. The most important of these new kingdoms was Magadha, in southern Bihar, with its capital at Rajagriha.

AJIVIKAS c. 550 BCE
Ajivikas was an ancient philosophical and ascetic movement of North India. Its members, being strict fatalists, believed that everything that happens in the world and in individual lives is unalterably fixed by fate.

BIMBISARA c. 542–494 BCE
The expansion of the kingdom of Magadha was initiated by Bimbisara of the Sisunaga dynasty. Through wars, strategic marriage alliances, and rigorous administrative policies, he made Magadha the most powerful kingdom in ancient India.

THE AGE OF TRANSITION

TERRITORIAL STATES AND NEW RELIGIONS, 700–362 BCE

jainism

Vardhamana (c.540–468 BCE), the "founder" of Jainism (*see p.240*), was the son of Siddhartha, a chieftain of the Jnatrika clan of North India. He is believed to have brought prosperity to the kingdom while still in his mother's womb—an auspicious sign that foretold his greatness. Despite leading a princely life, Vardhamana was spiritually inclined from childhood and became an ascetic at the age of 30, thereafter living naked and without any possessions. He attained enlightenment after 13 years of rigorous austerities and took on the title *Mahavira* (Great Hero). He spent the next 30 years of his life in incessant missionary work, acquiring hundreds of thousands of followers. Mahavira's preachings and his efforts to promote Jain philosophy were responsible for making Jainism one of the major religions of ancient India.

A depiction of Mahavira in a Jain scripture

BLACK POTTERY c. 480 BCE
Glossy black pottery, known as Northern Black Polished Ware (NBPW), appeared in the 5th century BCE, reflecting the prosperity of the times. Making pottery was big business, and Buddhist texts even speak of millionaire potters.

PATALIPUTRA c. 478 BCE
Bimbisara's son, Ajatasatru, built the fortified township of Patali. Later known as Pataliputra, it would remain one of India's major cities for more than a thousand years.

500 — 480 — 460 — 440 — 420 — 400 — 380

PERSIAN RULE c. 518 BCE
King Darius I of Persia invaded and occupied the western Indus Valley in the 6th century BCE. This period of Persian rule had enduring political and cultural consequences, influencing the art and administration of future dynasties. Moreover, their occupation opened the door to future invasions of India.

The Persian ruler Darius I in his court

Fragment of an inscription in *Brahmi* script

BRAHMI SCRIPT c. 500 BCE
The Aryans developed writing around 500 BCE. Known as *Brahmi*, this script was the precursor to all other Indian scripts and was used in the Ashokan inscriptions (*see p.73*), the first written documents of India.

YASKA'S NIRUKTA c. 450 BCE
Grammar was seen as a sacred subject in ancient India. Sanskrit grammarian Yaska's *Nirukta*, dealing with the origins of Vedic words, is the earliest existing grammatical work in Sanskrit.

MONEY c. 450 BCE
Coinage was first introduced in India by trading guilds. These coins were flat bars of silver, bearing punched marks that identified the issuing guild and certified the weight and purity of the coins.

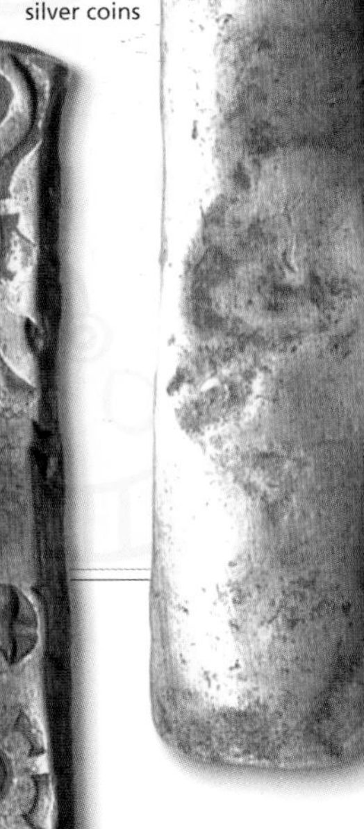

Punch-marked silver coins

Buddha with disciples Buddha addresses his five most important disciples. He founded a community of Buddhist monks and nuns (the *Sangha*) to continue his missionary work after his death.

gautama buddha

Buddhism is a religion of compassion and practical wisdom, not of blind faith. Its central teaching is that man should lead a life of prudence and righteousness, and that this is the means to avoid misery. Founded by the ancient Indian sage Gautama Buddha, the religion has today more than 300 million adherents across Asia, and is now gaining followers in Europe and North America.

early life

Buddha was born as Siddhartha Gautama to the royal family of the Sakyas on the full-moon day of the lunar month of Vaisakha, around 560 BCE in Lumbini, Nepal. A prediction that Siddhartha would become a sage distressed his father, Shuddhodana, who wanted his son to be a great king. Shuddhodana sought to prevent his son's portended fate by cocooning the child in luxury, and insulating him from the bitter realities of life. As a teenager, Siddhartha was married to his "fair-bosomed" cousin, Yasodhara.

Four things that Buddha saw on a venture into the royal park opened his eyes to the suffering in the world: an old man, a sick man, a corpse, and a serene ascetic. Siddhartha was depressed by what he had seen. How could old age, illness, and death be overcome? On the night after the birth of his son, he left the palace for the woods in search of spiritual solace.

enlightenment

After initially studying traditional wisdom under various gurus, Siddhartha practiced severe penances and self-mortification for a while, but enlightenment eluded him. "These so-called austerities only confuse the mind, which is overpowered by the body's exhaustion," he later remarked.

Siddhartha eventually decided to follow a new, "middle way" between asceticism and a life of pleasure. He began to eat food regularly, which restored his health and mental composure. Renewing his spiritual quest, he sat cross-legged in a yogic posture facing east, under a pipal tree in a lush meadow, and resolved not to rise until he had found enlightenment. For 49 days he sat in deep meditation, finally attaining enlightenment (*nirvana*) at the age of 35 on the full-moon day of May, after a night of mystic raptures. From then he was the Buddha, or "Awakened One." Over the next 45 years, until his death at about age 80, Buddha expounded his doctrines in a tireless missionary effort.

Stone footprints These "footprints" of Buddha, on the Great Stupa in Amaravati, Andhra Pradesh, each bear a *Dharmachakra* (Wheel of Righteousness) on the sole.

May all be happy and safe; may all be blessed with peace always . . . May none deceive another, nor scorn another, nor, in anger or ill-will, desire another's sorrow . . .

Sutta-nipata, ancient Buddhist scripture

उद्धरण

The passing of Buddha
This sculpture is from the Mahaparinirvana Temple in Kushinagar, Uttar Pradesh, where Buddha is said to have entered *parinirvana*, the final deathless state, at the end of his life.

THE FIRST EMPIRE

THE NANDA AND MAURYAN DYNASTIES, 362–185 BCE

The Persian occupation of the Indus Valley inevitably drew the Greek king, Alexander the Great, into India, to complete his conquest of the Persian Empire. Although his campaigns were confined to the Indus Valley and lasted for only two years, the interaction between the Indian and Greek civilizations endured for a long time. Meanwhile, the consolidation and expansion of the Indo-Gangetic kingdoms continued, culminating in the establishment of the Mauryan Empire. The largest and most rigorously administered kingdom in ancient India, it endured for well over a century, but collapsed after the death of Ashoka, the greatest of all Mauryan rulers. During this period, Buddhism emerged as the dominant religion of India.

A Sanskrit scroll

the arthashastra

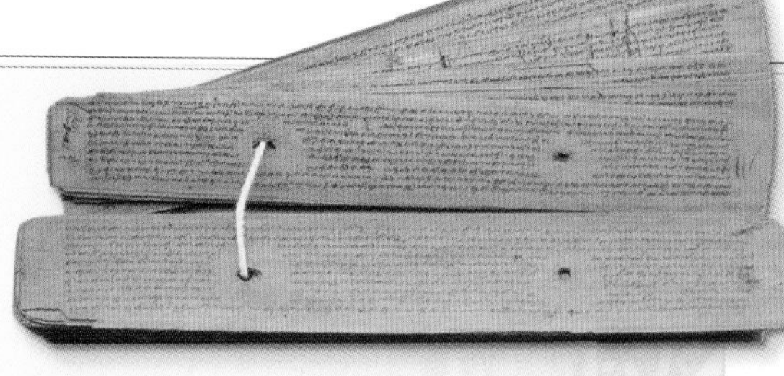

Manuscript of the *Arthashastra*

The *Arthashastra*, India's oldest political treatise on statecraft, is attributed to Kautilya, also known as Chanakya, the chief minister of the Mauryan ruler, Chandragupta. A work of forbidding intelligence and brutal candor, it is entirely unsentimental in its approach. It promotes a totalitarian state, which controls all aspects of society and the lives of its citizens through complex bureaucratic procedures. These involve tracking every event and overseeing every transaction, from births and deaths and the movements of individuals to the total control of all economic activities. It also mandates consumer protection by the state against unscrupulous traders, as well as protection against medical malpractice and the exploitation of laborers. Although the *Arthashastra* is a theoretical work, it is quite likely that Kautilya's ideas were based on Mauryan practices.

380 · 360 · 340 · 320 · 300 · 280 · 260 · 220

PANINI'S GRAMMAR
c. 350 BCE
The archaic Sanskrit of the Aryans was codified by the grammarian Panini in his treatise, *Astadhyayi*. It defined the structure and syntax of the language and is recognized as the most scientific grammar composed before modern times.

THE NANDA DYNASTY
c. 362–21 BCE
Despite his low social origin, Mahapadma Nanda took control of the Magadhan throne and established the Nanda dynasty. Due to his ruthless conquests, Nanda rule extended over the entire Gangetic plains.

ALEXANDER'S INDIAN CAMPAIGNS c. 326–25 BCE
In early 326 BCE, Alexander the Great crossed the Indus "into the country of the Indians." Advancing east, he defeated Porus, a local king, on the banks of the Jhelum River, but had to retreat from India soon after, as his battle-weary soldiers mutinied.

Alexander the Great at the Battle of Hydaspes

Battle elephants ▷
The Greek ruler, Seleucus Nikotar, is said to have ceded nearly all of Afghanistan to the Mauryas in exchange for 500 elephants.

THE MAURYAN EMPIRE c. 320–185 BCE
The Magadhan kingdom transformed into an empire under the Mauryas, a dynasty founded by Chandragupta (r. 320–298 BCE). With its capital at Pataliputra, the Mauryan Empire stretched over virtually the entire Indian subcontinent, and extended well into modern-day Afghanistan.

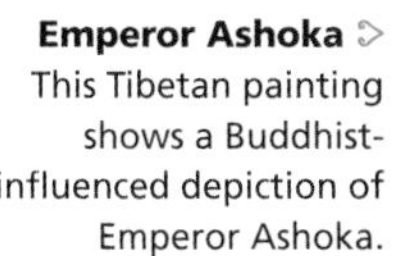

Emperor Ashoka ▷
This Tibetan painting shows a Buddhist-influenced depiction of Emperor Ashoka.

MILITARY COUP
c. 185 BCE
The Mauryan dynasty lasted for about 50 years after Ashoka's death. The last Mauryan ruler, Brihadratha, was assassinated by his commander-in-chief, Pushyamitra, who usurped the throne and founded the Sunga dynasty.

180

200

TAMIL LANGUAGE
c. 200 BCE
Tamil inscriptions from the early 2nd century BCE have been discovered in Tamil Nadu, making it one of India's oldest languages. Found in caves occupied by Jain or Buddhist monks, these short inscriptions are mostly just names, probably of their benefactors. The script is a variation of *Brahmi*, adapted to suit Tamil phonetics.

ashoka

Ashokavardhana, better known as Emperor Ashoka ("Without Sorrow"), was the grandson of Chandragupta Maurya. Today, he is recognized as one of India's greatest rulers and his *dharma-chakra* (wheel of righteousness) adorns the country's national flag. However, he was entirely unknown in India until British scholars, having deciphered the *Brahmi* script, identified him in the mid-19th century and revealed his greatness.

early life

Ashoka's mother, Subhadrangi, is said to have been one of the 16 wives of the Mauryan ruler, Bindusara. Not being the eldest son, Ashoka had to fight a brutal war of succession with his brothers before he could ascend the Mauryan throne around 268 BCE. A domineering and strong-willed ruler, he ruthlessly crushed the internal revolts taking place across the Mauryan Empire and soon acquired a reputation for cold-blooded efficiency. His only external conquest was that of Kalinga (a central-Indian kingdom), but the bitterly fought war claimed more than 100,000 lives.

conversion to Buddhism

Profoundly affected by such violence, Ashoka renounced war and accepted Buddhism to seek solace for his troubled conscience. Subsequently, his value system and the orientation of his government underwent a radical change. He began to emphasize social and familial values, deeming the stability of the family to be the basis of social order. He laid equal stress on fairness in dealings, proper treatment of slaves and servants, and gentleness toward all living beings. Despite being a devout Buddhist, he continued to honor all religions, believing that "all seek self-control and purity of mind."

Ashoka labored incessantly for the good of his subjects, and he commanded his officers to regularly tour the districts to check on the well-being of the people and to guide them to lead a virtuous life. His humanistic ideals were inscribed in different languages on rocks and pillars all over his empire, so that they could be followed even after his death.

No ruler had ever set themselves nobler goals or worked as hard to achieve them as Ashoka. However, all his aspirations turned to ashes after his death in c. 231 BCE, as the Mauryan Empire disintegrated and was usurped by the Sungas less than 50 years later.

◁ **The Lion Capital**
Ashoka's Lion Capital from Sarnath, Uttar Pradesh, has been adopted as the national emblem of India.

Around the time the Mauryan Empire declined, Greeks again invaded India. Alexander the Great's empire splintered soon after his death, and it was from Bactria (present-day Afghanistan), the easternmost fragment of the empire, that the Greeks extended their power into India. The Bactrian-Greek power lasted until the establishment of the Indo-Central Asian kingdoms of the Parthians, Sakas, and Kushanas. This period saw vast expansion of the Indian economy, nourished by flourishing foreign trade, particularly with the Roman Empire. Buddhism spread across Asia, although the religion declined in India. This was also a time of great cultural development, from the creation of the rock shrines of Ajanta, to the writing of great literary works.

Sunga figure ▷ This Sunga portrayal of a *yakshi* (demigoddess) is different in style from the formalism of Mauryan sculptures.

SUNGA DYNASTY
c. 185–73 BCE
After ousting the Mauryas, the Sungas ruled the core area of the old Mauryan Empire in the Gangetic plains for a little over 100 years, until about the first quarter of the 1st century BCE.

menander

The best known of the Indo-Greek kings is Menander (r. 155–130 BCE), who ruled over an extensive kingdom in northwestern India around the middle of the 2nd century BCE. Menander had his capital at Sagala (modern-day Sialkot, in Punjab). The *Milanda-panha*, an ancient Buddhist text in Pali (an Aryan language), describes him as "learned, eloquent, wise, and able . . . Many are the arts and sciences he knows . . . And as in wisdom so in strength of body, swiftness, and valor there was found none equal to Menander in all India."

Buddhist tradition holds that, in his old age, Menander abdicated in favor of his son and retired to a Buddhist monastery. According to the Greek historian, Plutarch, so great was the renown of Menander that on his death, many cities in his kingdom contended with each other to share his ashes, just as several cities had once contended for Buddha's ashes.

◁ **Coin of Menander** Menander's coins were among the finest in the ancient world.

DEVADASI SYSTEM c. 130 BCE
Devadasis were young females, trained as musicians and singers, who not only participated in Hindu temple rituals, but also provided sexual services to temple functionaries and devotees.

PAHLAVAS c. 100 BCE
The Pahlavas (Parthians) established their power in northwestern India toward the close of the 2nd century BCE, but were subsequently overwhelmed by the Sakas and Kushanas.

◁ **An Indo-Greek copper plate** *Kharoshthi* (Persian Aramaic) inscriptions have been found in Taxila, northwestern India.

SAKA KINGDOMS c. 80 BCE
After entering the Indus Valley in the 1st century BCE, the Sakas (Scythians) extended their power farther into India. Although ousted from the Indus Valley by the Kushanas, they held on to power in Central India and the western Deccan for several centuries.

INDO-GREEK KINGDOMS c. 180 BCE
The Greeks, who had settled around Bactria (Afghanistan) after Alexander's campaigns, were the first major migrant people to enter India after the Aryans. They formed a number of autonomous Indo-Greek kingdoms, which ruled over the western Indo-Gangetic Valley for around 100 years.

A Scythian horseman

AN EMPIRE DIVIDED

THE RISE OF REGIONAL KINGDOMS, 185 BCE–100 CE

rock-cut shrines

Some of the most renowned art treasures of ancient India, in sculpture as well as painting, are in the rock-cut shrines at Ajanta and Ellora in Maharashtra. These shrines, hollowed out of granite cliffs, are magnificent works of art in themselves. Between the 2nd century BCE and the 8th century CE, around 1,000 rock-cut structures were built in India, nearly all of them in Central India and the Deccan Plateau. Some of these shrines are rather bare and small, but most of them are large and richly adorned with sculptures and paintings. The largest of all is the shrine at Karli, which measures 125 ft (38 m) long, 50 ft (14 m) wide, and 50 ft (14 m) high.

buddhist shrines

The construction of rock-cut shrines was initiated by Buddhists, and the largest number of these monuments are Buddhist shrines. Later, when Buddhism declined during the late Gupta period (c. 450 CE), Hindus (and Jains, to a lesser extent) also built a number of these structures.

In Ajanta, all of the 30 shrines belong to Buddhists. Typically, these cave structures consist of a shrine (the *chaitya* hall) and an attached monastery (the *vihara*). The *chaitya* hall is designed for group worship; it is usually a long apsidal hall, with a stupa (hemispherical solid mound) carved out of solid rock in the apse. In the shrines of Mahayana Buddhists (who believe in an afterlife, rather than extinction after death), the stupa has a relief statue of Buddha in a niche at the front.

cave art

The stupa, as well as the pillars and cornices in the caves, are usually embellished with carvings, and in most cases their walls are covered with paintings illustrating the life of Buddha or other Buddhist themes. These paintings were executed in the *fresco-secco* method, by applying watercolors to dry plaster. The main emphasis in classical Indian paintings was on creating fluid lines, which were usually drawn with exceptional subtlety and expressiveness (although Indian artists generally disregarded perspective). The Ajanta paintings are among the greatest masterpieces of world art. But what remains today is only a fraction of what was there originally, and nearly all of the surviving paintings are badly damaged, ravaged by time.

Kailasanatha Temple

Among the rock-cut structures of the period, the most remarkable is the 8th-century Kailasanatha Temple at Ellora, in Maharashtra. The entire Kailasanatha Temple, some 100 ft (30 m) in height, is a sculpture. Carved out of a single outcropping of rock, it is considered to be the largest free-standing sculpture in the world. The sculpted temple itself is richly adorned with finely executed carvings of animals, people, and deities.

A column at Ajanta ▷ This figure of a standing Buddha is carved in a niche at the front of a stupa in a Mahayana Buddhist shrine.

▽ **Detail of an Ajanta fresco** Buddha as King Mahajanaka (*right*); many of the Ajanta frescoes depict episodes from Buddha's previous lives.

◁ **Satavahana carving**
The Amaravati stupa in Andhra Pradesh, which was built by the Satavahanas, has some of the most delicately carved sculptures of ancient India.

Traditional Indian chess pieces

CHESS BCE/CE
Chess originated in India in the early centuries of the Common Era. From India, it spread to Persia and the Middle East, and finally to Europe, where it was widespread by the 13th century. Over the centuries, the game changed considerably into its modern form.

SATAVAHANA DYNASTY c. 50 BCE–250 CE
The Satavahanas (also known as the Andhras), a non-Aryan people mentioned in the edicts of Ashoka, established an independent kingdom in the mid-1st century BCE. At its height, the kingdom extended from Central India down the peninsula as far as the Krishna River. Satavahana power endured for about three centuries, until around the middle of the 3rd century CE.

BHAGAVAD GITA c. 10 BCE
The *Bhagavad Gita* (*see pp.270–271*), a 700-stanza-long poem in which Krishna expounds the various philosophical theories of the age, is the most revered philosophical text in Hinduism. Composed around the 1st century BCE, it was a late addition to the epic *Mahabharata*.

60 · 50 · 40 · 20 · 10 · BCE/CE

indo-roman trade

The half-millennium spanning the centuries just before and just after the Common Era began was a period of spectacular expansion for the Indian economy. A crucial factor in this was India's flourishing trade with Rome, fueled by the incessant Roman demand for Asian silks, spices, condiments, and curiosities. Most of these products either originated in India, or passed through Indian hands.

trade boost

Around this time, India's trade with the Western world received a great boost from the discovery (or popularization) of the use of the monsoon winds to sail from Red Sea ports directly to India across the Arabian Sea, instead of taking the slow and hazardous route along the coastline. The balance of the Indo-Roman trade was heavily in India's favor. "There is no year in which India does not attract at least 50 million coins," groused the Roman philosopher, Pliny.

△ **Begrum ivory**
This Indian ivory plaque depicting two demigoddesses is from Begram, Afghanistan, which lay on the Indo-Roman trade route.

CHARAKA BCE/CE
Ayurveda, the Indian system of medicine, was given its definitive form by the scholar Charaka in the 1st century CE. Ayurveda places strong emphasis on maintaining health and preventing disease.

TAMIL SANGAM LITERATURE BCE/CE
Sangam literature, the oldest surviving Tamil works, consists of three poetry anthologies: *Ettuthokai*, *Pathuppattu*, and *Padinenkilkanakku*. These are huge collections, the first two books alone containing some 2,300 poems. *Tolkappiyam*, a work on grammar, was also composed during this period.

◁ **Bimaran reliquary**
This cylindrical gold reliquary (relic holder) from Bimaran, Afghanistan, bears one of the earliest depictions of Buddha in human form.

GANDHARA ART 50 CE
The Gandhara school of sculpture flourished between the 1st century BCE and the 5th century CE. Under Greco-Roman influence, it produced some of the best-known stone sculptures of Buddha in ancient India.

the pan-asian spread of buddhism

While Buddhism was on the decline in India in the 6th century CE, it thrived everywhere else in Asia. Its spread outside India began during the reign of Ashoka (*see p.73*), who initiated Buddhist missionary activities in Central Asia and the Middle East. A crucial development in the pan-Asian spread of Buddhism was its patronage by the Kushana ruler, Kanishka. By about the 6th century CE, Buddhism had spread all over Asia, having reached as far as Japan. Like Christianity in Europe, Buddhism is a strong common cultural factor in most of East and South Asia.

The spread of Buddhism was solely the result of peaceful missionary activity, and involved no military action at all. The religion had an ennobling influence on local cultures everywhere; indeed, the most brilliant periods in the history of most countries in Asia were those in which Buddhism was in bloom.

Emerald Buddha statue from Vietnam

SAKA ERA 78 CE
The Saka era, which began in 78 CE, is today the starting point for India's national calendar (used along with Gregorian calendar dates).

20 50 60 70 80 90 100

Stained-glass window depicting St. Thomas

ST. THOMAS 50 CE
The first major foreign religion to establish itself in India was Christianity. According to ancient tradition, Thomas, an Apostle of Christ, arrived in Kerala in the mid-1st century CE and converted some of the local families to Christianity. From these early converts grew the flourishing Eastern Churches of India (*see p.242*).

KANISHKA 78 CE
Of the many invaders who entered India in this period, the most prominent were the Kushanas (Yueh-chi). Under Kanishka, their greatest king, the vast Kushana Empire stretched across much of Central Asia and North India. He convened the 4th Buddhist council in Kashmir, which led to the emergence of Mahayana Buddhism.

MANU-SMRITI 100 CE
The *Manu-smriti*, the most authoritative law book on the Hindu social order, took its final form in the early centuries of the Common Era.

MAHAYANA BUDDHISM 100 CE
Over the centuries, the Buddhist religion split into several sects, the most important of which are the orthodox Hinayana and the reformist Mahayana. The Mahayana doctrines (*see p.239*) crystallized toward the close of the 1st millennium BCE.

THE GOLDEN AGE

THE RISE AND FALL OF THE GUPTA EMPIRE, 100–500

After the decline of the Kushana Empire, the main theater of political action shifted for a while to peninsular India, particularly to the Satavahana kingdom in the northeast of the peninsula, and to the Chera, Pandya, and Chola kingdoms of South India. This period also saw the rapid progress in the Aryanization of South India. The founding of the Gupta Empire in the mid-4th century brought North India into prominence again. The reign of the Guptas, who dominated the political scene for about two centuries, is known as the Golden or Classical Age of India. It was a time of unprecedented progress in the country, a culmination of the growing cultural and scientific expansion that had been witnessed in India throughout the previous several centuries.

SOUTH INDIAN KINGDOMS c. 100
South India was divided into three distinct political units in the early centuries of the Common Era—the Cholas and Pandyas in the East, and the Cheras in the West. These kingdoms constantly vied with each other for both military and cultural supremacy.

NATYA SHASTRA c. 100
The definitive text on Classical Indian performing arts, the *Natya Shastra* (see *pp.246–47*), was composed by the sage Bharata during the early 2nd century.

A Pandya sculpture of the god Vishnu

GAUTAMIPUTRA SATAKARNI c. 106–130
Gautamiputra Satakarni is considered to be the greatest of all Satavahana rulers. He revived the fallen fortunes of the empire through conquests and repossession of territories lost under previous inept rulers.

KAMASUTRA c. 150
A guidebook for the enjoyment of sensual and sexual pleasures, the *Kamasutra* was formulated by the philosopher Vatsyayana in the mid-2nd century. It describes in detail the art of seduction, the techniques of foreplay and coitus, and prescribes a variety of performance-enhancing concoctions and talismans.

An illustration from the *Kamasutra*

NAGARJUNA c. 150
The Mahayana sage, Nagarjuna, who is believed to have lived sometime between 15 and 250, is considered the greatest metaphysician of India. He founded the *Madhyamaka* (middle path) school of Mahayana Buddhism.

trade and cultural links with southeast asia

Concurrent with North India's overland foreign trade, kingdoms in South India began to develop maritime trade, with the Cholas and Pallavas concentrating on Southeast Asia and China, and the Pandyas and Cheras on the Middle East and the Mediterranean. India's commercial ties with Southeast Asia, involving the trade of textiles, spices, and ivory among other goods, began in the closing centuries before the Common Era, but gradually extended eastward into China and southward into the Indonesian islands. This trade peaked in the late Classical period (c. 400 onward), and remained active until the 13th century.

In Southeast Asia, Indians were more than just traders; they were also disseminators of culture and religion, who radically transformed the ethos of the region and turned it into what is sometimes called "Greater India." Both Hinduism and Buddhism came to have a strong presence, and Sanskrit became the region's sacred language.

Carved ivory elephant figurine

YOGASUTRA c. 200
The *Yogasutra,* the earliest and most authoritative text on yoga, was written by the sage Patanjali in the early 2nd century. It propounds *Rajayoga*, which emphasizes mental discipline to achieve spiritual goals.

Sage Agastya
The Aryanization of South India is associated with the mythical sage Agastya, about whom there are many colorful and contradictory Hindu legends.

aryanization of south india

The introduction of Aryan culture and beliefs into peninsular India is poorly documented. It was evidently initiated by Jain and Buddhist monks in the second half of the 1st millennium BCE, and these religions remained influential in South India for several centuries. Eventually, Hinduism gained popularity, as its inclusive character accommodated the folk cults of the local people, which neither Buddhism nor Jainism could do. By the early centuries of the Common Era, the influence of Hinduism began to trickle into the peninsula, gradually gathering momentum, and in time spreading as far as the southern state of Kerala. However, this was essentially a cultural sweep; there was no extensive migration of Aryans into the peninsula. The process primarily involved the superimposition of Hindu gods—Vishnu and Shiva—on local cults. South India never became as completely Aryanized as the North, and the region has largely retained its distinctive racial, linguistic, and cultural identity throughout its history.

HINDU TEMPLES c. 350
Early Hindu temples were flat-roofed structures, but by the Gupta period, they began to acquire a towered appearance. The oldest existing structure of this type is the Vishnu Temple at Deogarh, Madhya Pradesh.

The Vishnu Temple at Deogarh

260 300 340

240 280 320 360

A Pallava temple at Mamallapuram, Tamil Nadu

THE PALLAVAS c. 300–800
The Pallavas ruled over the northeastern tract of South India for about 600 years, from the 4th to the 9th centuries, with their capital at Kanchipuram, Tamil Nadu. They patronized music, painting, and literature, especially during the later stages of their reign. However, their greatest achievements were in architecture, in particular the majestic Shore Temple and the Ratha (Chariot) temples at Mamallapuram.

THE GUPTA DYNASTY c. 320–550
The long period of chaos in North India that followed the decline of the Kushanas ended with the rise of the Guptas, a dynasty of low caste or tribal origin. Chandra Gupta I was its first sovereign ruler.

SUSRUTA c. 350
An authority on Indian medicine, Susruta formulated the treatise on surgery, *Susruta-samhita*, which deals with complex procedures, such as cosmetic surgery. His original work has been lost; what exists today is a later compilation.

SAMUDRA GUPTA c. 335–380
The Gupta kingdom expanded into a vast empire under Samudra Gupta, who made extensive conquests in North India, and then swept into the peninsula as far south as Kanchipuram. But Samudra Gupta sought to establish his influence in the peninsula by forming alliances, and not via direct rule, which was confined to the Indo-Gangetic plains.

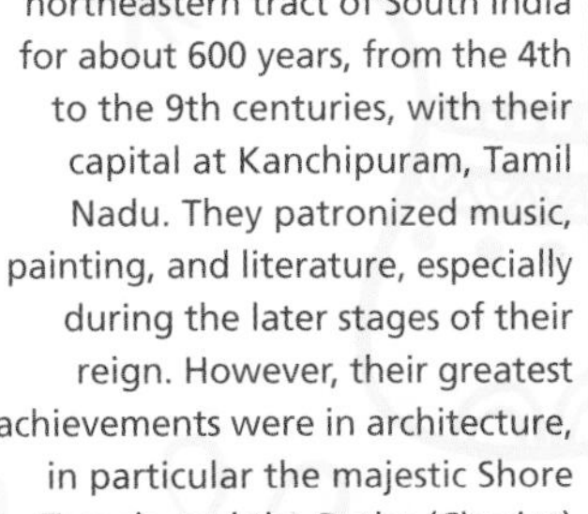

Coin of Samudra Gupta

Ruins of Nalanda, Bihar

A statue of Aryabhata

NALANDA c. 450
Nalanda, founded in the 5th century, was the most celebrated educational center in ancient India. Students from many lands and of different creeds came here for higher education, ranging from Buddhist philosophy to the arts and sciences. It was destroyed by Turkish invaders in the 13th century.

KALIDASA c. 400
The noted 5th-century Sanskrit dramatist and poet Kalidasa is renowned for his romantic plays: *Malavikagnimitra* (*Malavika and Agnimitra*), *Vikramorvasi* (*Urvasi Won by Valor*), and *Shakuntala*.

Scene from *Shakuntala*
Kalidasa's *Abhijnanashakuntala* (*The Recognition of Shakuntala*, or *Shakuntala*), is still popular today.

FA-HSIEN c. 405–411
The Chinese Buddhist pilgrim, Fa-Hsien, spent a decade in India, the last six years of which were spent in the Gupta Empire. His records speak highly of the prosperity and peace in the land.

ARYABHATA c. 460
Aryabhata, ancient India's greatest scientist, made seminal contributions in astronomy and mathematics. He was the first to propose that Earth moves around the Sun.

360 | 380 | 400 | 420 | 440 | 460

CHANDRA GUPTA II c. 375–415
Gupta power reached its apogee under Chandra Gupta II, the son of Samudra Gupta. His empire covered almost the entire Indo-Gangetic plains and most of Central India. His reign was a period of great prosperity and marked the climax of the Classical Indian civilization.

THE MAHABHARATA AND RAMAYANA c. 400
The *Mahabharata* and *Ramayana* are India's most famous religious epics to which numerous poets have contributed since 500 BCE. Both epics were composed orally, and for several centuries, transmitted orally. However, they took their final form by the beginning of the 5th century.

A scene from the Mahabharata
The epics find expression in other art forms as well. A textile motif here depicts Lord Krishna speaking to Arjuna before going to battle in the *Mahabharata*.

Rustproof technology
The iron pillar in Delhi is considered a marvel of ancient Indian metallurgy. It dates to the time of Chandra Gupta II and has not rusted in over 15 centuries.

Temple frieze
Stone carving of lovers enjoying a dance performance. Dance was an essential part of religious rituals and everyday life in Classical India.

480

500

END OF THE GUPTAS c. 500
The Gupta Empire declined by the 6th century due to the collapse of its commercial economy and military exhaustion, caused by the incessant wars waged over the preceding centuries.

VARAHAMIHIRA c. 500
Another great Indian scientist of this age was Varahamihira, who was marvelously versatile and excelled in several fields, including astronomy, astrology, meteorology, and architecture.

sophisticated urban life

The Gupta age was a time of unprecedented prosperity in India, as trade, which had expanded considerably in the previous centuries, reached its peak. Commercial and manufacturing activities flourished, with goods being produced not only for export but also for the expanding domestic market. Moreover, after years of military campaigns, the empire remained stable and peaceful, encouraging growth in the economy, as well as in the arts, particularly in the areas of sculpture, painting, poetry, and drama.

The impact of this wealth and prosperity was felt most in the urban areas of the empire, where affluent city-dwellers began to live in comfort and ease, devoting their time to various refinements of life. A Gupta city, according to Kalidasa in *Shakuntala*, was "sunk in pleasures." It catered to every indulgence—for the hedonists, there were restaurants and taverns, brothels, and gambling dens; for the cultured, literary gatherings, music, dance, and theater. Religious festivals, royal celebrations, and sports and games, including animal fights and gladiatorial contests, were also common.

However, the ideal urbanite of Gupta cities was not a mindless sensualist. He was a highly cultivated person, well-versed in literature and the fine arts, and someone who enjoyed the company of the learned as much as of courtesans. A gentleman of leisure, he had the means and the time to enjoy all the pleasures of life. "Having completed his education, and having acquired wealth by gifts, conquest, commerce, or by inheritance from his ancestors, he should become a householder and pass the life of a *nagarika* (city-dweller)," dedicating himself to the enjoyment of life, advises the *Kamasutra*.

Musician with lute
A terra-cotta tile from a Gupta-age Hindu temple depicts a "semi-divine" musician with a lute—a popular instrument of Classical India.

Priest performing rituals Men take part in *pooja* (a holy ceremony) performed by a Brahmin priest on the beach at Papanasam, Kerala. The Brahmins were at the top of the caste-system hierarchy.

the caste system

The caste system has defined Indian society from the late Gupta period until modern times. It divided people into four *varnas* (classes) with designated social roles: Brahmins (priests), Kshatriyas (rulers and warriors), Vaisyas (farmers, artisans, and traders), and Sudras (serfs and laborers). *Varnas* were subdivided into *jatis* (castes), each with a specific occupation. *Jati* means birth; birth determined a person's caste, and caste determined his class. Neither caste nor class could be changed, and inter-class and inter-caste marriages were forbidden. There were only four classes, but the number of castes varied as old castes died out and new ones emerged.

discrimination and separation

While the four *varnas* were all part of Aryan society, they were not equal, with the Sudras being especially discriminated against. The other *varnas* were *dvijas*, meaning twice-born; their "second birth" was their initiation into Aryan society via the sacred-thread ceremony. But Sudras had no initiation ceremony, and were kept at the periphery of Aryan society.

The outcastes, who formed a major segment of the population, suffered the worst discrimination. Excluded from *varna* society, the outcastes had their own segregated society, itself divided into castes. They lived at the edges of the towns and villages of the *varnas*, for whom the very touch or sight of an outcaste was considered polluting.

preservation of privilege

The caste system regulated every aspect of people's lives, from the gods they should worship and their occupations, to the education they were entitled to and where they should live. Its rules, laid down in the law books of the Brahmins, projected the Brahmins' world-view and interests.

The caste system took its final form by the late Gupta period, and by 1000 CE, it was considered divinely ordained and unalterable. Since then, it has preserved the privileges of the higher castes and has remained unchallenged until modern times. The system has endured because it was based on religious functions and ideas of purity and impurity, rather than wealth and power. Even today, it is an integral part of Indian society, marginalizing some people but providing a sense of community and belonging to others.

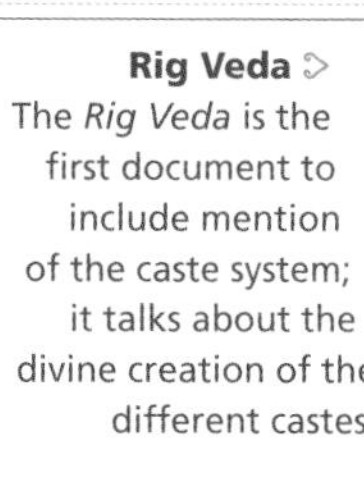

Rig Veda The *Rig Veda* is the first document to include mention of the caste system; it talks about the divine creation of the different castes.

He is a Brahmin . . . in whom truthfulness, liberality, patience, deportment, mildness, self-control and compassion are found . . . Personal virtues are the means to greatness, and not birth or family.

The Mahabharata

उद्धरण

Warrior wall-painting
The Kshatriya (warrior) class prepares to go into battle. Kshatriyas were second only to Brahmins in the social hierarchy.

THE DARK AGES

POWER MOVES SOUTH, 500–997

The age of prosperity and creative brilliance in India ended with the Guptas. By the 6th century, the marauding Huns brought much of western India under their control and, in the south, the Pallavas and the Chalukyas began to fight for regional supremacy. The country gradually slid into the dark ages as its commercial economy collapsed, towns became derelict, and few cultural advances were made. The period also saw the sharp decline of Buddhism and the revival of Hinduism. While these regressive developments particularly affected the north, a "Golden Age" gradually dawned in South India with the rise of the Cholas.

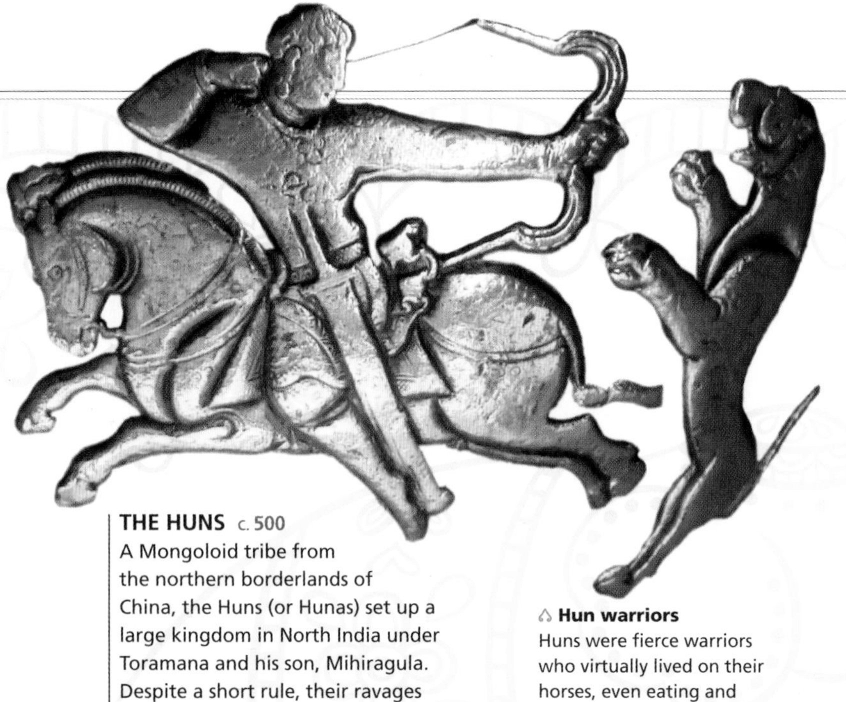

Hun warriors
Huns were fierce warriors who virtually lived on their horses, even eating and sleeping in the saddle.

The Chalukyan Virupaksha Temple at Pattadakal, Karnataka

THE HUNS c. 500
A Mongoloid tribe from the northern borderlands of China, the Huns (or Hunas) set up a large kingdom in North India under Toramana and his son, Mihiragula. Despite a short rule, their ravages ruined India's commercial economy.

THE CHALUKYAS
c. 543–1189
The Chalukyas, originally local chieftains, formed a separate kingdom in the Deccan under Pulakesin I in 543. During their six-century-long reign, they built a large number of spectacular temples at Aihole, Badami, and Pattadakal in Karnataka.

An intricately carved relief from a temple in Badami

DECIMAL SYSTEM c. 595
Invented in India sometime before the 6th century, the decimal system is first alluded to in an inscription of 595.

MAHENDRA-VARMAN I
c. 600–630
The Pallava culture reached a high point under Mahendra-Varman I. A man of many interests, he authored Sanskrit plays, and was a painter, musician-composer, and architect. He bore such titles as *Chitrakara-puli* (*Tiger among Painters*) and *Matthavilasa* (*Drunken Frolicker*).

PULAKESIN II
c. 608–42
The Chalukyas, under Pulakesin II, emerged as the dominant power in peninsular India, controlling vast territories, including parts of Central India.

HSUAN TSANG c. 630
The Chinese pilgrim Hsuan Tsang spent 13 years in India, most of them in the kingdom of Harsha, a prominent ruler in North India. His accounts provide vital information about the history and culture of the age.

ARAB INVASION c. 712
The conquest of Sindh (in present-day Pakistan) by the Arab general, Muhammad Bin Qasim, set the stage for future Islamic invasions of India.

500 520 540 560 580 600 620 640 660 680 720

changing religious scene

The post-Gupta period saw the rapid decline and eventual disappearance of Buddhism in India, as its support base eroded with the collapse of the economy and urban culture. Its decline coincided with the revival of Hinduism, which surged ahead by absorbing several regional folk cults, and new gods, beliefs, rituals, and practices. Indra and Varuna, the great Aryan gods, were replaced by Shiva and Vishnu as the dominant gods. The social expression of Hinduism was the caste system, which along with the intrinsic Hindu attitudes of passivity and fatalism, sought to thwart change and progress, thereby contributing to India's slide into the dark ages.

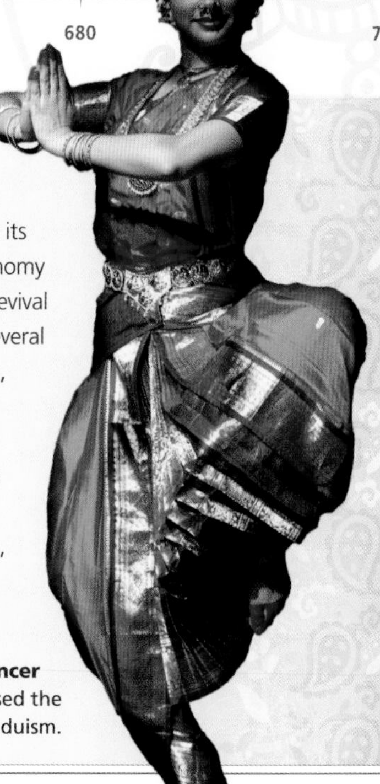

Classical dancer
Classical Indian dance expressed the devotional ardency of Hinduism.

the cholas

The dominant power in South India during the first few centuries of the Common Era, the Cholas virtually disappeared from history for several centuries, only to reemerge as an empire in the late 10th century. Under Rajaraja Chola (r. 985–1014), their rule stretched across the whole of South India and over much of Orissa in the east. The Chola power reached its zenith under Rajendra Chola I (r. 1014–1044), who continued the expansionist policies of his father. During his 30-year reign, he defeated the Palas of Magadha, annexed Sri Lanka, and brought much of Southeast Asia under his influence, creating the most extensive kingdom of the time.

The reign of the later Cholas marks the "Golden Age" of South India, a time of prosperity and high culture. Being patrons of the arts and architecture, they commissioned magnificent sculptures and temples. A flourishing trade with Southeast Asia brought in unprecedented wealth, and during this period, Hinduism spread across much of the region. Chola rule endured for about a century after Rajendra's death in 1044, disappearing completely by the mid-13th century.

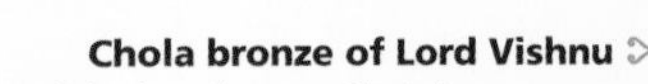

Chola bronze of Lord Vishnu
Some of the best-known Chola bronzes were made between the 10th and 12th centuries.

DHILLIKA c. 736
Dhillika, which later became Delhi, was founded in 736 by the Tomaras, a powerful Rajput clan in North India.

ELLORA TEMPLES c. 775
By the mid-8th century, the Rashtrakutas, former feudatories of the Chalukyas, emerged as the dominant power in the Deccan. To celebrate their victories, the Rashtrakuta king, Krishna I, built the Kailasanatha Temple in Ellora, dedicating it to Shiva.

740 | 760 | 780 | 800 | 820 | 840 | 860 | 880 | 900 | 980

SHANKARA c. 775
A philosopher and theologian from South India, Shankara played an important role in the continual revival of Hinduism in the late 8th century. He gave a definitive form to *Advaita*, a philosophy initially expounded in the Upanishads, which considers the *brahman*—the constant essence of the universe—to be real as opposed to the material world, which is believed to be illusory.

A Pratihara figurine

PRATIHARAS c. 850–950
The Rajput kingdom of the Pratiharas, a migrant Gurjara tribe, dominated North India for well over a century. At its peak, their empire stretched over Gujarat, Rajasthan, and Madhya Pradesh.

ZOROASTRIANISM c. 900
Known in India as Parsis, the Zoroastrians (followers of the prophet Zoroaster) fled to India after Persia was overrun by the Arabs during their imperial expansion in the mid-7th century. Most Parsis migrated to Western India, settling initially in Gujarat, and then spread to Maharashtra, where they occupied themselves with agriculture and trade.

Parsi New Year
A Parsi Head Priest offers annual prayers at a Fire Temple in Mumbai on the occasion of the Parsi New Year.

Tantric yantra
A yantra is a Tantric symbol of cosmic unity, and a tool of ritual and meditation. Yantras are aids to make the journey into the inner self, to perceive the ultimate unity of self and cosmos.

Tantrism

Of all the religious sects in India, the most mysterious is Tantrism. The Sanskrit word *tantra* means "technique", and what distinguishes Tantrism is its practices, not its doctrines. Tantrics, in fact, do not see their cult as an independent religious movement, but rather as an occult practice within the existing religions.

rites and rituals

The Tantric view is that everything in the universe is fundamentally the same, and that all perceived worldly distinctions—including those between good and evil, and the divine and the mundane—are illusory. Tantrics thus feel free of conventional restraints and inhibitions, and may deliberately violate cultural and social norms to equate themselves with gods by doing whatever they please. Tantrics hold that any human activity can be transformed into a spiritual act through occult rites, regardless of morality. "Those evil deeds that cause a man to burn in hell are the same as those by which the yogi attains salvation," states the ancient Tantric text, the *Kularnava-tantra*.

Ritual sex, often performed in a group in a shrine or in a cremation ground, was common practice. This was not an orgy, but an elaborate, formal rite within a consecrated circle. Rather than pleasure, the object was to reach a spiritual plane by transforming sexual energy into spiritual energy.

origins

Tantrism probably existed as a religious undercurrent in India long before it surfaced in history around the middle of the first millennium CE. Over the next few centuries, Tantric cults became prominent in Buddhism, Hinduism, and even in the highly puritanical Jainism. Between the 7th and 9th centuries, the Buddhist version of Tantrism spread to Nepal, Tibet, China, and Southeast Asia.

Tantrism's popularity in India peaked around the 8th century, then gradually declined. In medieval times, Tantrism went underground, and its centers shifted to frontier regions such as Assam, Kashmir, and Kerala as Muslim rulers (and later the British) sought to suppress its practices.

Tara
Female deities figure prominently in Tantrism. Tara is a female Buddha and a focus for Tantric yoga.

A man poisoned may be cured with another poison, its antidote . . .
So the wise purge themselves of passion with yet more passion.

Aryadeva, 7th-century Tantric sage

उद्धरण

Temple relief at Khajuraho Tantrism exerted great influence on social mores and the arts, as evident from these erotic temple sculptures at Khajuraho, Madhya Pradesh.

THE COMING OF ISLAM

RISE OF MUSLIM DYNASTIES IN INDIA, 997–1526

The beginning of the 11th century heralded radical changes for the Indian subcontinent, as raiders from Central Asia paved the way for the establishment of the first Islamic kingdom in 1206: the Delhi Sultanate, led by the Turk Qutb al-Din Aibak. The new rulers were deeply influenced by Indian traditions, especially in the areas of art and architecture. In the South, a powerful kingdom flourished at Vijayanagar; its splendor is still visible in the ruins at Hampi. This was also a time of creative spiritual inquiry, reflected in poetry and music, and in the emergence of Sikhism as a new religion. Toward the end of this period, the Portuguese explorer Vasco da Gama reached Indian shores, leading to the eventual Portuguese occupation of Goa.

A Rajput shield

AL-BIRUNI c. 1017
The noted Persian astronomer and scholar Al-Biruni, came to India in 1017 with Mahmud of Ghazni. During his ten-year stay, he mastered Sanskrit, and studied Indian philosophy and sciences in detail. His accounts, *Tarikh al-Hind* (*A History of India*), published in 1030, give invaluable insights into 11th-century India.

rajput kingdoms

The Rajputs (literally "sons of kings") were Hindu Kshatriya (warrior) clans who attributed their lineages to mythical solar and lunar origins. The most dominant among them, including the Pratiharas, Tomaras, and Chauhans, were rulers of powerful kingdoms spread across much of North and Central India. Others, like the Chandellas—builders of the Khajuraho temples (*see pp.274–275 and pp.352–355*)—reached high levels of artistic and creative achievement. By the 11th century, their power was undermined by serious intergroup rivalry, which enabled Mahmud of Ghazni, the Muslim Turkish chieftain, to plunder their kingdoms. Only the Chandellas, who agreed to pay him tribute, saved Khajuraho from destruction. Subsequently, several Rajput kingdoms attempted to form alliances in order to discourage future invasions. However, following an invasion by Mohamad of Ghori—an Afghan warlord—in the late 12th century, the Rajputs lost their hold over most of North India and failed to stem the rapid spread of Islam into the subcontinent.

980 | 1010 | 1070 | 1100 | 1130

GHAZNAVID INVASION c. 997
Mahmud of Ghazni, a Turkish chieftain from Afghanistan, was the first Muslim ruler to invade India. Between 997 and 1027, he made 17 expeditions across the Punjab and the North Indian plains, sacking Hindu kingdoms and temples for gold and jewels.

Invasion of India
Mahmud's superior Central Asian horses gave his cavalry a decisive edge over Indian horsemen.

the slave dynasty

Before returning to Afghanistan, Mohamad of Ghori instructed his generals to consolidate a new kingdom in India. This marked the beginning of a new epoch in Indian history, where Islam became the ruling culture of the subcontinent, and Persian the ruling language. One of Ghori's generals, Qutb al-Din Aibak, established the Delhi Sultanate in 1206, with its capital at Lahore (Pakistan). His was the first Turkish dynasty in India, and it was known as the Slave dynasty, because Aibak was a former slave who had risen up the ranks. Upon his death in 1210, Aibak was succeeded by his son-in-law, Iltutmish, who, along with his daughter, Raziya Sultana, extended the Sultanate's territories. Despite several differences, the Slave rulers had much in common with preexisting Indian kingdoms. They used military might to subjugate the countryside, and extracted taxation in much the same way as their non-Muslim predecessors.

Iltutmish's tomb at the Qutb Minar, Delhi

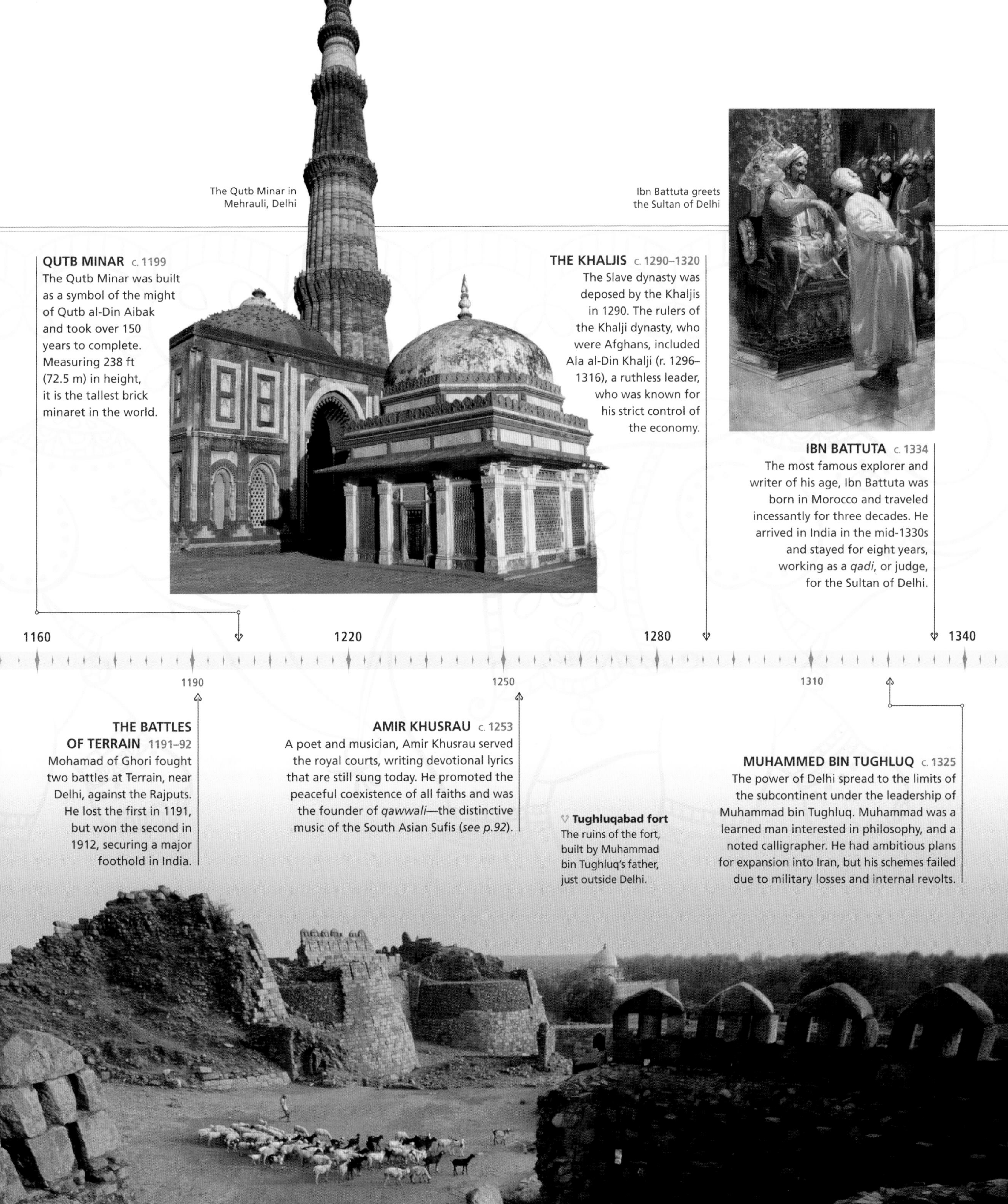

The Qutb Minar in Mehrauli, Delhi

Ibn Battuta greets the Sultan of Delhi

QUTB MINAR c. 1199
The Qutb Minar was built as a symbol of the might of Qutb al-Din Aibak and took over 150 years to complete. Measuring 238 ft (72.5 m) in height, it is the tallest brick minaret in the world.

THE KHALJIS c. 1290–1320
The Slave dynasty was deposed by the Khaljis in 1290. The rulers of the Khalji dynasty, who were Afghans, included Ala al-Din Khalji (r. 1296–1316), a ruthless leader, who was known for his strict control of the economy.

IBN BATTUTA c. 1334
The most famous explorer and writer of his age, Ibn Battuta was born in Morocco and traveled incessantly for three decades. He arrived in India in the mid-1330s and stayed for eight years, working as a *qadi*, or judge, for the Sultan of Delhi.

1160 | 1190 | 1220 | 1250 | 1280 | 1310 | 1340

THE BATTLES OF TERRAIN 1191–92
Mohamad of Ghori fought two battles at Terrain, near Delhi, against the Rajputs. He lost the first in 1191, but won the second in 1912, securing a major foothold in India.

AMIR KHUSRAU c. 1253
A poet and musician, Amir Khusrau served the royal courts, writing devotional lyrics that are still sung today. He promoted the peaceful coexistence of all faiths and was the founder of *qawwali*—the distinctive music of the South Asian Sufis (*see p.92*).

Tughluqabad fort
The ruins of the fort, built by Muhammad bin Tughluq's father, just outside Delhi.

MUHAMMED BIN TUGHLUQ c. 1325
The power of Delhi spread to the limits of the subcontinent under the leadership of Muhammad bin Tughluq. Muhammad was a learned man interested in philosophy, and a noted calligrapher. He had ambitious plans for expansion into Iran, but his schemes failed due to military losses and internal revolts.

Ruins of Vijayanagar ▷
The deserted ruins of monuments and temples can still be visited at the village of Hampi in Karnataka, built at the site of the capital of the Vijayanagar Empire.

VIJAYANAGAR c. 1336–1646
The vast and prosperous Vijayanagar Empire lasted for more than two centuries and dominated South India. The powerful king, Krishnadevaraya (r. 1509–29), presided over the empire at its zenith. Militarily advanced, the kingdom was in persistent conflict with the kingdom of Bijapur and the other Deccan Sultanates, who in the late 16th century banded together to eradicate the empire. Vijayanagar never recovered, and the kingdom crumbled less than a hundred years later.

Chariot shrine at Hampi, Karnataka

1340 · 1355 · 1370 · 1400 · 1415

guru nanak and sikhism

A radical philosopher and saint, Guru Nanak (1469–1539) made spiritual journeys through India, Tibet, and Arabia that lasted many years. During his travels, he studied different faiths and debated with learned men. He founded his own religion of Sikhism (*see p.241*) based on the knowledge he had gained, and became the first of the ten Sikh gurus. Many disciples were attracted to his influential teachings, which are based on the belief that there is only one god and that everyone is equal, regardless of gender or caste. Nanak's final years were spent at Kartarpur in the Punjab, surrounded by Hindu and Muslim disciples. His followers later came to be known as Sikhs ("learners").

◁ **The khanda**
The symbol of Sikhism is made up of a *khanda* (a double-edged sword), a *chakkar* (a throwing disk), and two *kirpans* (swords).

A portrait of Timur

TIMUR INVADES 1398
The Central Asian ruler, Timur, also known as Tamerlaine, sought to expand his power base by invading India. The sack of Delhi by Timur's forces in 1398 was a contributing factor to the fall of the Tughluq dynasty.

THE SAIYID DYNASTY 1414–51
Khidr Khan and his Saiyid dynasty, who succeeded the Tughluqs, claimed to be descended from the prophet Muhammad. In the wake of Timur's invasion, they did not control much territory, and faced constant challenges from other kingdoms and Timurid incursions.

New weaponry ▷ The first battle of Panipat was one of the earliest engagements in the world to involve field artillery.

Tomb of Sikandar Lodhi, Delhi

THE LODHIS 1451–1526
An Afghan dynasty, the Lodhis gained decisive control of Delhi after the fall of the Saiyids. The second sultan, Sikandar Lodhi (r. 1489–1517), made great territorial gains; he also founded the city of Agra. However, after his death, the dynasty struggled to exert its authority, and gradually gave way to Mughal power.

VASCO DA GAMA 1498
The noted Portuguese explorer of Asia and Africa was the first European to create overseas trading routes to India, establishing a port at Calicut, Kerala, after bloody conflict with the local population.

Vasco da Gama

THE FIRST BATTLE OF PANIPAT 1526
Under Babur, the Mughals of Central Asia challenged the Delhi Sultans; the two armies met at the battle of Panipat. The Lodhis resisted their 12,000 attackers with 100,000 men and 1,000 elephants. Though outnumbered, the Mughals had the advantage of gunpowder and light cannon. Their victory marked the beginning of the Mughal Empire.

1430 1445 1460 1475 1490 1505 1520

KABIR 1440
The work of Kabir, a mystic poet, greatly influenced Islamic, Sikh, and Hindu movements in South Asia.

GOA UNDER PORTUGUESE RULE c. 1500–1961
The Portuguese explorer Vasco da Gama first weighed anchor off the Indian coast in 1498, beginning a long period of Portuguese influence in South India. By 1510, attracted by the possibility of seizing control of the spice trade, Portugal had annexed the state of Goa, which became the hub of its maritime empire in Asia. The Portuguese brought their language and government system to Goa, as well as Christian missionaries and European-style architecture, furniture, and craftsmanship.

NOBLES' REVOLT 1519
During their reigns, each of the dynasties of the Delhi Sultanate faced revolts challenging their leadership. Some coups were staged by members of their own families, some by other noblemen. Ibrahim Lodhi (r. 1517–26), a weaker ruler than his father, Sikandar, faced just such a nobles' revolt in the early years of his reign. Risings were sometimes crushed using brute force, but on other occasions proved successful.

▽ **Indo-Portuguese arts and crafts**
Portuguese influence led to a fusion of European and Indian artistic styles, as seen in this miniature cabinet and fan.

THE MUGHAL EMPIRE

INDIA'S GREATEST ISLAMIC RULERS, 1526–1757

The victory of Babur over the last ruler of the Delhi Sultanate in the battle of Panipat (1526) marked the foundation of Mughal rule in India. Babur's dynasty transformed the history of India—the new line of emperors proved to be able rulers who created a vast and powerful empire. The unique Indo-Persianate culture of the Mughals was firmly established during this time. Successive rulers promoted state-building, and brought about revolutionary changes in administration and warfare. Under the Mughals, royal patronage of the arts resulted in a high level of artistic and architectural activity. However, by the 18th century, after 200 years of successful rule, the great empire had begun to weaken, with regional kingdoms breaking away from Delhi's control.

BABURNAMA 1529
Babur's memoirs in the *Baburnama* record his struggle to establish Mughal rule in Delhi. It also reflects his interest in politics, economics, nature, and society in general.

A page from the *Baburnama*

BABUR 1526–30
Founder of the Mughal Empire, Babur defeated every army that stood in his way from 1526 to 1530. He ruled from Agra and Delhi, the twin capitals of the Mughal Empire. More than just a great general, Babur was also a generous patron of the arts.

HUMAYUN 1530–56
Babur's son, Humayun, inherited one of the largest empires in the world, but lost most of it due to internal rebellions. He was forced to flee to Persia by the incursions of Sher Shah Suri, an Afghan warlord from Bihar. He returned after a decade and restored Mughal power, but died shortly afterward.

Humayun's tomb, New Delhi

1520 1530 1540 1550 1560 1570

hunting and polo

Babur was very fond of the game of polo and spread its popularity from Central to South Asia. Polo matches were major events, accompanied by music and large crowds. Hunting was the other great Mughal pastime, with hunting falcons, bows and arrows, and guns commonly used for prey that included tigers, wild birds, and deer. Jahangir, Babur's great-grandson, was known to have kept a pet hunting antelope named "Mansraj." Hunting scenes were also widely depicted in the art of the time. Fine horsemanship was a skill highly regarded in women as well as men. The Mughals developed beautiful hunting grounds, such as the Hiran Minar in Punjab, and cultivated a refined and specialized hunting tradition, which also served as valuable training for battle.

A Mughal hunting jacket

ABOLITION OF SLAVERY 1560
Following debates regarding slavery—a common practice permitted by Islamic law—Emperor Akbar prohibited the slave trade within his kingdom and banned the practice of enslaving prisoners of war, as well as their forcible conversion to Islam.

SUFISM 1562
The Sufi tradition of Islam stresses inner experience of God through meditation and mysticism. The Mughals patronized Sufi saints and their devotees, particularly the Chishti and Naqshbandi Sufi orders. The present structure in Delhi of the tomb of the great Sufi saint Nizamuddin Aulia was constructed in 1562, during Emperor Akbar's time.

Emperor Akbar

Jalaluddin Muhammad Akbar (1542–1605), who ascended to the throne at the young age of 14, was perhaps the greatest of the Mughal leaders. Under the tutelage of his guardian, Bairam Khan, the young prince suppressed revolts successfully, and won the second battle of Panipat in 1556 against Hemu, the last Hindu ruler of North India. He subdued the Rajput kingdoms of Rajasthan, and won their allegiance through matrimonial alliances. Akbar was as successful in peace as in war. He reformed the system of taxation, promoted commerce between regions, encouraged dialogue between religious groups, and gave autonomy to trusted provincial governors. Known for his religious tolerance and spiritual inquiry, he initiated religious debates between scholars of Islam, Sikhism, Hinduism, and even Christian Jesuits from Portugal, and abolished the hated *jizya*, a poll tax on non-Muslims. A great patron of literature, he commissioned a scholar, Abul Fazl, to write the *Akbarnama* (Akbar's biography) and the *Ain-i-Akbar* (Akbar's administration), but never learned to read or write himself, leading some scholars to speculate that he may have been dyslexic.

Emperor Akbar
A miniature painting showing Akbar seated on a throne with the emblem of peace—a dove—on his hand.

Ganjifa playing cards
Made of lacquered cloth and hand- painted, these circular *ganjifa* playing cards depict life in the court of Akbar.

1580 1590 1600 1610 1620 1630

CITY BUILDERS 1590
The Mughals were prolific builders and ruled from fort-cities. Towns such as Agra, Lahore, Delhi, and the now-deserted Fatehpur Sikri (*see pp.302–309*) saw a sharp growth in population and became busy commercial and administrative centers.

ADI GRANTH 1604
The *Adi Granth*, a precursor to the *Guru Granth Sahib*, the holiest book of the Sikhs, was compiled under the guidance of Arjun Das, the Fifth Sikh Guru, in 1604.

JAHANGIR 1605–1627
Highly educated and an art connoisseur, especially of miniature painting, Jahangir ruled the Mughal Empire at its height of military and economic might. His wife, Noor Jahan, shared much of the state power after Jahangir's addiction to alcohol in later life.

EAST INDIA COMPANY 1612
After arriving in Surat on the coast of Gujarat in 1608, the East India Company set up its first factory in 1612. Soon, it was competing with the Dutch, French, and Portuguese for textiles, indigo, and saltpeter.

SIR THOMAS ROE 1616
The first English ambassador to India, Sir Thomas Roe, stayed at Jahangir's court for four years, exchanging letters between Queen Elizabeth I and the emperor. He later published his memoirs of his time in India.

Qawwali singers
A recital of Sufi songs by *qawwali* singers. These songs of human love often have an underlying spiritual meaning.

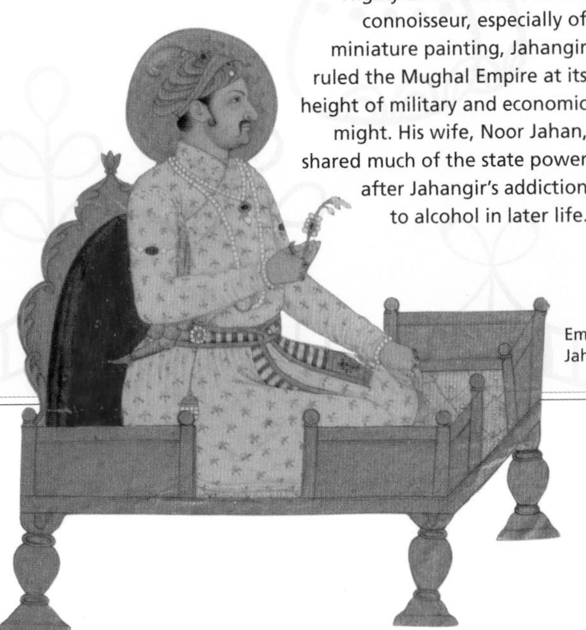

Emperor Jahangir

East India Company ships en route to India

Miniature painting
The Mughals introduced the art of miniature painting as book illustration. This 18th-century scene shows the Hindu god Krishna with ladies in a garden.

Mughal architecture
Shah Jahan's Diwan-I-Khas (Hall of Private Audience) in the Red Fort, Agra, is one of the finest Mughal buildings.

mughal arts and crafts

The Mughal era (1526–1757) was a golden age for Indian creative arts. The Mughals surpassed the earlier sultanates in jewelry-making, painting, garden design, calligraphy, the making of musical instruments, and especially architecture. Visitors from around the world marveled at the craftsmanship of the grand Mughal courts.

emperor patrons

Akbar was the greatest Mughal patron: he commissioned many illustrated manuscripts and employed artists of all religious traditions, from across the empire and beyond. One of the greatest works was *The Adventures of Hamza*. This book of popular legends containing over 1,400 paintings was directed by two Iranian master painters, and took more than 15 years to complete. Mughal rulers were personally involved in overseeing production and sponsoring artists. Akbar's son, Jahangir, was especially fond of painting, and claimed that he could instantly identify the work of any artist. Jahangir's interest in European painting (he had a copy made of Raphael's *Deposition from the Cross*) meant that Mughal artists were exposed to, and influenced by, European techniques of perspective and shading. Individual portraiture developed under Jahangir, as did naturalistic depictions of birds, animals, and wild flowers.

great craftsmanship

Mughal craftsmen transformed everyday objects into beautiful artifacts, from dagger hilts, drinking cups, and spoons to turban ornaments, mirrors, and chess sets. Favorite patterns included scrolling vines of gold inset with gems, and radiating floral patterns. Jade carving was highly valued, too. New techniques such as inlay work, glass engraving, and enameling also became established.

The most lavish Mughal creation of all was the emperor's Peacock Throne in Delhi. Made during the reign of Shah Jahan, it was wrought from over 2,200 lb (1,000 kg) of gold and decorated with 440 lb (200 kg) of precious stones, including diamonds, emeralds, and rubies. Tragically, the throne was looted in Nadir Shah's raid of 1739, and was later destroyed.

Mughal jewelry
This 18th-century gold necklace is etched with grooved patterns and set with precious stones. The smaller piece is a 17th-century enameled gold pendant.

No jeweler can ever determine its worth. How can an ounce scale weigh a mountain? It has no price but whatever else you want it is: Splendour, grandeur, dignity, pomp, beauty, and elegance.

Poet *Kalim* describes the Peacock Throne at the Red Fort, Delhi, 1635

उद्धरण

Inlay detail of Diwan-I-Khas ▷
The inlays of the walls and archway frames depict highly stylized vines, flowers, and fruits. The inlay stones themselves are yellow marble, jasper, and jade, leveled and polished to the surface of the walls.

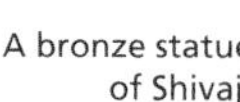

A bronze statue of Shivaji

Mughal women

The Mughal harem (women's quarters) was a self-contained world forbidden to men, where the queens, princesses, and concubines lived in pomp, splendor, and luxury in separate apartments under the guard of eunuchs. However, Mughal women did not just lead cloistered lives; they also shaped the outside political world in many ways—as wives, patrons, courtiers, and power brokers. Noor Jahan (Light of the World), the favored wife of Emperor Jahangir, was the real power behind the throne. She shared and sometimes took political decisions on behalf of her husband. Building projects bore her stamp of approval and even coins were minted in her name. Princess Jahanara, the eldest daughter of Shah Jahan, never married and aided her father in his duties as emperor. She headed his harem, commissioned poetry, and contributed significantly to the architecture of Old Delhi. But perhaps the Mughal woman best immortalized was her mother, Mumtaz Mahal, the beloved queen of Shah Jahan, who died in childbirth and for whom he built the mausoleum called the Taj Mahal.

◁ **Harem life**
Mughal women listen to music in a palace garden.

SHIVAJI 1674–80
The Marathas were clans of Hindu warriors from western India. Shivaji, a Maratha chief, was fiercely independent and used guerrilla tactics to conquer large parts of the Mughal Empire. When forced to submit to the Mughal court in 1666, he made a bold escape from Agra and won back all his lost territories. He founded the Maratha Kingdom in 1674, which grew in power even after his death in 1680.

1630 1635 1640 1645 1650 1655 1660 1665 1670 1675 1680 1685

SHAH JAHAN 1628–58
The third son of Jahangir, Shah Jahan, was the greatest Mughal patron of architecture. He was dethroned and imprisoned by his son, Aurangzeb.

Emperor Shah Jahan

STRUGGLE FOR THE THRONE 1657
Two of Shah Jahan's sons, Aurangzeb and Darah Shikoh, fought a bitter and bloody battle of succession in 1657 to claim his throne. It is said that Aurangzeb celebrated his victory by sending his brother's severed head to his imprisoned father.

THE TAJ MAHAL 1653
Completed in Agra, Uttar Pradesh, in 1653, the royal tomb complex of the Taj Mahal (*see pp.324–331*) took more than 20 years to build. It was constructed from marble brought from Rajasthan, and decorated with precious gems imported from all over the world.

AURANGZEB 1658–1707
After securing his right to the throne, Aurangzeb extended Mughal boundaries through constant wars, thereby weakening the empire considerably. Moreover, his narrow-minded approach to non-Muslims led to resentment against his rule. The last 25 years of his reign were spent fighting in the Deccan, and losing territory to rival states.

Emperor Aurangzeb

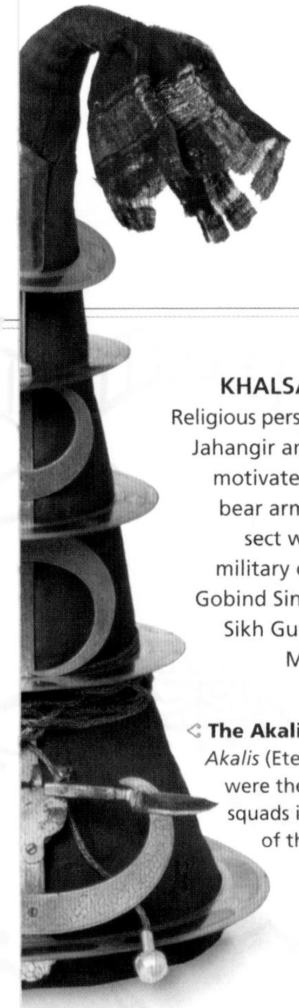

KHALSA SECT 1699
Religious persecution under Jahangir and Aurangzeb motivated the Sikhs to bear arms. The Khalsa sect was set up as a military order by Guru Gobind Singh, the Tenth Sikh Guru, to counter Mughal power.

◁ **The Akali headgear**
Akalis (Eternal Ones) were the suicide squads in the armies of the Sikhs.

◁ **The Peacock Throne**
The original Peacock Throne was destroyed in the chaos that followed Nadir Shah's death, but later Iranian kings created their own versions of the priceless artifact.

NADIR SHAH'S INVASION 1739
Nadir Shah, an Iranian ruler and conqueror, led a daring raid on Delhi in 1739 from his base in Afghanistan. The city was plundered for its riches, which included the *Koh-i-noor* diamond and the Peacock Throne at the Red Fort. Thousands were slaughtered in the city.

1690 1695 1700 1705 1710 1715 1720 1725 1730 1735 1740 1745 1750

ANGLO-INDIAN WAR 1689
The East India Company used both diplomacy and warfare to gain a foothold in India. They courted Aurangzeb with costly gifts, but also attacked Mughal vessels off the coast of Bombay, leading to the First Anglo-Indian War in 1689.

Mughal gardens

The Mughals took great delight in constructing elaborate geometric gardens that were integral to their architecture. Highly maintained and carefully planned, some were built on the banks of rivers, others around tomb-complexes and mosques. Water features and pools were common. The image of the garden, as a metaphor for paradise, pervaded Mughal culture and poetry, along with a deep appreciation for roses. The memoirs of Akbar and Babur also refer to their love of gardens; Babur was fond of the *Charbagh*—a style of garden divided into four quarters and separated by paths. Some of these gardens still exist today, such as the Shalimar Gardens in Kashmir and Lahore, which are famous for their flower beds, terraced lawns, and fountains.

Shalimar Gardens in Lahore

THE FOUNDING OF JAIPUR 1727
The "pink city" of Jaipur was founded by Maharaja Jai Singh II of the Kachwaha Rajput clan. Based on ancient Hindu architectural manuals, the city is planned with a strict geometric layout.

DISINTEGRATION OF THE EMPIRE 1722
The Mughal Empire steadily declined after Aurangzeb's death as successive rulers failed to control external attacks, rural uprisings, and the challenge of breakaway states. In 1724, Hyderabad became one of the first provinces to declare its independence.

Workers at a Lipton tea plantation

TEA 1835
A surging demand in Europe, and the end of the trade monopoly in China in the early 19th century, led the EIC to cultivate tea in India. By 1835, plantations were started in Assam, Darjeeling, and the Nilgiri Hills of South India.

The Fairy Queen
Built in 1855 for the Indian Railways, the *Fairy Queen* is the oldest functioning steam locomotive in the world.

MACAULAY'S MINUTE ON EDUCATION 1835
English was made the language of instruction in schools associated with the EIC in 1835 on the recommendations of Thomas Macaulay, a member of the Governor-General's council, in order to expose Indians to Western arts and sciences.

INDIAN RAILWAYS 1853
The first train service in India ran between Thane and Bombay, a distance of 21 miles (32 km). It was initially for trade and military use, but passenger services grew rapidly.

EMPRESS VICTORIA 1858
In the wake of the 1857 rebellion, the administrative rights of the EIC were annulled, and control of India was handed over to Queen Victoria in 1858.

1830 1835 1840 1845 1850 1855 1860 1865 1870

THUGS 1830
Secret cults, known as "thugs" (Hindi for "thieves"), terrorized parts of North and Central India by robbing and murdering travelers, until a major British campaign succeeded in curbing the menace in the 1830s.

DALHOUSIE'S ANNEXATIONS 1848–56
As the Governor-General of India, James Broun-Ramsay, better known as Lord Dalhousie, brought most of India under British control by taking over several princely states. He started the policy of "Doctrine of Lapse," wherein any states that did not have legitimate male heirs were forcibly annexed by the British.

POSTAL SYSTEM 1853
Postal reforms in the 1850s brought about the beginnings of the modern postal network in India and the launch of postage stamps in 1853. The stamps were called the *Scinde Dawks* because they were introduced in Sindh, in present-day Pakistan.

Dalhousie's forces clash with Sikhs in the Punjab in 1849

Thug menace
A group of "thugs," also called "thuggees," ambush and rob an unsuspecting traveler.

great uprising of 1857

The Great Uprising was a mass revolt against British rule that began in May 1857 as a *sepoy* (native soldier) mutiny in Meerut and rapidly spread to large parts of North and Central India. It was triggered by the introduction of the new Enfield rifles, which used cartridges greased with animal fat. This offended the religious sentiments of the Hindu and Muslim *sepoys* in the British India Army and caused widespread discontent among its ranks. The *sepoys* joined forces with several different groups who had grievances against the British, and marched to Delhi where they proclaimed the Mughal heir, Bahadur Shah Jafar, as their leader. Meanwhile, uprisings against the British continued in Lucknow and Kanpur, leading to the massacre of British men, women, and children. Despite fresh British reinforcements, it took more than a year to completely suppress the rebellion. Reprisals against the rebels were indiscriminate and cruel, involving mass executions. Bahadur Shah was exiled to Rangoon (in present-day Myanmar) and members of his family were executed, formally marking the end of the great Mughal dynasty. In the aftermath of the revolt, the British parliament terminated the East India Company.

The mutiny in Meerut, Uttar Pradesh

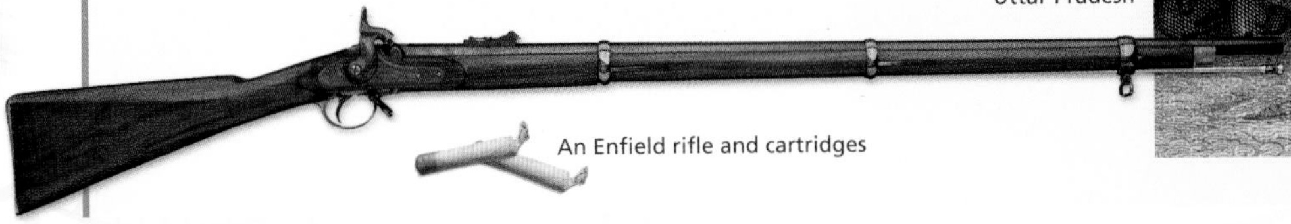

An Enfield rifle and cartridges

FIRST CENSUS 1881
The first comprehensive census, conducted in 1881, pegged India's population at over 250 million. The most complete record of the country's demographics at the time, it classified Indians into groups by religion, caste, and occupation.

INDIAN NATIONAL CONGRESS 1885
Originally an annual meeting of lawyers, the Indian National Congress (INC) emerged as a powerful nationalist force embracing millions of Indians.

ROYAL CORONATION 1903
To celebrate Edward VII's crowning as the King of England, a two-week long ceremony was organized in Delhi in 1903. Eight years later, a similar ceremony was held for the coronation of George V. Events such as these were an ideal way to display the glory and political might of the British Empire to its Indian subjects.

PARTITION OF BENGAL 1905
The Bengal Presidency was divided into Western and Eastern Bengal by the British. In protest, the INC called for a mass boycott of British goods.

1875 1880 1885 1895 1900 1905 1910

The Delhi durbar
The coronation ceremony of Edward VII included a majestic elephant procession through the streets of Delhi.

The young Gandhi
During his years as a practicing lawyer, Gandhi became, in appearance at least, the quintessential English gentleman. He later gave up all material possessions, wearing only a loincloth and shawl made of cheap home-spun cotton, called *khadi.*

mahatma gandhi

Known as the "Father of the Nation," Mahatma Gandhi was the leading figure of the Indian Independence movement. His philosophy of *Satyagraha*—a form of passive, nonviolent resistance—not only led India to independence but also influenced civil rights and anticolonial movements all over the world.

early career

Mohandas Karamchand Gandhi was born in 1869 at Porbander, a small principality in present-day Gujarat. As a young man, he went to London to study law. After qualifying as a barrister in 1891, he relocated to South Africa to begin his law practice. It was here that Gandhi's political ideals took shape. Deeply affected by his eviction from a train carriage because of his skin color, he developed his ideas of *Swaraj* (self-rule) and *Satyagraha,* and organized successful campaigns against racial discrimination.

leading the freedom struggle

Upon his return to India in 1915, Gandhi began to organize small protests in support of the poor, piloting the techniques of strikes, nonviolent processions, and fasts. He called for a nationwide *Satyagraha* in 1919 against the Rowlatt Bills, a harsh British legislation that allowed for the imprisonment without trial of any Indian suspected of terrorism. In 1920, he assumed leadership of the Indian National Congress (INC), and over the following decades he combined spiritual leadership with astute political action. Leading nationwide campaigns for women's rights, religious harmony, an end to caste discrimination, and alleviation of poverty, he was idolized by those marginalized in Indian society and politics.

Gandhi's greatest challenge was to secure the end of rule by the British. Between 1920 and 1942, his three major campaigns—the Noncooperation, Civil Disobedience, and Quit India movements—decisively undermined British authority. He was also closely involved in constitutional negotiations with the British concerning the future of India. At the time of India's independence in 1947, deeply distressed by the partition of the country, which he opposed, Gandhi worked ceaselessly to stem the resulting communal violence. He was assassinated on January 30, 1948 by a Hindu fanatic opposed to interreligious harmony, but Gandhi's legacy remains, and he continues to be revered by millions across India, who celebrate his birthday on October 2 as a national holiday.

The Salt March
In 1930, to protest against the tax imposed on salt by the British, Gandhi led thousands in a 200-mile (320-km) march from Ahmedabad to Dandi to make salt from sea water.

I have nothing new to teach the world. Truth and nonviolence are as old as the hills. All I have done is to try experiments in both on as vast a scale as I could.

Mahatma Gandhi, *Harijan* (March 28, 1936)

उद्धरण

Charkha

Economic self-reliance for India was an important feature of Gandhi's ideology. Calling all Indians to reject imported textiles, he promoted the *charkha* (spinning wheel) to encourage pride in homespun cloth.

Capital complex
Inaugurated in 1931, Delhi's capital complex presents an imposing mix of Eastern and Western architectural styles.

1910 · 1920 · 1930 · 1940 · 1950

DELHI BECOMES CAPITAL 1911
Delhi replaced Calcutta as the capital of India in 1911, because of its central location. The majestic architecture of New Delhi, laid out in a radial design to the south of the old city, was conceived by British architects Edward Lutyens and Herbert Baker.

FIRST FEATURE FILM 1913
India's first full-length feature film, *Raja Harishchandra*, was a silent movie directed by Dadasaheb Phalke.

RABINDRANATH TAGORE 1913
The Bengali poet and philosopher Rabindranath Tagore became the first Indian to win the Nobel prize in 1913 for his work, *Gitanjali*.

Rabindranath Tagore

Jallianwala Bagh after the massacre

JALLIANWALA BAGH 1919
Hundreds of unarmed people were fired upon and killed by troops under Brigadier Dyer at the Jallianwala Bagh enclosure in Amritsar in 1919, sparking widespread unrest against British rule.

NONCOOPERATION MOVEMENT 1920
The first national movement of resistance against the British, Gandhi's Noncooperation Movement encouraged the boycott of British institutions and goods.

MUHAMMAD IQBAL 1930
A leading poet and intellectual, Muhammad Iqbal gave a speech to the All-India Muslim League arguing for a separate Muslim state.

CIVIL DISOBEDIENCE MOVEMENT 1930
In 1930, Mahatma Gandhi launched a nationwide Civil Disobedience Movement in protest of the British salt laws in colonial India.

WORLD WAR II 1939
Indian troops played a major role in World War II, fighting for the British forces in Africa, Asia, and Europe. India generated the largest volunteer army in world history, comprising over 2.5 million soldiers.

BENGAL FAMINE 1943
A devastating year-long famine in Bengal, due to a massive shortage of rice, resulted in over 3 million deaths.

INDEPENDENCE 1947
India became independent at the stroke of midnight on August 15, 1947.

Indians at the Front
This magazine cover depicts a *sepoy* a for Britain and its allies in Italy.

the partition of india

The British Empire in India was divided into the independent nations of India and Pakistan in August 1947. The partition, which occurred along religious lines, not only resulted in one of the largest mass migrations in human history, but also led to unprecedented violence between Hindus, Muslims, and Sikhs in the riots that accompanied the British withdrawal.

reasons for partition

The Indian Nationalist Movement, which had been steadily growing since the late 19th century, intensified in the early 20th century. An increasing Hindu dominance in the Indian National Congress (INC) led to the formation of the All-India Muslim League as an alternate platform for the representation of Muslim interests in the freedom struggle. The Muslims feared cultural suppression in a Hindu-dominated society, and the deep-rooted ideological differences between the Hindus and Muslims seeded communal conflicts across India. With the prospects of independence looming large, political differences sharpened between the INC and the Muslim League, and thus partition of India was agreed upon as the only viable solution.

the partition and its aftermath

The actual demarcation of territories was decided on June 3, 1947 by Viceroy Lord Mountbatten, the INC, the Muslim League, and other parties. Muslims, who constituted 25 percent of the population, were mainly concentrated in the northeast and northwest regions, which became East and West Pakistan. This demarcation had unfortunate consequences in the provinces of Punjab and Bengal, where mixed communities of different religions lived closely together in small towns and villages, which straddled both sides of the new borders. Following the division of resources, such as the military, government administration, and treasury, between the two nations, the British hurriedly withdrew, which led to a complete breakdown of law and order.

The impact of the partition was devastating and caused an unexpected mass migration or "population exchange," wherein over 15 million people crossed the border, with Muslims fleeing to Pakistan, and Hindus and Sikhs to India. Refugees traveled by train, bullock cart, or on foot, often carrying few possessions. Violent riots, murders, lootings, and rapes were common, and an estimated one million people died in the aftermath of the partition. Afterward, both countries spent extensive amounts of money on the rehabilitation and housing of the refugees.

The years following the partition have seen recurrent hostility between India and Pakistan, and a deadlock over the state of Kashmir—which both India and Pakistan lay claim to—that exists to this day.

LA DOMENICA DEL CORRIERE

Supplemento settimanale illustrato del NUOVO CORRIERE DELLA SERA - Abbonamenti: Italia, anno L. 930, sem. L. 500, - Estero, anno L. 1230, sem. L. 650

Anno 49 — N. 35 — 31 Agosto 1947 — L. 20 (Arretrati L. 25)

L'India indipendente. Dopo lunghi anni di lotta l'India ha ottenuto l'autonomia: divisa in due grandi Stati, l'Indostan (in maggioranza indù) e il Pakistan (musulmano), essa è diventata una parte libera della Comunità britannica. A Londra, i rappresentanti dei due nuovi Stati annunciano lo storico avvenimento, presentando le rispettive bandiere: quella dell'Indostan, gialla bianca e verde, quella del Pakistan, bianca e verde.

India and Pakistan
This newspaper clipping from August 1947 shows the flags of the newly formed countries of India and Pakistan post-independence.

Mass exodus
Thousands of refugees gather at the train station in Amritsar, Punjab, in October 1947. Amritsar was a hub for the exchange of refugees due to its proximity to the border between India and Pakistan.

After Independence, India became a democratic republic, with a constitution that promoted liberty and equality for all its citizens. With India's first prime minister, Jawaharlal Nehru, at the helm, the country slowly began to take steps toward becoming a modern nation. After years of foreign dependence, self-sufficiency became the new mantra for its policy makers, and gradually, impressive gains were made in agriculture and industrial development. Despite ongoing social and religious tensions, the democratic fabric of the country that was set in 1947 remained intact over the following decades. After 1991, sweeping economic reforms were introduced, which brought unprecedented levels of growth to most sectors of the economy.

CONSTITUTION 1950
The Indian constitution, one of the longest in the world, was adopted on January 26, 1950. Considered the supreme law, it defines the rights and duties of citizens, as well as the structures and powers of the government. It paved the way for the first general elections, held under universal suffrage in 1951–52.

Republic Day parade January 26 is celebrated as the Republic Day of India, with an annual military and cultural parade in New Delhi.

FIVE-YEAR PLANS 1951
After Independence, the Indian government began to boost infrastructure and economic growth through a series of five-year plans. The first plan, introduced in 1951, focused on irrigation, communications, heavy industries, and energy.

1950 1955 1960 1965

MOTHER TERESA 1950
Mother Teresa, an Albanian Roman Catholic nun, founded the "Missionaries of Charity" in Kolkata in 1950 to aid and empower the poor and helpless. She was awarded the Nobel Peace prize in 1979 for her outstanding service to humanity.

Mother Teresa in Kolkata

KASHMIR 1947
Following a Pakistani invasion of the Muslim-dominated princely state of Kashmir, its Hindu ruler, Hari Singh, acceded to India in exchange for military support. The kingdom was split into two, with both nations laying claim to the lost territories.

GREEN REVOLUTION 1965
India, which had relied heavily on food imports, managed to achieve self-sufficiency in food grains by investing in new high-yielding seeds, fertilizers, and several other agricultural innovations—collectively known as the Green Revolution.

INDIRA GANDHI 1966
Indira Gandhi, India's first female prime minister, dominated Indian politics during the 1970s and early 1980s. She was killed by her Sikh bodyguards in 1984, after the Indian army entered the Golden Temple in Amritsar to flush out Sikh militants.

INDEPENDENT INDIA

ENTERING THE MODERN AGE, 1947–2010

Nehru

Jawaharlal Nehru (1889–1964) was a leading figure in Indian politics from the 1930s until his death, first as an influential leader of the Indian National Congress (INC) and the nationalist struggle, and after independence, as India's first prime minister. Born to a prominent lawyer family, he rose in the INC as a left-wing leader and developed a close relationship with Mahatma Gandhi. As prime minister, he steered the country toward a democratic and pluralistic constitution. A firm believer in socialism, Nehru favored a closed economy and a central role of the government in promoting economic development. He supervised the introduction of the five-year plans that helped stabilize India's economy. Nehru also pioneered India's foreign policy of nonalignment, resisting pressures to join ranks with the US or USSR during the Cold War. His charisma and affable personality made him popular among Indians, especially children, who still celebrate his birthday on November 14 as Children's Day.

Prime Minister Nehru
Nehru was the prime minister of India for 17 years, serving four successive terms.

New TV audiences
Moving beyond urban centers, satellite television has also made great inroads into rural India.

SATELLITE TELEVISION 1991
The advent of 24-hour satellite television in 1991 offered audiences a multitude of foreign and domestic channels for the first time, stimulating growth in the entertainment and advertising industries.

1970 1975 1980 1985 1990

WAR WITH PAKISTAN 1971
A two-week war broke out between India and Pakistan in December 1971, over the separatist movement in East Pakistan. An Indian victory led to the creation of an independent Bangladesh.

FIRST NUCLEAR TEST 1974
India joined the elite league of nuclear nations after conducting its first nuclear test in 1974 in the Thar Desert of Rajasthan.

Bhabha Atomic Research Center, Trombay, Maharashtra

THE EMERGENCY 1975
Under pressure from opposition parties over alleged electoral fraud, Indira Gandhi suspended civil liberties from June 1975 to March 1977. During this period, known in India as the Emergency, many rival leaders were jailed and the freedom of the press was curtailed.

MANDAL COMMISSION 1979
The Mandal Commission, formed in 1979 to identify marginalized sections of society, proposed higher quotas of tribal people, lower castes, and women in public jobs and educational institutions. Its suggestions, implemented in 1991, polarized Indian society and caused a political backlash.

CRICKET WORLD CUP 1983
India became the first Asian country to win the Cricket World Cup when it beat the West Indies in England. The unexpected victory sent the entire country into a mass frenzy.

MARUTI 800 1983
A government-backed project in collaboration with Suzuki, the Maruti 800 car was produced as the first affordable car for India's middle classes. Over 2.5 million units have been sold since 1983.

The Indian cricket team with the World Cup in 1983

Maruti Suzuki's Maruti 800 car

◁ The Bombay Stock Exchange
The Bombay Stock Exchange (BSE) has seen record growth since its markets were opened up to foreign capital.

NEW ECONOMIC REFORMS 1991

Unable to repay its external debts, the Indian government was forced to open up the economy in 1991. Over time, state-owned industries were sold, restrictions on foreign trade and investments were reduced, and private participation was encouraged. Today, India's economy is growing at more than 9 percent a year—one of the fastest in the world.

SATYAJIT RAY 1992

The prolific Bengali film-maker Satyajit Ray (1921–92) was given an honorary Academy Award for his contribution to cinema. Ray, who made over 35 films, was renowned for his character-driven plots and realistic depictions of human life.

COUNCIL SEATS FOR WOMEN 1992

The 73rd constitutional amendment formalized local governance by *Panchayats* (village councils), elections for which are held every five years. For the first time, one-third of the council seats were reserved for women.

Sushmita Sen, winner of Miss Universe in 1994

BEAUTY QUEENS 1994

The crowning of Aishwarya Rai as Miss World and Sushmita Sen as Miss Universe in 1994 started a winning streak for Indians at global beauty pageants. Despite criticism from some women's groups, such wins have helped promote the growth of India's budding fashion industry.

ARUNDHATI ROY 1997

Arundhati Roy became the first native Indian writer to win the Booker Prize in 1997. Her work, *The God of Small Things*, was one of the first books to popularize contemporary Anglo-Indian literature.

1990

1995

ASSASSINATION OF RAJIV GANDHI 1991

Former prime minister Rajiv Gandhi, who sent Indian soldiers to fight Tamil separatists in Sri Lanka, was killed by a Tamil suicide bomber during an election rally in May 1991.

BABRI MOSQUE DEMOLITION 1992

The 16th-century Babri mosque in Ayodhya, Uttar Pradesh, was demolished by Hindu extremists who believed that it stood over a temple marking the birthplace of Lord Rama. The event precipitated widespread Hindu–Muslim riots across India.

▽ Religious extremism
Hindu extremists stand atop the razed Babri mosque on December 6, 1992.

AMARTYA SEN 1998

The prominent economist and philosopher Amartya Sen was the first Indian to win the Nobel Prize for Economics in 1998, for his work on welfare economics.

Madhuri Dixit
One of Bollywood's leading actresses in the late 1980s and early 90s, Madhuri Dixit appeared in more than 60 movies.

bollywood goes global

Film-making in Bollywood (*see pp.256–57*) saw a subtle shift in the 1990s. Innovative storylines, technical advancements, and lavish production led to a rapid growth in revenues in the Asian, North American, and European markets. The rising international popularity of Bollywood was exemplified by such breakthrough films as *Lagaan*, which was nominated for the best foreign-language film at the Academy Awards in 2001. Bollywood films also evolved to reach expanding nonresident Indian audiences in the US and elsewhere, by reflecting their aspirations and lifestyles. One of the highest grossing Hindi films in the UK and US was *Kabhi Khushi, Kabhi Gham*. Aimed at the diasporic audiences and set in both London and India, it celebrated traditional values juxtaposed with a rapidly changing modern world.

A poster for *Kabhi Khushi, Kabhi Gham*

COMMONWEALTH GAMES 2010
The 2010 Commonwealth Games are to be hosted in Delhi. The forthcoming event has accelerated urban development, including the expansion of road networks, overpasses, and mass transit systems, and the construction of a Games Village on the banks of the Yamuna River.

2000

2005

2010

POPULATION TOPS ONE BILLION 2000
The population of India exceeded the one billion mark in 2000. Today, India has one of the youngest populations in the world, with over a third of its people under 15 years old.

GUJARAT EARTHQUAKE 2001
On January 26, 2001, a devastating earthquake measuring 7.9 on the Richter scale hit Gujarat. Over 20,000 people perished and hundreds of thousands were injured, besides economic losses worth billions of US dollars.

INDIA–PAKISTAN BUS SERVICE 2005
Following the launch of the first bus service between Lahore and Delhi in 2001, another bus service was initiated in 2005 between Muzzafarabad, in Pakistan-occupied Kashmir (POK), and Srinagar, in Jammu and Kashmir in India. For the first time since 1947, Kashmiri people from both sides could travel freely across the disputed border. This has been one of the highlights of the ongoing peace process between India and Pakistan.

growth of megacities

India's largest cities—Mumbai (Bombay), Delhi, Kolkata (Calcutta), and Chennai (Madras)—have been growing at a tremendous pace since Independence. While approximately three-quarters of the Indian population continues to live in rural areas, and India's overall level of urbanization is low, these megalopolises attract incessant migration because of greater opportunities for employment and a higher standard of living. Delhi's population has increased more than ten-fold since 1951, to approximately 16.5 million in 2006. Almost half of Mumbai's population is estimated to be living in slums. The burden on the infrastructure of these cities will be one of the greatest challenges that India will face in the 21st century.

Mumbai
A major commercial hub, Mumbai is the most populous city in India.

THE FUTURE OF INDIA

INDIA BEYOND 2010

As India's economy continues to expand, the country looks well placed to be a leading power in the 21st century. Its growing upper and middle classes are ready to enjoy the benefits of globalization—from tourism and travel to modern shopping malls. Nevertheless, India's economic growth will come at a cost. The impact on the environment will increase as the population grows, cities and towns expand, and more and more natural resources are consumed to fuel development. The large percentage of the population who live below the poverty line will continue to struggle unless they are made a part of the development process. In the future, the country and its leadership will have to adapt and devise new and innovative strategies to overcome these problems.

ECONOMY

INFORMATION TECHNOLOGY

India's information technology industry is currently generating over US$11 billion of business a year. Cities such as Bangalore have become global hubs of programming and outsourcing. With a huge resource pool yet to be tapped, the IT industry is predicted to grow beyond US$50 billion by 2012.

LOW-COST AIRLINES

The recent emergence of low-cost airlines in India has made air travel affordable for millions of middle-class consumers. It is projected that by 2020, the number of domestic passengers will double to surpass 60 million. As more and more Indians take to the skies, many smaller cities will be opened up to business and domestic tourism.

One of India's low-cost airlines

RETAIL REVOLUTION

India is in the midst of a retail revolution, with supermarkets and shopping malls offering a variety of goods to consumers who have traditionally relied on neighborhood shops for their needs. With overseas retailers eager to enter the markets, consumers will have even more choice in the near future.

A shopping mall in Bangalore

SOCIETY

Precious commodity Indian tribal women filling their pitchers with drinking water from water tankers in Gujarat.

WATER SCARCITY

India's water tables are falling due to excessive use, and pollution of its rivers has reached alarming levels. Rural farmers still rely on seasonal rains for irrigation, while cities and villages are facing severe shortages of drinking water. The country faces a turbulent future unless management of its water resources is radically improved.

POPULATION GROWTH

By 2050, India's population—which is currently second only to China—is set to become the world's largest. With over 35 percent of its population under 18 years of age, India will reap the benefits of a growing workforce. However, providing education and social security to all will be a huge task for future governments.

INDIANS OVERSEAS

The 20 million Indians living overseas are an important political and economic group for India. Some have been living abroad for decades, while others are recent migrants. In the future, the Indian government may ease their access into the country by allowing them dual citizenship.

Voices of dissent ▷ Female daycare workers gather on the streets of Delhi to protest against government policies.

POLITICS

WOMEN IN POLITICS

Indian women have traditionally held limited power in politics, largely due to the country's male-dominated society. However, in recent years, several women have emerged as influential politicians. Today, one-third of seats on village councils are reserved for women. In the future, such quotas will also be present in state assemblies and the Parliament.

AN INTERNATIONAL FORCE

As an emerging economic and military force, India desires to play a greater role on the world stage. Its aspirations for a permanent seat on the United Nations' Security Council may be realized in the future.

PEACE WITH PAKISTAN

After nearly six decades of incessant rivalry, India and Pakistan have been involved in peace talks for the last five years, with hopes that good relations will continue to flourish in the future.

TECHNOLOGY

SPACE PROGRAM

India is among the few countries to have realized the potential of space technology. After launching a series of satellites into orbit since 1975, it is now planning crewed missions into space and manned expeditions to the moon.

An Indian satellite launch vehicle

PHARMACEUTICALS AND MEDICINE

In the recent past, India's network of private hospitals and its pharmaceutical industry have grown rapidly due to low research and production costs, and a rising demand for affordable healthcare. India is set to become a global center for low-cost but world-class medical facilities.

ENVIRONMENT

ALTERNATIVE ENERGY

A limited supply of fossil fuels and surging demand for power has forced India to search for alternative energy sources. Besides nuclear power, sizable investments have been made in renewable sources of energy, such as wind and solar power.

CARBON EMISSIONS

India's carbon emissions have risen by more than 50 percent since the 1990s. Although per capita emissions are still low, a growing population and rising living standards may push emissions much higher, contributing to global warming.

Clean energy ▷ A wind farm in Gudihalli, Karnataka. Wind power is rapidly emerging as an alternative to energy produced from fossil fuels.

PEOPLE

A DAY IN THE LIFE

India's people are its greatest strength and greatest challenge. A kaleidoscopic range of ethnicities, social groups, religions, castes, languages, customs, and allegiances make for a vibrant but volatile social fabric, which is represented on a global scale in the world's largest democracy of over 1.1 billion people. Despite the lingering effect of centuries of social and political oppression under British rule, India is emerging as an economic powerhouse; industry and services are growing exponentially, super-rich Indians feature regularly in *Forbes* magazine's lists of billionaires, and a huge middle class has emerged. However, vast disparities remain—60 percent of the population survives by labor-intensive agriculture, and 300 million people still live on incomes of under $1 a day. As India negotiates the tricky path between development and human cost, its government must work to ensure that this vast group is not ignored or forgotten. This chapter follows 14 individuals from all walks of life to give a sense of the social diversity found in India today.

HINDU PRIEST

PRAYERS ON THE BANKS OF THE GANGES, VARANASI

Vinay Kumar Tiwari looks out at the Ganges from the steps of Ahilyabai Ghat on the western bank of the river. "The city of Varanasi is so ancient that every single street has a story and something which is holy for someone," he says. "This is where the great poet Tulsidas sat and where the sage Ved Vyas conversed with the gods. It is the center of the universe."

Tiwari, one of the many Hindu Brahmin priests (*paandas*) who populate this city, rarely leaves the *ghats*, the stone steps that line the Ganges River. He has lived all of his 54 years in the 250-year-old stone house nearby in which he was born, and is known by the nickname "Gullu Paanda." "My family originates from Maharashtra, and were the priests of the Holkar clan. They moved to Varanasi with the Holkar royal family. My house used to be one of the royal outhouses. My father was a priest, too." Gullu Paanda studied Hindi and Theology at university, and now takes care of Ahilyabai's temple to the goddess Kali, next to the famous Dasashvamedha Ghat.

Varanasi, also known as Kashi and Benares, is the spiritual capital of India. It has always drawn holy men, pilgrims, and tourists, many of whom rely on *paandas* to conduct their prayers and rituals. Of all the prayer ceremonies on the *ghats*, the autumn festival of Diwali, or the festival of lights, is particularly beautiful. It celebrates the return of the god-king Rama to his realm on a moonless night, so people set out oil lamps to light his way. As the residents of Varanasi are followers of Shiva, rather than Vishnu, the city concentrates its celebrations on Dev Deepavali, 15 days after Diwali. In the evening, the city is ablaze with lights and candles; the houses are decorated with oil lamps and colored patterns outside the front door. Firecrackers light up the sky. There are processions of carved deities in the streets, and oil lamps are set afloat on the river.

Life as a priest is financially hard. Gullu Paanda once attempted to run a business selling rosaries in Delhi and Mumbai, but now makes a very modest living renting out rooms in his house for 150 rupees per night, and from leasing wooden platforms on his *ghat* to priests from lower orders. "It's a challenge to keep one's faith. *Shraddha* (devotion) is disappearing," he says. "Modern-day children only worship success. What do they care for poor priests?" His own 22-year-old son has firmly rejected priesthood in favor of an MBA course and a corporate job.

Varanasi is spiritually significant not just for Hindus, but also for Muslims, Jains, and Buddhists. Gullu Paanda says, "There's no divide here. My Muslim friends visit me and eat with me. When you come here, take a dip in the river and visit the temples of all the gods. This is God's own city."

THE GHATS
The *ghats* along the Ganges are always alive with people. In addition to tourists and pilgrims, most residents of Varanasi bathe and pray in the holy water every day.

DAILY IMMERSION
Gullu Paanda bathes in the river every morning, even drinking the water. He is unfazed by talk of pollution from industry effluents and by corpses floating in the Ganges from the cremation *ghats*.

RITUAL PRAYERS
Gullu Paanda immerses himself, ritually ducking his head, and prays to the sun. The water of the Ganges is believed to wash away sins and purify the soul.

GETTING DRESSED
Once Gullu Paanda emerges from the sacred water, he refastens his *dhoti*, or lower-body wrap. Its saffron color is typical of the Hindu religion.

APPLYING FACE PAINT
He smears a paste on his forehead and scrapes three lines in it, marking himself as a worshipper of Shiva, the Destroyer. Varanasi's Hindus are mostly Shaivites.

PRAYING ON THE GHAT
Gullu Paanda conducts a prayer in honor of his forefathers, a ritual especially auspicious in the two weeks of the new moon.

PERFORMING A SACRED RITE
A priest of the *ghats* is lower than a temple priest, so a priest of a higher level sometimes helps Gullu Paanda to conduct ceremonies.

Mother Ganga is a living goddess, holy and pure. We pray to her every day.

पुरोहित

Varanasi was once made of gold, but because of the people's wickedness, it turned to stone.

पुरोहित

DAILY PRAYERS
Gullu Paanda conducts a small prayer as part of his daily routine. Prayers are a regular occurrence in most Indian households, for all faiths.

BUYING FLOWERS
He buys garlands and ropes of flowers to decorate his home and the Kali temple, of which he is the caretaker. Stands selling flowers and earthen lamps do a brisk trade during Diwali.

SHOPPING FOR DIWALI
Gullu Paanda buys statues of Ganesha, the elephant-headed god, and Lakshmi, the goddess who brings luck and prosperity, as well as some colorful tinsel and cloth.

▽ **FAMILY LUNCH**
In the early afternoon, Gullu Paanda stops at his home, which is close to Ahilyabai *ghat*, for a quick meal with his wife and son.

◁ **CHECKING ON HIS GUESTHOUSE**
Gullu Paanda looks in on the rooms he rents in his house. Most priests have to rely on additional sources of income as patronage is increasingly rare.

▽ **PRAYING AT THE KALI TEMPLE**
On his way to the local tea shop for a drink, Gullu Paanda pauses to say a brief prayer at his small temple on Ahilyabai *ghat*, which is dedicated to the fearsome goddess Kali.

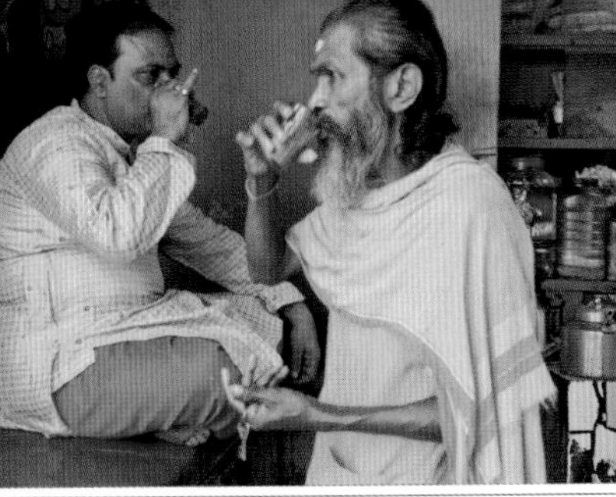

◁ △ **DRINKING TEA WITH A FRIEND**
Varanasi has a thriving and laid-back street culture, with refreshment stands, people, and even animals crowding the tiny lanes that make up the heart of the city.

△ ▷ **EATING PAAN**
Varanasi is famous for betel-leaf rolls, a digestive known as *paan*. Connoisseurs of *paan* claim to be able to distinguish the individual maker by the blend.

EVENING BOAT RIDE
It is traditional on most evenings, but especially during Diwali and the Dev Deepavali celebrations, to go out on the water and set an oil lamp afloat.

OFFERINGS ON THE GHAT
With candles and oil lamps on the steps of the *ghat*, Gullu Paanda makes an offering of purifying incense and then sits down to pray. The string around his chest is the mark of a Brahmin.

ARTI AT DASASHVAMEDHA GHAT
Dasashvamedha Ghat is the most holy in Varanasi. A spectacular *arti* prayer to the goddess Ganga is performed nightly. Priests with blazing oil lamps move in unison.

ARTI RITUALS
A priest performs the *arti* ritual at the shrine of Ganga, circulating flames around the statue of the goddess while singing. The crowd assembled on the *ghat* sings along.

FAMILY OFFERINGS
Statues of Ganesha and Lakshmi are encircled with flowers. A tiny oil lamp, a bowl of sweets, and red powder to anoint the statues and the worshippers complete the offerings.

FAMILY PRAYERS
Diwali is essentially a family festival conducted at home. Even if people visit each other in the evening, they begin with a small prayer at home. Windows and doors are left open to welcome Lakshmi, the goddess of abundance.

PRAYERS AT THE TEMPLE
Gullu Paanda goes to his Kali temple on Ahilyabai *ghat*, which is decorated with the auspicious marigold flowers and leaves that he bought at the market earlier in the day, and conducts a prayer ceremony with another priest.

EVENING CROWDS
In the excitement created by the Diwali festival, residents of Varanasi stay out late in the narrow lanes of the city to shop, eat and meet and chat with friends.

◁ **HINDU IDOLS**
Statues of the many Hindu gods, made of wood, marble, stone, or painted pottery, are used in Hindu worship, both at home and in the temple.

Prayer is woven into the fabric of life in every part of India, whether the ritual is Hindu, Muslim, Christian, Buddhist, or Zoroastrian. Hinduism is the most prevalent religion in India, and Hindu prayer has a rich panoply of gods on which to call. Most Hindus conduct their own personal rituals, known as *pooja* (or *puja*), with no more than a small flame, incense, a dab of *sindoor* (red powder), a few grains of rice, and a few words. More complex rituals often involve hiring a priest, a *pundit* (Hindu scholar), or another knowledgeable guide to assist. This is the case for a Vedic *havan*, an elaborate purification ritual using Sanskrit *shlokas* (verses) with which many ordinary people are not acquainted. There are specific rituals for birth, death, and everything in between, including the start of a journey, buying a new car, moving into a new house, getting married, warding off illness and the evil eye, and giving thanks. Hindu rituals are carefully prescribed in terms of timing, the particular god to be worshipped, the choice of words or songs, and the gestures to be used.

THE RITUAL OF PRAYER

▷ **KALASH**
Copper *kalashes* (pots) are filled with water from the Ganges River and topped with auspicious mango leaves and a coconut. Such pots have many symbolic meanings and are important in Hindu and Jain prayer rituals.

RITUAL INGREDIENTS
The Hindu *pooja* is an elaborate holy ceremony requiring several items (*samagri*), each of which is steeped in religious significance. They include offerings such as fruits; auspicious flower garlands; a sacred fire; and purifying turmeric, camphor, and incense.

▷ **DAYBREAK IN HIJJA**
Early morning mist surrounds the village as its inhabitants begin their day. The bamboo fences provide protection from fire.

▽ **BEFORE DAWN**
Yadd and Ba Khang wake, sooty and tousled, by the square brick-lined hearth that forms the center of their house. They sleep on a mat next to the hearth.

Although she is a 64-year-old grandmother, Atta (aunt) Yadd never sits still. Her tiny bent body moves constantly around her home and the rice fields of Hijja, a mist-wreathed village in the far northeastern state of Arunachal Pradesh. "We Apatanis are better than any other tribe," she says firmly. "We are better farmers, wealthier, and more beautiful!"

The Apatani, one of hundreds of indigenous peoples in India, were originally Mongolian nomads who settled on the Ziro plateau. Unlike other tribes, they practice fixed agriculture, and are also foresters, planting trees on the rim of the plateau to make a basin they believe will hold rain-bearing clouds. The cool, damp climate is good for bamboo, from which the Apatani create their whole world, from houses to aqueducts to household containers. They cultivate the bamboo carefully, believing that if it is allowed to flower and die, the tribe will die out as well.

Bamboo is easily grown, easily fashioned, and easily recycled; Yadd's house has been rebuilt several times using materials from her family's bamboo grove. "This one is not as elegant as the last," she reflects. Still, the number of sacrificed cattle skulls hanging on the wall is a measure of her wealth; she giggles that she made a good marriage to her teetotal husband, Ba Khang, who is a respected village elder and to whom she has been married for half a century. They have a son, who lives with his wife in the same village, and a daughter who lives with her own family in another village. "The secret is choosing the man well," she says.

Yadd and Ba Khang live off their fields and livestock and sacrifice a few *mithun* (cattle) every year in accordance with their religious beliefs. Ba Khang has a bank account in town, but they are mainly self-sufficient and only buy sugar, tea, tobacco, or a few treats.

In addition to the traditional facial markings of her tribe, Yadd still wears the distinctive cane nose and ear plugs that Apatani women adopt as an expression of beauty. Younger Apatanis no longer choose to wear these, as nontribal people with whom they come in contact see them as defacing. Yadd says that she does not understand what it means to be nontribal, although she has met white people. "Isn't everyone part of a tribe?" she asks.

Modernity has touched the Ziro region in the form of electricity and municipal water. There are now a few corrugated tin roofs and wooden doors among the bamboo houses in Hijja. Yadd worries about the fact that younger Apatanis are moving away from cultivation to work as government clerks in towns like Ziro and Itanagar. Yet she thinks that the traditional Apatani life will endure. "Things must change as they always have," she says, "and the young will bring the new."

△ **MAKING TEA**
Yadd puts a kettle of water on the stove to make a cup of strong, black sweetened tea for herself and her husband.

▷ **FRESHENING UP**
The couple wash on a bamboo platform at the back of the house, using a mug of icy or warm water. Sometimes they wash at the pigsty so that the waste water flows into the pig trough.

APATANI TRIBESWOMAN

A TRIBAL ELDER'S WIFE, ARUNACHAL PRADESH

TENDING TO THE POULTRY
Yadd releases her chickens from their coop so that they can roam freely during the day. The Apatani practice farming and animal husbandry.

LEAVING FOR WORK
With the basket she always wears on her back, Yadd leaves for her fields. She wears blue glass beads, and a skirt of the dark indigo color favored by older Apatanis.

WORKING IN THE FIELDS
Yadd and her friends re-contour the rice fields, bare after the harvest, to change the water channels. They also raise fish spawn in the irrigation channels.

SHARING THE BURDEN
Yadd's daughter-in-law fetches a lunch of rice, soup, roast pork, chili peppers, and rice beer from her home. The women work on each other's fields on a *quid pro quo* basis; when her friends require her help, Yadd works for free. The field's owner always provides the day's lunch.

BACK TO WORK
While her friends hoe the ground and create new banks, Yadd levels the embankments with her feet, doing a little dance to press the soil flat.

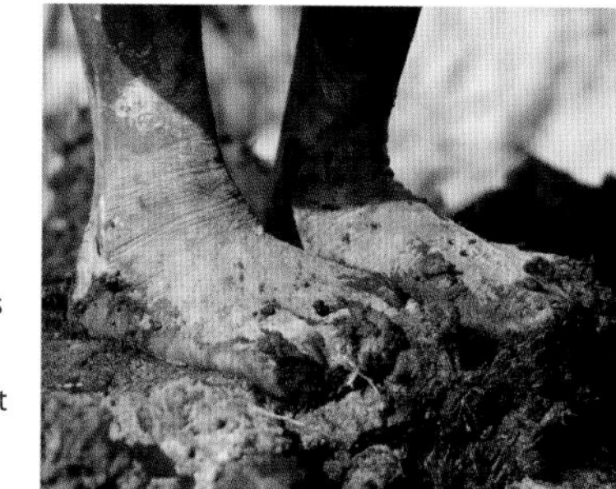

HARD-WORKING FEET
The dark gray soil cakes Yadd's feet, splayed, calloused, and cracked from walking barefoot and from hard labor.

LEAVING THE FIELDS
By mid-afternoon, the women set off home, each carrying her own handwoven bamboo basket.

THE KITCHEN GARDEN
Yadd harvests tomatoes, *lai saag* (mustard leaves), and peppers as a thank-you for her friends' work.

DRYING THE RICE
On the platform behind her house, Yadd spreads the rice grain on a bamboo mat, where it can dry in the sun and be sifted for grit.

FETCHING RICE
Yadd stops by at her granary, on the outskirts of the village. It's a raised, windowless wooden room with a padlock, built at a safe distance from the village to protect it from fire. She fills her basket with whole-grain rice.

FEEDING THE LIVESTOCK
After she has given the chickens their daily feed, Yadd throws the slops from her kitchen to the pigs in the pigsty.

ethnic minorities

India is the world's second most populous country after China, with over a billion people, and comprising one-sixth of the world's population. India's population is incredibly diverse, speaking 22 official languages and thousands of dialects, and including people of all the major races—Australoid, Mongoloid, Europoid, Caucasian, and Negroid. The Constitution of India recognizes upwards of 500 indigenous peoples categorized as Scheduled Tribes. According to the 2001 Census, tribals (often called *adivasis*, or forest-dwellers) account for 8.3% of the population, about 84 million people. From the 7.4 million Gond tribals in Andhra Pradesh to just 18 Chaimals in the Andaman islands, India's tribal peoples retain their distinct character, language, religion, and largely self-sufficient relationship with their immediate environment.

△ COLLECTING BAMBOO
Yadd meets her husband in their bamboo grove, where he has been cutting the flexible, young green bamboo.

◁ BEARING THE LOAD
Ba Khang helps load strips of bamboo into Yadd's basket, which she carries with the strap resting against her forehead for support.

▽ BACK HOME
After a long, hard day of work, Yadd builds a bamboo fire on which she makes some tea.

▷ WEAVING
When she arrives home, Yadd settles down at her hand loom to weave the dark blue cloth that older Apatani women wear.

◁ AN EVENING SNACK
Ba Khang returns home from work with a large rat, which he caught in a trap he set in the bamboo grove. The couple roast the animal over the open fire and eat it as a snack before the main evening meal.

I don't think much about change. Our lives are complete. We don't have any modern needs.

आदिवासी

FAMILY DINNER
At the end of the day, Yadd and her husband go to visit their neighbors. As they do most days, the couple eat their evening meal at their son and daughter-in-law's house nearby in the village.

◁ **FISHING BASKETS**
Weaving grass, cane, or bamboo into baskets is one of the most ancient human skills. These baskets from Assam are used by fishermen to carry the day's catch.

India's diverse tribal groups, based in the hilly forest areas of central India, the northeast, and the island archipelagos, have a vibrant tradition of arts and crafts that is famous across the globe. Each tribe expresses its identity through the creation of objects that are unique in style and technique to their place of origin. While the majority of the pieces primarily serve a utilitarian purpose for use in agriculture, hunting, food-making and serving, and storage, they can also be highly decorative.

Art is an integral part of the culture of a tribe, reflecting every aspect of life. Tribal jewelry uses not just silver and gold, but also brass, beads, wood, copper, shells, and rope. Tribal craft has to compete in an increasingly industrialized society, which has made mass-produced, and, therefore, more affordable, products widely available. However, in recent years, the Indian government has set up emporiums to showcase and sell tribal arts and crafts, thereby helping to preserve these ancient traditions for future generations.

TRIBAL ARTS AND CRAFTS

▷ **PAINTED CLAY MASK**
Masks of deities, such as the Tibetan guardian, Mahakala, are used to ward off evil spirits and protect the village. Tribal ceremonies often use masks made of painted clay, wood, paper, or even hollowed-out pumpkins.

HANDCRAFTED OBJECTS
Handmade, utilitarian objects created from natural materials such as wood, bamboo, metal, and clay have become highly prized around the world for their simple elegance and quality of craftsmanship in a world dominated by mass-produced goods.

BIRD-WATCHING
Taking a stroll on the villa's terrace before breakfast, Rao Saheb, an avid naturalist, looks out for the bird life that frequents Raghav Sagar lake.

Rawat Nahar Singhji peers over the walls of Deogarh Mahal to the water below. "I shot crocodiles at this lake in my youth," the 74-year-old recalls. Deogarh Mahal, now a heritage hotel, is also a 340-year-old palace where Nahar Singhji, known as Rao Saheb, grew up to become an *Umrao* (baron) of Mewar, the 15th of his line and a relation of the Maharana of Udaipur.

When India gained independence in 1947, its 400-odd independent regional rulers continued to receive recognition, as well as a hereditary grant from the government. However, in 1971, these payments were abolished. Today, many erstwhile royals and aristocrats have either sold their ancestral holdings outright, or have turned them into revenue-earning hospitality ventures.

Rao Saheb, his wife, Rani Saheb, and their three children moved out of Deogarh Mahal in 1966 when it became too difficult to maintain, and moved into the nearby lakeside villa. The fortress lay unused for 30 years until, in 1996, Rao's sons decided to rescue the crumbling building. They offered it to hotel chains, but the proliferation of such properties in Rajasthan made it hard to sell, so the family raised funds themselves. "My sons are really the upholders of our tradition," says Rao Saheb. "They restored Deogarh using local artisans and skills. The biggest problems were to introduce modern plumbing and conserve the frescoes on the walls."

After moving out of the fortress, Rao Saheb became a schoolteacher at Mayo College, Ajmer, teaching history and photography. Now retired, he still plays an active role in the community, and also helps his family run the hotel, which employs 150 people from the surrounding villages. The hotel brings about 100,000 rupees a day to the local economy. Rao Saheb's wife, to whom he has been married for 50 years, is chief decorator; their elder son is the operations manager, and their younger son is the marketing manager. Their daughter lives in Australia, where they go every year to visit their grandchildren.

"I spend my days bird-watching and meeting family," says Rao Saheb. "I used to be an avid hunter, but am now the district's Chief Wildlife Warden, and I educate the village children about the environment." He also researches and lectures on Rajasthani art, and has cowritten a book on the Deogarh school of painters with a friend. "My forefathers commissioned some local Deogarh artists, who had their own style, to decorate the palace. The collection of frescoes by them that now adorn our walls is invaluable."

Rao Saheb does not lose sight of the changing social context around people like himself. "My family has a history of aristocracy," he says. "But today, we are normal citizens of India. I am just an ordinary person."

FAMILY BREAKFAST
Rao Saheb enjoys a sumptuous breakfast in the sun-dappled dining room, presided over by his wife and served by uniformed waiters. All members of the family eat breakfast together when in Deogarh.

DRIVING TO THE HOTEL
Villagers and Rao Saheb greet each other as he drives his jeep to the hotel. They show their respect by bowing deeply, and he folds his hands in a traditional *namaste* greeting.

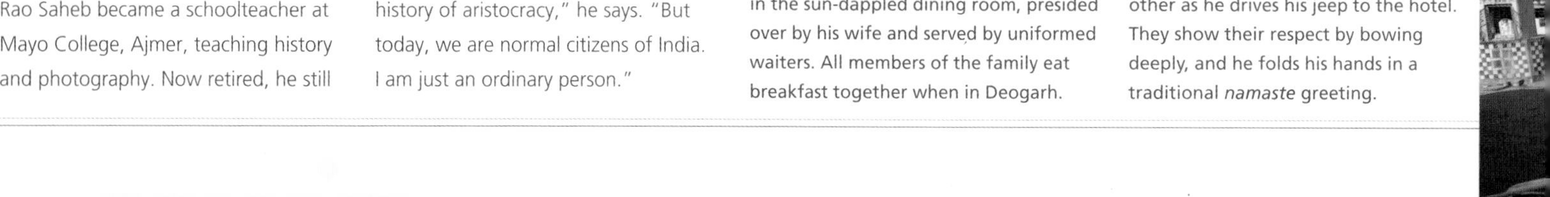

NOBLEMAN

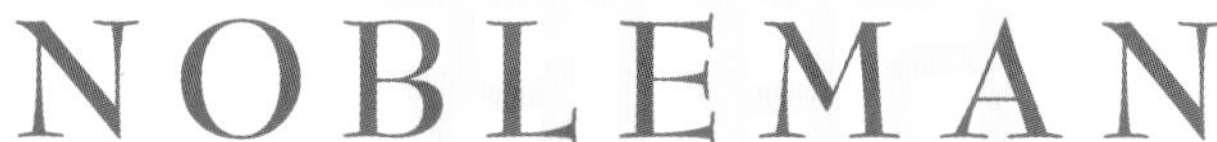

AN UMRAO OF MEWAR, RAJASTHAN

◁ **AT THE HOTEL**
He leaves his car in front of the decorated portal. The fort entrance is small by design, built to control the number of entrants.

▷ **MEETING THE STAFF**
Rao Saheb greets the hotel staff, who are largely local inhabitants. The relationship between the former aristocracy and their one-time subjects is formal but warm.

△ **OVERSEEING BUSINESS**
He catches up briefly with his son, who runs the hotel. Rao Saheb manages the estate, but spends more time on his other interests.

◁ **CHECKING FRESCOES**
Rao Saheb is passionate about art, and frequently looks over the palace frescoes—to enjoy them as well as to check for any damage.

▽ **NEW DESIGNS**
In the Sheesh Mahal room, Rao Saheb helps his wife, who is the principal interior decorator, to make her design decisions.

> My years of teaching were very rewarding. I taught many *maharajas* and senior politicians throughout the years.

सामंत

DRIVING TO SCHOOL
After leaving the hotel, Rao Saheb and his wife drive out of Deogarh town to keep a scheduled appointment at a local village school.

WELCOMING COMMITTEE
The teachers of the village school come out to greet Rao Saheb and Rani Saheb, who are honored visitors. The couple are involved with Deogarh's community on many levels.

MEETING STUDENTS
Today the couple are donating school uniforms, each student touching Rani Saheb's feet in thanks. They visit a classroom to see the teaching in progress.

BACK HOME
Besides his involvement with the hotel and his community work, Rao Saheb leads a quiet life; after lunch, he often bird-watches and then retires to read and relax.

◁ ▽ **HOMEOPATHY CLINIC**
Assisted by his daughter-in-law, Rao Saheb distributes homeopathic medicines to the hotel staff and women from the nearby villages.

▷ **DRESSING FOR TEA**
In preparation for afternoon tea, Rao Saheb changes into traditional formal wear, including the *padgi*, the official headdress of Udaipur.

◁ △ **TEA IN THE GARDEN**
The family meets for a genteel cup of afternoon tea on the well-kept lawns of their home, in the company of their six Labrador puppies. Dogs and horses are the main topics of conversation.

▷ **ROYAL SETTING**
Looking every inch the royal couple, Rao Saheb and his wife relax on a terrace overlooking the courtyard of Deogarh Mahal, formerly their hereditary home, as the evening falls.

ELEPHANT HANDLERS

MAHOUTS AT SONEPUR CATTLE FAIR, BIHAR

ARRIVING AT THE FAIR
Elephants and their *mahouts* are a common sight on the roads around Sonepur during the month-long fair.

FAIRGROUNDS
The Sonepur Mela is held among the trees on the banks of the Gandak River. Buyers and sellers bring their own bedding and food supplies.

Gul Mohammed watches over his elephant, Lachmi, in a shady mango grove beside the Gandak River. Gul and his helper Zaheer are one of 70 pairs of *mahouts* (elephant handlers) here. The air is full of bells, clinking iron chains, and the chatter of prospective buyers—the sounds of the elephant bazaar at the month-long Sonepur Mela, one of the largest animal trading fairs in India.

Mahouts are well-respected individuals who go through rigorous training to learn how to domesticate, train, and care for elephants. The *mahouts* of Assam state are particularly famous for their skill at capturing wild elephants, which were once widely used for heavy labor, hunting, transportation, and war. Today, Indian elephants are a protected species, so only those born in captivity can be used as working animals.

A *mahout* cares for one elephant at a time, often from when the animal is barely a few months old, building an emotional bond and a relationship of mutual trust over many years. "The elephant is a noble, intelligent, sensitive animal," says Gul, who has tended two elephants before Lachmi. "To care for one is to amass blessings." Though the *mahouts* care for the elephants, they do not own them. Some *mahouts* will find it difficult to let go of their charges after so many years together, but each animal is worth between 600,000 and 1,200,000 rupees ($15,000–30,000) to its owner. Since elephant trading is officially banned, the animals will be "gifted" to their purchasers at the fair.

Sonepur Mela is many centuries old. Like most fairs in India, it has a religious background, commemorating the night of *Kartik Purnima* (the full moon in the Hindu month of Kartik, usually November) when the god Vishnu rescued an elephant from a crocodile in the Gandak River. Unlike other fairs, however, Sonepur trades in all kinds of animals—elephants, horses, mules, donkeys, cattle, goats, and sheep—and attracts close to a million visitors from the rural heartland of India every year. The day before the fair starts, roads are closed to vehicles and the area beside the river becomes a mass of pedestrians and animals in an improvised township full of campsites, hanging laundry, and food stands.

In recent years, each Sonepur Mela has seen around 100 elephants brought to the fair for trading; far fewer than in the 1950s, when the animal was seen as an important status symbol. Most of the elephants are now bought by South Indian temples for ceremonial purposes, and by a few landowners as a sign of prosperity. The *mahouts*, who earn around 800 rupees ($20) a month, don't see much of a future in their line of work. "We are poor people," Gul says. "The elephant is our livelihood. We have been doing this for many generations, but I would rather my children went to school."

THE ELEPHANT'S AREA
The elephant bazaar is located in a grove of mango trees. Two *mahouts* tend to each animal; one drives the elephant, and the other cuts its food.

DRINKING AT THE RIVER
The *mahouts* take their elephants down to the water for a drink. Though often held in November, the fair can still get hot and dusty.

◁ **OIL RUB**
The elephants' heads are rubbed with mustard oil, which helps keep them cool and prevents their skin from drying out.

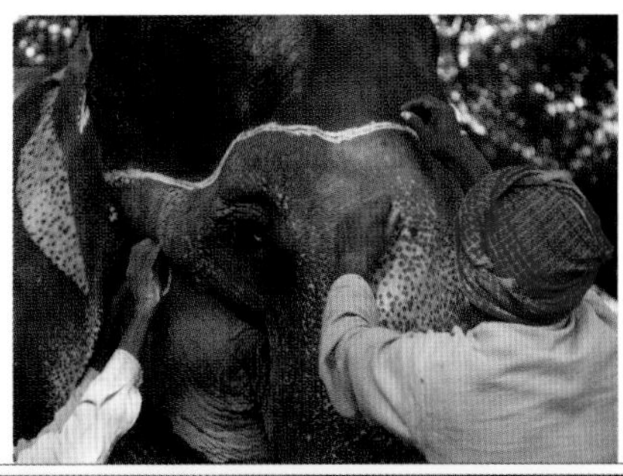

▽ ▷ **CHALK DECORATION**
The *mahouts* decorate the animals' foreheads and ears with patterns drawn in colored chalk, to make them more appealing to potential buyers.

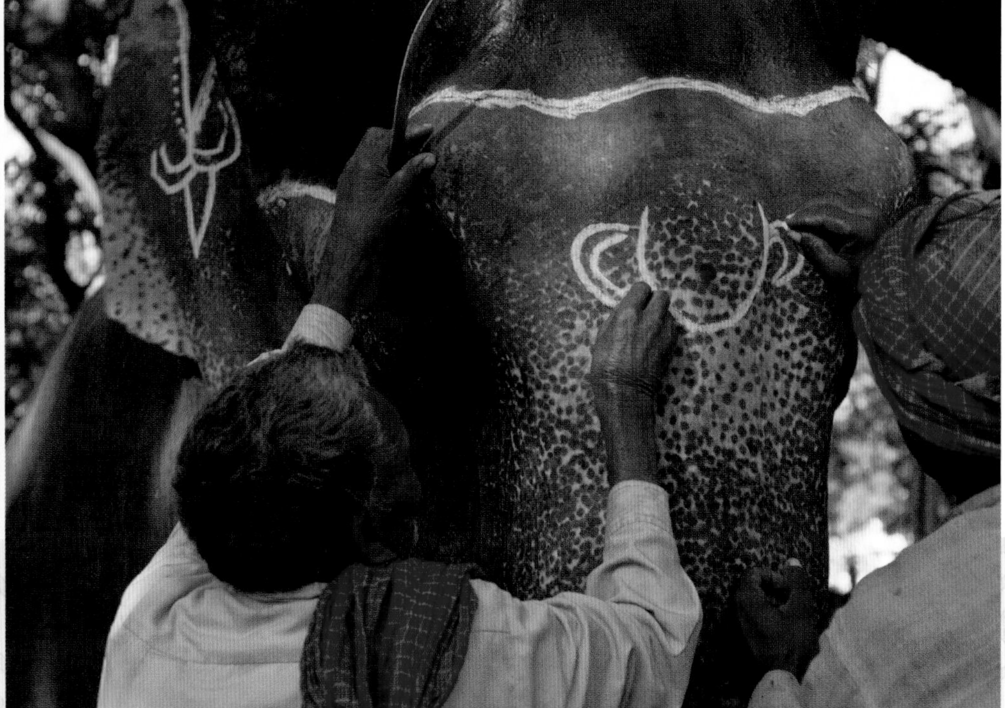

◁ **ELEPHANTS FOR SALE**
The elephants are lined up so that each can be seen clearly. Because of their size and their association with the god Ganesha, they get a lot of attention, even from non-buyers.

▽ **INSPECTING THE GOODS**
Prospective buyers look for a nicely domed forehead and well-shaped back, broad ears, a short tail, good height, and a balanced gait.

▷ **MOUNTING AN ELEPHANT**
The *mahout* climbs up onto the elephant's trunk, grips its ears, and directs it to lift its trunk so that he can clamber easily up its forehead.

Because they love the water so much, it's often difficult to coax the elephants out of the river when it's time to leave.

महावत

BATHING IN THE RIVER
The *mahouts* take the elephants down to the river for a drink and a wallow. People also bathe regularly in the river during the fair, particularly on the auspicious day following the full moon.

RETURNING TO THE FAIR
After a good splash and scrub in the water to cool off, the elephants and their keepers make their way back to the mango grove for a rest.

TAKING A BREAK
After lunch, the *mahouts* sleep, though at least one stays awake to watch over the animals and keep the curious at bay.

AFTERNOON CROWDS
From early afternoon onward, the lanes of the cattle fair become busier – crowded with spectators, buyers, sellers, residents, and pilgrims.

THE CATTLE MARKET
Sonepur Mela is widely known as an event at which elephants are traded; however, it is the more mundane cattle market that sees the largest amount of business at the fair.

GOATS FOR SALE
The Sonepur sells in every type of livestock a farmer might want or need on his farm; trade in each animal is conducted in its own specific area.

THE HORSE MARKET
After the elephants, the horses attract the most attention from bystanders at the fair; their riders often perform tricks for the crowds.

◁ **SHOPPING AT THE BAZAAR**
The lanes of the fair are lined with stands that sell everything from food to trinkets and toys, and embellishments for animals.

▽ ▷ **STAND MERCHANDISE**
Powdered paints, bangles, necklaces, and hairpieces are on sale, as well as deep-fried snacks such as *jalebi* (spirals of sweet batter) and samosas cooked on portable stoves.

◁ △ **DUSK IN THE MANGO GROVE**
On waking, the *mahouts* lay out fresh straw and feed the elephants a treat of bananas to supplement their usual diet of sugar cane.

▷ **DAY'S END**
By 8:00 p.m., most people at the fair are either asleep or relaxing and exchanging stories and gossip. The grounds glow with the lights of campfires as people settle down for the night.

◁ **RELIGIOUS PARAPHERNALIA**
Gods are everywhere, with images of Hindu, Sikh, Christian, and Buddhist deities printed on merchandise ranging from money purses to wall calendars.

While supersized, air-conditioned shopping malls are on the rise, most of India's merchandise is still sold at local weekly street markets, or by the wandering sellers who wheel their goods through the neighborhood calling out for business. These local sellers are the cornerstone of every Indian householder's life. Weekly markets set up for one frenetic day, filling the streets with fragrance and color, and then disappear as quickly as they arrive. Often a noisy and chaotic experience, browsing through a market anywhere in India can be as enthralling as it is bewildering. The small shops and sidewalk stands are filled with a boundless array of inexpensive and eye-catching goods ranging from simple household items to fanciful children's toys and religious paraphernalia, and it's likely that the man selling toothpaste and soap out of a tiny storefront also has cell phones and ceiling fans for sale. While the prices are never exorbitant, they are rarely fixed, and bargaining is a way of life for Indian shoppers and sellers.

STREET-MARKET GOODS

▷ **SHOPPING BAGS**
Indians are inclined to conserve and recycle, and there is a drive to use less plastic, so many shoppers buy reusable cloth bags to carry their daily groceries. Here, as almost everywhere, religious images are prevalent.

LOCAL MARKET GOODS
Indian markets are a veritable treasure trove of color and sparkle. Traditional sequins, *bindis*, jewelry, and embroidered decorations compete for attention with brightly packaged CDs and DVDs, cigarettes, and myriad other products.

▷ **DARJEELING TOWN**
The route starts in the foothills of the Kanchenjunga range at Darjeeling, also known as the Queen of the Hills.

▽ **TRAIN CREW ARRIVE**
When the crew arrives at the yard in the morning, it is bitterly cold. The men warm themselves at a fire made from embers raked from the engine.

"A steam engine is like an old wife—you have to listen carefully to her mutters and grumbles, or she comes to a grinding halt," jokes Birkh Bahadur Dattani, as he lovingly polishes the dials and brass on the locomotive that runs between the hill stations of Darjeeling and Kurseong, in West Bengal. "My job is to drive the engine, not to clean it," says Birkh, "but I like to make it shine."

The Scottish-made engine called Victor, also known as the Queen of Himalayas, pulls the charming two-carriage toy train of the Darjeeling Himalayan Railway (DHR). The DHR is one of the few steam railroad routes left in India, and because of its romance as well as its engineering achievements, including loops and reverses in the track, it is now classed as a World Heritage Site.

Birkh, 58, has worked on this train for 40 years. One of many Nepalese born and brought up in the Darjeeling area, he studied at a mission school before joining the railroad at the age of 18. He began with the tough job of coal loader on the four-man engine cab team, moved on to stoking the coal, then maintaining the boilers, and is today the most senior locomotive pilot on the Darjeeling–Kurseong–Siliguri line.

"I love my job. The railways have been good to me," says Birkh, "and they've looked after my family. Maybe we should be getting bigger salaries, closer to those of private jobs, but I've done okay; I have free accommodation, a full medical plan, and a pension." Birkh's wife and children live 12 miles (20 km) along the track from Kurseong in quarters at Tindharia, where there is a railroad workshop that manufactures spare parts for steam engines. Birkh usually spends his nights in the railroad running room, a board and lodging facility provided for railroad staff.

He sometimes drives trains from Siliguri to Darjeeling, but often drives the shorter daily runs from Kurseong to Darjeeling. Victor the engine runs on the latter route, covering a distance of 20 miles (32 km) and climbing about 2,543 ft (775 m) in the space of three hours. "A car can make that journey in 45 minutes," says Birkh. "Earlier, there was only one road up to Darjeeling but now, with more new roads, there are fewer passengers on the train."

The train passes within touching distance of shops and homes at most stations, and passengers include tourists, schoolboys, and wandering ascetics. "In the old days," says Birkh, "rich people were the only ones who could afford the price of a train ticket. But I don't care who the passengers are, as long as they still choose to travel by train."

Birkh is aware that cars and planes are fast replacing rail travel for millions of people—his own sons make good money as tourist taxi drivers—but he remains optimistic. "I don't believe trains will become obsolete. Maybe steam travel will, but not trains."

△ **BOILERMAN'S TASKS**
The boilerman, who is responsible for maintaining the temperature and pressure of the water and its steam, stokes the engine to its full capacity.

▷ **COAL LOADING**
The men who carry the heavy baskets of coal that keep the engine well stoked perform a crucial but back-breaking task.

TRAIN DRIVER

ABOARD THE DARJEELING HIMALAYAN RAILWAY, WEST BENGAL

SIGNING IN
At 8:15 a.m., Birkh signs in at the chief supervising engineer's office, located above the station floor.

TEA WITH THE CREW
Birkh's work doesn't begin until 9:00 a.m., but he gets in early to watch the preparations, and to drink tea with his colleagues.

TICKET COUNTER
Passengers, who are mostly local commuters, line up for tickets to stations on the Darjeeling–Kurseong route.

CLEANING THE ENGINE
Birkh finds the engine is not up to his perfectionist standards. He sets about cleaning the dials and running board himself.

WASHING UP
When he's satisfied, Birkh washes the soot off his hands under a stream of water from the engine. He wears a blue Nepali cap over his standard-issue railroad uniform.

READY TO GO
After some last-minute polishing, the engine is shunted from the train shed into the station platforms, where it will be attached to two passenger carriages before it begins its journey.

▽ ▷ **DARJEELING STATION**
The locomotive waits on the platform as the passengers board the train cars. The station forms a flat open space in an otherwise hilly and crowded town.

△ **FIRED UP**
The crew stokes the fire to achieve the burst of energy that will be required to make the steep ascent from Darjeeling to Ghum station.

▷ **DARJEELING TO GHUM**
The railroad tracks often sit by the side of the road, and local traffic easily passes the locomotive as it struggles to pull its cars uphill.

△ **GHUM TO SONADA**
At an altitude of 7,407 ft (2,260 m), Ghum is the second-highest station in the world, and the engine travels in reverse for more brake control on the area's steep slopes.

◁ ▽ **TRAIN PASSENGERS**
A boisterous party of local Nepalese women make use of the cheap transit. A first-class ticket costs 100 rupees ($2.50); second-class tickets cost just a tenth of this price.

△ **DISEMBARKING**
The Nepalese party gets off at Sonada to attend a birthday lunch. The train's timing suits them perfectly.

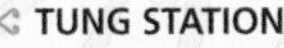

◁ **ON TO TUNG**
A whistle and flag announce the train's departure from Sonada on the downhill stretch to Tung station.

◁ **TUNG STATION**
A ramshackle board marks the small station at Tung, the last stop before Kurseong, at an altitude of 5,656 ft (1,725 m).

▽ **KURSEONG**
The train steams in to the fourth and final station of Kurseong, at the end of its three-hour journey.

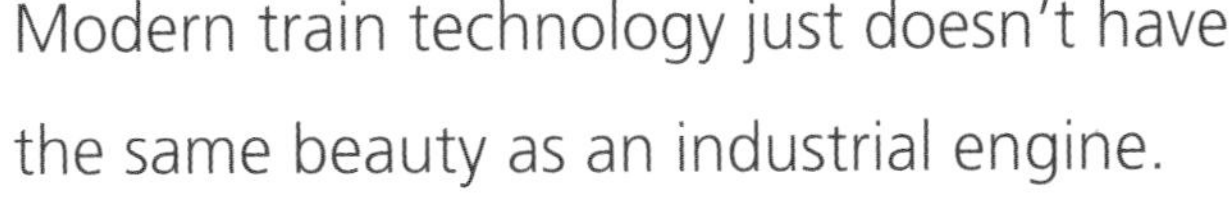

Modern train technology just doesn't have the same beauty as an industrial engine.

रेल चालक

FAMILY MONEY
At Kurseong, Birkh meets his daughter-in-law in the station's running room, and hands over his salary for her to take home.

QUICK LUNCH
The running room provides hot meals for all train staff; Birkh eats a lunch of fish and rice.

KURSEONG STATION
Kurseong is a picturesque station in the middle of tea country, halfway between Siliguri and Darjeeling.

KURSEONG TICKET OFFICE
Tickets are available for travel toward either Darjeeling or Siliguri; the latter town links the Himalayan Railway to the rest of India's train network.

TOPPING OFF
The engine is taken to the locomotive shed for extra water, coal, oil, and a brake check. Topped off once more, Victor is ready for the return trip.

CATCHING UP
Birkh exchanges news and views with a colleague as the train is shunted back to the station. The locomotive will face the right way for the return journey.

◁ **READY TO DEPART**
Birkh waits patiently for passengers to board the train, and for the green signal that will allow him to begin the journey back to Darjeeling.

As a perk of the job, I get free rail travel anywhere in India. So when the children were younger, we used to go on trips all over the country.

रेल चालक

△ **THROUGH THE BAZAAR**
The train steams through the colorful bazaar at Kurseong, which almost spills onto the tracks. People move out of the way to let the train through.

▷ **ENGINE CREW**
The brakeman and second boilerman flank the front of the train to watch out for any hindrances on the track, while the stoker sits atop the engine.

REPAIR STOP
The well-maintained engine is nevertheless an old one, and to keep it running at its best, the crew must sometimes make an unscheduled stop to carry out repairs.

YOUNG PASSENGERS HOLDING ON
Children and other locals who don't possess their own means of travel often skip on and off the train, as a cheap way to travel small distances.

EVENING FALLS
The return journey becomes magical as daylight fades and the train's main headlight switches on. On the flatter sections of the route, the train can reach speeds of around 18 mph (30 km/h).

INSIDE THE CAB
As it gets dark, 15-watt lamps are switched on in the engine cab to allow the crew to continue their work.

BACK THROUGH SONADA
Catching the last of the day's light, the train revisits the bazaar in the town of Sonada on its climb back to Ghum.

STOP AT GHUM
The train stops long enough for everyone to take a tea break at Ghum station, and some curious passengers are also given the opportunity to peek into the engine cab.

public transportation

Moving people and goods over the vast Indian subcontinent is a challenge. The huge network of the state-owned Indian Railways—today the second-largest employer in the world—connects thousands of settlements, from metropolises to remote hamlets. With 16 million passengers and a million tons of freight a day, it is not uncommon to see trains chugging along with people hanging out of the doors and crammed together on the roof. While trains remain by far the most popular mode of transport, aviation is catching up. As airline tickets get cheaper, the profile of the air traveler is changing to include a far greater cross-section of people. India is also trying to improve its road infrastructure, to keep up with a burgeoning population and galloping sales of cars and motorcycles—India is on the move in every way.

PAAN SHOP
Still hot from the day's work, Birkh heads over to the *paan* shop to buy some cigarettes, which he will only smoke once he is off duty for the day, back at his quarters.

IN THE DORMITORY
Birkh chats and laughs with the crew in the running-room dormitory before retiring for the night.

BACK AT DARJEELING
At the end of the journey, Birkh and the crew stoke up the boiler to burn for the rest of the night, as the engine is never allowed to cool.

HINDU BRIDE

WEDDING CELEBRATIONS, RAJASTHAN

THE MEHENDI CEREMONY
The reddish dye made from henna leaves, also called *mehendi*, has been used for thousands of years to decorate the body on special occasions, especially for a bride and her female guests.

Shweta Singhal is an atypical bride in her community of Marwaris, Rajasthani traders known for their business acumen and social conservatism. A qualified banker, she left her home in Jaipur to live and work in Mumbai, and is marrying a man of her own choice. "My parents were just happy that Rohit is a Hindu," she says. "I don't think they would have accepted a non-Hindu."

Shweta's family is also pleased that their son-in-law, who comes from a comparatively liberal South Indian family from Tamil Nadu, has a college degree, an MBA, and a good position as a consultant. Like many urban Marwaris, the Singhals value education and financial security. Shweta's father, a trained engineer who trades in copper, insisted that both his children study further. It meant that after completing her school years in Jaipur, Shweta went on to gain an MBA in finance, and then traveled to the United States to undertake a three-year course to qualify as a chartered financial analyst. She has been working in private banking for six years.

"Rohit and I are both career-oriented," she says. "Today, if we were in Mumbai having dinner, he'd set the table and I'd heat the dinner. I'm too strong-minded to marry into a traditional Marwari family. I would have made myself and them miserable."

She laughs about how she met Rohit in Mumbai, through a friend of a friend who set them up on a blind date, having misheard Shweta's last name as "single." "We met for a drink and had dinner, and it was an instant connection," she says. A year and a half later, they are getting married at a beautiful historic property near Delhi. She stresses that they are "romantic but realistic," and believes that it's a good thing for couples to live together before getting married in order to get to know each other better.

More and more young Indians are resisting the pressure to get married at a young age to a person of their parents' choice, preferring instead to study and concentrate on their careers. Although being married is important to 28-year-old Shweta, she does not expect it to change her relationship with Rohit significantly. "Life goes on," she says. "Marriage is just one more facet of your life." She will have to make some changes, moving from Mumbai to the suburb of Delhi where Rohit lives, and supervising a household for two, but she plans to keep working, and understands how the demands of a profession can impact one's life.

"I will support Rohit's career completely," she says. "In 2009, he is going to have an international posting. If we have to be apart for six months, that's fine. I'm ready to make those adjustments. But," she smiles, "when I have children, I don't want to be working 14 hours a day like I do now."

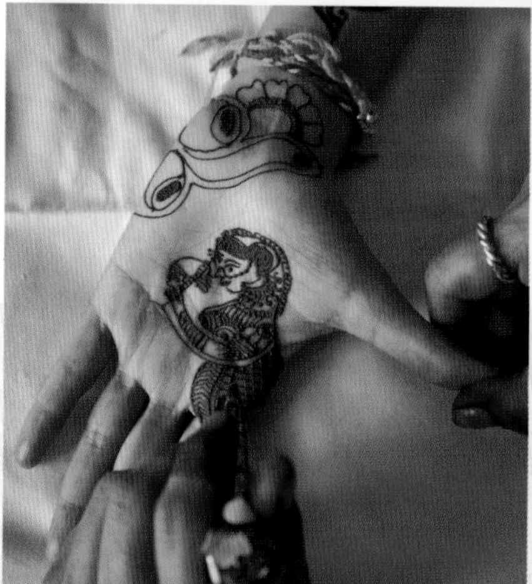

THE ART OF HENNA
Using a cone filled with henna paste, the artist creates decorative patterns—on Shweta's left palm a bride, on her right a groom. Sometimes the groom's name is hidden in the patterns.

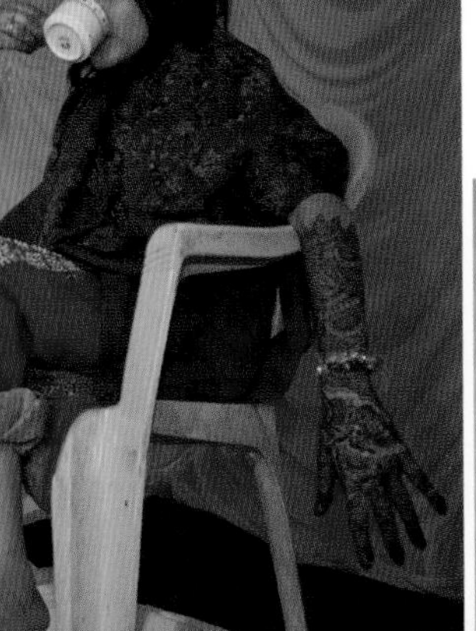

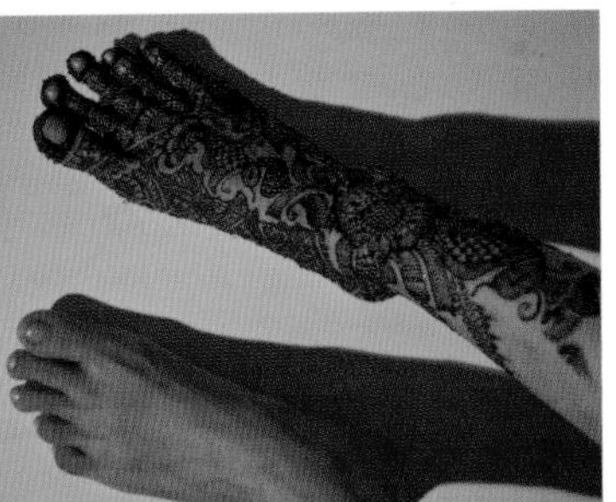

BRIDAL MEHENDI
As a bride, Shweta's henna is much more elaborate than that of the other women, reaching to her elbow and her mid-calf.

CELEBRATORY SINGING
The bride's brightly dressed female relatives and friends sing marriage songs to the accompaniment of a *dholak*, a drumlike instrument.

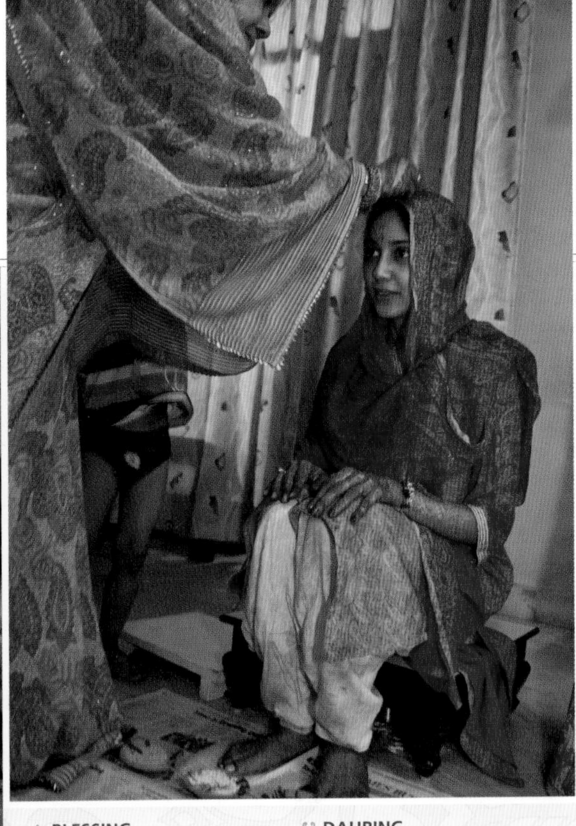

BLESSING
On the wedding morning, elders from Shweta's family bathe her, touching her head, shoulders, knees, and feet with *doob* grass.

DAUBING
After prayers, Shweta's forehead is smeared with saffron and marked with sandalwood, dried turmeric, and vermilion; her face is bathed with buttermilk.

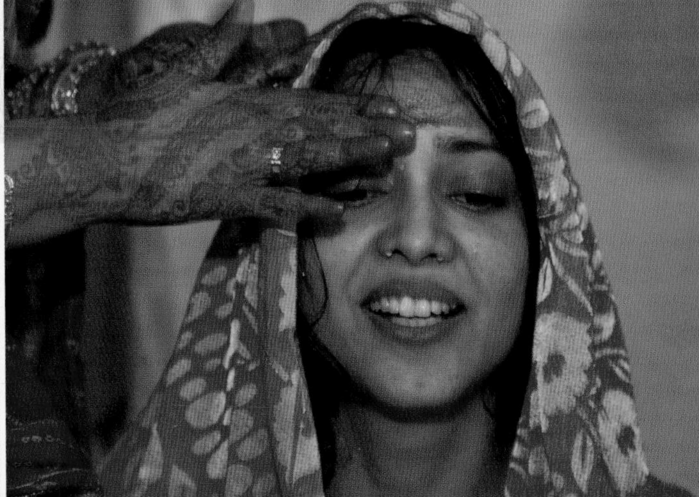

LEAVING HOME
Ritually blessed and wished good luck by her family, Shweta leaves her home for the wedding venue.

Tonight I must say farewell to my family home. After the wedding, I will be a part of my husband's family.

THE VENUE
Around two hours' drive from Delhi, Neemrana Fort-Palace is a 15th-century fortress restored as a hotel.

DRESSING FOR THE EVENING
A professional makeup artist helps Shweta get ready. The bride wears a jewel-encrusted designer *choli* (blouse) and *lehenga* (skirt), bought from a couture store in Mumbai.

ORNAMENTING THE BRIDE
Shweta's elaborate gold and emerald bridal jewelry—necklace, earrings, and forehead ornament—complements her wedding outfit, and her hair is adorned with red roses.

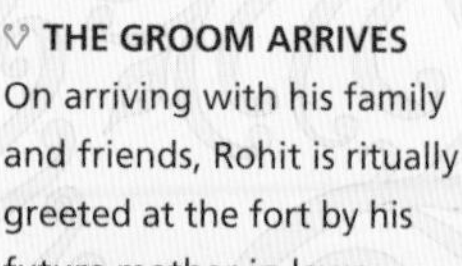

VIP GUEST
The arrival of the Chief Minister of Delhi adds a touch of celebrity glamour to the day's proceedings.

THE GROOM ARRIVES
On arriving with his family and friends, Rohit is ritually greeted at the fort by his future mother-in-law.

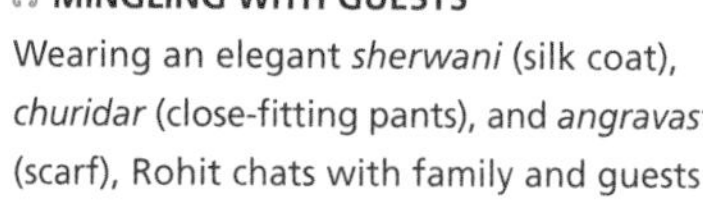

MINGLING WITH GUESTS
Wearing an elegant *sherwani* (silk coat), *churidar* (close-fitting pants), and *angravasta* (scarf), Rohit chats with family and guests while he waits for the arrival of Shweta.

THE RING CEREMONY
Standing in a pillared pavilion, Rohit places a ring on Shweta's finger. The act symbolizes their engagement, and is followed by a photo session for the couple and their families.

◁ **LIVERIED SERVICE**
The hotel staff and waiters are beautifully presented, with colorful turbans and spotless white uniforms.

▷ **WATCHING THE DANCES**
The couple sit under an umbrella and watch their family members perform rehearsed dances, before they also join in themselves.

▽ **BEAUTIFUL SETTING**
Lit by the warm glow of chandeliers, fairy lights, lanterns, oil lamps, and candles, the vegetarian-only dinner has an old-world romance about it.

My only expectation of the marriage is that the way we treat each other doesn't change.

दुल्हन

MUSICAL ACCOMPANIMENT
The wedding day includes many elements of Rohit's South Indian culture. Musicians play the *nadaswaram*, a classical wind instrument from the south that is played in pairs and accompanied by *thavil* drums.

SACRED FIRE
The priest prepares for the wedding ceremony before the sacred fire (*vedi*). Items that will be used include coconuts, betel leaves, fruit, sandalwood, incense, money, and flowers.

THE VRIDHAM CEREMONY
The priest ties a yellow string (*rakshai*) around Rohit's wrist, which signifies that he will take on the responsibility of being a good husband.

GARLANDING EACH OTHER
The couple place three garlands around each other's necks in a ceremony called *jaimaal*. Newlyweds often pretend to resist being garlanded, as here, where Shweta's friends playfully make it difficult for Rohit to reach over her head.

BEING FED MILK AND BANANAS
In another part of the *oonjal* ritual, the couple are fed bananas and milk to ward off the evil eye. Many of the symbolic gestures and practices that form a part of this wedding stem from Rohit's South Indian Tamil heritage.

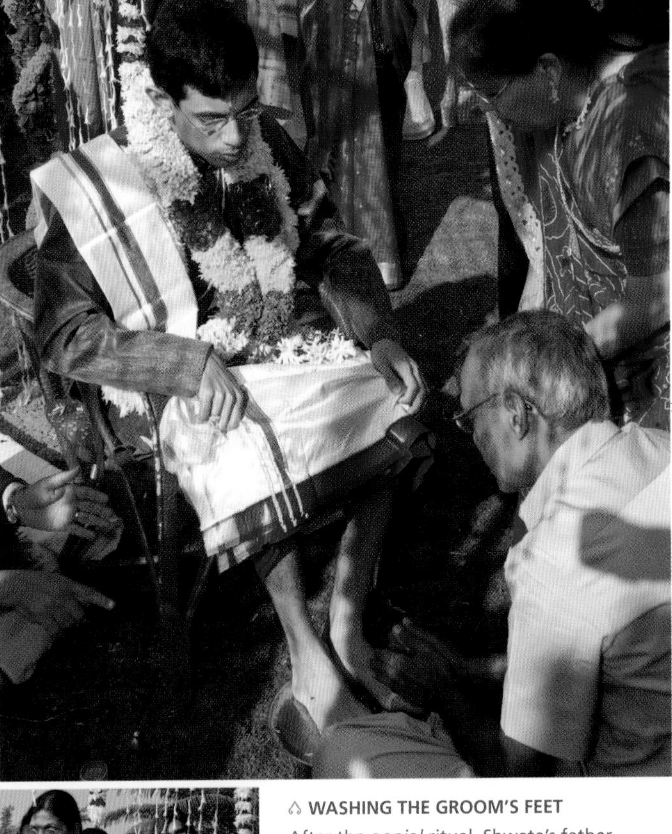

SWING RITUAL
Shweta and Rohit sit on a swing during the ritual known as *oonjal*, in which the forces of good are propitiated to keep the couple safe from evil thoughts and curses.

CLASPING HANDS
Holding Shweta's hand, Rohit recites Vedic hymns asking the goddess Saraswati to bless their marriage and any future children.

WASHING THE GROOM'S FEET
After the *oonjal* ritual, Shweta's father symbolically washes Rohit's feet, as a bridegroom is considered to be an incarnation of Lord Vishnu, the Protector.

NEW SARI
Rohit's mother gives Shweta a new wedding sari, reflecting the fact that the bride has joined her new family. Generally, Indian weddings involve gift-giving on both sides.

GIVING THE BRIDE AWAY
Changed into her new sari, Shweta sits on her father's lap as the priest recites verses meant to purify the bride. Her father then gives Shweta away to her new husband as a gift.

My father is giving me away so completely that I will even take on my new husband's caste.

दुल्हन्

△ **FINALIZING THE CEREMONY**
Having placed a necklace (the sign of a married woman) with a gold locket around Shweta's neck, Rohit stands with his new wife. They prepare to walk around the fire to complete the ceremony.

middle-class india

Economic reform in the 1990s opened India's doors to foreign investment and helped pave the way for India's budding entrepreneurs. It also had the effect of unleashing a huge pool of dynamic, skilled people with aspirations ranging from setting up their own businesses, to buying consumer goods, to traveling the world. In the booming India of today, this middle-class population of around 300 million now has more lifestyle options than ever before, and is no longer so firmly tied to the traditional social roles that previous generations grew up with. It is estimated that by the year 2023, India will leap from the 12th– to the 5th–largest consumer market in the world.

PUFFED RICE OFFERING
As the couple circle the fire three times, a male relative places puffed rice into Shweta's hands, which she throws into the fire. This is an offering to the fire god, Agni.

▽ **ANOTHER GIFT**
The marriage is now formalized and the fire has been extinguished. Rohit's mother offers Shweta the present of another sari as a welcome into her new home and family.

▷ **FLOWER HAIRPIECE**
A traditional floral hairpiece is placed on Shweta's head and flows down her back. Fresh flowers are an important part of a wedding ceremony as they signify beauty.

△ **MARK OF MARRIAGE**
Rohit dips his wedding ring in the red powder called *sindoor*, and marks Shweta's forehead.

◁ **DAUBING THE GROOM**
An auspicious mark called a *tilak*, made of red powder, sandalwood and a few grains of rice, is made on Rohit's forehead to bless him.

△ ▷ **EMOTIONAL FAREWELLS**
The *doli* is when the bride's family symbolically bids her farewell. Rohit and Shweta then leave the fort to establish their new life together.

△ **WEDDING CEREMONY INGREDIENTS**
Debris accumulates on the ground as objects used in the ceremony pile up, including cups of ground sandalwood and turmeric called *samagri*, which are thrown into the fire as the ceremonial verses are recited.

GLASS WEDDING BANGLES
A bride often wears glass bangles from her wrist to her elbow. She puts them on for her wedding day, and continues to wear them until they break naturally.

When you wear a piece of Indian jewelry, you are taking part in a tradition dating back more than 5,000 years. There are few places in the world where jewelry is afforded such importance, both spiritually and as a social and cultural marker. In a land where women do not traditionally inherit property, jewelry is considered a woman's *stridhan*, or personal wealth. Although men wear jewelry, such as the hoops in the ears of Rajasthani men and the rings favored by urban businessmen, jewelry is mainly the special preserve of women. Baby girls are given gold jewelry by their relatives at birth, and a bride is given a substantial amount of jewelry as a wedding gift by her parents and in-laws. Specific kinds of jewelry, such as the *mangalsutra* or *thali* necklace and toe rings, are used to signal a woman's married status. Indian jewelry is famous for its delicacy, inspired by the real flowers women used in ancient times to enhance their beauty. Some jewelry is prescribed by astrologers as a protective talisman, especially gemstone jewelry.

TRADITIONAL JEWELRY

GOLD BANGLES
Gold is prized, not just for its beauty, but also as security against hard times. Gifts of gold, particularly wedding gifts, form a woman's personal wealth, as she is entitled to keep these pieces under any circumstances.

HEAD-TO-TOE ADORNMENT
From hair decorations to toe rings, there is a form of Indian jewelry to beautify every part of the body. Finely carved metals, *kundan* work (stone inset work in gold), and *meenakari* (the decoration of metal with enamel) are just some of the popular traditions.

AYURVEDIC MASSEUR

TRADITIONAL MEDICINE AND MARTIAL ARTS, KERALA

THE SETTING
The ten-acre estate of Kalari Kovilakom has several buildings, which contain treatment centers and accommodations.

PLANTS FOR TREATMENTS
The resort maintains its own herb and vegetable gardens, where the medicinal plants used in some of the Ayurvedic treatments are grown.

Tony Menon, 30, is the chief masseur at Kalari Kovilakom, an Ayurvedic treatment center set in a 19th-century palace near Kollengode, Kerala. He is also a practitioner of *kalari payattu*, a martial art from South India. "*Kalari payattu* training includes massage," he says, "and I trained in massage at an Ayurvedic school, so becoming a *kalari* masseur was natural for me."

Ayurveda is a holistic system of Indian traditional medicine that is classified in ancient texts; in Sanskrit, *ayu* means "life" and *veda* means "knowledge." It views illness as a disturbance in the healthy balance of the three elements (*doshas*) that regulate the body and influence a person's temperament: *vata*, or air, which governs movement in the mind and body; *pitta*, or fire mixed with water, which governs metabolism and transformation; and *kapha*, or water, which is the medium within which the body is structured.

Ayurvedic diagnosis relies on observation of both the body and the mind of the patient, with treatment consisting of detoxification therapy and modifications in lifestyle to restore a beneficial balance of the *doshas* particular to each person. It is therefore customized for every individual, from diet and exercise to mental attitude. Ayurveda aims to heal body and mind in an integrated fashion and in that sense is an entire way of life.

"Kalari Kovilakom considers itself to be an Ayurvedic hospital, so we have doctors as well as masseurs," says Tony. "No one person can do everything. I can give a strong massage because *kalari payattu* strengthens the spine, limbs, and musculature. Sometimes the tissue to be massaged is deep, or in a difficult position. For example, a patient sits on a stool and we massage the spine while in a half-squat position to maintain absolute control of pressure and direction on the vertebrae. *Kalari* keeps our energy and aura strong so we can help people who are not well."

Tony was trained in his martial art by his guru, and is a *kalari payattu* champion. There are several forms of *kalari*, and though many are defensive, others use weapons such as swords, lances, and shields. The art draws its style of movement from examples found in the animal kingdom, and involves meditation and prayer as much as it does physical training and massage. The *kalari* massage called *uzhichil* is based in Ayurveda, and serves to increase the body's suppleness and stimulate its self-healing properties.

The palace at Kovilakom is called Kalari because it was built at the site of a gymnasium dedicated to the martial art. The beautiful heritage property attracts people looking to indulge in a short but intense cleansing treatment. "For most people today, Ayurveda is a spa treatment," says Tony, "but for me, it is a complete way of life."

PREPARING MASSAGE OIL
At the start of a treatment, hot oil is infused with medicinal herbs and a lamp is lit to symbolize that an enlightened spirit is necessary to the healing process.

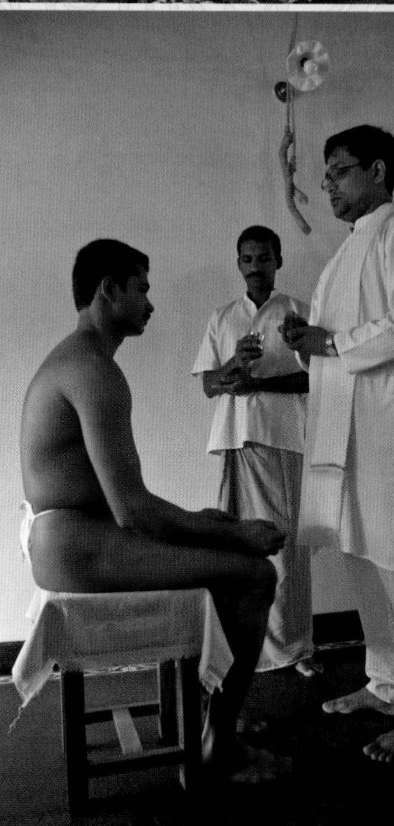

THE ANOINTMENT PROCESS
With Tony standing alongside, the doctor chants a Sanskrit verse invoking divine blessings, and anoints the patient with oil.

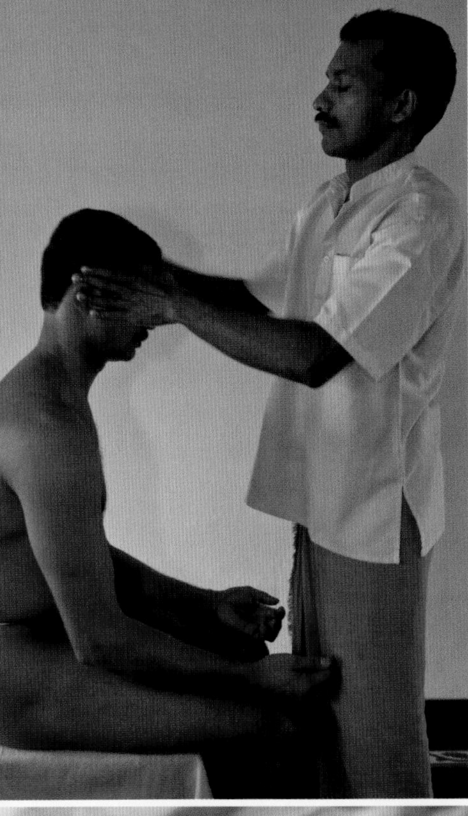

◁ ▽ **HEAD MASSAGE**
Kalari uzhichil is one of the preparatory steps before treatment begins. The gentle head massage is aimed at moving toxins toward the gastrointestinal tract.

▽ **SHOULDERS AND SPINE**
Tony massages the deep tissue in the patient's shoulders and spine. This limbers up the musculoskeletal structure and prepares the body to receive treatment.

▽ **MASSAGE BY FOOT**
Uzhichil can also be done with the feet. Here, Tony stands over the patient and dips his foot in the oil as he prepares to work.

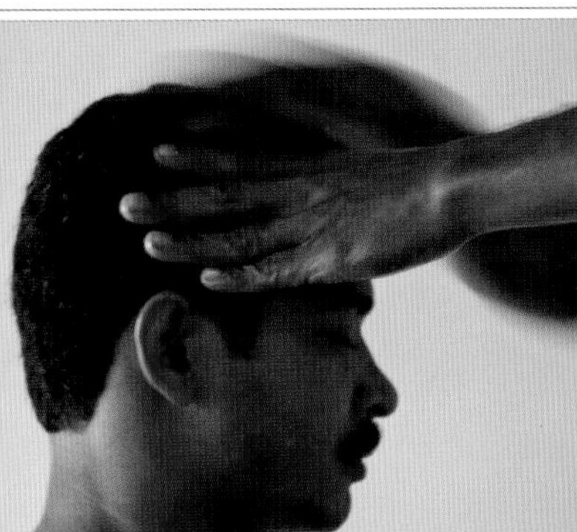

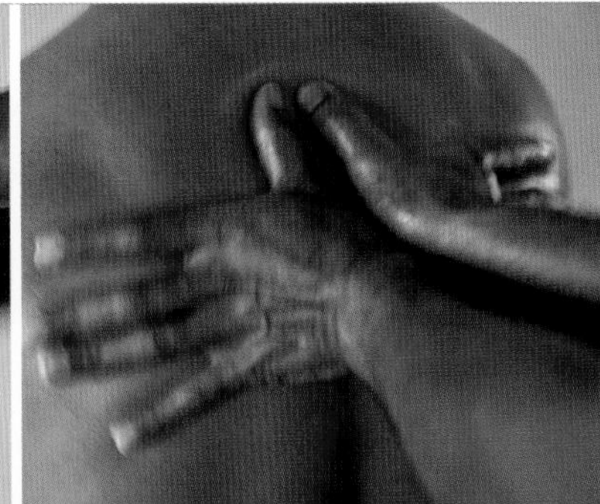

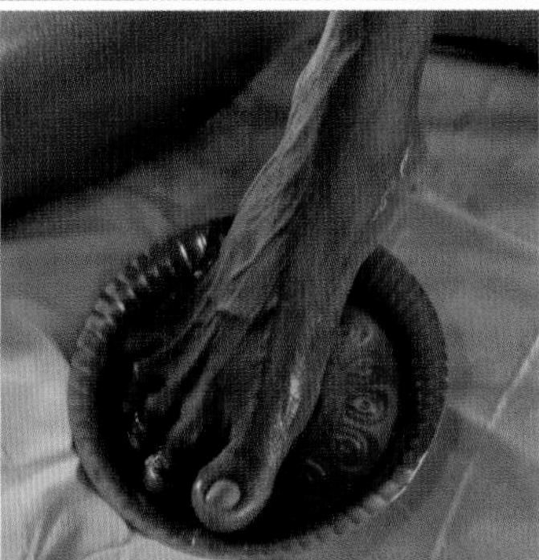

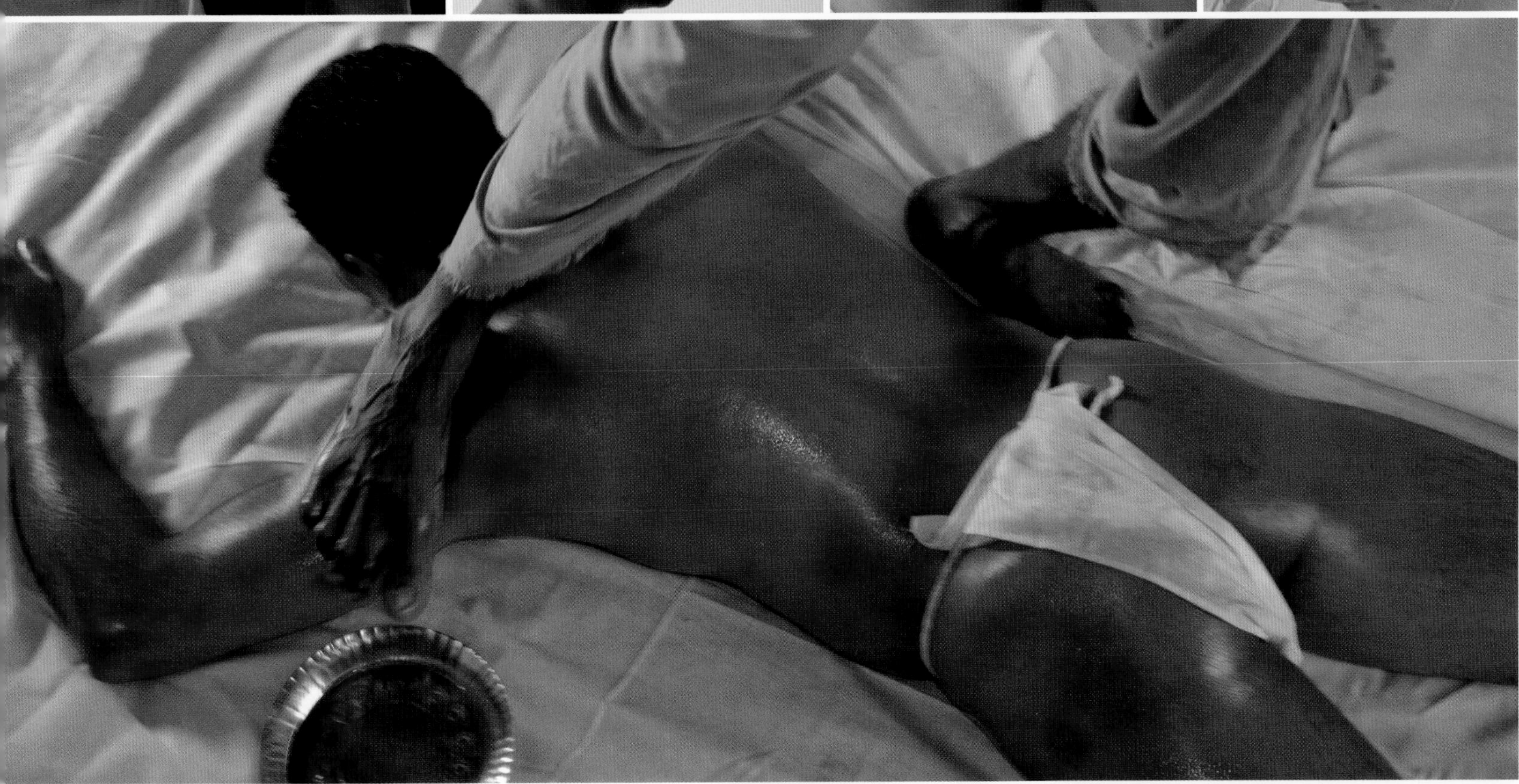

◁ △ **ROPE MASSAGE**
The patient lies face down on the floor and, in the massage technique known as *Padabhyarngam*, Tony performs a massage with one foot, balancing himself on the other while hanging from two ropes that are attached to the ceiling.

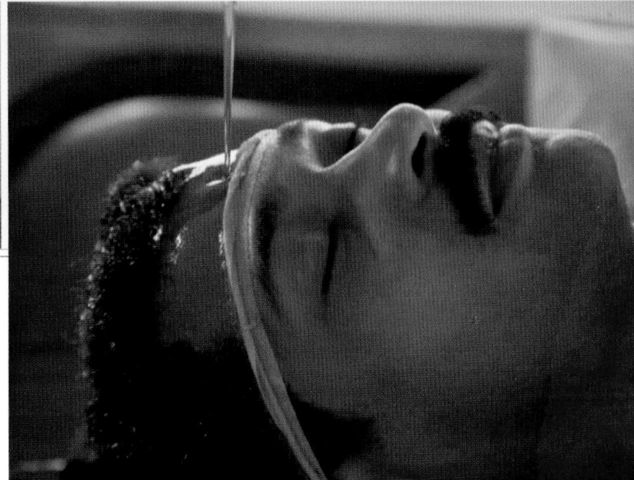

△ ▷ **SIRODHARA TREATMENT**
This rejuvenation treatment involves pouring a continuous flow (*dhara*) of hot medicated oil from a clay pot onto the patient's head. Tony ties a cloth above the patient's eyebrows to protect his eyes, and directs the flow in specific directions to soothe mental tension.

> Ayurveda is not only a science, it is an art; the art of a balanced and healthy lifestyle.
>
> मालिशी

PREPARING INGREDIENTS All food at the resort is prepared from fresh ingredients; each meal is tailored to the doctor's prescription, which includes dietary requirements.

AYURVEDIC KITCHEN The vessels and implements used in the kitchen are made of stone or brass, as aluminum is considered to add harmful toxins to food.

A BALANCED LUNCH A cup of medicated water is drunk before a meal to prime the stomach. The meals are presented in small bowls on a section of banana leaf; they are served in the resort's refectory, and eaten in silence.

PREPARING THE HERBAL BATH After a post-meal interval, it's time for a bath. A tub is filled with water and herbs beneficial to the patient's condition.

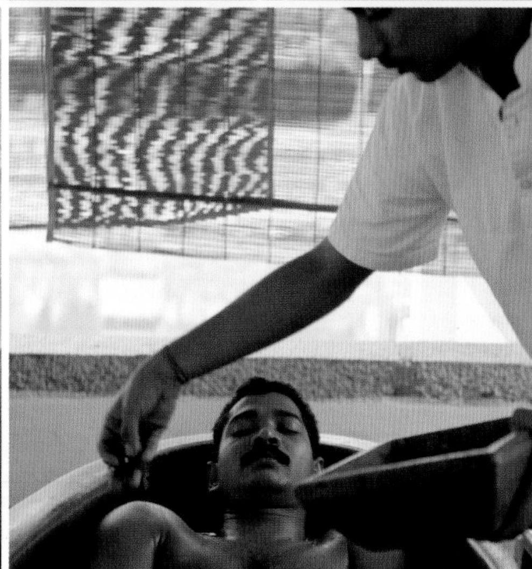

HERBAL BATH The patient lies almost fully submerged in the tub of herb-infused water. Herbal baths are part of the resort's daily regimen of detoxification and relaxation that promotes both physical and spiritual healing.

POULTICE INGREDIENTS
For the next treatment, called *narangakizhi*, lemon (*naranga*) and medicinal herbs are mixed together.

MUSLIN MIXTURE
Once the correct proportions have been attained, the cooked herb and lemon mixture is placed in the center of a square piece of muslin cloth.

MAKING THE POUCH
The muslin is tied up to create a medicated pouch (*kizhi*) that will be rubbed over the patient's body—the mixture seeps through the fine holes in the muslin.

OLEATION PRIOR TO MASSAGE
Tony first rubs the patient down with oil. External oleation (*snehana)* is a preparatory detoxification step designed to prime the body to receive the treatment.

POULTICE MASSAGE
When the patient's skin is thoroughly oiled and his muscles are relaxed, Tony begins to rub his body with the poultice dipped in medicated oils.

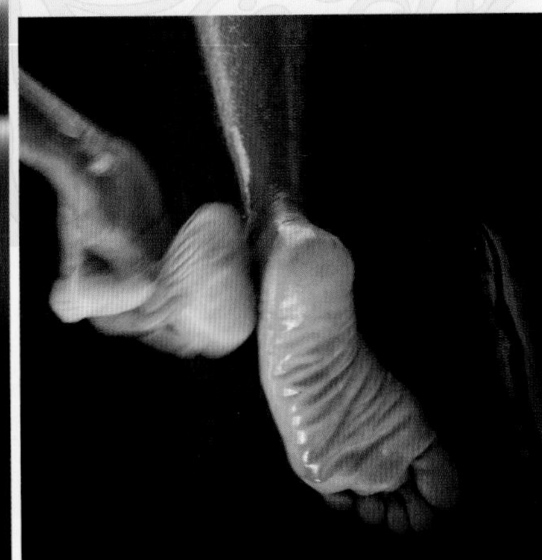

POST-MASSAGE GLOW
After the *narangakizhi* treatment, which is intended to rejuvenate and add a glow to the body, more oil is poured on the patient.

RUBBING IN THE OIL
Two masseurs finish off the treatment with a rhythmic, synchronized massage that penetrates through to the deep tissue.

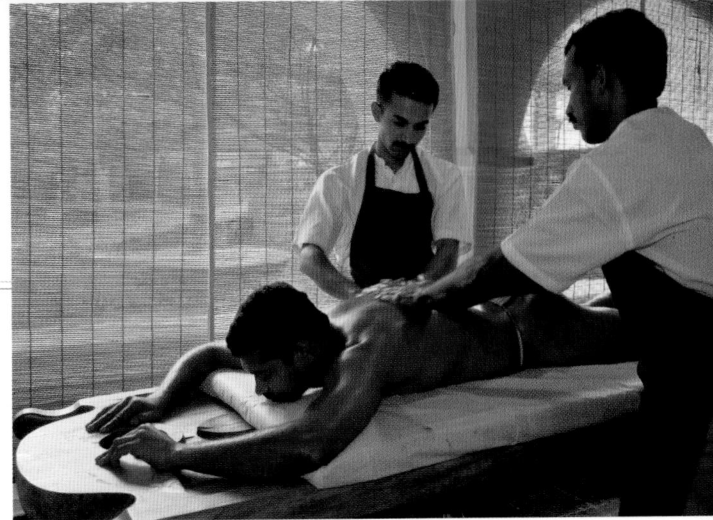

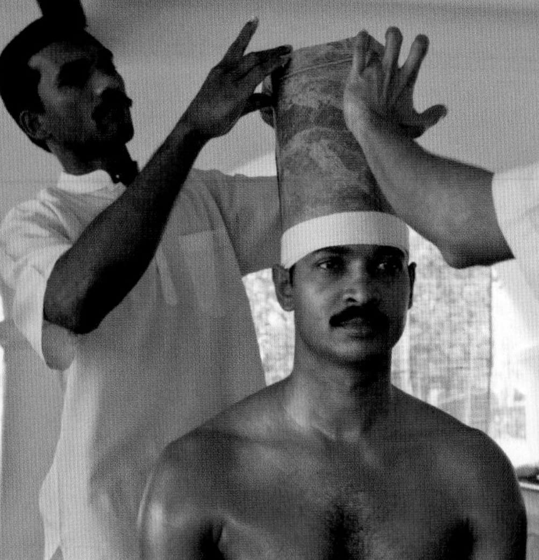

SIROVASTHI TREATMENT
Tony pours medicated oil into a cap on the patient's head, which will be worn for up to an hour. This treatment, also known as the "Nefertiti cap," benefits mental function.

the growth of medical tourism

India's ancient traditions of alternative healing (through disciplines such as Ayurveda and yoga), its reputation for high-quality, low-cost mainstream medicine and surgery, and its burgeoning number of spa facilities are attracting increasing interest from overseas visitors. The result is a new, highly specialized form of tourist travel known as medical tourism, in which foreign visitors combine a trip to India with a desire for healing, whether this takes the form of rejuvenation therapy or Ayurvedic treatment at a luxury spa, or surgery at a mainstream hospital. As well as enjoying all the benefits of a conventional vacation, medical tourists save money and time on treatments that would often be much more expensive and have a much longer waiting list if performed in their home country.

Though it is a relative newcomer as a destination for medical tourism, India's high standard of healthcare and comparatively low costs make it an increasingly popular choice. It is estimated that by 2012 the industry will be worth in excess of US$2 billion to the Indian economy.

UDVARTHANAM TREATMENT
Performed with a dry medicated powder, this treatment is aimed at reducing fat. It helps to drain fat-carrying lymphatic fluid from the body, improves the metabolism, and reduces accumulations of cellulite.

FOUR-HANDED MASSAGE
Tony and a colleague each use both hands to rub the powder onto the patient's back in upward strokes. *Udvarthanam* has the added effect of cleansing and nourishing the patient's skin through exfoliation.

KALARI PAYATTU PRAYERS
Tony begins a session of *kalari payattu*. As it is as much a mental as a physical discipline, every session starts with prayers designed to focus the mind.

STRETCHING WARM-UP
The practitioners undertake a series of gentle stretching exercises to awaken their *prana* (vital energies), after which they move on to practice a set of *kalari payattu* movements.

COMBAT TRAINING
On the ocher-colored floor of the *kalari* pit—which is medicated with herbs and antiseptic turmeric—Tony and his colleagues practice kicks, jumps, leaps, and battle training with staffs and other wooden weapons.

POST-WORKOUT STRETCH
Yoga and stretching are an important part of *kalari* practice—in fact, the harder yogic poses, or *asanas*, are part of *kalari* movements—and each session finishes with a stretching period to ease the body back into stillness.

Breathing correctly is vital in *kalari payattu*; breath control adds to the impact of each movement.

मालिशी

END OF THE DAY
Forbidden the distractions of music, alcohol, and television, and with the prospect of a dawn start in the morning, patients get to bed early in the quiet surroundings.

FEEDING THE CHICKENS
Jasbir rises at 5:00 a.m., brushes her teeth, studies, and then starts her chores. She is responsible for feeding the family chickens.

WASHING UP
Before having breakfast and preparing for her morning at school, Jasbir helps her mother wash last night's dishes in the courtyard of their home.

Twelve-year-old Jasbir Kaur, bright and bespectacled, looks around the village of Chita Kalaan, close to the town of Amritsar, Punjab. "I like my village," she says, "but it would be nice to have a house and a car, and all my family doing well." This determined and gregarious little girl might be speaking for millions of children throughout rural India.

Like her parents before her, Jasbir was born in Chita Kalaan. Her father is a reader of the Sikh holy book in Amritsar, and her mother is a housewife; the family is poor but well educated, and they value learning. Her grandparents, who live with them in a two-room home, lost their land, and now her grandfather drives a rickshaw, in which he takes Jasbir and her two brothers for rides in between transporting customers.

Jasbir attends the government high school in Chita Kalaan, which also attracts schoolchildren from surrounding villages. The school covers the standard Punjab high school curriculum, and teaches the basics of using a computer. Jasbir speaks Punjabi, Hindi, and a little English. Her parents encourage her to study and make something of her life, and she complies. Thanks to television, she is alive to the possibilities of modern India, and is confident of achieving her dreams. "I would live anywhere. I want to be a pilot or a singer when I grow up. I'm a good singer," she says, "or I'll be on TV." When there is electricity, she watches movies and the Discovery Channel in Hindi, but she loves reading most of all. She says, with a touch of pride, "Nobody disturbs me when I study, because I do so well in my exams." However, Jasbir, like many children in rural communities, has to balance her studies and her playtime with serious responsibilities at home. After school, she helps her mother around the house and watches her younger brothers. "I cook, clean, take out the trash, help to weed the fields, and cut fodder for the animals," she says. "My little brothers need watching. Omkar is extremely naughty, but Robin is younger and he still listens to me."

Many rural children share Jasbir's eagerness to do well and improve their circumstances, building on their parents' dreams and achievements. "My father has traveled to Singapore and Malaysia. I'd like for him to fulfill his wish to go abroad again and make something more of his life."

In the future, Jasbir will probably become part of a growing demographic of young, increasingly competent Indians who migrate to urban centers in search of careers ranging from office or call-center worker to politician or even TV actor. But if she does leave her village community, Jasbir is likely to feel a wrench. "I love my family," she says. "And I love my pet chickens, they make me happiest."

BRAIDING HER HAIR
Like most other schoolgirls, Jasbir has long hair that is faithfully braided by her mother into two braids every morning and tied with blue ribbon.

EATING BREAKFAST
Wrapped up against the cold of a winter morning, her head covered with a warm scarf—even indoors—Jasbir sits down with her grandfather to enjoy a breakfast of *roti* bread with herbs.

SCHOOLCHILD
A RURAL STUDENT, PUNJAB

WALKING TO SCHOOL
Jasbir sets off in the morning mist, carrying her books and supplies in a plastic bag.

ASSEMBLY
All the students fall in for assembly, standing in rows, to say their morning prayers.

HINDI EXAM
The pupils sit on mats in the yard for a Hindi exam. Their first language is Punjabi, but Hindi is a mandatory language in most Indian schools.

WARMING HANDS
Punjab winter temperatures can dip below freezing; the students warm their hands over a coal fire.

STUDYING IN THE YARD
Jasbir's teacher holds a revision class to go over the exam answers in the yard, to take advantage of the growing warmth of the sun.

ROADSIDE SNACK
After school, the children pause by a roadside seller to buy and eat *golgappas*, a puffed wheat snack filled with spiced water.

WALKING HOME
At 1:00 p.m., her schooling over for the day, Jasbir begins the short journey home through the fields with her close friends.

WALKING IN THE MUSTARD FIELDS
Jasbir takes a stroll with her grandfather and brother through the flowering mustard fields around her village. The agricultural revolution in Punjab has made it the "breadbasket" of India.

When I'm not studying or doing my chores, I like to play in the fields with my family and friends.

छात्रा

I wish we had more land so that we weren't so poor, but I like it that we are all happy.

छात्रा

△ **EATING LUNCH**
Hungry after school, Jasbir sits on a cot and eats lunch while her mother works on some sewing and darning.

▷ **HOMEWORK**
Taking advantage of the afternoon sun, Jasbir takes her schoolbooks up to the roof terrace to do her homework.

▽ **RICKSHAW RIDE**
One of Jasbir's favorite pastimes is to ride on her grandfather's rickshaw with her friends. Her grandfather is very popular with the village children.

▷ **CLEANING UP**
Like most of the village children, Jasbir has to find time for a variety of household chores, including taking out the trash.

△ **SHELLING PEAS**
Jasbir sits with her mother on the cot in the courtyard and chats as she helps her shell peas and chop vegetables for the evening meal.

◁ **MAKING THE FIRE**
Jasbir puts wood on the fire, as her grandfather sips his afternoon tea. The cooking is done on an earthen stove called a *chulha*, often outside the house.

▽ **EMBROIDERY**
Jasbir's mother helps her embellish a piece of clothing with floral embroidery, sequins, and colored beads.

rural life

India lives in its villages. Whether on a farm in Haryana, in a mountain settlement in Ladakh, or in the forests of Andhra Pradesh, three-quarters of the country's 1.1 billion people live in rural settlements. There is a world of difference between a village in Punjab, where a farmer might own a Mercedes, and one in Orissa, where crippling poverty can lead a farmer into heavy debt. However, India's countryside is beginning to prosper, led by growth in the cities. Many villages suffer from a lack of electricity, drinking water, healthcare, and education, but rural credit, new roads, and burgeoning aspirations are slowly changing daily life. The rural middle class forms a formidable market for low-priced consumer goods, and while villages are still largely mired in the caste system and social conservatism, the increased expectations of their populations are driving social change.

△ **FAMILY DINNER**
When Jasbir's father comes back from work at the *gurudwara* (Sikh temple), the family sits down together in the courtyard for dinner.

◁ **FINISHING HOMEWORK**
After dinner, Jasbir finishes her homework and studying. She is ambitious, and therefore diligent about doing her schoolwork.

▽ **EVENING PRAYERS**
Jasbir and her younger brother end the day by saying their prayers in front of an image of Guru Nanak, the spiritual guide of Sikhism.

◁ **BOARD GAMES**
Snakes & Ladders (*far left*) and Ludo (*left*) are classic favorites, as is chess, and *pachisi*, which is played on a cross-shaped board with cowrie shells.

Throughout India, there is a rich tradition of making simple but beautiful toys that remain firm favorites with children in spite of competition from expensive high-tech rivals. Street markets around the country brim with a mind-boggling assortment of bright, attractive, and sometimes mystifying trinkets for children. The town of Channapatna, near Bangalore in Karnataka, is famous for its exquisite wooden toys, traditionally made from lacquered wood, known as *aale mara* (ivory wood), and in Kondapalli, in Andhra Pradesh, artisans carve beautiful toys from a distinctive white-colored wood, called *Puniki*, which is then stuffed with sawdust and tamarind seed paste.

Puppetry has been popular in rural India since antiquity, often depicting characters from classical Indian tales, such as the *Ramayana* and *Mahabharata*. Board games are very popular, particularly chess, which originated in India. India's national obsession with cricket means that cricket bats and balls are an enduring favorite with children of all ages.

TRADITIONAL TOYS AND GAMES

▷ **RAJASTHANI PUPPET**
Traditional puppets, or *kathputalis*, have a good range of motion and can be made of wood, clay, leather, or cloth. The tradition of handmade string puppets in Rajasthan dates back more than a thousand years.

TRADITIONAL TOYS
Indian toys are decorated in dazzling colors created using everything from simple vegetable dyes for inexpensive children's playthings, to exquisite enamel paints and lacquerwork used to embellish pieces made as collector's items.

DABBAWALLAH

DELIVERING TIFFIN LUNCHBOXES, MUMBAI

LEAVING HOME
At 8:30 a.m. Vitthal leaves his home in a tenement, or *chawl*, in the Mumbai suburb of Andheri West. *Chawls* are often close-knit communities.

Cycle rides through a heaving metropolis, the crush of packed train platforms, and a series of strict deadlines structure the day for Vitthal Sawant, a young delivery man from Mumbai. "I pedal about 20 kilometers a day," he says, "to pick up lunches from homes, deliver them to offices, and drop the empty boxes back home. This way people get fresh, home-cooked food at work."

Vitthal is part of a unique 125-year-old institution known as the Mumbai dabbawallahs (or tiffinwallahs). For a nominal charge of 250–300 rupees (US$6–8) a month, Vitthal and his colleagues service office workers who would prefer to eat a hot packed lunch (*dabba*, or tiffin) cooked in their own kitchens rather than having to order junk food or eat out. The dabbawallahs are famous for two reasons: they have become integral to the life of Mumbai, and their near-perfect efficiency has gained them international attention.

"Each of us has to contribute two bicycles, a wooden crate for the tiffins, white cotton kurta-pajama clothing, and a white Gandhi cap," says Vitthal. With these accessories, a sharp eye on the time, and great conscientiousness, 5,000 dabbawallahs move 200,000 lunches throughout the city every day, using bicycles and the excellent Mumbai commuter trains to implement a formidable relay system.

"We don't ever go on strike. There's a standby man in case I fall sick," says Vitthal. He works through Mumbai's intense monsoon season, wading through floods if necessary to make his deliveries. In hundreds of thousands of deliveries all over the city, barely any *dabbas* are lost, stolen, or delivered to the wrong address. The dabbawallahs' dedication and excellence has earned them *Forbes* magazine's Six Sigma quality rating (one error in six million transactions—a record which puts them on a par with companies such as Motorola) and a place in business school case studies.

Like most dabbawallahs, Vitthal comes from a village, and lives in a Mumbai tenement house. "My father was also a dabbawallah," he says. "My brother is a farmer in the village, but the rest of my family lives in Mumbai." Vitthal went to school until he was 16 years old, but many of his colleagues are uneducated. Their delivery system doesn't require literacy, instead using a simple color-coded alphanumeric system to mark the destination of each individual tiffin box.

Vitthal has been a dabbawallah for ten years. There isn't much change in the nature of the job, but everyone gets a pay raise every two years, meaning that Vitthal's starting salary has now tripled. The dabbawallahs also move with the times; the telecommunications revolution has made it easier to keep up-to-date with travel conditions, and bookings can now even be made online.

DAILY PRAYERS
Like many dabbawallahs, Vitthal is a devout Hindu. He stops at two temples before work to perform his daily *pooja* (prayer) in front of statues of Hanuman and Ganesha.

READY FOR THE DAY
Vitthal picks up the bicycle that he uses to collect *dabbas* throughout the morning. There is a second bike waiting at the end of his train ride.

SETTING OFF
Vitthal starts his working day cycling through the suburbs to various homes. In the heavy but fairly ordered traffic of Mumbai, a bicycle is easily maneuverable and avoids the inconveniences of traffic jams and parking.

◁ **TEA BREAK**
Mumbai is typically a hot and humid city, so Vitthal stops cycling briefly to fortify himself with a quick drink at a roadside tea stand.

▽ **MORNING ROUNDS**
Vitthal sets off with a colleague alongside a milkman carrying his load in steel canisters. Dabbawallahs are recognizable by their impeccable white clothes and Gandhi cap.

△ **COLLECTING DABBAS**
Like most dabbawallahs, Vitthal has many regular customers with whom he has struck up a personal rapport, as he visits them at home on a daily basis.

▽ **LOADING UP**
As he goes about his morning's work, Vitthal attaches each lunch to the back of his bicycle. It takes skill and strength to cycle with this load.

◁ △ **ARRIVING AT THE TRAIN STATION**
His bicycle almost disappearing under his bags, Vitthal arrives at Andheri station, where he unloads and sorts his *dabbas* according to their final destination.

△ **CARRYING DABBAS TO THE TRAIN**
Loading the packets onto a long wooden cratelike shelf, Vitthal carries them across the tracks to the train that will take him to Dadar, about 10 miles (16 km) away.

The only thing that keeps us from delivering lunches is if the trains stop running, and then it's a day off.

डब्बावाला

TRAIN JOURNEY TO DADAR
Sitting with other dabbawallahs, Vitthal spends the hour-long trip to Dadar station relaxing and chatting. This is also a good time for him to eat breakfast before making his deliveries.

REACHING DADAR
Vitthal arrives at Dadar station. The platform is relatively empty, but he must be able to carry his *dabbas* even when it is thronged with people.

STARTING TO DELIVER
He and his colleagues sort the *dabbas*, redistributing them among themselves by delivery area, and each sets off to load up his bicycle and start making deliveries.

DELIVERING LUNCH
Vitthal hands over hot, home-cooked lunches with a smile. His customers range from small shop-owners to white-collar executives at large corporations.

ON THE BIKE AGAIN
His bicycle laden with packages again, Vitthal sets off once more on chaotic streets. Dabbawallahs pride themselves on not letting the hectic traffic of Mumbai impede their deliveries.

STAYING IN TOUCH
The telecommunications revolution in India has benefited dabbawallahs greatly; Vitthal can use a cell phone to fine-tune delivery times and places.

DABBA CODIFICATION
Lunches are marked with an alphanumeric code that indicates the destination area, building, and floor, and identifies the collecting and delivering dabbawallahs.

> My colleagues and I are proud that we have never made a mistake with a delivery.
>
> डब्बावाला

BACK ON THE BIKE
From mid-morning, when he gets off at Dadar, until lunch time, Vitthal whirls through the streets delivering tiffins.

COLLECTING EMPTIES
After lunch it's time to do the whole round in reverse, as Vitthal goes back along his route to collect the empty lunchboxes.

BACK AT DADAR STATION
At the train station with all of the empty boxes, the dabbawallahs re-sort them for delivery back to each home.

RETURN JOURNEY
The train ride home is spent taking a well-earned rest, reading newspapers, and catching up on the day's events.

BACK HOME
After a tiring day, Vitthal enjoys a cup of tea in the family kitchen with his wife and young son.

◁ **TEA-MAKER'S EQUIPMENT**
North Indians drink tea *dhaba*-style, which is boiled, with a lot of milk, and is very sweet. Tea is often spiced with cardamom or ginger.

Indians love to eat, preferably well and cheaply, and whenever the urge strikes. The result is an astonishing range of delicious freshly cooked, sweet and savory street foods. From the humble stuffed *samosa* to the curly *jalebi* (a deep-fried sweet), from the single-morsel *golgappa* (a puffed-wheat snack filled with spiced water) to the satisfying spiced vegetable *pao bhaji*, made of curry and bread, there is something for every occasion. Refreshing beverages are available from the tea stand, the sugarcane juice vendor, and the wandering coconut-water seller. On rainy days, people love *pakoras* (hot, deep-fried savory snacks); on hot days, they yearn for *kulfi* (an iced milk dessert) with cold *dahi vada* (lentil or potato doughnuts dipped in yogurt). A late-night worker can always find someone selling *anda-parantha* (fried unleavened dough with scrambled egg) or chicken or lamb morsels wrapped in *rotis* (bread). Vendors adapt to the season, time of day, and clientele with consummate ease, and every street in India reflects the distinct palate of the area.

TEA STANDS AND STREET FOOD

▷ **ANTIQUE TIFFIN BOX**
Although working Indians increasingly opt for fast food, many people bring lunch such as rice, *rotis*, lentils, and vegetables from home in a tiffin box. The separate compartments prevent the dishes from mixing.

INDIAN FAST FOOD
The mouthwatering array of food available on an average Indian street ranges from a basic paper cone of roasted peanuts to meticulously prepared *chaat* (fried pastries in spiced yogurt with onions, coriander, and potato pieces).

DANCE TEACHER

TEACHING AND PERFORMING CLASSICAL DANCE, CHENNAI

A south Indian sari accentuates Ganga Thampi's graceful form as she moves from class to class at the prestigious Kalakshetra school for the arts in Chennai, Tamil Nadu. This is where the 34-year-old dancer was trained in Bharatnatyam, the oldest Indian classical dance form. She lives close to the school, and for the past ten years, her life has been measured by its routine.

Like many artists, Ganga became interested in classical dance at a very young age, in her hometown of Koilon in Kerala. Her father, a well-known Kathakali dancer and the principal of a dance school, encouraged her to follow her passion. Talent and grit earned her a place at Kalakshetra, the most highly regarded arts academy in India, and the toughest to get into. "It was a grueling entrance process," she recalls.

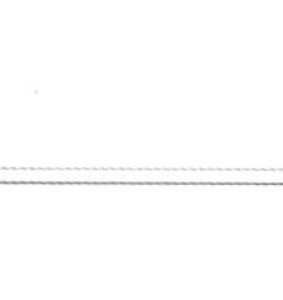

The Kalakshetra academy was founded in 1936 to nurture the most traditional forms of India's rich cultural heritage. The school recruits master artists to pass on their discipline to younger people in a "living chain" of artistic heritage that dates back to the *Natya Shastra*, the 2,000-year-old text that lays down the principles of Indian dramatic theory and performance.

Kalakshetra school revived the Bharatnatyam style of the *devadasis*, temple dancers whose performances were banned during the British occupation (1750–1947). Today's curriculum is exactly as it was at the school's inception more than 80 years ago, and Ganga dances the role of Sita, from the revered *Ramayana* epic, exactly as it was first choreographed by the school's founders, down to the same costumes and masks. Though the academy is a secular establishment, Ganga believes that dancing in this place is a spiritual experience; "the vibrations of great artists and musicians are present in the school," she says.

Her husband teaches yoga, a discipline that Ganga has incorporated into her daily routine, though dance remains her greatest focus. She was taught by Leela Samson, one of India's best-known dancers, and now passes on her commitment and skill through the traditional Indian *guru–shishya* (mentor–disciple) relationship. She corrects her students as they practice on a floor burnished to a shine by the rhythmic striking of many feet. Ganga is popular with her students for her soft-spoken manner, but loses her shyness on stage, transformed by the drama and passion of classical dance.

In today's India, where commerce and innovation are high priorities for many young Indians, dancers like Ganga and academies like Kalakshetra ensure that traditional art forms do not lose their place and meaning. "People dance because it is their calling," says Ganga. "It comes from within. My greatest reward is to bring out the talent that is hidden in a student."

GETTING TO WORK Ganga arrives at Kalakshetra on a scooter, though sometimes she walks. She wakes very early and has already spent the early morning meditating, praying, and practicing yoga for fitness.

THE STUDENTS ARRIVE Students walk to assembly, wearing the traditional clothes that are compulsory dress for both students and teachers when they are on school grounds.

GATHERING FOR ASSEMBLY Usually held under a banyan tree, assembly is taken indoors when it rains. The entire school files in, leaving their rubber sandals outside.

MORNING PRAYERS
The school director leads prayers invoking the school's gurus, past and present. The students then sing prayers from across many religions.

WALKING TO CLASS
Ganga walks to her first class. She usually has the first period free, and spends it reading in the library or chatting with colleagues.

STRETCHING EXERCISES
Before Ganga arrives, her students start their stretching exercises in the classroom, having touched the floor as they enter in a gesture of respect to their place of learning.

PRACTICING BEFORE CLASS
Students practice their movements while waiting for Ganga. The classroom has a traditional red oxide floor, and is well lit and ventilated by large latticework windows.

TRADITIONAL GREETING
When Ganga enters the class, the students offer her a respectful *namaste*, a traditional greeting with palms joined at the heart.

The school's motto is "Art without vulgarity, beauty without cruelty, education without fear."

नृत्य गुरू

BEATING TIME
Ganga uses a wooden stick to sound the *taal*, or rhythm. Bharatnatyam is a highly structured dance form.

TEACHING
The class is learning *nritya*, the combination of rhythm and expression. Ganga walks among them as they practice, correcting their mistakes.

CORRECTING GESTURES
She adjusts a student's hand in the *mudra* (gesture) called *katakamukh*, which is one of 12 ways of holding the hand in dance, and demonstrates how to hold the foot as her students pause and watch.

DEMONSTRATING MOVEMENT
Ganga demonstrates a movement and the class practices it with her. Ganga's great skill inspires her junior students to reach for greater heights.

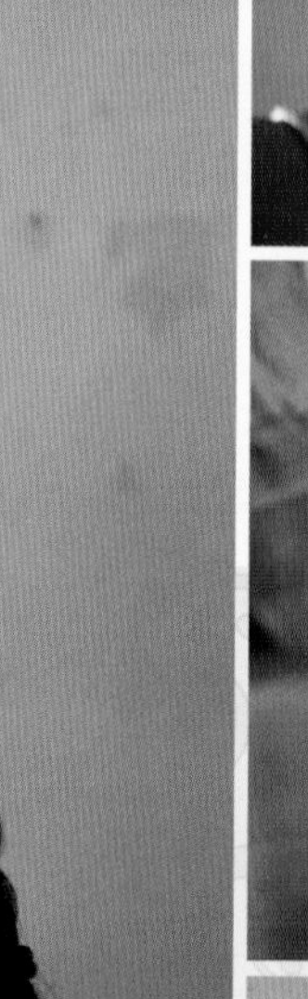

CORRECTING FORM
Ganga shows a student the correct angle at which to hold his arms as he performs a movement. A dancer's strength, flexibility, and balance are critical to their art.

the role of women in india

Being a woman in India has always had both positive and negative consequences. In the past (and in many rural areas today), the Indian mother was revered, just as the Indian daughter-in-law was oppressed; and while becoming a bride was a state of grace, widows were relegated to a life of lonely neglect. But just as India's cities have modernized in recent decades, urban Indian women have stepped outside the role of teacher, homemaker, or caretaker to become entrepreneurs, executives, pilots, artists, and athletes. Today, women lead major political parties, and have also held the highest political offices of President and Prime Minister. As India continues down the road of commercial and cultural globalization, its women are increasingly challenging the country's rigid traditional social structure as well as its outdated patriarchal attitudes, but still face a long, uphill struggle for full emancipation.

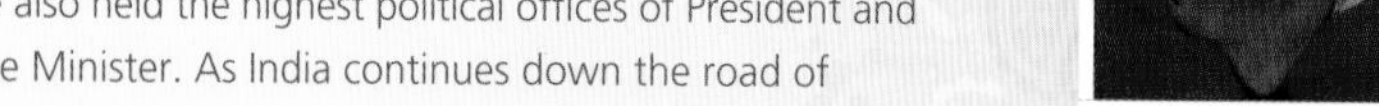

SCHOOL LUNCH
At lunch time, students and teachers go to the dining hall in the dormitory area, where a self-service cafeteria provides a basic South Indian meal.

◁ **EXPRESSIONS CLASS**
Ganga holds a class on *abhinaya*, or stylized expressions, which are important to the storytelling component of Bharatnatyam.

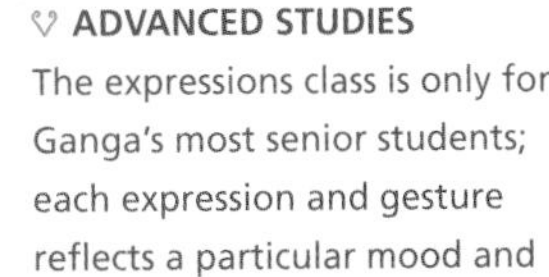

▽ **ADVANCED STUDIES**
The expressions class is only for Ganga's most senior students; each expression and gesture reflects a particular mood and must be carefully distinguished.

△ **LEAVING SCHOOL**
As soon as the day's lessons are over, Ganga heads home to prepare for the dance performance that she is to give at a theater in the evening.

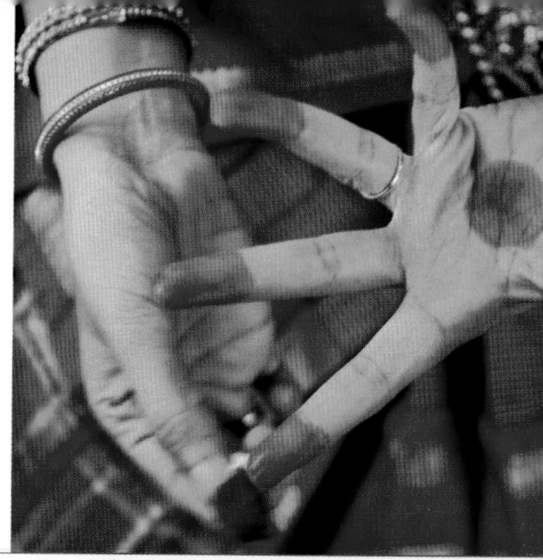

Art and life is almost one in India—it is not separated. There is no difference between an artist and her life.

नृत्य गुरू

APPLYING EYE MAKEUP
At the theater, Ganga readies herself for the role of Sita in the choreographed dance-drama of the *Ramayana* epic. Once she has changed into her costume, she applies striking eye makeup that emphasizes her expressions.

APPLYING A BINDI
She traces a bindi on her forehead. Bindis are standard ornamentation for women, but those applied for performances are more emphatic. Ganga highlights hers with a stroke of gold under the red to match her eyebrow makeup.

DANCE JEWELRY
The elaborate costume jewelry worn by Bharatnatyam dancers is made of silver dipped in gold leaf, and inset with semiprecious green and red stones. A full set comprises ten pieces.

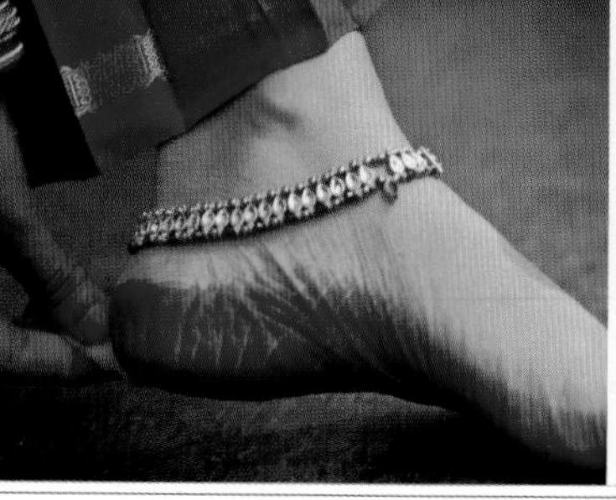

FOOT DECORATION
Ganga's feet are painted with red *alta* (a variety of henna), to emphasize them. She wears anklets heavy with tiny bells that ring with every step.

◁ **HAND DECORATION**
Ganga's hands are also painted with *alta*. The circular design serves to highlight the body's *chakras*, or energy points.

▽ **FINAL ADJUSTMENTS**
A colleague helps to place Ganga's ornaments. The costume, makeup, and jewelry used in a performance vary dramatically from role to role.

▷ **PAYING RESPECT**
Ganga touches her guru's feet. It is said that a dancer must bow to her teacher before bowing to God, because the teacher is the one who shows her the way to God.

◁ △ **THE PERFORMANCE**
Ganga plays the role of Sita, the wronged wife of the exiled King Rama. The performance is being enacted exactly as the founder of Kalakshetra choreographed it.

CLASSICAL MUSICIANS
A traveling Hindustani band plays to a village audience in Udaipur, Rajasthan. It requires a lifelong commitment to learn and memorize traditional Indian music.

Indian classical music is a remarkably complex and sophisticated art. The northern Hindustani classical tradition is based on a melody often improvised around a steady drone from the four-stringed *tanpura*, and given complex rhythmic structure by the *tabla* drum. Carnatic classical music from the South is more structured, and uses violins and *mridangam* percussion but emphasizes vocals. Highly skilled players can create music of almost unbelievable subtlety, exploiting every nuance of predominantly simple instruments. To hear a *tabla* player create incredible rhythmic patterns and variations in tone from a simple skin drum, using just the strength of his hands, is a wonderful experience.

Unlike in the Western tradition, Indian music is not written down, instead the tunes are passed down from generation to generation. Instrument-makers usually come from generations of highly skilled craftsmen, but as young people increasingly have a wider choice of professions, such traditional skills are in danger of becoming lost.

CLASSICAL MUSIC-MAKING

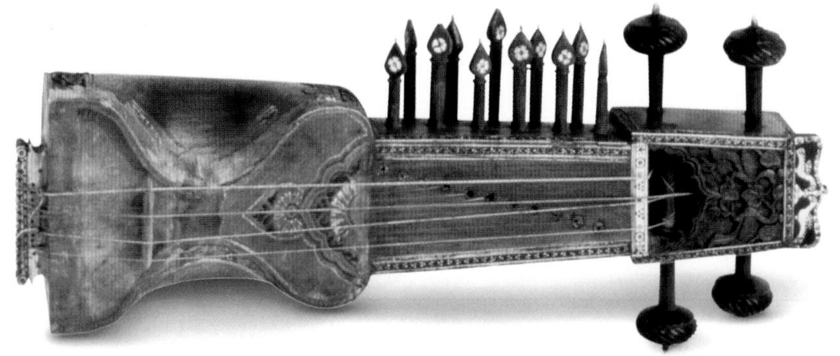

NORTH INDIAN SARANGI
The *sarangi* is one of the oldest Indian instruments. It has three or four playing strings, and many unplayed "sympathetic" strings, which resonate to create the hum characteristic of Indian music.

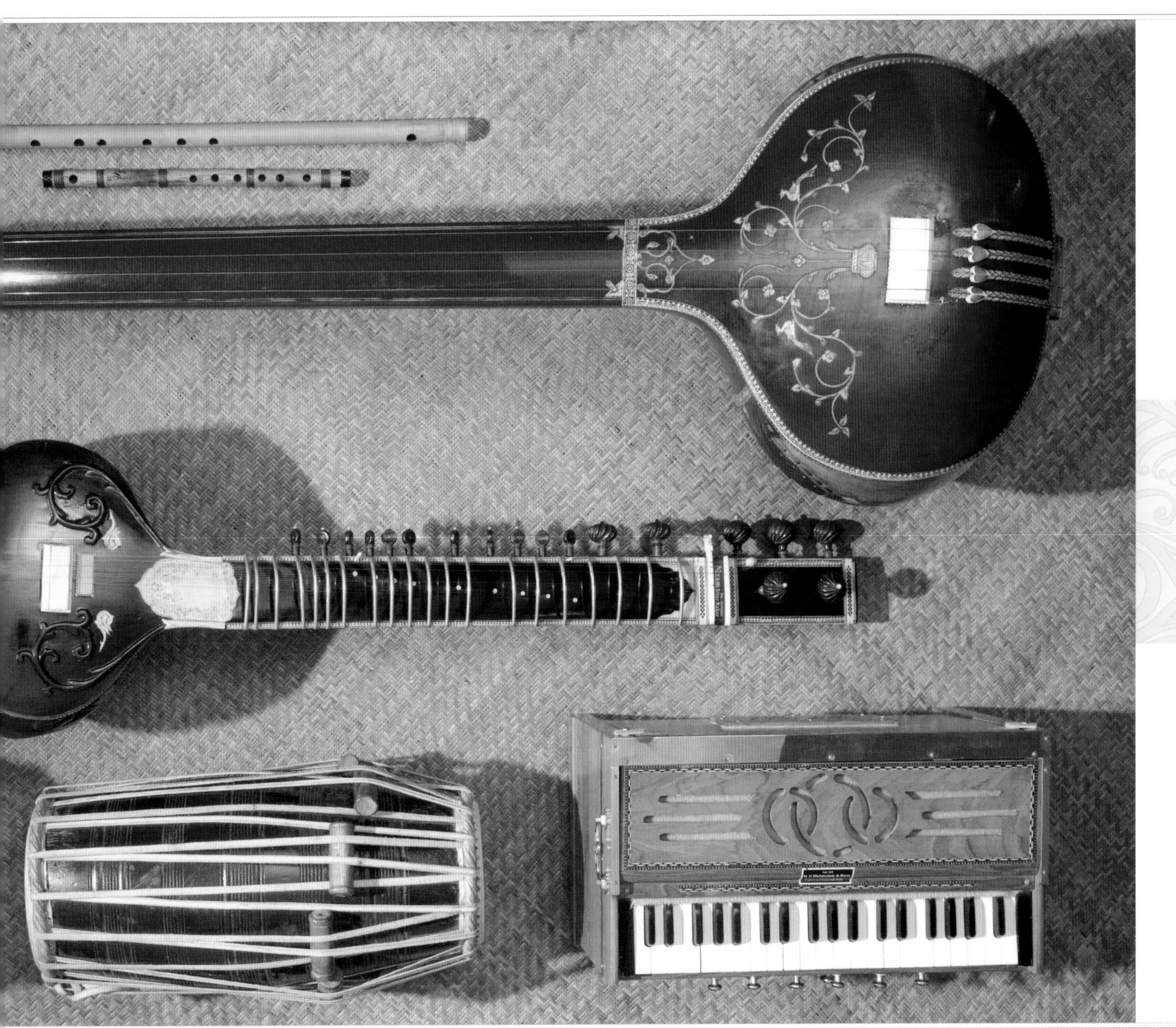

HINDUSTANI INSTRUMENTS
Hindustani classical music frequently uses a combination of stringed instruments, such as the *tanpura* and *sitar*, blown-air instruments, like the flute and harmonium, and percussion, including the *dholak* and *tabla* drums.

Monindro Nath Mondol, or Moni-da, is a man seasoned by sun, salt water, and hard physical labor. The 54-year-old fisherman and farmer has spent the majority of his life in the Sunderbans Delta, the vast braid of marsh, mangrove forest, and tidal water at the entrance to the Bay of Bengal, in a landscape that is constantly being reshaped by surging seas and epic storms.

Like many other village farmers of their generation, Moni-da's parents moved to this watery land after the Bengal Famine of 1943. They were pioneering settlers on Bali Island, and Moni-da had to drop out of school when he was 13 in order to help his parents clear the jungle, plant fields, and gather honey from the forests. Now a father himself, Moni-da has lived on Bali for 41 years, in a thatched mud homestead that is surrounded by two acres of rice fields.

When he is not working his farm, Moni-da also has a job as a fisherman at Help Tourism's Sunderbans Jungle Camp lodge. He thinks that ecotourism is good for the Sunderbans; "all the poaching has stopped now that there is alternative employment," he says. As well as working for the ecotourism industry, many former poachers now farm and spawn fish, and are able to sell directly to buyers who travel from the mainland. "People can now afford permanent houses," says Moni-da.

Large swaths of the Sunderbans region are World Heritage protected territory, but this region is famous for bloody clashes between people and unusually aggressive man-eating tigers. Honey-gatherers working in the forest wear masks on the back of their heads, as tigers always attack from the rear. Moni-da prefers to gather his honey from the fields, though like many inhabitants he has had a terrifying encounter there, too: a tiger charged him as he was cutting firewood about 100 yards from his house. "I dropped my ax, jumped into the river, and swam for my life. Luckily, a nearby wedding party heard the roars and they came to chase the tiger away," he remembers.

The World Wildlife Fund has erected a tiger net on the perimeter of the forest, but like most inhabitants of the Sunderbans, Moni-da believes that the best defense against tiger attacks is Bonbibi, the all-powerful goddess of the forest in the local religion. He prays for protection at her shrine in his house every day before he sets out for work.

Life in the Sundarbans is difficult. The only electricity on Bali is provided by a generator at the tourist lodge and a few solar panels. People suffering from serious illnesses must be treated outside the region. Entertainment consists of professional storytellers, fairs, and chats at the local tea stand. Still, Moni-da wouldn't change things for the world. "The city is too noisy and selfish for me. There is nothing as beautiful as the river, the stars, and the fields of Bali."

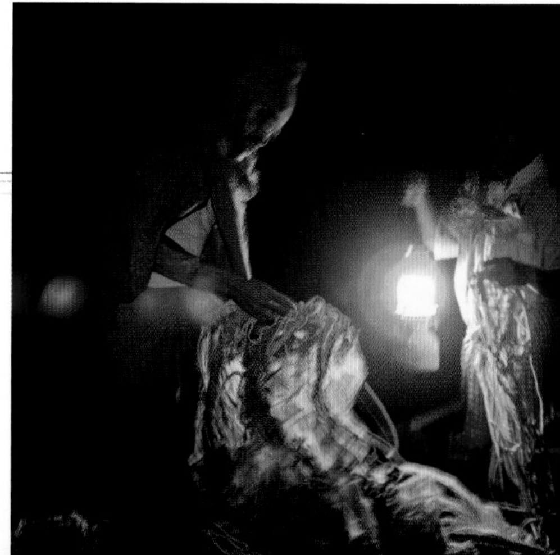

LOADING THE BOAT
With a lantern cutting through the darkness, Moni-da and his brother-in-law pack the boat with nets and food for the day.

PREDAWN BREAKFAST
Once on board, the men eat a quick breakfast of *pantha*—rice left to soak in water, and spiced with salt and chilis.

PREPARING TO FISH
The men row out across the tributary toward the jungle, and anchor their boat near buoys that mark good fishing spots. Once tethered against the rising tide, they are ready to begin fishing.

MANGROVE BOATMAN

FISHING AND FARMING IN THE SUNDERBANS, WEST BENGAL

◁ LETTING OUT THE NET
After half an hour of careful positioning, the long blue net is finally placed in a central current.

▷ WAITING FOR THE CATCH
The men place a bamboo stick across the mouth of the net to keep it open, and begin a long, patient vigil on the quiet water.

▽ THE THROWING NET
Moni-da flings a throwing net that he normally uses in ponds out onto the water, as it may help supplement the main catch.

△ ▷ DRAWING IN THE NETS
The men reel in the blue net. The white socklike end contains the morning's slim catch, which is emptied into a bowl. They draw in the nets heavy with water, draining them as much as possible to lighten the load.

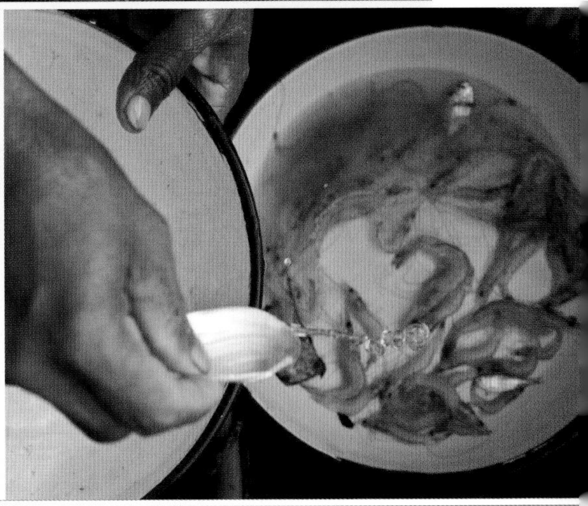

△ SIFTING THE CATCH
Despite the poor size of the catch, Moni-da is pleased to have netted some tiger prawn spawn, which fetches two rupees per piece. At other times of the year, he will catch sea perch and hilsa, both local delicacies.

TAKING A BATH
Moni-da bathes in the pond to wash off the clay from the river banks before heading out to work in the rice fields.

HARVESTING RICE
Sickle in hand, Moni-da makes the short walk out to his paddy fields, where his winter crop of rice must be harvested before it is lost to frost or heavy rain.

BACK ON LAND
At 8:30 a.m., the men return to the shore. Their neighbors, waiting at the bank, help hoist the boat to higher ground.

UNLOADING THE BOAT
Moni-da's family all pitch in to unload the boat and carry the catch and equipment home.

RETURNING HOME
Moni-da and his family live in a compound of thatched mud huts close to a pond. When he arrives home, Moni-da puts away the washed and neatly folded nets.

THE FAMILY LUNCH
Moni-da's wife prepares a meal of spinach, lentils, and rice, which is served on steel plates to the rest of the family sitting on the veranda.

> I want people to see my beautiful island, and tourism has brought the world to my door.
>
> नाविक

◁ **THRESHING RICE**
Moni-da and his sister beat bushels of rice stalks on a bamboo lattice to separate out the grain, which falls through gaps in the lattice and collects at the bottom.

▽ **MENDING NETS**
After a short break it's back to work. Fishing nets are frequently subject to wear and tear, and these spares must be repaired for future fishing expeditions.

△ **VISITING THE IRONMONGER**
In the early evening, at the end of his day's work, Moni-da pays a visit to the local ironmonger to have his knives sharpened and to buy some new tools.

△ **DOWNTIME**
Evening is a time to meet friends for a gossip, a smoke, or a game of cards at the village tea shop, before returning home for dinner as darkness falls.

ecotourism in india

India's varied terrain and vast wildernesses, which include over 90 national parks and about 500 wildlife sanctuaries, make it one of the biodiversity hot spots of the world. Its delicate ecosystems, both on land and at sea, are subject to intense pressures from a booming population and rising economic development, which has driven species like the tiger and the rhinoceros to the brink of extinction. With greater public awareness, however, rising numbers of visitors to these areas are turning to a more responsible form of tourism. Hoteliers and guides increasingly try to bridge the demands of tourism, local employment, and conservation by offering ecotourism trips that both delight and educate visitors while leaving little or no impact on the environment.

THE TEMPLE AT NIGHT
At 3:00 a.m., Gurdayal gets up to start work; the Golden Temple is still lit up for the night.

In the vast kitchen of the Golden Temple in Amritsar, Punjab, head cook, Gurdayal Singh, is making lentil and chickpea flour curry. "I can't tell you the exact proportions," he says. "I don't measure things out, it's all instinct." He relies on flair and more than 30 years of experience to feed the 30,000–40,000 people who eat at the temple's *langar*, or free kitchen, each day.

LIGHTING THE FIRE
As the head cook, Gurdayal is responsible for starting the vast wood fire in the main kitchen.

MORNING PRAYER
Gurdayal prays before starting to cook. *Kar seva* permeates his whole life, so every act he performs is an act of devotion.

Every *gurdwara* (Sikh house of worship) maintains this charitable institution, and the Golden Temple is the holiest of India's *gurdwaras*. Charity is central to Sikhism, as is the concept of *kar seva*, or selfless duty. Donating time, energy, and funds to benefit others is a way of offering thanks to God through good deeds. The *langar*, which is manned by volunteers and maintained with community support, provides simple vegetarian fare to anyone who wants a meal, regardless of religion, caste, or class. The food is served in a communal space where all people sit together. "Actors, politicians, and officials have eaten on the floor here," says Gurdayal. "Everyone is equal in the eyes of God."

Gurdayal came to the Golden Temple at the age of 16 to follow a spiritual calling, leaving his farmland in the village of Raj Oki in the care of his brother. "I used to work in the village *gurdwara*," he says, "and when my father and I visited the Golden Temple they were taking interns, so I decided to stay. I began as an apprentice, stacking supplies in the warehouse." Soon Gurdayal moved up to become the sous chef; now he is the head cook, managing the wood fires and training up two younger cooks for the temple.

The kitchen is an enormous operation manned by more than 40 Sikh men and women, mostly volunteers, who make *rotis* (flat bread), manage the gas ovens, store the supplies, cook the food, wash up, and clean the kitchens. The *langar* is open around the clock; if a full meal is not available, the kitchen will at least provide a cup of tea and a *roti*. Gurdayal estimates that on regular days, he will cook 20 sacks of wheat and 3,300 lb (1,500 kg) of lentils, but these figures multiply on Sundays, when the number of people eating at the *langar* might go up to 150,000, and on festival days, when numbers might reach 500,000. An automated *roti*-making machine is pressed into service for these occasions.

Gurdayal has a wife and two sons back in Raj Oki village. He gets time off from his duties to go home and see his family for a month every year, but for the last 35 years he has lived within the *gurdwara* complex, in the enormous kitchen shed full of firewood and vats, sleeping on a cot next to a box that contains all of his worldly possessions—two sets of clothes and a thick woollen blanket to stave off the winter cold. Yet these meager possessions are enough for Gurdayal. "I want to spend my life in the service of the Guru," he says.

EARLY MORNING TEA
The holy book, called the Guru Granth Sahib, will be brought to the temple at 5:00 a.m., so the kitchen staff make tea to supply to the early worshippers.

LANGAR COOK

FREE KITCHEN AT THE GOLDEN TEMPLE, AMRITSAR

◁ **THE HOLY BOOK**
While the kitchen prepares the morning tea, the Guru Granth Sahib is placed on a canopied throne (*takht*) and carried into the Golden Temple's main hall for the day's prayers.

▽ **BEGINNING THE LANGAR**
After making the tea, Gurdayal starts on the first *langar* of the day. He whirls between pans in the kitchen, stirring constantly.

▽ **CLEANING VESSELS**
The enormous vats used to cook food dedicated to God must be spotless; while cooking continues in the rest of the kitchen, the used vats are thoroughly cleaned.

△ **BATHING**
At 6:00 a.m., Gurdayal immerses himself in the freezing water surrounding the temple for a bath. He ties his *kirpan* (sword) to his turban while he prays.

◁ ▽ **SIKH OBJECTS**
After bathing, he uses his *kangha* (comb) on his long hair, sharpens his *kirpan* with sand and ash, and reties his turban, which is worn to protect the hair and is wrapped around the head in various ways.

◁ **TAKING A BREAK**
As the supervisor of all the kitchen activity at the Golden Temple, Gurdayal rarely has time to take a break, but occasionally finds a moment to relax with a cup of tea.

PRAYERS AT AMRITSAGAR
Getting away from the heat of the kitchens, Gurdiyal prays on the edge of the Amritsagar ("Pool of Nectar") surrounding the temple, for which the town of Amritsar is named.

I am dedicated to my work because a visit to the Golden Temple is not complete without sharing a meal with others.

बावर्ची

▷ **SUPPLIES ARRIVE**
The food supplies for the Golden Temple kitchens are donated by the Sikh community, who give what they can when they can.

▽ **MAKING ROTI BREAD**
A small area of the kitchen turns into a *roti* production line as a group of volunteers help to knead and flatten the dough.

▷ **FOOD IS READY**
Gurdayal says a prayer over all the food before it is taken out to the dining hall. He remains in the kitchen while volunteer workers at the temple serve the *langar*.

▽ **EATING AT THE LANGAR**
People sit cross-legged in rows on the floor on mats set with plates, and once served they eat in silence. Everyone must cover their head in a *gurdwara*.

△ ▷ **A STAPLE FOOD**
Once it is flattened, the bread is cooked. *Roti* makes a good accompaniment to many foods, so large quantities are made.

◁ ▽ WASHING UP

At the end of the meal, empty plates are handed over to be stacked in large metal tubs. Once full, these are taken away so that the plates can be cleaned for the next user.

▽ EVENING PRAYER

After cooking the second *langar* of the day for the evening visitors, Gurdayal can rest. He goes out to pray by the water and listen to the hymns that float out of the temple's main hall.

◁ EVENING MEAL

With the temple visitors fed, Gurdayal and his colleagues sit on sacks on the kitchen floor to have their own evening meal.

▽ EARLY TO BED

Gurdayal is in bed by 8:00 p.m. because of his early start; he has a quilt and a cot in the sleeping area at the back of the kitchen.

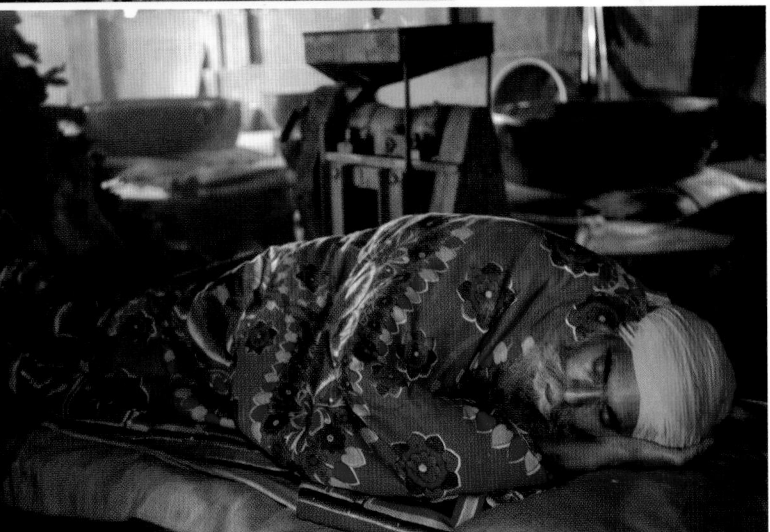

I do not taste any of the dishes before they are served; *langar* food is dedicated to God.

बावर्ची

LEAVING FOR WORK
Like many rural women, Kuki covers her head in public. The *adobe* houses in Salawas are painted the same distinctive blue as those in nearby Jodhpur.

In the courtyard of her house, Kuki Devi sits cross-legged on the floor in front of a pit loom, preparing to weave one of the exquisite *dhurries* (floor coverings) for which the village of Salawas in Rajasthan is famous. Making *dhurries* is a family enterprise, and everyone is involved in weaving, washing, and drying the rugs, which are prized around the globe.

Kuki lives in the family home across a low wall from her brother-in-law, the shared space reflecting their joint family structure. Kuki is uneducated and lives with her daughter-in-law, the wife of her elder son who lives and works as an electrician in Jodhpur. Her younger son visits often. "My family are all from Salawas," she says. "I married a man from the village too, but he died of pneumonia just a few years ago."

All the weavers of Salawas are related. They belong to a tribe of the Prajapati caste, who left their drought-parched village a century ago and settled in the fallow land that was then part of the Jodhpur estate, gradually creating the settlement of Salawas out of the thickly forested area. Originally a tribe of potters, their skills also included weaving *dhurries* and fabric for local customers to use as blankets or shawls. Today, weaving still constitutes the backbone of the village economy.

"I work for Nenu Bhobaria's *dhurrie* factory," says Kuki. The factory owner supplies her with silk, cotton, camel-hair, or goat-hair yarn, selects colors with her, and shows her the designs that he wants her to make. Entrepreneurs and designers discovered the weavers of Salawas in the 1970s and 80s, encouraging them to create *dhurries*, throws, and other furnishings in a variety of patterns and colors, and introducing them to chemical dyes and fast color, instead of the vegetable dyes the villagers traditionally used. The interlocked weave of the *dhurries* makes the pieces reversible. Today, the products of Salawas are in demand from the Middle East to New Zealand.

"I can weave about 30 cm [1 ft] of fabric a day," says Kuki, who is paid 15 rupees (US$0.38) for a day's work, "and it usually takes me a week to make a *dhurrie*." People like Kuki are the base of a giant business, and many weavers like herself have joined together to form cooperatives to organize their craft and guard against exploitation.

During the wedding season, Kuki supplements her income by helping to cook the wedding food, although it is hard to accommodate this extra work. Her day begins before dawn and ends close to midnight, although she works a few hours less in the brutal heat of summer. She has to find time to take grain to the mill, clean the house, and collect cooking fuel, but she doesn't complain. "My daughter-in-law is here to help with the chores," she says, "and she keeps me company."

MAKING ROTIS
Kuki and other village women spend the early morning kneading and rolling out wheat dough for the *roti* bread that will be served at a local wedding.

WEAVING AT HOME
Kuki works at the pit loom in her courtyard. The patterns of the *dhurries* are typically geometric, and woven using an interlocking technique.

DHURRIE WEAVER

COTTAGE INDUSTRY WORKER, RAJASTHAN

WORKING WITH THE FAMILY
Kuki works with her sister-in-law on the same *dhurrie*, using short wooden rods to beat the threads back tightly against one another. Other relatives help at various stages of the production.

COLLECTING DUNG CAKES
Kuki picks up some of the cakes of dung that she has dried in the courtyard to use for the day's cooking on an earthen stove. Cattle dung is a vital source of fuel in rural India.

DRYING POPPADOMS
As Kuki chats with her mother-in-law, her sister-in-law checks the *poppadoms*. *Poppadoms* are long-lasting lentil flour wafers that are dried and then roasted.

RANGOLI
Auspicious patterns on the floor, called *rangoli*, are drawn in white and colored powder every day. They are common in rural homes.

HOUSEWORK
Kuki sweeps the dust from the courtyard around the *rangoli* with a long switch as she chats to her daughter-in-law and grandson.

VISITING THE FACTORY
Kuki heads for Nenu Bhobaria's factory to get more yarn for the next *dhurrie*. She carries a sack of grain on her head, which she will drop off at the mill on the way.

The designs that we use on our *dhurries* have been passed down through the generations.

दस्तकार

WASHING YARNS
The yarns that Kuki will use to create her next *dhurrie* are washed in a large vat of water before dyeing. The yarn must be wetted to ensure that the color is even.

PREPARING YARNS
The wet material is arranged on poles that will hold the yarns while they are dyeing. *Dhurries* can be made of cotton, silk, linen, jute, or wool, or any combination of these.

MEASURING DYES
Dyes are selected and carefully weighed according to the size of the *dhurrie* and the length of yarn to be dyed. Each handwoven piece will have a unique coloration.

▷ **MIXING COLORS**
The dye is placed in a vat of heated water to create the desired shade. The factory chooses colors with Kuki, according to the wishes of the particular client.

cottage industries

Over 18 million Indians are employed in a variety of cottage and small-scale industries across the country. This sector of the economy contributes 40% of India's gross manufacturing value, and around a third of its exports. Typically found in rural areas, cottage industries use cheap, family-based labor and traditional skills to make handcrafted products with simple tools and little or no infrastructure. These industries include hand-loom and textile weaving, toy manufacture, silk production, and handicrafts in jute, terra-cotta, metal, wood, leather, and cane. In 1948, the government set up the Central Cottage Industries Emporium, to sell and promote India's artisan traditions. In recent years, that challenge has been taken up by many nongovernmental organizations.

◁ **DYING THE YARN**
To make the yarns multicolored, only one end of the yarn is dipped into the solution, which is kept hot to allow the dye to penetrate.

▽ **TWISTING DRY**
Each section of dyed yarn must be thoroughly washed and dried out before Kuki can take it home to be used in a new *dhurrie*.

◁ **EVENING PRAYERS**
While Kuki makes her way home, her daughter-in-law prays at the family's household altar, lined with pictures and statues of deities.

△ **FAMILY MEAL**
Later on, the family sits down for dinner. Kuki eats first, sitting on the floor as her daughter-in-law cooks fresh *rotis* on the earthen stove.

◁ **TIE-DYE FABRIC**
Bandhini cotton and silk is renowned for its brilliant color, and is made primarily in Rajasthan, Gujarat, and Madhya Pradesh.

India's 4,000-year-old textile tradition is admired around the world for its astonishing beauty, variety, and craftsmanship. Along with traditional expertise in weaving fine cotton and silk, textile makers and designers have evolved enormous skill in the art of embellishing cloth. In addition to woven patterns, embroidery, crewelwork, appliqué, and mirrorwork, textiles are decorated using techniques such as block printing, *batik* (literally meaning "wax writing," which uses wax to create a pattern on dyed fabric), *bhandini* or tie-dye (similar to *batik*, but masking fabric with string, beads, and grain), and the ancient art of *kalamkari* hand-painting popular in Andhra Pradesh. This intricate process involves 17 separate steps to turn a length of cloth into an exquisite work of art. Traditional textiles are colored with vegetable dyes such as madder (red) and indigo (blue), and today, as more people turn away from the use of chemical dyes, these beautiful, naturally colored textiles are experiencing a resurgence in popularity.

FABRIC DECORATION

▷ **PRINTING BLOCK**
To make a printing block, a pattern painted on paper is fixed to a block of wood. A master craftsman then carves the pattern into the wood, which is then dipped in ink and pressed to the cloth.

TRADITIONAL BLOCK PRINTING
To achieve a variety of patterns, craftsmen use wooden blocks of differing sizes and shapes, chiseled with carving implements into fantastically delicate floral, paisley, or geometric patterns.

PRESIDENT'S BODYGUARD

LANCE DAFFADAR OF THE INDIAN ARMY, NEW DELHI

POLISHING BOOTS
At the beginning of his day, Girdhari sits in the sun in his regular soldier's uniform and cleans his boots, which need to be buffed to a good shine for the parade.

"The biggest challenge in the army is learning discipline, but once you've overcome that, discipline becomes your life," says Girdhari Lal, a member of the Indian military unit known as the President's Bodyguard. Girdhari holds the rank of lance daffadar (equivalent to a corporal), and is proud of his role: "Ours is the oldest and most prestigious regiment in the Indian Army."

Girdhari Lal, originally from a farming family in Lochib village, Rajasthan, has many relatives in his extended family who have careers in the armed forces. On leaving school, he signed up with the President's Bodyguard (PBG) on the recommendation of a cousin.

The PBG is the preeminent regiment of the Indian Army, first raised in 1773 during the British occupation. The handpicked unit began with just 50 men, but now has a strength of 160 soldiers, plus an additional 50 support staff. The regiment has a dual role; it acts as the ceremonial guard of the President of India, and is present in its magnificent finery at state functions, but it is also an elite operational unit of the Indian Army that has seen action on many battlefields. "I haven't been in any action myself, but I completed a tour of duty at Siachen Glacier," says Girdhari. Siachen is an area held by India in the volatile region of Kashmir on the border with Pakistan, where PBG troops are stationed to this day.

On top of their regular guard duties, soldiers of the PBG must also find time for horse grooming and weapons training, as well as practicing their parade formations, showjumping, and riding skills. Every Saturday at 10:00 a.m., the troops must also take part in the 40-minute Changing of the Guard ceremony. "We have a full life, and very little time to relax," Girdhari laughs. "When we do, we play games, watch television, and chat. Sometimes we catch up on our sleep, because we have night duties during the week."

The unit is stationed in Delhi, and the soldiers' families can join them by rotation. Girdhari Lal's wife, daughter, and son live a four-hour bus ride away in Lochib village. "I break up my two months' leave into a few days at a time," says Girdhari, "so I get to go home every couple of months—except in January, when we're rehearsing for the Republic Day Parade; nobody takes their leave during that busy period."

Girdhari earns 10,000 rupees ($254) a month, and receives free accommodations, medical care, and other perks. "The free train rides are useful," he smiles. As a lance daffadar, Girdhari can rise to the post of rissaldar major. "When they retire, most PBG soldiers find a second career as security guards," he says, "because of their height and attitude. When I retire, I would like to join a private security firm. There's a lot of money in that, and we have the training to protect VIPs."

INSPECTION LINEUP
The Bodyguards line up for early morning inspection, at which the commanding officer will ensure that they are impeccably turned out.

WEAPONS TRAINING
The PBG is an elite corps of paratroopers who can be called to active duty in times of war; they must undergo regular weapons training to keep their skills sharp.

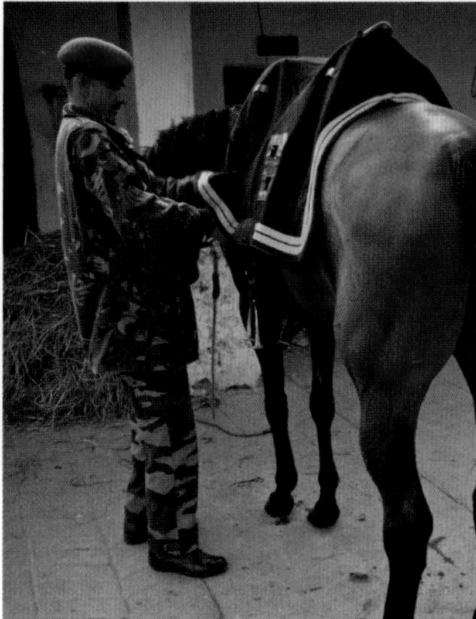

READYING THE HORSES
In preparation for the morning's parade, the PBG horses' manes are braided, their tails combed, and their saddles fixed.

DONNING THE PARADE TUNIC
Girdhari dresses in his red parade tunic, decorated with the PBG insignia and full medals. The two chevrons on his sleeves denote his rank as a lance daffadar.

ARMY TURBAN
He puts on his blue and gold ceremonial turban with its distinctive fan. The Indian Army has different kinds of parade headgear depending on the regiment's location and function.

READY FOR PARADE
The men fall in at the barracks entrance in full ceremonial dress, which is finished with a gold girdle, white buckskin gloves, white breeches, and spurred knee-length boots.

LEAVING FOR THE CEREMONY
The cavalry sets off for the Changing of the Guard at Rashtrapati Bhavan (the presidential palace). Girdhari is part of the New Guard—the troops who will take over guard duty.

BEGINNING THE PARADE
The parade begins at 10:00 a.m. sharp as the New Guard marches away from the Iron Gate of the Rashtrapati Bhavan along the ceremonial avenue known as the Rajpath.

INSPECTION AT CENTRAL SECRETARIAT
On reaching the Central Secretariat, which houses India's Ministry of Defense, the New Guard lines up for inspection in front of flags that display the official colors of India.

During parades, we all ride on bay-colored horses, except for the Regimental Trumpeter, who rides a gray charger.

अंगरक्षक

BACK TO THE PALACE
After inspection, the New Guard slowly troops back to the Iron Gate of Rashtrapati Bhavan in perfect military tandem. In the forecourt past the Iron Gate, the New Guard ranges itself alongside the waiting Old Guard, in readiness for the ceremony's formal salutation.

CHANGING THE GUARD
In the shadow of the Jaipur Column in front of Rashtrapati Bhavan, the sentry of the New Guard salutes the Old Guard, to show that they are prepared for duty. The Old Guard then hands over the ceremonial keys and marches away, while the New Guard assumes its posts.

RETURNING TO BARRACKS
The troops return to barracks after the ceremony, their bamboo lances—with their red and white cavalry pennants—carried in stirrup buckets.

CHANGING UNIFORM
The Bodyguards change out of their parade finery into less formal uniforms that are more suitable attire for the rest of the morning's activities.

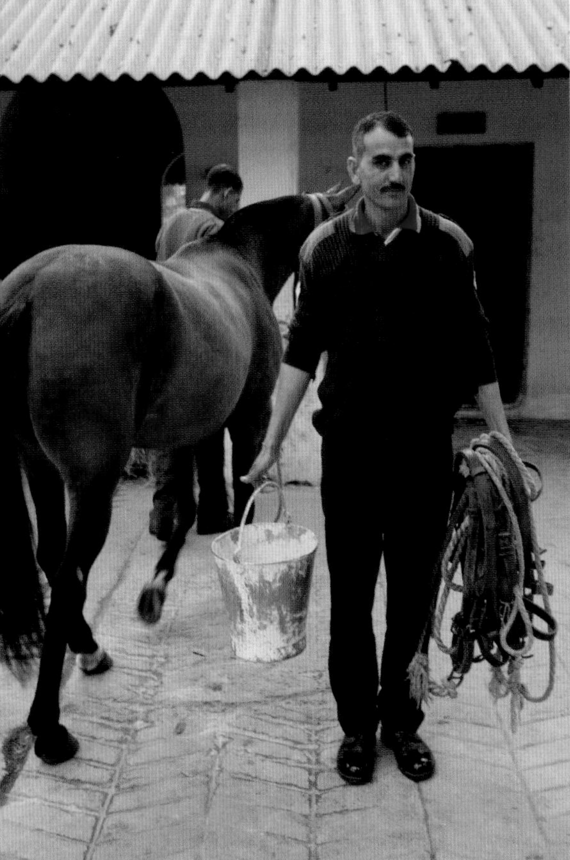

◁ **CARING FOR THE HORSES**
Once dressed, the first priority is to water and feed the mounts, which are then taken for a walk to help aid their digestion.

▽ **CLEANING EQUIPMENT**
The men sit down in the barracks yard to clean and maintain their tack and harness—the equipment used to ride a horse.

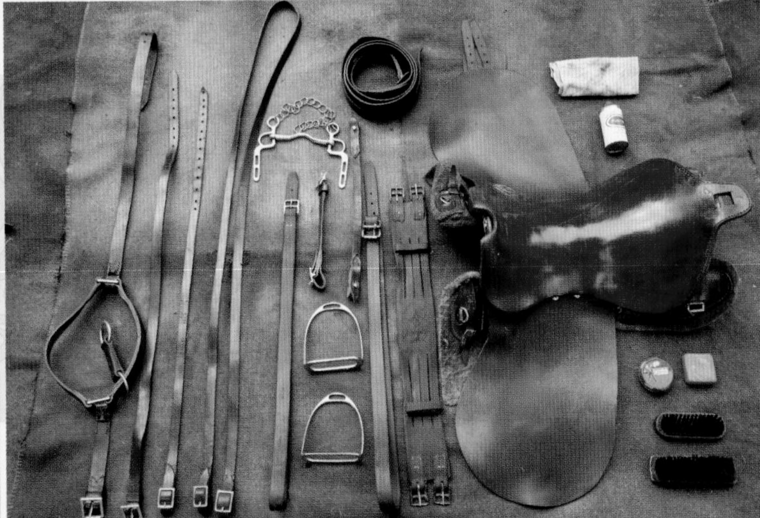

△ **TACK AND HARNESS**
All of the PBG riding equipment, including the leather saddles, bridles, and reins, as well as the bits and stirrups, needs to be brushed and polished regularly.

◁ **POLISHING MEDALS**
Once the horses' equipment is in good shape, it's time for Girdhari to start maintenance on his own attire. He begins by polishing the brass buttons and medals that are attached to his parade uniform.

◁ **CLEANING UNIFORMS**
Many of the soldiers spend some time before lunch cleaning their uniforms. After polishing the medals and buttons, dust from the morning's parade is brushed off fabric, insignias, and embroidery.

▷ CAVALRY UNIFORM
Before lunch, Girdhari changes into standard cavalry uniform, with its maroon, long-tailed turban. The insignia on the shirt shows a winged parachute, the symbol of this paratrooper unit.

△ LUNCH
The soldiers go to the large mess hall for lunch, where Girdhari has a small meal and a cup of water before afternoon guard duty.

▷ GUARD DUTY
For the early part of the afternoon, Girdhari and two of his colleagues are on sentry duty outside the headquarters of the PBG, at a spot from which the dome of the Rashtrapati Bhavan can be seen.

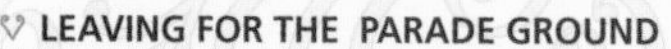

▽ LEAVING FOR THE PARADE GROUND
By around 4:00 p.m., the Bodyguards, still in standard uniform, are back on horseback and heading for the parade practice ground, which lies just across the road from the PBG barracks.

▷ PRACTICING HORSEMANSHIP
The Bodyguards spend the late afternoon practicing polo, showjumping, daredevil riding, and trick riding. The horses are as highly trained as their riders, as they are taken out for practice daily.

As a soldier, the needs of my country and my regiment take precedence over everything else.

अंगरक्षक

◁ ▽ **PRACTICING FOR PARADE**
The riders drill their horses for the precise, finely timed maneuvers that are required for parades. It is essential for the rider to have complete control over his mount.

△ **UNHARNESSING THE HORSE**
Back at the stables, Girdhari unharnesses his horse for the last time that day. The horses of the PBG are allowed to wear full manes, unlike other horses of the Army.

◁ **LOWERING THE FLAG**
At Retreat—the official end of the military day—Girdhari takes down the regimental flag that flies outside PBG headquarters.

▽ **EVENING DUTY**
The evening guards outside headquarters rotate according to a roster; tonight it is Girdhari's turn to remain on guard duty.

CULTURE

THE SPIRIT OF INDIA

India is one of the world's most ancient civilizations, dating back some 5,000 years. Despite an onslaught of invaders and colonizers, Indian culture has survived and even thrived, its ancient forms and ideas adapting and renewing themselves in a never-ending process. Home to over a billion people, India's linguistic, cultural, and ethnic diversity has long been its strength, allied as it is to a supreme openness and a belief in both the oneness and interdependence of all things. The theme of "the many and the one" plays out across all of its arts and philosophies. This holistic viewpoint, coupled with a highly developed sense of symbolism and ritual, has made India the birthplace for some of the world's most valuable concepts, including key religions such as Hinduism and Buddhism; mathematical phenomena, such as the misnamed "Arabic" numerals, negative numbers, and the number zero; and cultural activities as diverse as chess, weaving, and yoga. This rich culture forever changes and stays the same, playfully teaching us the wisdom of its gods and gurus.

THE CYCLE OF LIFE

THE ANCIENT ROOTS OF INDIAN CULTURE

The Hindu culture is extraordinarily adaptable and tolerant; ideas, like people, are endlessly reborn in various guises. Nothing is permanent, and the world is seen as just a great revolving door between life and death. Even time moves in cycles, broken down into *yugas* (ages) that span periods of 400,000–2,000,000 years. We are said to be living in the fourth and most corrupt of all ages: the Kali Yuga. This era began in 3102 BCE, at around the time of India's first recognizable culture: the Indus Valley Civilization.

the indigenous culture

India has been home to intensely creative civilizations for over 5,000 years. The inhabitants of the ancient Indus Valley cities, home to India's oldest known culture, were both innovative and social; they built huge cities on recognizable grid systems, featuring two-story town houses that, astonishingly, featured kitchens, bathrooms, plumbing, and polished floors as long ago as 3000 BCE.

The Indus Valley people were farmers and craftworkers; they wove fabrics and fashioned items from bricks to fine jewelry in clay, metal, and precious metals and stones. Their craftsmanship was such that they were able to produce fired pottery to standard shapes and capacities for their kitchens, uniform bricks for their houses, and exact weights and measures—which were critical to their lively trade with Sumeria, Babylonia, and Egypt. This urban population was also literate and cultured; they developed a written language, and archaeologists have unearthed glorious works of art from the twin "capitals" of Harappa and Mohenjo-daro, including terra-cotta figurines, stone sculptures, and fine bronzes, such as the Mohenjo-daro *Dancing Girl* (*see p.258*).

Although they are thought to have worshipped a mother goddess, the Indus Valley people produced intricately carved seals that often featured a three-headed male figure surrounded by animals, who may prefigure Shiva as Prajapati, Lord of the Beasts. The later Hindu culture may also owe its reverence for nature—plants, trees, and animals—to the Indus Valley people, who held water in especially high regard, both as a vital practical commodity and as a purifying force in a more ritualistic sense.

> Offer to Agni, oh my friends, your seemly food, your seemly praise; to him supremest o'er the folk, the Son of Strength, the mighty Lord. Him in whose presence, men rejoice.
>
> The *Rig Veda*, Book 5

This sophisticated culture, however, seems to have paid no attention to military weaponry or fortifications; and this oversight may have played a part in its sudden downfall. Agricultural production dwindled and cities decayed leaving them vulnerable to invaders, and by around 1500 BCE, the Indus Valley Civilization had disappeared, and the Aryans—an Indo-European race—had become the dominant culture.

THE VEDIC AGE BEGINS

Where the Indus people had built urban environments, the Aryans lived initially in smaller, simpler rural settlements. The Indus script was abandoned, and the Sanskrit language of the Aryans became the dominant language, moving southward through the subcontinent with the Aryan people. The Aryans became adept at absorbing change while maintaining a continuity of culture, beginning a tradition of inclusion

THE GIFT OF THE VEDAS
The Vedas are said to have issued from the four heads of Brahma, the creator god, and presented to the seers, who handed them down through generations.

that has reigned in India ever since. The Aryans' gods and values were also hugely influential; they are known to us through the ancient texts of the Vedas.

VEDIC INHERITANCE

The four books of the ancient Vedas—*Rig Veda, Yajur Veda, Sama Veda,* and *Atharva Veda*—were memorized by the *Brahmins* (priests) and initially passed down through recitation, c.1500 BCE. They are thought to have been collected into a written form around 400 years later.

The Vedas are considered to be *sruti* ("that which is heard"), having been spoken by the gods to the *rishis,* or seers, rather than *smrti* ("that which is remembered"). They are sacred texts (*see pp.266–267*) honoring the Vedic gods, and they form the cornerstone of the Hindu culture. Many of the righteous gods portrayed in the Vedas personify natural forces, such as Indra, the storm god; Agni, the god of fire; Surya, the sun god; Ap, the god of water; Varuna, god of the sky; Saraswati, the goddess of learning; and Shakti, the goddess of power. Varuna also observes the world and judges the acts of humankind; he decides whether they should be sent to heaven or its opposite—The House of Clay—after their death. Rebirth was not a part of the Vedic cosmology. The Vedas did, however, introduce many concepts that were to remain within the Indian culture in a continually evolving form. The most important of these is *rta*, an unchanging, natural law, or truth, which gives order to the world. It is the way things are meant to be. *Dharma*—a Hindu concept which decrees that for each person there is a "righteous path"—springs from *rta*, as it is part of the cosmic order and the law that literally "upholds" the world and society.

> The essence of man is speech, the essence of speech is the *Rig Veda*, the essence of the *Rig Veda* is the *Sama Veda*, the essence of the *Sama Veda* is the *udgîtha* —which is *Om*.
>
> From the *Khandogya Upanishad*

The *Rig Veda* also outlines the *varnas* (groups) into which people fall, which in turn determines their *dharma*. The four initial groups, which were later recognized as castes or classes, are said to have emerged from Purusha, the primeval man, who was larger than the Earth itself. As the gods sacrificed him, the moon was born from his mind, and the sun from his eye; the *Brahmins* (priests) from his head, the *Kshatriyas* (warriors) from his arms, the *Vaisyas* (traders, landowners) from his thighs, and the *Sudras* (the servant class) from his feet.

A later body of sacred texts—the Brahmanas, the Arayankas, and the Upanishads—were commentaries on Vedic thought (*see pp.266–267*). They are Vedantic (post-Vedic) observations on nature, mind, matter, and spirit, and they introduced key ideas such as *atman* (the true self or soul), *maya* (illusion), *karma* (the law of action and reaction), and *samsara* (the repeating cycle of death and rebirth). These texts ultimately led the *Brahmins* to transcend the personal gods, focusing instead on an absolute oneness—the Supreme Being—that existed beyond the cosmos.

As this process evolved, leading ultimately to the creation of Hinduism, two new non-Aryan religions were born in India: Buddhism and Jainism, which were both to influence countries throughout Asia and beyond. By the beginning of the Common era, India was home to a vibrant plethora of rituals, philosophies, and gods.

AGNI—VEDIC GOD OF FIRE
Agni is one of the most important Vedic gods: he is the fire of sacrifice, the heat of the sun, the light of the stars, and the vital spark of life itself.

Hindu mythology

At first sight, Hinduism seems almost impossibly complicated—its pantheon is said to include 330 million gods. However, Hinduism states that the godhead lives in every human being, and this huge figure simply reflects the fact that when the notion first crystallized in ancient times, the world was thought to consist of 330 million people—or gods.

Every Hindu god or goddess represents one particular aspect of the universal truth, or Supreme Being. In this sense, Hinduism is a polytheistic belief system that is, at its core, totally monotheistic. The three most important gods—Brahma, Vishnu, and Shiva—who make up a trimurti, or Hindu trinity, are not three independent deities. They represent three sides of the same cosmic task that the universe is ceaselessly engaged in creation, preservation, and destruction, leading to re-creation. Just as the same person is a doctor, a parent, or a lover, according to the tasks he or she performs, so the Supreme Being is referred to variously as Brahma (creator), Vishnu (preserver), or Shiva (destroyer), according to the task that is being accomplished. This enables Hindus to freely select a favorite god (*deva*) or goddess (*devi*) with whom they feel a connection, and thereby establish a direct link with divinity.

Although post-Vedic texts of the Upanishads (*see p.267*) discuss the concept of the formless and absolute infinite (Brahman), over time the intellectual rigor of this idea yielded to that of a personal god with whom the ordinary man or woman could comfortably bond. This transition occurred naturally, almost imperceptibly. In selecting a particular aspect of the Supreme Being to worship, the important concept of *upaj*, improvisation, also comes into play, just as it does in music and dance; in a religious context this concept grants each person the freedom to choose their own deity and worship it in their own way.

▷ **KRISHNA**
The eighth incarnation of Vishnu, Krishna is the embodiment of love.

BRAHMA THE CREATOR

Brahma is the god of creation. In one legend, he is said to have grown from a golden egg; in another, from a lotus that sprang from Vishnu's navel. As the lotus grew, it was bathed in light, and as the light spread, so did Brahma, becoming one with the whole universe. Brahma is traditionally depicted with four arms and four heads, from which the ancient scriptures of the Vedas (*see pp.266–267*) are said to have emerged. Some accounts say that Brahma at first had only one head, but he became obsessed with a female deity he had created, called Gayatri (sometimes Shatarupa or Saraswati). As she moved around, trying to escape his gaze, Brahma sprouted four new heads to follow her. Seeing this, Shiva flew into a rage, thinking it wrong for a god to fall in love with a daughter he had created. He cut off the highest of Brahma's five heads, and declared that he was not to be worshipped. Either for this reason or, in some accounts, because his work was considered to be finished once the creation of the world was complete, Brahma has been worshipped in only one temple in India: the Temple of Lord Brahma in Pushkar.

> Whenever goodness declines and wickedness increases, I make myself a body; in every age I come back to protect the good, to destroy the sin of the sinner, and to establish righteousness.
>
> Vishnu speaks, as Krishna, in the *Bhagavad Gita*, Chapter 4

VISHNU THE PRESERVER

The Hindu gods reincarnate many times, assuming different forms and shapes, from human to animal. Vishnu, the preserver, comes to Earth in ten different incarnations, or avatars, which are surprisingly close to the evolutionary ladder. At first, primeval waters covered the Earth; hence Vishnu's first incarnation as a fish (Matsya). His second incarnation was as a tortoise (Koorma), symbolic of the amphibian stage. The third, Varaha the boar, symbolizes the first stage of animal life on land. The transition from animals to humans is imaginatively portrayed by a half-man-half-lion—Narasimha—in the fourth incarnation.

His fifth incarnation demonstrates the appearance of early *Homo sapiens*—symbolized by the dwarf Vamana. Then came fierce savages wielding primitive weapons, like Vishnu's sixth incarnation: Parashuram. The human form later became more sophisticated in both mind and body, and this is exemplified by Rama, the seventh incarnation—the epitome of rectitude and courage.

Krishna, the eighth incarnation, is the moral teacher, who delivers the magnificent sermon of the *Bhagavad Gita* (see pp. 270–71) from the battlefield of the *Mahabharata* (see pp. 268–69). Gautama, the Buddha, is Vishnu's ninth incarnation: the messenger of peace and the futility of war, and the avatar that comes nearest to *nirvana* (salvation). Vishnu's tenth incarnation, Kalki, is yet to be manifested. He is the ultimate terminator, who will one day finish the evolutionary process, and end the world in one mighty holocaust.

SHIVA THE DESTROYER

Shiva is the divine dancer; poised between the twin forces of destruction and creation. He represents the creativity of change, through the cycle of death and rebirth. Shiva is a contradictory figure: he is the great ascetic but also the symbol of fertility; the ideal and the worst of husbands; the Lord of Beasts and the destroyer of humankind; and, in one of his forms, half-man, half-woman: the Ardhanarishwar. Shiva combines matter and energy, mind and body, male and female; he defies the dualism of Western philosophy that separates mind and body, and he demonstrates the inseparable unity of the universe. Shiva is often depicted in a fearsome guise, clothed in elephant hides, with skulls and a serpent around his neck, his body white from the ashes of corpses. He has three eyes; his fearsome third eye destroys everything on which it alights.

The relationship between Shiva and his wives holds special significance in Hindu mythology. The goddess Sati married Shiva despite deep misgivings on the part of her father, King Daksha, who disliked Shiva's beggarlike appearance and habits. Shortly after their marriage, the king organized a great sacrifice to which he invited all the gods except Shiva. Sati was outraged, but went to the gathering, where the king insulted Shiva again, causing the enraged Sati to throw herself into the sacrificial fire. When Shiva learned of her death, he stormed the gathering with an army of ghouls, killing the king and all his men. Then, lifting Sati above his head, he began to dance the *Tandava*: the cosmic dance of death (see p.259), signaling the end of the world. Unable to stop him, Vishnu and Brahma cut Sati's body in portions and allowed them to fall to Earth. Each of the 57 spots where the parts fell are still today venerated as *shakti-peeths*, stations of power and sacred pilgrim spots. Sati was then reincarnated as the gentle Parvati, venerated with Shiva as part of the ideal couple. They had two sons: the demon-killer Kartikeya (see p.224) and the much-loved Ganesha (see p.223).

BRAHMA, THE CREATOR GOD
Creation starts anew each day for Brahma; each of his days is said to last for 4.32 billion human years.

THE GREAT GODDESS

The pre-Aryan (*see p.218*) cult of the mother goddess lives on in Devi, the Great Goddess of Hinduism; all of the Hindu goddesses can be seen as manifestations of this female power. She can only be understood with reference to the term *shakti*, the life-force, or animating energy. While the gods—embodying the masculine principle of *shaktiman*—are wielders of power, the goddesses—embodying the feminine principle, *shakti*—are the power itself. Shakti and Devi appear in Hindu mythology as goddesses in their own right, but this powerful female energy also appears in many other manifestations, such as the gentle Parvati or Uma, the wealthy Lakshmi, the knowledgeable Saraswati, and the terrifying Kali and Durga.

Durga is the invincible warrior goddess, whose story is told in the sacred verses of the *Devi Mahatmya*. When the cosmos comes under attack from Mahishasura, the buffalo demon, the gods are unable to defeat him because a boon, or spell, has made him invulnerable to men and gods. Vishnu fights him unsuccessfully, first as Narasimha the man-lion and then as Varaha the boar, before Shiva turns his third eye toward the demon, destroying three worlds but leaving the evil Mahishasura unharmed. The gods begin to fear that nature

▷ THE GREAT GODDESS DURGA
The powerful, fearless Durga is invoked for protection by gods and humankind. In the *Ramayana*, Rama is prepared to pluck out his eye to ensure her protection.

herself will be conquered, so they release *shaktis*—pure energy in female form—from their bodies. The seven *shaktis* rise to the sky and merge into one goddess: the all-powerful Durga. The gods salute her and equip her with all of their powers and weapons: into her many arms—some say eight, others a thousand—they place the trident of Shiva, the discus of Vishnu, the spear of Agni, the thunderbolt of Indra, the bow of Vayu, and the sword and shield of Vishvakarman. Durga then rides into battle on a lion; the mountains shake and the oceans tremble as Mahishasura the buffalo demon attacks her. Some accounts say that she finally kills him by pinning him down with her foot and plunging Shiva's trident into his neck, others that the demon survives the onslaught of all of her weapons, so finally she leaps from her lion and kills the demon with her many bare hands.

The mighty Durga is symbolic of courage and the fight for justice that every human has to wage, at all levels of life. Her victory over the buffalo demon is still celebrated in India today in the festival of Durga Pooja, or Navaratri—the Festival of Nine Nights (*see pp.230–231*).

The terrifying goddess Kali—the Dark Mother—is the ferocious aspect of womanhood, and she is invoked for dealing with challenges in daily life. Kali's black or dark blue body is traditionally depicted garlanded with skulls, and with weapons in every hand except two, which are held in gestures of protection and fearlessness. Kali's three eyes represent the past, present, and future. As Shiva's wife, she is often shown standing on his body; she is Shiva's *shakti*, or life force, without which he is unable to act.

THE GENTLE GODDESS

Later forms of the Great Goddess are more benevolent and bountiful, and they are often known essentially as part of a spousal pair, such as Parvati and Shiva, Sita and Rama, and Lakshmi and Vishnu. The beautiful Parvati—also known as Uma—symbolizes all that is noble and kind, and she tames even Shiva's fierce nature as his wife. Their perfect union leads to lovemaking so intense that it shakes the cosmos, and the gods become so fearful about the power of a potential child that they send first Vishnu and then Agni to interrupt the couple. But even this perfect marriage endures its fair share of very humanlike arguments. On one occasion, Shiva finally agrees to tell Parvati the secret of immortality while they are resting in the quiet of the Amarnath caves, only to witness her falling asleep during the telling. When he complains, Parvati explains that she concentrates better with her eyes closed. Legend has it that two pigeons who were hiding in the caves consequently became immortal, and they can still be seen there every year in the Hindu month of *Shravana*.

> I am Great Nature, consciousness, bliss, the quintessence, devotedly praised. Where I am there is no attachment, happiness, sadness, liberation, faith, guru or disciple.
>
> Devi, speaking in the *Kulachudamani Tantra*

GANESHA, REMOVER OF OBSTACLES
Ganesha is Shiva and Parvati's wise son, whose name is invoked before any other god at Hindu ceremonies and events to ensure their smooth running.

Lakshmi, Vishnu's consort, is the goddess of wealth and good fortune, who is said to have taken many different forms in order to remain with Vishnu through his ten incarnations. Rama and Sita, the hero and heroine from the *Ramayana*, and Radha and Krishna are both said to be incarnations of Vishnu and Lakshmi. Another gentle goddess, Saraswati, is the goddess of learning and the arts. She is also considered to be a later form of Vak, the Vedic goddess of speech, who enabled Brahma to hear the primordial sound—*Om*—which led to the world's creation. Clothed in white, Saraswati is often shown riding a swan—to symbolize knowledge—or sitting on a white lotus holding a book, prayer beads, and musical instruments in her four hands.

THE ANIMAL GODS

The ease with which the Hindu mind juxtaposes different forms of human and animal life is demonstrated by two favorite gods: Ganesha, the elephant-headed son of Shiva and Parvati, a symbol of both wisdom and auspicious beginnings (*see pp.268–269*); and Hanuman, the monkey god, faithful lieutenant of Lord Rama (*see pp.272–273*); progenitor of scores of monkey fables in East Asian literature and performance arts.

The story of Ganesha's elephant head recounts that the goddess Parvati, while bathing one day, created a puppet from the dirt washed off her body. Then she breathed life into it, called it her son, Ganesha, and set him to stand guard outside her door of her chamber while she finished bathing. When her husband, Shiva, returned home and found the way to Parvati's chamber blocked, he angrily asked the unknown young boy to leave. When Ganesha refused, Shiva cut off his head in anger. Parvati then came out, and seeing the dead Ganesha, was inconsolable. Shiva realized his mistake, and to mend matters sent the palace guards out to bring back the first living being they could encounter. This happened to be an elephant, whose head Shiva then cut off and attached to Ganesha's dead body, bringing the demigod back to life.

nature worship

A respectful reverence toward the natural world is central to Indian religion and mythology. Many natural objects, from streams to trees, are said to have spirits, and numerous animals are either linked closely with the gods or revered in their own right. India's rich and varied wildlife influenced both the mythology and the religion of the subcontinent.

Some of the Hindu gods take animal form at times. Vishnu, for example, appeared on Earth at different times as a fish, a tortoise, a boar, and a "man-lion" in order to put right the wrongs of the world (*see p.221*). Many of the gods are associated with a *vahana* (vehicle), a creature that accompanies the deity and acts as his or her mount. Shiva's *vahana* is a bull called Nandi or Nandin; Vishnu is borne by an eagle called Garuda; and Ganesha is always seen accompanied by a small mouse. Among the goddesses, Durga rides a lion, Saraswati a swan or peacock, Lakshmi an owl, and Ganga a *makara*: a mythical creature resembling a crocodile. The *vahanas* act as symbols of the deity's qualities—Nandi represents Shiva's strength and virility, while Saraswati's swan suggests beauty and wisdom. The creatures also give their deities practical help: Ganesha's mouse enables the elephant-headed god to spread his influence into tight spaces.

Many animals are revered, ranging from monkeys to bees. Even serpents, known as *nagas,* are seen as semidivine creatures who guard treasures beneath the earth. But the animal afforded most reverence is the cow. Cattle played a part in religion as far back as the Indus Valley Civilization, when there seems to have been a cult of the bull, and the cow came to religious prominence in the Vedic period, when it became forbidden to slaughter milk cows. Everything associated with the cow is considered sacred, even the dung—which is mixed with water and used as an insecticide in rural areas.

BANYAN TREE SHRINE
Trees are often festooned with bells and auspicious red fabric. Bowing before a tree brings inner harmony.

THE SPIRITS OF THE TREES

Trees have always played a prominent role in the religion of India. This reflects their importance to people, who benefit from their sheltering branches and their nutritious fruit. Archaeologists believe that the people of the Indus Valley Civilization counted trees among their deities some 4,500 years ago. Trees play a major role within Buddhism and Jainism, because the Buddha and Mahavira, a Jain prophet (*see p.240*), both achieved enlightenment following a period of meditation beneath a tree.

In rural areas, trees are still venerated and believed to be home to spirits; traditional prayers are sometimes said when a tree is felled, to appease the spirits living there. Among the tree spirits are the Salabhanjika and the Yaskshi, worshipped as symbols of fertility. In art they are portrayed as beautiful young women sheltering beneath foliage, and they sometimes indicate their identity with the tree by holding one of the branches or touching the trunk with a leg or foot. This pose relates to an ancient ritual in which worshippers would bring a tree back to life at the end of winter. A young woman or girl would break a twig from the tree while striking its trunk with her

> In the background of the whole process of creation is the Primal Matter, pulsating with its own life, vibrating with inherent force, seeded with potentialities.
>
> The *Rig Veda*, Book 10

KARTIKEYA, THE GOD OF WAR
The six-headed Kartikeya rides a peacock, which destroys the desires and harmful habits of the ego, symbolized by a snake.

foot. These actions were said to "wake" the tree and herald spring. There is a lasting tradition that says that some kinds of tree are even more responsive to the touch or attention of young women—certain species are said to blossom when a girl touches the trunk with her foot.

SACRED RIVERS

With their life-giving, cleansing waters, rivers have always been especially significant in India. Seven rivers, in particular, are seen as sacred in Hinduism: the Ganges, Yamuna (Jumna), Saraswati, Godavari, Narmada, Indus, and Kaveri. Their importance is such that they are said to be the veins of Earth's body. Rivers are mostly seen as female (the male Indus is a major exception) and certain parts of them—such as their source, the places where they turn toward the north, and the points at which they join other rivers—are held to be particularly holy.

The holiest of all these rivers is the Ganges, and its goddess, who is called Ganga, is greatly revered. The river's waters are beneficial on several levels. They are said to be medicinal, curing many ills; they wash away the sins of those who bathe in them; and the soul of a dead person whose ashes are scattered on the river will be released from the Earth.

▷ **NANDI CARRYING SHIVA AND PARVATI** Shiva's *vahana* is the white bull, Nandi ("the joyful"). It represents Shiva's strength, fertility, and sexual energy, and his ability to control these powers.

discipline and practice

Indian belief systems have always valued the life of the ascetic, and they lay heavy stress on the idea of self-discipline or self-training. The term used for this traditional discipline is "yoga," which comes from the Sanskrit word *yuj*, to join. Yoga involves an inward searching; the discipline is a means of finding one's true self, and potentially, *moksha* (liberation). The way this is done varies according to which of the many traditions of yoga the believer follows, but it involves both a demanding physical regimen embracing exercise and diet (such as Hatha yoga) and a mental and spiritual discipline that includes meditation and studied concentration (such as Raja or Patanjala yoga). These two strands combined are so central to the Indian religions that many people today use the word "yoga" to refer both to their religious practice and to their philosophy of religion.

> When thy mind, that may be wavering in the contradictions of many scriptures, shall rest unshaken in divine contemplation, then the goal of Yoga is thine.
>
> The *Bhagavad Gita*, Chapter 2

Yoga is practiced widely in India, especially among those who have reached the final, spiritual stage of life (*see pp. 236–237*): that of the *sanyasi*, who becomes detached from the senses and from the world in general. It is a demanding discipline for newcomer and adept alike, and it is usually practiced under the supervision of a teacher or guru. This notion of a guru, or spiritual guide, is a very strong one in Indian religion. Both Buddhism, with its great founder and teacher, Siddhartha Gautama, and Sikhism, with its succession of gurus, draw heavily on the teachings of revered spiritual leaders. Spiritual leadership is also important in the practice of martial arts such as Kalari, which, like yoga, involves both mental and physical discipline. Hinduism, too, greatly values the thoughts and teachings of guru figures who aim to lead their followers to a higher spiritual plane. The discipline of yoga is often the route to this spiritual liberation.

Yoga is not a religious practice that is done regularly on set days and then put aside. It permeates a person's whole life, must be practiced continuously, and incorporates several moral precepts, of a deep and pervasive influence. One of these, *ahimsa* (nonviolence), is a common thread in many of the Indian religions. Among other things, it means that practitioners can only eat food that has been prepared without violence—vegetarian food, in other words. Yoga also discourages the eating of strong-tasting foods, aiming for a diet that will help the mind to stay calm and focused. It is said that the three requisites of practicing yoga are purity (in mind and body), patience, and perseverance. Stillness of mind is gained only through concentrated, long-term practice.

YOGA: THE ULTIMATE UNION
The aim of yoga is to unite the individual soul (*atman*) with the cosmic consciousness (*Brahman*).

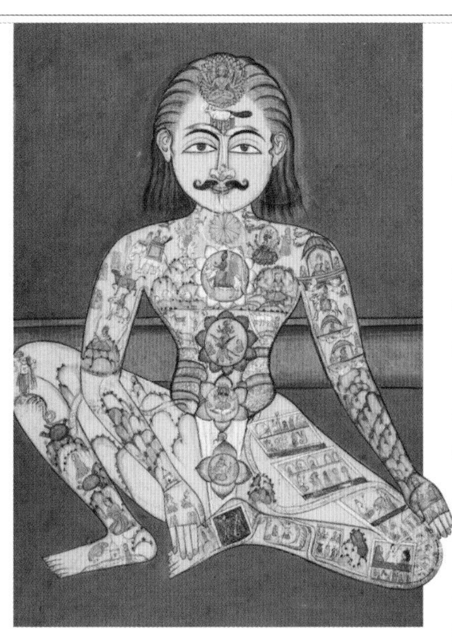

CHAKRAS OF KUNDALINI YOGA
Kundalini is the body's dormant spiritual energy, which unwinds through the seven *chakras*, or energy centers, of the body during yoga to expand consciousness.

A SPIRITUAL PATH

In Hatha yoga, the practitioner aims to awaken a kind of latent spiritual energy called *kundalini*, which exists in the body. A combination of physical exercises and breath control is used to awaken the energy, which then travels along a spiritual channel through the person's "subtle body," passing as it does so across seven points in the body called *chakras* (energy points). When the *kundalini* has traveled across all the *chakras*, it achieves union with the god Shiva. The awakening of this powerful spiritual energy can be potentially dangerous for the practitioner, and people are therefore advised to practice this form of yoga only under the guidance of a teacher or guru.

Although Hatha yoga appears to concentrate mainly on bodily exercises and to resemble the kind of yoga-as-exercise most often practiced in the West, it is truly spiritual at heart. In some Hindu texts, it is seen as a form of preparation, after which one progresses to Raja yoga.

The yogic route to liberation is described in the *Yoga Sutras*, a collection of aphorisms attributed to the healer and writer Patanjali, who lived in the 2nd century BCE. The aim of this form of yoga is the achievement of a kind of inner or spiritual freedom that comes from the stripping away of illusion. To do this, the practitioner follows a regimen involving eight steps. The first step, Restraints, involves observing five key moral precepts: nonviolence; truthfulness (in the sense of keeping one's thoughts and actions consistent); honesty; continence (controlling sexual desire); and nonacceptance of gifts (leading to detachment from material things). The second step is called Observances, and this embraces five further moral disciplines: purity; contentment; austerity; study of the scriptures; and concentration on *Ishvara* (the Absolute Being).

The third stage requires the practitioner to practice various postures, the *asanas* that are familiar to Western devotees of yoga. However, the *Yoga Sutras* say that the main objective is not to practice a variety of postures or to exercise in an extreme way, but to find one posture that the person finds agreeable and enables them to meditate for long periods; the *asanas* are therefore steps on the road to clearing the mind rather than ends in themselves.

The fourth stage is Breath Control. Some people achieve remarkable feats of breath control, slowing down their breathing until their metabolism slows down too, but, again, the *Sutras* do not encourage this extreme version of the discipline. The aim is to attain mental control, because controlling the breath can control and still the mind. The fifth stage entails the withdrawal of the senses, so that the person becomes protected from outside sensory influences and the mind can follow its own path undistracted.

The last three elements are linked by the concept of *samyama*, or effort. They act to separate the consciousness from exterior things, including the body, and enable the person to achieve a heightened state of mind and being. The sixth element is Concentration, which slows down the mind by making it focus on one thing. The seventh is Contemplation, which is achieved when the mind's attention flows in an uninterrupted way toward the focus of meditation. The eighth and final step is called *Enstasis*, when the ego or identity of the self itself is lost. According to the *Sutras*, the person who can achieve the final step attains the ultimate goal; he or she will find liberation from this world, become free of *karma*, and reach *moksha*: liberation from *samsara*, the endless cycle of life and death.

> The senses of the one
> with understanding,
> With the mind ever disciplined,
> Are under his control,
> Like good horses of a charioteer.
>
> *Katha Upanishad*

KALARI FIGHTERS
Kalari is the martial art of Kerala, and its adherents learn the art of exerting the perfect force for a particular action.

BODY DECORATION
Before a Hindu wedding, the bride's hands and feet are decorated with intricate patterns—often auspicious symbols—in natural dyes.

rituals and symbols

Rituals pervade life in India, from those that are used daily to the most significant events in life, such as weddings and funerals. At the simplest, everyday level, Indians traditionally greet each other by saying the Sanskrit word *Namaskar* ("I bow to you") or its Hindi equivalent, *Namaste*, while holding the palms together in front of the chest and bowing the head slightly. The gesture recognizes the divine in both the person performing the bow, and the person receiving it, thereby paying honor to the sacredness of all. Placing the hands at the forehead heightens the gesture, to indicate deep respect, while to honor a deity, the person may hold the hands above the head. These forms of greeting have deep symbolic and religious significance, especially in Hinduism, but the greeting and gesture are used widely across all faiths.

Daily worship, known as *pooja*, or *puja*, is an important part of Indian ritual. Hindu deities are worshipped in the form of images—especially statues in the temple or home shrine—and in the form of symbolic objects, such as the phallic linga that is often used to represent Shiva. The image or object is seen as a dwelling-place for the deity, and is treated as an honored guest. The rituals of *puja* vary widely, but there are a number of common elements. Objects are often washed—literally or symbolically—by touching them with flowers dipped in water. Devotees may make offerings to the god or goddess in the form of food, fragrant incense, or lights. They may honor the deity by singing hymns, and show respect by bowing to the image. The focus of all this activity is the notion of *darshan*, which means viewing or having an audience with a deity, through which devotees receive a blessing. One common way of performing *darshan* is to walk around the image in a clockwise direction, or to sit cross-legged in front of it, maintaining eye contact.

> Whatever you do, whatever you eat, whatever you offer in sacrifice, whatever you give, whatever austerity you practice... do that as an offering to me.
>
> Krishna, from the *Bhagavad Gita*, Chapter 9

SYMBOLS AND DECORATION

India's rich culture has produced many symbols with religious significance. Foremost among these is the "primal syllable," the Sanskrit *Aum* or *Om* (*see p.266*). The three letters, a-u-m, represent the three worlds of Heaven, Earth, and Atmosphere, and the Hindu trimuriti: Brahma, Shiva, and Vishnu. Unified, these in turn represent the Absolute Being, or "all that is." The sound is used as a *mantra*—a repeated silent word during meditation—when it is believed to penetrate a person's deepest consciousness. The symbol, or written form, is also seen everywhere— from the beginning of an Upanishad to the opening statement of a letter. Another prominent symbol is the *swastika* ("all is well"). This is a cross with four arms of equal length, each of which is bent at right angles. The arms of the Hindu version are angled to the right, or clockwise, while the Buddhist version points counterclockwise. The symbol is used to represent good fortune and well-being in Hinduism, Jainism, and Buddhism, as well as other faiths across the world. A third symbol, the lotus, is an image of the human soul, which can blossom and reach enlightenment even in the most unpromising circumstances. Many of these symbols are incorporated into Indian paintings and sculpture (*see pp.260–261*).

Symbols are not only used at temples and religious sites. They appear at the threshold of people's homes and in public buildings, especially when used as patterns in a popular form of decoration called *rangoli*. This is a type of design, usually created on the floor, using colored powders. When placed near a front door or at the entrance to a building such as a hotel, *rangoli* are seen as a sign of welcome, and are especially associated with Lakshmi, goddess of wealth. They are popular at weddings and festivals, such as *Diwali*, when people visit each other and when they hope their home will be visited by Lakshmi, too. The motifs used in *rangoli* range from abstract patterns through natural forms such as flowers and leaves to symbols such as the lotus.

RANGOLI: INDIAN FLOOR ART
The forms depicted in *rangoli* can be realistic or symbolic, but they must always use an unbroken line, to prevent evil spirits from entering the house.

CEREMONIES

Marriage is considered to be very important in India because it bonds two people and two families, and represents a stable way for producing and raising children. Wedding ceremonies are therefore traditionally very solemn and complex, although they can vary greatly in form. Preparations typically include evoking deities such as Ganesha, god of good fortune, anointing the bride and groom on the days before the wedding itself, erecting a canopy called a *mandap* under which the ceremony takes place, and adorning the bride's hands and feet with henna. The ceremony itself may last several hours, and includes a ritual in which the couple walk around a sacred fire, the threading of a cord to link the bride and groom, and a ritual where the couple take seven steps together, to symbolize seven things the couple hope for in their relationship, such as food, strength, wealth, good fortune, children, longevity, and friendship. There are also many prayers for the good fortune of the couple.

Although Hindus and followers of the other major Indian faiths believe in the continuous cycle of death and rebirth, their funeral rituals are designed to send the deceased, who becomes a *preta* (ghost) on death, safely on his or her journey to join their ancestors. The body is washed and wrapped in a shroud, carried to a place of cremation in a procession led by the son of the deceased, and traditionally, placed on a pyre. Today, especially in towns and cities, more modern methods of cremation are generally used. The deceased then begins the transition from the *preta* to *pitri* (ancestral spirit), in a spiritual journey that takes 12 days. Rites in honor of the dead continue long after the funeral itself, and include a funeral meal, known as *shraddha*, which takes place once a month, for a year. The food eaten is said to nourish the departed ancestors and help them to move to a higher plane.

▽ **THE BURNING GHATS OF VARANASI** Traditionally, Indian cremations take place beside a holy river, such as on the *ghats* (riverside steps) of the Ganges.

festivals and seasons

Somewhere in India a festival is taking place, on every day of the year. Yearly celebrations vary in times and content from one part of the country to another, and between faiths. Buddhists celebrate key events, such as the birthday and enlightenment of the Buddha, while the Sikh holy days commemorate the gurus who were the early leaders of their religion. Hindus celebrate a rich variety of festivals that mark key events in the lives of the deities and important points in the round of the seasons and the solar year. Poorams, for example, are annual summer festivals that take place after the harvest. They usually involve colorful processions with at least one lavishly decorated elephant.

Mythological, seasonal, and even astronomical patterns are frequently linked in a festival, so that, for example, the journey of Rama to Lanka is celebrated at the festival of *Shravani-purnima*, which also marks the full moon in the month of *Shravana*, in the middle of the monsoon season. Another example is Shiva's night, or *Shivaratri*, which takes place at the first full moon in the month of *Magha* (January/ February) and is a major event in the year for devotees of Shiva all around the subcontinent. Hindu festivals like these are celebrated throughout India with music, processions, and feasting.

Although many celebrations are small in scale, involving a single village or local community, India's festivals include some of the largest in the world. Most famous of all is *Kumbh Mela*, "the festival of the pot" (*see pp.232–233*). Legends attribute the origins of this festival to a fight that once took place between the gods and demons, who were tussling over the pot of immortal nectar. During the battle, drops of the nectar fell to Earth in four places that later became the cities of Prayaga (Allahabad), Hardwar, Nasik, and Ujjain. The festival takes place at each of these cities in turn, once every three years. The largest *Kumbh Melas* are those that take place at Prayaga every 12 years, when the sun enters the constellation of Aries and Jupiter is in Aquarius. Millions come to this festival, when it is believed that bathing in the rivers at Prayaga will bring purity and salvation and wash away the sins of 88 previous generations.

ANNUAL FESTIVALS

One of the most popular annual festivals is *Diwali*, which takes place in the month of *Kartika* (October/November), a joyful five-day festival of lights associated especially with various Hindu goddesses and the god Rama. The opening of the festival is devoted to the gentle goddesses Parvati and Lakshmi (*see pp.222–223*). Householders open their doors and windows to invite the goddesses to enter and bless their home; traders settle their bills and place coins and account books on images of Lakshmi in the hope that she will bring them prosperity. On the fourth day of the festival, houses, terraces, and gardens are adorned with small oil lamps, and the land lights up to celebrate

THRISSUR POORAM
The Thrissur Pooram festival of Kerala is essentially secular, featuring parasol exchanges atop bejeweled elephants, drum concerts, and fireworks displays.

HOLI—THE FESTIVAL OF COLORS
Holi, the spring festival also known as *Holaka* or *Phagwa*, celebrates nature's return to color and liveliness with the throwing of brightly colored paints.

the triumphant return of Rama to his home after his 14-year exile and defeat of Ravana, as described in the *Ramayana* (*see pp.272–273*).

Holi is one of the most riotous of festivals worldwide. It takes place on the day of the full moon in the month of *Phalguna* (February/March), and for several days beforehand, to mark the beginning of spring. All the rules of respect relating to caste, status, age, and gender are temporarily cast aside, colored paint is thrown with abandon, and licentious behavior and jokes abound. As a spring festival it also pays homage to Krishna and his consort Radha, and spring *ragas* (*see pp.248–249*) are sung. *Holi* bonfires are lit—symbolizing the god Vishnu's defeat of the demon Holika by burning—which are said to burn away past evils.

The fall equinox in the month of *Asvina* (September/October) is marked by *Navaratri* ("nine nights"), which is linked with different deities in different parts of India. In the north, it is very much a festival of Rama, while in southern and eastern India it is associated with the goddess Durga and her defeat of the buffalo-headed demon Mahishasura (*see pp.222–223*). In these regions it is often known as *Durga Pooja* ("worship of Durga"). In Bengal, after nine days of worshipping Durga, her images are taken to a river or to the sea to be cleansed, and bulls are sacrificed to the goddess. In many other places, especially in northern India, the tenth day after the beginning of the festival is called *Dusshera*; it celebrates Rama's defeat of Ravana, as told in the epic of the *Ramayana* (*see pp.272–273*). A dramatic re-enactment of the tale, the *Ramlila*, dramatizes episodes from the epic over several days. Processions carrying huge images of the demon Ravana, his brother Kumbhakarna, and his son Indrajit, wind through the streets. Afterward, the images are burned, making a dramatic spectacle, as they are often stuffed with fireworks. The ritual forges a colorful celebration from the remembered triumph of good over evil.

> If one desires a world of singing and music, at one's will singing and music appear—and one triumphs, blessed with a world of singing and music.
>
> *Chandogya Upanishad*

KUMBH MELA FESTIVAL
The Kumbh Mela festival, which takes place every three years, is attended by large numbers of ascetics called *Naga* (naked) *Sadhus*, worshippers of Shiva.

LAND OF MANY FAITHS

SHARED BELIEFS AND PRACTICES

India is home to many religions. Several of the major faiths of the world—Hinduism, Buddhism, Jainism, and Sikhism—have their roots in India. Other faiths from outside the subcontinent, especially Islam, have also found many adherents there. These belief systems came to prominence at different times; Buddhism, for example, which began in northern India with the teachings of the Buddha c.500 BCE, became widespread in the 3rd century BCE, and a Hindu and Buddhist civilization flourished for most of the first millennium CE; while Islam expanded hugely during the reign of the Mughal emperors (1526–1750).

shared beliefs

In many ways the Indian religions seem very different from one another. They include Hinduism, which has millions of gods; Sikhism, which recognizes only one God; and Jainism, which does not recognize a supreme being at all. But there are a number of important areas in which the religions of India coincide. These common themes can be seen in religious narratives, belief and doctrine, ethics, religious practice, and in society.

Narrative is extremely important within Indian religions and culture. Hinduism, with its myriad gods, has a vast body of stories about the deeds of the deities. Tales of the Buddha, of the gurus, and of Mahavira are also central in Buddhism, Sikhism, and Jainism, respectively. The supernatural tales of Hinduism, the stories of the Buddha's lives, and the teachings of the Sikh gurus all reflect the importance of the great hero or teacher, who appears on Earth in order to set the world to rights. This pattern is visible, for example, in the interventions made by Krishna in the *Mahabharata*, and by the way both the Buddha and the Sikh Guru Nanak show their followers a new moral direction. This kind of intervention, in which sainted or supernatural beings correct the balance of good and evil in the world, is a major theme across Indian culture.

In the area of belief and doctrine, one key common element in the religions of India is the notion of reincarnation or rebirth. Buddhists, Hindus, Sikhs, and Jains all believe in the concept of existence as a continuous cycle of birth, death, and rebirth, known as *samsara*. The state in which one is reborn (whether as a human or an animal, for example) is controlled by the moral law of cause and effect, called *karma*: good deeds in one life cause good *karma*, and a favorable rebirth in the next. Even better than a favorable rebirth is to break out of the cycle of *samsara* altogether, by reaching a heightened spiritual state known as enlightenment, *nirvana* or *moksha*. This exalted goal is recognized by most people as just that—a supreme achievement that is only likely to be afforded to the very few. Most people are content to work toward a more favorable rebirth.

> The worship of different sects,
> which are like so many small streams,
> move together, to meet God,
> Who is like the Ocean.
>
> Rajjab, Hindu saint

Ethically, the Indian religions share the notion of living correctly in order to guarantee a favorable rebirth. How one achieves this varies from one faith to another, but several faiths share the ideal of avoiding harm or violence to living things. This is an especially strong notion in Jainism, and plays a key part in Buddhism. The nonviolence of both these faiths has proved inspirational to people throughout the world, and has had a strong influence on many Hindus. *Brahmin* priests, and many other Hindus, are vegetarian, for example. The ethic of nonviolence was crucially influential on Mahatma Gandhi (*see pp.102–03*) when he was campaigning for Indian independence from British rule.

PRACTICE IN SOCIETY

In the practice of religion, many Indian faiths share an element of discipline or self-training, typified by the discipline of yoga (*see pp.226–227*), which is seen as a way of training the body and the mind as part of an inward spiritual search. In some Indian faiths, especially Jainism and Hinduism, the related practice of austerity or asceticism is seen as an important aspect of spiritual life.

In most Indian religions, the concept of devotion also plays a major part. Followers are devoted to one or more of the Hindu deities, to the one God of Sikhism, to the Buddha, or to the Jain prophet Mahavira. Worship, or *pooja*, can take many forms (*see p.228*), from performing a sacrifice to making eye contact with the image of a deity. The kind of animal sacrifices carried out in early religions were not acceptable to the nonviolent belief systems, and so more symbolic offerings evolved. In all of these faiths, frequent worship is fundamental, and many people worship regularly both at a home shrine and at a temple. The practice of pilgrimage is an extension of this devotion, and it plays an important part in Hinduism, Buddhism, and Jainism.

Religion also makes its mark on the social system in India. Hinduism is rooted in the country's complex system of castes and classes, which has been important in two ways. First, Hindu ceremony was always deeply concerned with ritual purity, and this concept became identified with the caste system: a member of an upper caste could be "contaminated" by contact with those lower down the social scale, so there were elaborate rules about inter-caste contact. Second, Hinduism is concerned with how believers follow their own *dharma*, or allotted path through life. The social caste to which a person belonged determined their role in life, their employment, and their *dharma*. Other religions were also affected by the caste system, but Buddhism and Jainism tried to overcome its constraints. They had their own classes of exalted people—the monks of the Buddhist order and the Jain ascetics—who were afforded special respect and reverence.

▷ **DHARMACHAKRA MUDRA**
This Buddhist hand gesture (*mudra*) represents the "wheel of *dharma*." It was performed by the Buddha at the first sermon he gave after enlightenment.

▽ **HARIMANDIR: THE GOLDEN TEMPLE**
The principal place of worship for Sikhs, Harimandir lies on the lake of Amritsar ("pool of nectar"), which is regarded as having miraculous powers of healing.

hinduism

India's most ancient religion has developed over thousands of years. It has a multitude of gods and goddesses (*see pp.220–223*), many different religious texts, and no body of doctrine or practice that is seen as orthodox. Although only a handful of the myriad deities attract the most worshipers—especially Shiva, Rama, Krishna, various forms of the Great Goddess, and the animal gods Ganesha and Hanuman—and although all of these deities are seen as being encompassed by the one ultimate reality, Brahman, Hinduism is still the most diverse of all the major religions of the world. There are, however, a number of common elements. One constant theme in Hindu thought is the struggle between good and evil. This is because Hinduism sees human life as a cycle of birth, life, death, and rebirth, known as *samsara*, where the constant choice between good or evil action is paramount: the deeds of one lifetime will dictate one's type of rebirth in the next.

The law of *karma* dictates that whatever we do—in word, thought, or deed—has consequences. Bad or negative actions cause negative *karma*, while good or positive actions accrue positive *karma*. Some *karma* has an immediate effect in our everyday lives, but other karma has a more lasting power and affects how we will be reborn in the next life; whether we will be born as a human being, for example, or as a member of an animal species. Rama and Krishna, the two most popular avatars of the mighty Vishnu, personify the "good"—and their battles with evil demons reflect an individual's struggle to follow the "righteous path" through the course of a lifetime.

> Homage to you, peaceful self,
> Homage to you, greatest secret,
> Unthinkable, immeasurable,
> Without beginning or end.
>
> *Maitri Upanishad*

KRISHNA VICTORIOUS Krishna represents the victory of good over evil, and is often depicted dancing on the many heads of the serpent demon, Kaliya.

In order to live well, Hindus are guided by *dharma*, a term that can be translated as "moral law," but which is more flexible than this implies. *Dharma* first of all encompasses general morality, and it guides Hindus towards a number of key virtues, including forgiveness, charity, wisdom, and truthfulness. But in addition, *dharma* means what is right for each social class, or caste, what is right for people following specific trades or professions, and what is right for a person at each stage of life. It is the law of one's being. Each person therefore has their own specific *dharma*—or righteous path—and Hindus aim to follow their *svadharma* ("own *dharma*"). This is the lesson that Arjuna learns in the *Bhagavad Gita* (see *pp.270–271*). It is only through following *svadharma* that a person can evolve morally and move toward a favorable rebirth.

FINDING SALVATION

An endless series of good rebirths is not the ultimate goal of Hinduism. Hindus hope that eventually, after many rebirths, they will reach a state in which they break free of *samsara*. To achieve this, they must leave behind the world of the ego and the self through three forms of practice: *gyana marga*—the study and meditation on the unmanifest aspect of Brahman; *karma marga*—actively engaging in selfless and righteous acts; and *bhakti marga*—deep devotion to the divine.

These practices lead to the dissolution of the self, at which point there is nothing for either positive or negative *karma* to attach to, and the person's inner soul, the *atman*, is manifested. The *atman* then merges with the Supreme Being or Absolute Brahman, and the person finally achieves *moksha*: liberation from the constant cycle of *samsara*.

THE FOUR STAGES

Hinduism's exalted ultimate goal, the attainment of *moksha*, involves leaving behind the world of the ego and *karma*. But Hinduism is a practical belief system that recognizes that attachment to worldly things, together with marriage, social status, and wealth, is also necessary if human society is to function well. The religion defines a series of four *ashramas* (stages), through which a person must pass during their lifetime.

These vary in the extent to which the individual is expected to embrace or renounce the world and the self. The *ashramas* define the life of the Hindu male; the woman's role is defined traditionally in terms of her support of her husband, running the household, and, above all, being a mother.

The first *ashrama* is that of the *brahmachari* (student), who lives a life of celibacy and education, learning how to become a good member of society. During the second stage, the *grihasta* (householder) phase, the Hindu is expected to marry and work hard at a trade or profession in order to support a family. He should also help others in his community. At this time of life, the pursuit of worldly goals such as wealth and pleasure are permissible—provided that the basic moral laws of *karma* and *dharma* are followed. This is the only stage that allows intimate contact between men and women.

The third stage, *vanaprasta* (the anchorite), arrives when the man becomes a grandfather or when his children begin to reach adulthood. At this stage the individual leaves behind the hopes of youth and retires from more worldly attachments, seeking to explore his inner self and the ultimate truth. The fourth *ashrama* is that of the *sanyasi*, or aged ascetic, who turns completely away from the world and society, in order to prepare to merge with God. Few Hindu men today adhere literally to the traditional *ashramas*. But they still see them as important because they embody the message that a person should behave in a way befitting their age and time of life. This overall principle is still central for many Hindus, even if they do not strictly practice the *ashramas*.

A HINDU PRIEST OFFERING PRAYERS Hindus believe all existence is made up of fire, earth, water, wind, and *akash* (ether), and make offerings symbolizing these elements at dawn and dusk.

buddhism

Buddhism is the belief system that evolved in India in the middle of the first millennium BCE from the teachings of Siddhartha Gautama, known as the Buddha ("the enlightened one"). It arose during the Vedantic period, which was a time of great social change and religious unrest, when the higher-caste rights to religious ritual were being questioned, and asceticism seemed to offer a more personal spiritual experience. Buddhism was to become very popular in India in the 3rd century BCE, and it spread widely throughout South and Southeast Asia before declining in popularity in India during the 6th century. A resurgence in popularity at the beginning of the 20th century means that today there are once again many Buddhists living in India.

THE BUDDHA IS BORN

There are many conflicting historical accounts of the Buddha's birth and life, and scholars have been unable to agree on a definitive version. However, a traditional tale has developed, bringing together the most famous events of his life, and this is the story commonly given to explain the birth of Buddhism.

Siddhartha Gautama was born c.560 BCE in Lumbini, northern India (now in Nepal), to Queen Maha Maya and King Shuddhodana. Some accounts say that he was born from the arm of his mother and could walk and talk immediately, and that a lotus flower blossomed under each foot as he walked. His father hoped Siddhartha would grow up to become a ruler, but while he was still a child, a sage prophesied that he would instead become an enlightened being who would help people overcome their

THE MONASTIC LIFE
Boys cannot be ordained as monks until they are 20, but they may enter a monastery as a novice from the age of 7, the age at which Buddha's son Rahula was accepted into a monastery.

BUDDHIST ACTS OF DEVOTION Buddhists confirm their commitment to the Buddha through pilgrimages, meditation, offerings, and prostration.

suffering. The king acted to prevent this by confining Siddhartha to the palace, giving him every luxury, and shielding him from even setting eyes on poor, old, sick, or suffering people. But when he was a young man, Siddhartha at last managed to leave the palace—some accounts say literally, others that this was merely a vision—and he glimpsed normal life at last. He had four life-changing encounters: firstly with an old man, secondly with an ill person, thirdly with a funeral procession, and lastly with a serene ascetic. Soon afterward, Siddhartha left the palace to become an ascetic, seeking enlightenment and a way to overcome suffering. After years of wandering, he sat down beneath a pipal tree and vowed to meditate until he came up with the answer. Despite attacks by Mara, the god of desire, at the end of his extended meditation, Siddhartha reached a state of enlightenment known as *nirvana*—he had awakened from the sleep of ignorance and found a way for people to understand and ultimately escape human suffering.

THE FOUR NOBLE TRUTHS

The Buddha, as he had now become, realized that the key to existence was to follow a middle way between the harsh life of the ascetic and the luxurious life of the palace. This middle way should be illuminated by the Four Noble Truths: that all life involves suffering; that the cause of suffering is craving or desire; that release from this craving will bring an end to suffering; and that this release can come through following the Noble Eightfold Path. The eight aspects of the Buddhist path are correct thought, correct speech, correct understanding, correct action, correct livelihood, correct effort, correct mindfulness, and correct concentration. Buddhists see these eight aspects of the path as the eight spokes of a wheel—if you practice all of them together, the wheel will be able to turn and you will be able to move toward enlightenment.

> When the Sage entered *nirvana*, the Earth quivered like a ship struck by a squall, and firebrands fell from the sky. The heavens were lit up by a preternatural fire.
>
> Ashvaghosha, *Buddhacarita*

THE SPREAD OF BUDDHISM

Buddhism began as a small sect, but by the time of the Mauryan emperors, the first rulers to unify India, Buddhism had found many adherents. It flourished when the empire reached its height under the Emperor Ashoka in the 3rd century BCE. Ashoka converted to the faith, and deliberately set about rejuvenating it. He erected monuments at sites associated with the Buddha, went on pilgrimages to Lumbini (Buddha's birthplace) and Bodh Gaya (where Buddha reached enlightenment), and helped to spread Buddhist ideas by sending monks to all the regions of India and the countries beyond. Later rulers, including those of the Kushan Empire (1st to 3rd centuries CE), also supported Buddhism, and Buddhist art flourished under the Hindu Gupta rulers from 300–600 CE. After the 6th century there was a decline in support as Hinduism became more popular, and in the 16th century, when the Muslim Mughal emperors reigned, Buddhism had all but disappeared from India.

In the 1890s, a Buddhist revival began. It was spearheaded by Anagarika Dharmapala, a Buddhist leader from Sri Lanka, who visited the site of the Buddha's enlightenment at Bodh Gaya and was shocked to find the temple there being looked after by a Hindu priest. Dharmapala founded many Buddhist monasteries and temples in India and attracted many Indians to the faith. By the start of the 21st century there were around 17 million Buddhists in India.

FORMS OF BUDDHISM

During its long history, Buddhism has adapted and diversified and there are now two main strands of Buddhism, as well as numerous substrands. Theravada Buddhism is the form that claims to be closest to the original teachings of Buddha; it teaches the Eightfold Path but believes that actual Buddhahood is attainable by only a few. Followers of this kind of Buddhism aim to achieve the virtuous life of the *arhat*, a saintly figure who devotes a lifetime to helping others. The other main strand, Mahayana Buddhism, developed in northern India and produced many additional sacred texts, which are claimed to contain words either from the Buddha or inspired by him. Mahayana Buddhists believe that Buddhahood is available to all, but the most exalted beings are those who turn back at the point of becoming a Buddha, in order to help others reach enlightenment. These saintly beings are known as *bodhisattvas*.

When Indian Buddhism was revived in the 20th century, both Theravada and Mahayana traditions were firmly established, so there are now followers of both branches in India. In addition, there are also many Tibetan Buddhists in northern India who follow their own distinctive version of the faith.

BUDDHA MEDITATES The Buddha's right hand touches the Earth, calling it to witness his enlightenment.

jainism

Jainism is an ancient Indian religion based largely on the teachings of the spiritual leader Mahavira, who lived in the 6th century BCE. It arose in the same region—the Ganges Basin—and at around the same time as Buddhism, but it is a distinct religion. Its followers aim to achieve liberation from the cycle of death and rebirth by renouncing all luxuries and worldly concerns, and by avoiding causing harm to other living things.

Jains believe that humans, animals, and plants all have souls, and non-violence to all these living beings, *ahimsa,* is Jainism's most important moral principle. This highly exacting religion of self-help has no gods who can be called upon to rescue the soul—the soul destroys or liberates itself.

THE TIRTHANKARAS

Jains see time as a series of motions lasting many millions of years. In each era, 24 spiritual leaders called Tirthankaras appear in order to lead people to a higher spiritual plane. Followers believe that the 24 Tirthankaras of the current era were real, historical people, but records only survive of the final two: Parsva, who lived in the 9th century BCE, and Mahavira (540–468 BCE). Mahavira was a high-ranking member of the warrior caste who lived the life of the ascetic and achieved enlightenment. He attracted followers who collected the Jain scriptures.

THE PATH TO LIBERATION

Jains believe that adopting the life of the ascetic is the best way to avoid the cycle of death and rebirth and to move toward liberation. Jain ascetics adhere to the Five Great Vows: *ahimsa* (non-violence), *satya* (telling the truth), *brahmacharya* (sexual abstinence), *asteya* (not taking what is not given), and *aparigraha* (detachment). These vows are interpreted in a very rigorous way. Lay people try to come as close to these demands as they can, eating vegetarian foods and pursuing non-violent careers in areas such as the civil service, arts and crafts, agriculture, or commerce. By living up to these exacting standards as best they can, both ascetic and lay Jains hope to move gradually toward liberation through 14 stages of spiritual progress, from a state of delusion and spiritual sleep to complete detachment from the world and, ultimately, liberation.

In practice Jains see the higher stages of this spiritual hierarchy as distant goals, only achievable after many lifetimes of effort. In the 4th century CE, a split occurred between two main groups of Jains, the *Digambaras* ("sky-clad") who renounce even the wearing of clothes in their attempt to detach themselves from the world, and the Shvetambaras ("white-clad"), who see detachment as more of a mental process. Both groups are small, but their ideas have influenced many non-Jains, including Mahatma Gandhi.

> Homage to the Enlightened Ones! Homage to the Liberated Souls! Homage to the Leaders! Homage to the Teachers! Homage to all the Jain Monks in the world!
>
> The Jain Fivefold Salutation

PRAYING TO BAHUBALI During the Jain festival of Mahamastakabhiseka, pilgrims pray before the 59 ft (18 m) statue of the Jain saint Bahubali.

sikhism

The youngest of the Indian religions, Sikhism began toward the end of the 15th century with the teachings of Guru Nanak. Sikhs believe in one God—whom they refer to as *Sat Guru* ("true teacher")—and follow the teachings of Nanak and the nine gurus who came after him. The word *Sikh* means disciple or student. The faith has always been strongest in the Punjab, but its 22 million members live in many parts of the world. The faith recognizes everyone as equal, and has always granted full recognition and rights to women and members of all castes.

THE BEGINNINGS

Nanak was born in Talwandi, a village west of Lahore, in 1469, when the region was ruled by the Delhi Sultanate. In 1499, while bathing in a river, he received the call of God, who commanded him to "rejoice in my Name and teach others to do the same." Nanak announced that, "There is neither Hindu nor Muslim," which was taken to mean that members of these religions were not true to their faith. For this reason, Nanak decided to worship God in his own way, avoiding in the process the tensions that were rife between Hindus and Muslims in this period, when the Muslim Mughal Empire was establishing itself in Hindu India.

After Nanak, there were nine successor gurus who led the Sikh faith and spread its teachings. The last of these was Guru Gobind Singh, who founded the Khalsa, the community of initiated Sikhs, and declared that he would be the last human guru. Since then Sikhs have been guided by their sacred book, the Adi Granth, which itself became known as a guru, the Guru Granth Sahib ("Granth Personified"). This collection of prayers and hymns notably condemns any idea of caste.

Like the followers of other Indian religions, Sikhs believe in the concepts of *karma* and rebirth. They believe in the absolute sovereignty of God—they will bow to no one else—and they see God's will as being made clear through the teachings of the gurus. Sikhs have a strong sense of communal identity, and wear five items, all with names beginning with "K", as symbols of their Sikhhood. These "Five Ks" are the *kesh* (uncut hair as given by God), the *kanga* (a comb to symbolize cleanliness), the *kaccha* (special undergarments symbolizing their commitment to purity), the *kara* (a steel bracelet signifying bondage to the Truth), and the *kirpan* (a ceremonial sword symbolizing defence of the Truth).

Sikhs hope to progress from the concerns of everyday existence toward a life that is absorbed in and devoted to God, and meditation on God's name is an important way of directing their minds and souls towards this aim. But Sikhs also find God's way in their everyday lives, playing a full part in society and performing community service.

GURU NANAK AND MARDANA
Nanak traveled, taught, and composed hymns. He was accompanied everywhere by his childhood friend and rabab player, the minstrel Baba Mardana (*far right*).

ST. THOMAS OF KERALA
St. Thomas, the doubting apostle, was reputed to have been speared by a lance while praying on a hill and buried in a tomb on the Coromandel coast.

christianity

Christians follow the teachings of their founder, Jesus Christ, whom they believe to be the Son of God and whose life and teachings are described in the four books of the Christian Bible called the Gospels. By believing in Jesus, adopting his exacting moral code, and repenting their sins, Christians hope to achieve salvation when they die.

Beginning in Western Asia, the Christian faith spread quickly westward through the Roman Empire in the centuries after Jesus's death. It was also carried eastward to India, where it established itself in small pockets before expanding throughout the country.

INDIA'S FIRST CHRISTIANS

There is some debate among scholars regarding Christianity's exact route to the subcontinent, but according to a widespread tradition, the faith came to India in the 1st century CE, when St. Thomas the Apostle traveled to Kerala, on the coast of southwest India. Kerala was known as "the spice coast of India," and there was a well-established trade route from here to both the Middle East and Europe by this time. The saint is thought to have arrived on a trading vessel from Alexandria at the port of Cranganore in 52 CE.

St. Thomas is said to have converted both Jewish people and Hindus in Kerala, where his teachings also became integrated into the beliefs and traditions of the local communities. In some details the new Christians remained resolutely Hindu: many of the families converted were Brahmins and Kshatriyas, and continued to consider themselves high caste, while their churches resembled Hindu temples.

St. Thomas established seven churches before being martyred at Mylapur, Madras, c.72 CE. Many of the St. Thomas Christians left India to become fervent missionaries, taking the faith as far as Indonesia and the Maldives. In later centuries, Christianity in India expanded with the arrival of immigrant Christians from various parts of western Asia, including Persia and Syria, who followed the rites and traditions of the Eastern Churches (later known as the Orthodox Churches).

THE MISSIONARIES

Christian missionaries from France and Portugal began to arrive in the 14th and 15th centuries. They introduced Catholic Christianity to India, and converted both existing Christians and many Hindus to Roman Catholicism. The arrival of the explorer, Vasco da Gama, in 1498 signaled the first schism in Christianity within India, as the Portugese Catholics were opposed to the orthodox rites of the Eastern Churches, practiced by the St. Thomas Christians in Kerala. In the 16th century, Portuguese Jesuits, led by St. Francis Xavier, were especially active, converting many people in Goa, which to this day has a large Catholic population. Goa is still famous for its Catholic churches, which, with their rich architecture, woodwork, stone carving, and intricate metalwork, introduced European artistic forms into India on a large scale for the first time. The missionaries also played a major role in education. The Jesuits founded many schools, and set up India's first printing press in Goa in 1566; three of its earliest productions were grammar books by St. Francis Xavier and the English Jesuit Thomas Stephens, and a booklet of Christian doctrine by Diogo Ribeiro. By 1578, a similar booklet had been produced in the local Tamil language, which was later translated into Persian for the Mughal Court. The 18th and 19th centuries saw the arrival of British Protestant missionaries, who preached widely throughout India, founded churches, and made many converts. The Baptist missionary William Carey, who arrived in India in 1793, made the first translation of the Bible into Bengali.

> Love your enemies, bless them that curse you, do good to them that hate you, and pray for them that persecute you, that you may be the children of your father in heaven.
>
> The Bible, the Gospel of St. Matthew, Chapter 5

CHRISTIANITY TODAY

There are more than 24 million Christians in India today, and the number is said to be increasing. More than two-thirds are Roman Catholics, who are especially numerous in areas such as Goa that were once dominated by the Portuguese. The Christian population includes some three million members of the Oriental Orthodox Churches, some of whom trace their religious lineage back to Kerala and the time of St. Thomas.

There are also many different Protestant denominations, the largest being the Church of South India, an amalgamation of Indian Anglican, Methodist, and Reformed Churches that forms part of the Anglican Communion. Lutheran, Baptist, and Brethren groups are also represented. Most of these Protestant Churches trace their origins to missionary activity by the British in the 18th and 19th centuries. In addition, there are a number of more recent local Pentecostal Churches. Such growth indicates that Christianity in India has its own vigorous life.

islam

The religion of Islam was revealed to the Prophet Muhammad in the Arabian peninsula in the early 7th century. The Prophet Muhammad preached belief in one God, Allah, and taught that the Islamic sacred text, the Quran, was made up of the actual words of God, as revealed to the Prophet.

Muslims pray five times each day, support the poor with alms, fast during the month of Ramadan, and make the pilgrimage to the city of Mecca, where the Prophet Muhammad was born. Islam spread quickly across Northern Africa, through Western Asia to India, but the number of its Indian adherents grew significantly under the Mughals. The earliest of these, the Umayyad dynasty, ruled an Islamic empire that included both Syria and Iraq. In 711, they took control of the area now covered by Pakistan and western India, and persuaded local leaders—some of whom converted to Islam—to run the region on their behalf. Other Muslim leaders conquered parts of India from the 12th century onward, but bt far the most significant period was from 1526 to the 18th century, when the Muslim Mughal dynasty ruled all or part of India. The Mughals transformed the religious landscape of India, converting people to Islam and building many mosques. Some of the emperors, such as Aurangzeb (r.1658–1707), imposed Islam ruthlessly, but other Mughal rulers, such as Akbar the Great (r.1556–1605), were much more tolerant. Under his influence, Hindu and Muslim artists began to work together, creating new styles that heralded a golden age within Indian art.

In the 18th and 19th centuries, Islam survived the decline of the Mughal Empire, the resurgence of Hinduism, and the take-over of the British (who brought Christian missionaries in their wake). When the British pulled out of India in 1947, the Muslim northwest became the separate state of Pakistan.

Islam is quite diverse among India's 138 million Muslims. Many follow the path of Sufism, a mystical form of the faith that stresses a personal relationship with God and reveres saintly figures called *Pirs*. Others follow the more orthodox Sunni branch of the faith, some of whom learn about their religion at traditional Islamic schools (*madrasas*), while others attend Muslim universities with a modern curriculum.

JAMA MASJID, DELHI
Built by the Mughal emperor Shah Jahan in the 17th century, this mosque houses the footprint of the Prophet Muhammad.

zoroastrianism

The religion of ancient Persia (now Iran), Zoroastrianism was founded by the prophet Zarathustra, or Zoroaster, who is thought to have lived c.1200 BCE. Zarathustra taught his followers to worship Ahura Mazda, the Wise Lord. Ahura Mazda is seen as a wholly good and all-powerful deity who is nevertheless locked in perpetual conflict with an evil spirit, Angra Mainyu. As in Hinduism, the struggle between good and evil is acted out by the gods, just as humankind is free to choose between good and evil. Modern scholars believe that some aspects of the Zoroastrian conflict were influenced by early Indian writings, such as the Vedas.

Zarathustra and his followers aimed to help Ahura Mazda in his struggle by living well and worshiping him regularly at temples where a sacred flame, symbolizing truth and order, was kept continuously burning.

Zoroastrianism grew in popularity in Persia, where it was the state religion between the 6th century BCE and the 7th century CE. The sacred book of the faith, the Avesta, was compiled during the 2nd century BCE, preserving the words of Zarathustra and other teachers, and the religion flourished. But in the 7th century, as the Islamic faith spread rapidly across Western Asia, the Zoroastrians began to find themselves a persecuted minority. Ultimately a number of them therefore decided to seek asylum in India, where they were allowed to follow their faith freely, and became known as the Parsis, or people from Persia.

The first Parsis to arrive in India settled in Gujarat in the 10th century, breaking off virtually all communication with their Iranian counterparts until the mid-15th century. Under British rule they became much more prosperous, realizing financial success in areas as diverse as shipbuilding, banking, science, and the arts.

Today, the Parsis constitute a tiny minority in India—according to current estimates there are only around 70,000 Parsis in the subcontinent. Many live in Mumbai, but there are also Parsi communities in Delhi and Karachi, and in many villages in Gujarat.

baha'i

The Baha'i faith began in Persia (modern Iran) with the teachings of the prophet Baha'u'llah in the 19th century. Baha'u'llah believed that there is only one God, and that all faiths worship him. The various prophets and gods of the great religions—such as Abraham, Jesus, Muhammad, the Buddha, and Zarathustra—are all seen as manifestations of the one God.

The goal of the Baha'i faith is to unite the world's religions and peoples in this vision and thereby bring salvation to individual believers and peace to the world as a whole. Their holy writings state: "The religion of God is for love and unity; make it not the cause of enmity and dissension."

The religion does not have a priesthood, nor ceremonies, but it does impose certain rules, such as fasting for 19 days each year, attending a feast day each month, practicing monogamy, and abstaining from taking mind-altering substances.

The Baha'i faith was not well received in Muslim countries, where it was seen as heretical. But it has expanded widely outside its homeland of Iran. The world's largest Baha'i community is now in India, where there are over two million adherents to the Baha'i faith spread through more than 10,000 localities. The Baha'i House of Worship—the Mashriqu'l-Adhkar—in New Delhi, is also known as the Lotus Temple. This large temple has a striking roof that resembles the unfolding petals of a lotus flower (*see pp.338–341*).

◁ ZOROASTRIAN INITIATION CEREMONY **Between the ages of 7 and 15, children are welcomed into the Zoroastrian faith through the ceremony of Navjote.**

judaism

The Jewish people originated in the western Mediterranean, settling in the areas now known as Israel and Palestine some 3,500 years ago. Their religion is based on the Torah, the first five books of the Hebrew Bible, which Jews believe to contain the words of God as revealed to the Jewish leader Moses. It stresses above all the oneness of God and the importance of obeying his commandments. The Torah contains hundreds of commandments that govern the lives of practicing Jews.

There have been small Jewish communities in India for more than 2,000 years. One of the oldest is made up of the Cochin Jews, who made their home in Kerala, southern India, especially in the town of Kochi. Various traditions reveal how the Cochin Jews arrived in India. Some may have arrived as early as the time of King Solomon (10th century BCE) or when the Jews were exiled from their homeland when the Babylonian Nebuchadnezzar ruled in the 6th century BCE. Another tradition says that they arrived as exiles during the Roman period. There were probably several migrations to Kerala, but the precise dates are unknown. The other early arrivals were the group known as the Bene Israel ("Sons of Israel"), who settled in western India, especially in and around Mumbai. They are said to have arrived 2,100 years ago after seven Jewish families were shipwrecked.

The isolation of these early groups of Jewish settlers meant that they naturally absorbed some of the tenets and practices of the Hindu faith that surrounded them. Traditionally, they are also said to have lost their Bibles in the shipwreck. However, in the 19th century, they gained access to a Marathi-language Hebrew Bible through Christian missionaries, and came into contact with a much later group of immigrants who followed a more mainstream tradition. This Jewish community, known as the "Baghdadi Jews," were in fact fleeing from religious persecution in Iran, Afghanistan, Syria, and Yemen, as well as Iraq, and settled in India around Mumbai and Kolkata.

> Hear, O Israel, the Lord is our God, the Lord is One. And thou shalt love the Lord thy God with all thine heart, and with all thy soul, and with all thy might.
>
> The Bible, Deuteronomy 6:4–5 (The Shema)

The Jewish settlement of India came to spread over quite a wide geographical area, but involved a relatively small number of people. They developed successful communities, building businesses in oil pressing and trading as merchants. Judaism is not normally a religion that seeks to convert others to its beliefs, but India does also include some indigenous communities who have converted to the faith. However, since the foundation of the state of Israel in 1948, many Indian Jews have migrated to Israel, leaving a small community of only around 5,000 still in India today.

MAGEN DAVID SYNAGOGUE, MUMBAI The most prominent "Baghdadi Jew" was David Sassoon, who fled Iraq in 1826. He built many schools and synagogues in India, including the sky-blue Magen David.

ART AND PERFORMANCE

A HOLISTIC APPROACH

If there is a single window into the mysterious world of the Indian arts, it is via a holistic vision of the world—where every being and action is viewed in its relation to the whole universe, past and present. The fascination lies, as with Indian religion and philosophy, in exploring the relationship of the part to the whole, the many to the one, and the finite to the infinite. Every one of the arts explores our world and the world of the gods from this perspective. Man acquires special significance not because he is first among nature, but because he has a capacity for consciousness and the ability to transcend physicality through psychic discipline.

the arts entwined

Prana, the primal energy, is held to be the force behind every object, thought, action, and natural force. This single, unified source of energy is the starting point for the Indian artist, who feels free to express this wondrous energy in a multiplicity of forms, in an imaginative celebration of color, sound, touch, and smell.

The *Vishnudharmottara Purana*, a 7th-century sacred text of the Hindus, recounts the story of a king who wanted to learn the art of painting. He went to a master painter and asked to be taken on as his disciple, and the master said he would do so, but only after the king had learned to sculpt. The king therefore sought out a teacher who would help him learn the art of sculpture. But the sculptor asked him to come back once he had learned the art of dance. Once again, the king set out in search of a guru, this time to help him learn dance. But when he found the right master, this teacher asked him to first learn the arts of music and rhythm. Only after he had mastered all of these arts could the king learn how to paint.

This apocryphal story points to the holistic underpinning of Indian art and aesthetics, and also to the strong links between every art form. The links forge a purposeful interconnectedness, reflecting the interrelationship of all existence—a belief promoted by Indian religion and its concept of life cycles, dating back to ancient Hindu teachings. As the sages say: "All that exists is one. The wise call it by many names."

AN ARTISTIC BANQUET

Traditional Indian art is built around the concept of the *rasa*, as described by the sage Bharata in the ancient text of the *Natya Shastra*, written between 200 BCE and 200 CE. *Rasa* literally means "juice" or "sap," and the term is used to describe the quintessential flavor or "taste" of a work of art, as if it were a part of something served in a banquet of assorted flavors.

There are nine *rasas*, which are collectively known as *navarasa*. Each *rasa* represents a basic human emotion: love, humor, pity, courage, fear, anger, disgust, wonder, or spiritual peace. The artist endeavors to suggest a particular *rasa*, such as courage, distilling it within a work of art so vividly, but impersonally, that both he or she—and crucially, the audience—recognize and respond to the pure, abstract, and universal nature of the emotion.

Through this depersonalization of emotion, the artist tries to resolve the contradiction between the microcosm of the human body and the macrocosm of the universe; while simultaneously taking the sensuous on a journey to the super-sensuous, and ultimately, to the spiritual. A successful work of art transports the artist and the audience to a state of supreme bliss or joy (*ananda*), similar to that achieved through meditation. This state of being is art's ultimate purpose.

Dancers, musicians, painters, and actors from the folk and the classical streams routinely dance, paint, sing, and enact a vast variety of themes using the *navarasas*. One example of this is

RAMA AND SITA
The *Ramayana,* one of India's most famous stories, reflects the importance of an overriding theme within Indian arts: the triumph of good over evil.

the *Ramayana*, whose main *rasas* or flavor are said to be pity and pathos, but which also contains humor and heroics. Bharata's original text even relates the colors that correspond to each of the *rasas*, such as pale light green for the *rasa* of love and eroticism, and black for the *rasa* of storytelling.

> He whose body is in the sentiment of *Love* as he moves with Sita;
> In *Courage* as he breaks the mighty bow;
> In *Pity* as he protects the smitten crow;
> In *Wonder* as he looks at the bridge of stones across the ocean;
> In *Humor* as he watches Surpa-nakha;
> In *Fear* and *Disgust* as he gazes upon others, except Sita;
> In *Anger* as he kills Ravana;
> In *Peace* as he sees the Sages.

The nine *rasas,* as experienced by Rama, from an ancient *sloka* (prayer)

STORYTELLING

Katha, literally "story," is another pillar of Indian aesthetics. The stories are drawn from life, nature, moral fables, and mythology, and both the performing and visual arts depend on them for their themes.

India is sometimes referred to as the home of fairy tales, and its folk tales have acted as source material for countless works of literature around the world. The *Katha-saritsagara*, or Ocean of Stories, is an assemblage of tales around 2,000 years old, whose histories, legends, magical folk tales, and riddles seem to have acted as source material for, among others, Aesop's *Fables*, Boccaccio's *Decameron*, *The Arabian Nights*, and the fairy tales of Hans Christian Andersen. For thousands of years, India has maintained an oral tradition of storytelling, and supported specific castes of professional storytellers. These performers, known as *kathaks*, inherited their status. They would use music and dance to help tell their tales, and a major classical dance of the north, known as Kathak (*see pp.250–251*), is still a popular form of storytelling.

Classical texts, such as the group known as the Upanishads, exemplify the complex nature of Indian storytelling. The *Katha Upanishad*, written c.1000 BCE, is among the earliest examples of the Indian form, where a story is told within a story, itself encased within many other stories. This multilayered device is used to take the narrative forward, while allowing the stories to impact upon and interact with one another, just as the universe itself is made up of a dazzling array of multiple beings and stories.

The rich, artistic qualities of the Mughal period took *katha* to new heights. The masterpiece of illustrated storytelling, *Hamzanama* (*The Adventures of Amir Hamza*), was commissioned by Emperor Akbar (1542–1605). It is a magnificent storehouse of myths, legends, and "shaggy dog" stories. With over 1,400 huge illustrations, the book reflects the merging of two artistic worlds: Hindu India and Persian Islamic Central Asia. During the 19th and 20th centuries, Indian stories continued to fan out beyond the country's borders, to interact with new cultures. After visiting India in 1938, the British novelist Somerset Maugham wrote a novel called *The Razor's Edge*, which took its name from a story in the *Katha Upanishad*. He was inspired by the story, which includes the lines: "Arise! Awake! Approach the great and learn. Like the sharp edge of a razor is that path, so the wise say; hard to tread and difficult to cross." Entering the world of Indian aesthetics—a maze of rhythm, story, structure, and emotion—is akin to crossing the sharp edge of the razor.

ODISSI DANCE
Odissi dance is thought to be the oldest form of classical Indian dance; its roots lie in the Odra Magadhi dance style, mentioned in the ancient *Natya Shastra*.

classical music

Melody, rhythm, and a ground note ("droning") form the basis of Indian classical music, which has its roots in the ancient rhythmic chanting of the Vedas. While Western musicians explored the musical concepts of harmony and counterpoint, those in India stayed true to the simple power of melodic scale and rhythm, eschewing fixed, orchestrated scores for soaring demonstrations of *upaj* (improvisation) within the strict boundaries of *tala* (rhythm) and a range of notes known as a *raga*. Like the Hindu religion, India's classical music explores the many and the one, finding a form of perfect unity within limitless diversity.

Most of India's musical terminology derives from the *Natya Shastra* (*see pp.246–247*). However, the concept of the *raga*, which is central to Indian music, first emerged in the *Brihaddesi*, a 7th-century text. A *raga* is a melodic formula of five, six, or seven notes with particular intervals, or relationships, which sets the range for a piece of music. Broader in reach than a scale, but not fixed in order, the *raga* is described as "the very soul" of Indian music. Each *raga* embodies a particular *rasa* (emotion), such as wonder or tranquility, and in North India each was played at a specific time of day or year, such as morning or night, winter or summer.

The *raga* serves as the foundation for the musician's performance, and it is underpinned by the *tala*—long rhythmic cycles that are beaten out on a percussion instrument. Today's popular percussion instruments include the double vertical drums of the *tabla,* and the horizontal drums of the *pakhawaj* or *mridangam.*

M. S. SUBBULAKSHMI The Indian maestro M. S. Subbulakshmi found international fame in the 20th century singing Carnatic classical music.

THE CLASSICAL DIVIDE

Until the Mughal invasion, Indian classical music was generally religious in nature. The chanting of the *Sama Veda* led to the creation of the first form of Indian classical music, the seven-note form known as Raga Sangita. This in turn developed into Gandharva, a Sanskrit musical form celebrating the Hindu deities that accompanied all the Hindu festivals and court ceremonies and was codified in the *Natya Shastra.* The saint-musicians of the 12th century, such as Jayadeva of Orissa, who composed the *Gita Govinda* (*see p.265*), had a profound effect on Indian music. They gave rise to a new devotional form of song, variously called Bhajan, Kirtan, or Abhang, which used the vernacular languages. These songs moved away from the more rigid structures and techniques of classical music, toward a freer form that placed more emphasis on music as a mystical and emotional experience.

> I do not dwell in heaven, nor in the hearts of great yogis. There only I abide, O Narada, where my devotees sing.
>
> Shiva, from the *Narada Samhita*

From the 11th to 12th centuries, Indian music split into two systems: the north and the south. The northern style began to absorb the music of the great Mughals, and new *ragas* were invented, particularly for the Sufis, an esoteric sect within Islam that used music as a path to the divine. This new music was an amalgamation of Hindu and Islamic thought. The Mughal courts prized virtuosity and highly imaginative interpretation; under their influence, the slow, formal temple music of Dhrupad gradually developed into a school of music known as Khayal ("imagination"), which became the most popular form of music in the North. Other musical styles also developed, such as the romantic–devotional hymns of Thumri, and the brief love songs of Tappa. These North Indian styles of music became known as "Hindustani" music.

Meanwhile, southern India had become the center of Hindu learning, and Sanskrit continued to be used within its music. Highly theoretical and devotional, this form of music became known as Carnatic, or Karnataka. More popular forms developed alongside this, such as the devotional songs of Kirtana, and the music of the Bharat Natyam dance form (*see pp.250–251*).

FOLK MUSIC

There are numerous different tribal groups in India, mainly in the central and eastern hill regions, numbering more than 30 million people. Their music, and the folk traditions throughout the country, erupt in a myriad of forms which can only be defined in terms of context. One form is the ceremonial or "outdoor" type of music that is played and sung at important rituals and celebrations. Another is a group of more personal songs, which are performed at everyday occasions. These may be secular songs of love or humor, or religious songs giving thanks to the gods, such as the Onam harvest song of Kerala.

A VASANTA (SPRING) RAGAMALA
Ragamala paintings portray a particular musical *raga*, played at a certain time of year. Here Krishna dances to a spring *raga*, devoted to him.

CLASSICAL DANCE FORMS The Mughal influence on Kathak dance (*far left*) marks it out from the dances of Odissi (*center*) and Bharat Natyam (*right*).

classical and folk dance

All of the performing arts of India are sacred in origin, and they are encapsulated in the *Natya Shastra*—India's ancient guide to their purpose and content. The powerful spiritual aspect of dance is distilled in Shiva's dance of the Tandava, in which he spins a dance of such furious energy that it endlessly destroys and recreates the universe—an act famously portrayed in the Chola bronzes of the *Nataraja* (*see p.259*). This masculine dance of the divine was matched by a more graceful, feminine form (*Lasya*) by his wife Parvati, and these two aspects—male and female—are still important in Indian dance today.

Music forms the very basis of dance, which is said to be its visual expression. Until recently, the term *sangeet*, which is now used for vocal and instrumental music, was also used to refer to dance, and performers are expected to train in both of these arts. Dance revolves around three concepts: *natya* (drama), *nritya* (mime through hand gestures and facial *abhinaya* or "expression"), and *nritta* (pure dance, where the body movements do not express any specific mood or *rasa*, or convey any story). The dance forms of today emphasize *nritta* and *nritya*, while *natya*—dance as drama—is limited, except in Kathakali, the classical dance form of Kerala.

As in Indian theater, dance revolves around the *rasas* or emotions (*see pp.246–247*). The dancer must communicate these through four types of *abhinaya*, or modes of expression: the body, the words, the costumes, and *Satvika*, the dancer's state of mind. The physical expressions are subtle and the *rasas* are conveyed through small eye and facial movements combined with hand gestures (*mudras*). One of the most important parts of a dancer's training involves mastering the many highly stylized manners in which to express the nine *rasas* of love, compassion, valor, laughter, anger, disgust, wonder, fear, and peace.

DANCE FORMS

There are seven classical dance forms in India today: Bharat Natyam, Kathakali, Kuchipudi, Kathak, Manipuri, Odissi, and Sattriya (a tradition of monastic dance rituals that is now recognized as a classical form of dance). Each has its own movements, patterns, codified body language, grammar, techniques, and costumes.

One of the oldest forms of dance, with its roots in the *Natya Shastra*, is Bharat Natyam, a dance from southern India that is illustrated in the sculptures and paintings of several temples in Tamil Nadu. It started as a temple dance called Dasiyattam ("the dance of the maid-servants") and was kept alive by the *Devadasis*, the young girls who were offered by their parents to the deities in the temples, in a practice now outlawed. These girls learned dance and music and performed in the temple courtyard, and some of the most renowned performers of the last century belonged to the families of the *Devadasis*. Accompanied by classical Carnatic songs, the solo dancer presents a series of body movements that represent a kind of visual geometry. The dance is made up of two parts: *nritta* (pure dance) and *nritya* (mime). As in many other classical arts, the solo dancer takes on the role of all the characters in the story.

The Kathakali dance form of Kerala is a spectacular dance form that verges on theater—hence it is known more as a dance-drama. Some scholars believe that Kathakali originated from Kudiyattam, the only surviving Sanskrit theatre form in India. The stylized face makeup is extremely important: the colors to be used for the heroic characters, the villains, and the gods and goddesses are exactly specified, and the makeup may take up to seven hours to be applied. The exaggerated movements of the face and eye muscles are the defining characteristics of Kathakali, and training starts at a very young age. The dancers are accompanied by music from a small wind instrument, a vertical drum, and a vocalist.

The divine origins of dance are evident in many ways. Kuchipudi, a dance form named after the village

in which it originated, Kuchipudi in Andhra Pradesh, is said to have been created by Siddhendra Yogi after Krishna appeared to him in a dream and asked him to compose the dance about the god's own jealous wife, Satyabhama.

The Odissi dance form of the eastern region is portrayed in the temples of Orissa, where it is performed to local Odissi *ragas*. Its teachers were originally young boys who trained and performed in the temples, later passing on the tradition to the *Devadasis*.

Kathak, the most popular form of dance in the northern region, comes from the storytelling tradition, when traveling bards told mythological and moral tales, embellished by hand and eye movements. Kathak was highly influenced during the medieval period by the Mughal courts, and it is a perfect synthesis of Hindu storytelling and Persian dance. The dance places great emphasis on rhythm and pays extraordinary attention to precise footwork, but uses much simpler, more natural gestures than other classical dance forms.

Another regional dance from the northeast, the Manipuri, is purely devotional. This lyrical and graceful dance revolves around *Raslila*: the divine dance of Radha, Krishna, and the god's 16,000 devoted milkmaids.

The most recently recognized form of classical dance, Sattriya, evolved within the monastic tradition. It stems from plays by the Vaishnava saint and reformer, Shankaradeva of Assam, who focused on episodes from mythology and the epics. Distinctly regionalized, the hand gestures, choreographic patterns, and footwork are all specific to the northeastern region.

FOLK DANCE

India's large rural population has created a huge variety of regional dances, many of which are associated with festivals or ceremonies, some celebrating the seasons or the life cycle of humans, others acting to invoke the spirits or gods for removing evil. Folk dances tend to be influenced by local issues, ideologies, the prevailing climate, and the performance space available. The dances of coastal India, for instance, have gestures and songs related to boats and fishing, while those of the plains relate to the agricultural cycle; dances performed by the communities in the snowbound areas of the Himalayas depict slow movements, reflecting the restrictions of thick, warm clothing.

> Where the hand goes, the eye follows; where the eye goes, the mind goes; where the mind goes, so too the heart; where the heart is, lies the reality of being.
>
> From the ancient dance treatise, *Abhinaya Darpanam*

Indian dances are being given new life today by the government and other agencies, particularly in areas with rich dance traditions, such as Rajasthan and Madhya Pradesh. Their importance has also been recognized globally, and Indian classical dance is now an essential inclusion in international dance festivals. India's performing arts survive by moving like the flow of a river; new tributaries constantly join the mainstream. Schools of music and dance interact with each other, producing new forms and styles. Amid the bustle of modern India's technological and industrial growth, the movements and sounds of dance bring its people back to an essential connection with their aesthetic roots.

DANCING IN THE GREAT THAR DESERT
Rajasthani folk dances, with their vibrant colors, swirling movements, and rhythmic music, are a focus of the annual desert festival.

drama

The performing art traditions in India are like an old tree, its roots spreading all the way back to the ancient Vedas, its branches reaching out into myriad forms. The *Natya Shastra* treatise (*see p.246*) created the theatrical traditions by using words from the *Rig Veda*, music from the *Sama Veda*, and gestures from the *Yajur Veda*. It also suggested the reflection of the moods or *rasas* (*see pp.246–247*), that are embodied in the *Atharva Veda*. The Vedas specified very detailed and elaborate preparations for the Vedic rituals, all of which were carried through to the staging of classical dramatic productions. Some of today's more common practices have their origins in the Vedic tradition, such as the consecration of the performance space.

Most regional theater performances take place on village squares or in courtyards, beginning in the evening and continuing into the night. Many regional companies break a coconut, ritually "light the lamp," or invoke Ganesha before a performance, to bring it blessings. The lamp functions on many levels, from the practical one—of providing light for the performance—to a spiritual one, in which it embodies the concept of the Supreme or Divine Light, which is then bestowed on to the consecrated space.

CLASSICAL THEATER

Classical theater based itself on the rules of the *Natya Shastra*; it was performed in Sanskrit, was essentially religious and aristocratic in subject and style, and depicted tales from history, the epics, and mythology. It was performed in urban centers for audiences initiated in the classical texts, but the story was not the only factor of interest. Classical theater was concerned with *abhinaya*: "carrying forward" a character or emotion to the audience—exhibiting not just events, but also their meaning, through a series of face and hand gestures. *Abhinaya* could be achieved through two different types of production: *lokadharmi*—where realistic actions were performed within a natural presentation; or *natyadharmi*—where idealistic, stylized gestures were enacted within a symbolic landscape.

Plays written by the greatest playwrights of the classical era—such as Sudraka, who was best known for his 2nd-century play, *Mrichchakatikam* (*Little Clay Cart*), and Kalidasa, a secular 5th-century author—are still performed in theaters today. Their work exemplified the *natyadharmi* style of classical theater, in which entire episodes were acted out without recourse to decor or props, and the actor was restricted to gestures codified in the *Natya Shastra*. As the story moved along, the actor alone created the illusions of forests, people, rivers, heavens, and Earth using only body movements and the sung or spoken word.

> No one fails to feel delight when hearing Kalidasa's verses; they are sweet and dense, like clusters of buds.
>
> The 7th-century poet and novelist, Banabhatta

◁ CLASSICAL DRAMA
Indian classical theater centers around stories from history or mythology, and brings together an exciting mixture of mime, music, poetry, and dance.

FOLK THEATER

In the 7th to 8th centuries a new literary movement emerged that dominated Indian theater for the next thousand years. This was based on the oral folk tradition of storytelling. The storyteller, who sometimes elaborated the story with paintings and comic, exaggerated facial expressions, was often accompanied by musical companions. Folk theater put story at its heart, taking the myths and legends of India and the Buddhist Jataka tales as its inspiration. Where classical theater was urban, sophisticated, and fixed in performance and content, the folk tradition was rural, simple, and flexible. Whether played out by a single storyteller or a theater group on an open-air stage, rural theater is exciting, and may contain an unexpected element. It is often given a contemporary edge, even if the story is taken from the epics: an actor may choose to comment on the corrupt practices of the village head sitting in the audience, for example, or raise the issues of drinking water or education.

REGIONAL THEATER TODAY

The folk tradition gave birth to the wide variety of regional theater forms that exist today. This variety stemmed from the different languages of the regions, which influenced the melodic textures and patterns of plays, making them particular to the local dialect, and contributing greatly to the *rasa* of the performance. The tradition lives on in forms such as the Harikathas in Maharashtra, Gujarat, and Tamil Nadu; the Krishna Gathas of Uttar Pradesh; and the Burrakatha of Andhra Pradesh.

▽ SHAKUNTALA, THE MODEST MAIDEN
Kalidasa's most popular play, the tragic-romantic *Shakuntala*, is considered by many to be the most important piece of dramatic writing in India's history.

A DEMOCRATIC ART
Puppetry in India has always been used as a form of communication, for stories real and imagined. Performances took place in the palaces and on the streets.

puppetry

Puppetry has a long tradition in India, dating back to the Indus Valley Civilization, c.2500 BCE. The archaeological sites of Harappa and Mohenjo-daro have yielded ancient terra-cotta puppets in the form of a bull with a detachable head and a monkey that glides up and down a rod. The *Natya Shastra* (*see p.246*) and *Shilappadikaram*, a Tamil classic, c.200 CE, both mention a character called Sutradhar—literally, "the holder of strings." In traditional theater today, the role of Sutradhar belongs to the person who "controls" the story, by providing the links between different acts of the play. In the post-Vedic philosophical text, *Srimad Bhagavata*, the Supreme Being is described as a puppeteer who holds the three strings of the characteristics of the human being. People are seen as puppets in the hands of the Great God; and the puppeteer finds himself in a similar position—the puppets are called *puttalika* or *puttika* in Sanskrit, meaning "little sons." They are seen as an extension of the human being, and are treated reverentially by the puppeteers, who offer prayers before and after their performances. When at last the puppets have decayed beyond use, like humans they are immersed in a sacred river.

> The puppets danced with war-like vigor, just as goddess Durga danced to destroy the demons.
>
> Ilango Adigal, *Shilappadikaram*

Traditional puppet theater adopted stories from literature, as well as local myths and legends. Traveling troupes of puppeteers often told heroic stories about the royal family that supported them, and acted as a form of mass communication as they toured around a region. They were also seen as significant in a religious sense, and were often invited into villages to perform at ceremonies, or to invoke the gods' help. The tales of Krishna's love for Radha, and his devoted milkmaids, is one of the most popular themes, and these pieces of folk theater often use local dialogue and music, ensuring that style and presentation differ enormously from one region to another. Puppeteers today tend to choose their themes according to the occasion: at a wedding they might perform *Girija Kalyana* (Girija's Wedding) or at a funeral, *Swargarohana* (Ascent to Paradise).

THE FOUR PUPPET TYPES

All four varieties of Indian puppets—the glove, string, rod, and shadow—have long histories within India. Wherever they emerged, they incorporated the regional styles of dance, music, and theater, but also a broader range of local arts such as painting, sculpture, and costume design. The puppeteers were well versed in

RAJASTHANI STRING PUPPETS
The puppetry plays of Rajasthan are usually narrated by female puppeteers, accompanied by music, whistling, and the loud beats of a *dholak* drum.

Hindu philosophy, religion, and poetry; they acted as narrators, singers, and musicians, and most could perform in a wide range of languages and dialects.

Glove puppets are popular in Kerala, Orissa, Uttar Pradesh, and West Bengal. The most interesting ones are those from Kerala, where they are known as *Pavakoothu* or *Pavakathakali*. These ornate puppets stand around 2 ft (0.6 m) high, and they are delicately carved from wood into highly stylized versions of the Kathakali dancer, dressed in the traditional headgear and long flowing skirts. The Orissa glove puppets, in contrast, represent a rural folk tradition. Their stories center on Krishna and Radha, whose love stories are sung to local folk music and interspersed with comic sequences. The puppets are colorfully dressed and painted with definite expressions, leaving no doubt as to the emotions each represents.

String puppets are India's most common form of puppets. The Kathputli string puppets from Rajasthan are legendary, and their puppeteers claim an ancestry of royal patronage. The puppets are carved from a single piece of wood to stand around 18 in (0.5 m) high, and look like large dolls with exaggerated facial features. They have no legs, and are manipulated by strings running from their neck, shoulders, and hands to the puppeteer's fingers.

The tradition of shadow puppets derives from the visual arts, such as the scroll paintings of southern India, Bengal, and Rajasthan. These puppets are representative not of people but of their shadows, and this is demonstrated through the translucent quality of the leather from which they are made. During the performance, the flat puppets are moved behind a lighted screen—which may be as simple as a white sheet—while the surrounding area is kept dark for maximum dramatic effect. The shadow puppets of Orissa, Kerala, and Andhra Pradesh draw on the great epics for their material. The most exciting shadow puppetry comes from Orissa, where the "human" puppets are joined on stage by those of animals, trees, mountains, chariots, and other pieces of the landscape. Known as *Ravana Chhaya* (Shadow of Ravana), this form of puppetry is still very popular in both villages and urban areas.

> The movements of a man without a sensitive conscience are like the simulation of life by marionettes moved by strings.
>
> Thiruvalluvar, *Kurals*

India has a long history of rod puppets, although the traditional ones from West Bengal and Orissa that moved east to Java and Japan are now more or less extinct. Rod puppets can still be found today within the states of Orissa, Jharkhand, and West Bengal, where an operatic form of *Putul Nacha* (puppet dance) is performed by large teams of 15 to 18 people.

LEATHER SHADOW PUPPETS Shadow puppets, which may stand up to 6½ ft (2 m) tall, derive from the scroll paintings of India, and are mentioned in the Puranas and the Buddhist Jatakas.

the moving image

The world's most prolific movie-making country, India releases up to 1,200 new films every year, in 16 languages and 1,600 dialects. Hindi films are distributed nationally and they generate the largest box office numbers, but most films are also released in South Indian languages, such as Telugu, Tamil, and Malayalam. Overall, the Indian film market extends far beyond India's borders, into Asia, Europe, and the United States. The art of Indian filmmaking is equally far-reaching, drawing on Hollywood practices for studio-building, international cinema movements for techniques, and Indian history and culture for shape and themes. From renowned director Satyajit Ray to Bollywood, India's changing identity is reflected through its films.

India's film industry dates its beginnings to July 7, 1896, when six French films were exhibited at Bombay's exclusive Watson's Hotel. The ten-minute showing featured six scenes, including a train arrival and the demolition of a building. Two years later, Hiralal Sen, India's first film director, filmed stage productions from Calcutta's Classic Theatre and presented them as added theatrical attractions.

The first Indian feature film was 1913's *Raja Harischandra* by Dada Saheb Phalke, the father of Indian cinema. Phalke saw the European film *Life of Christ* at a time when the nationalist philosophy of *swadeshi*—promoting the use of Indian products and businesses within India—was becoming popular, and he decided to make a film centering on Indian mythology. Indian myths had always been a part of everyday life, and provided a shared narrative for the entire subcontinent. Phalke's faith in their enduring appeal was not misplaced. The resulting movie, centred on a story from the *Mahabharata*, was an immediate success. Several mythologicals followed, including *Mohini Bhasmasur* (1913), which introduced India's first screen actress, Kamalabai Gokhale, and Phalke's most successful film, *Lanka Dahan* (1917), based on the *Ramayana*.

> *Lanka Dahan* was a minor masterpiece ... The spectacle of Hanuman's figure becoming progressively diminutive as he flew higher and higher was simply awe-inspiring.
>
> J.B.H. Wadia, founder of Wadia Movietone Studios, Bombay

By 1920, India was producing nearly 30 films a year, and several studios, producers, and distribution companies had developed. The first was the Royal Bioscope Company, and this was followed by other major players, including Madan Theatres Limited, which released *Raja Harischandra*; New Theatres, which produced *Devdas* (1935), the story of a tragic love affair between a rich man and a poor woman; and Prabhat Film Companies, which released *Sant Tukaram* (1936), a film about the famous poet-saint of Maharashtra. Some movies, such as the hugely popular *Devdas*, went on to be remade many times and in many different Indian languages, including Hindu, Bengali, Telugu, and Tamil.

THE SOUND ERA

India's first film with sound dialogue, *Alam Ara*, appeared in 1931. Directed by Ardeshir Irani, it starred Prithviraj Kapoor, founder of one of Bollywood's acting dynasties. No copies of this landmark film remain, but its astounding success was attributed by many to its large number of popular songs, which numbered somewhere between seven and twenty. The film's popularity led the fledgling industry to drastically increase the number of songs in all of its movies—music had always been an essential component of India's arts, and with *Alam Ara*, it also became an important part of Indian cinema.

SALAAM BOMBAY
The director Mira Nair's award-winning debut film, *Salaam Bombay* (1988), portrayed the lives of homeless people in Bombay through the eyes of a child.

Despite the 1930s depression, Indian film production increased to 200 films per year, produced in its three major film centers: Bombay (Mumbai), Calcutta (Kolkata), and Madras (Chennai). The latter two cities produced regional films, while Bombay made national works. India's first color feature was *Kisan Kanya* (1937), and by the 1950s Indian movies had become large, glamorous, full-color musical vehicles producing Indian movie stars. These actors and actresses were often helped by the technological breakthrough of playback singing, through which they could lip-synch the songs of established Indian singers.

Equally important to the expanding breadth of Indian cinema was the development of popular films with social themes. Among them were Debaki Bose's *Chandidas* (1932), P.C. Barua's *Devdas* (1935), and *Sant Tukaram* (1937), the first Indian film to win an international award, at the Venice Film Festival. Melodramas also gained popularity in the 1930s, particularly the German Expressionist-influenced *Kunku* (1937).

INDEPENDENCE

Upon India's independence in 1947, changes in the film industry followed. During this period, studios were largely closed or transformed into freelance sites; taxation on filmmaking increased. The state also took more of a voice in the filmmaking process, and in 1961, it formed the Film Finance Corporation to support new filmmakers. Melodramas and socially conscious films gained import as art forms that represented the entire country. Serious filmmakers emerged, such as Bengali director Satayajit Ray, whose 1953 film, *Pather Panchali,* and subsequent works of the Apu Trilogy won recognition at the Cannes Film Festival and introduced the world to Indian cinema. Ray's realistic, humanistic style has influenced India's directors ever since, most notably Mrinal Sen and Ritwik Ghatak, who explored the realities of the lower middle class.

Socially conscious films such as Mehboob Khan's 1957 Oscar-winning *Mother India*, Guru Dutt's *Pyasa* (1957), and Bimal Roy's *Do Bigha Zamin* (1953) held sway during the 1950s, but the later part of the 20th century was dominated by big-budget, quirky films, such as Raj Kapoor's *Bobby* (1973), Ramesh Sippy's *Sholay* (1975), and Kamal Amrohi's *Pakeeza* (1972). In the 1980s, the state's Film Finance Corporation stepped in to support the pro–social justice films of directors Mrinal Sen and others.

Toward the end of the 20th century, the appeal of song-and-dance commercial movies grew even stronger. Film budgets were dominated by massive sets and star salaries, while music videos and plots about teenage romances also increased the musical film's appeal. The 1990s teen musical romance *Maine Pyar Kiya* became so popular that with new scenes added, it was re-released repeatedly. It is part of the "Bollywood" genre, named after India's best known movie region, Bombay, now renamed Mumbai. "Bollywood" is the popular name for a Hindi cinema that blends Mumbai and Hollywood influences to create a rich mix of music and topical themes. It is more active than Hollywood, making more films and selling more tickets to viewers, not only in India but throughout the Middle East and most of Asia. Bollywood films have enjoyed only limited success in the West, but their popularity is increasing, and some actors, such as former beauty queen Aishwarya Rai, have become international stars.

▽ **BOLLYWOOD MUSICALS**
Bollywood is best known for its extravagant song and dance movies, which often center on a powerful love story and carry a strong moral message.

painting and sculpture

The *Chitrasutra*, a section of the *Vishnudharmottara Purana* texts written in the 5th century, is thought to be the world's oldest treatise on art. It provides a detailed account of the various schools, techniques, and ideals of Indian painting, and specifies the two-fold aim of the fine arts: to communicate an emotion (*rasa*), and to induce particular spiritual states of mind (*bhava*). The painter's aesthetic, like all of the Indian arts, is defined by the *rasas* (*see pp. 246–247*)—the "taste" or "flavor" of a work of art. The artist aims to distill one of these emotions so purely that the viewer experiences it and recognizes its abstract, universal nature, and through this, begins to transcend his or her own subjectivity. The fine arts, like all of India's arts, are ultimately a path to the divine.

India's pictorial vision is a vivid, lively, sophisticated, bold, and, of course, colorful one. It combines a love of naturalism with an impulse to decorate all kinds of surfaces and spaces, from a scroll painting to the walls of a chamber or temple altar. The impulse to adorn and ornament is applied to mud, stone, metal, cloth, and paper through paint, and it emerges in a huge variety of forms in different parts of India.

THE DANCING GIRL
The sophisticated artistic modeling of the *Dancing Girl* of Mohenjo-daro prefigured Europe's similar Hellenistic forms by over 3,000 years.

THE ART OF AJANTA
The prayer halls of the Ajanta caves contain paintings and sculptures of such extraordinary beauty and grace they are considered masterpieces of Buddhist art.

EARLY ROCK AND CAVE PAINTINGS

The prehistoric cave paintings carved into the sandstone rocks of Bhimbetka, a World Heritage Site in Central India, were created some 10,000 years ago. They are a cornucopia of line drawings and engravings depicting scenes of hunting, feasting, and dancing. An engraving of a deer shows fronds of grass in its stomach, signifying its recent meal. This is just one example, perhaps the earliest, of the Indian artist's kinship with nature; a thread that continued to run through the entire story of Indian art.

Another important strand of prehistory is the Indus Valley Art, dating back to the 2nd century BCE, which is particularly known for its statuettes, such as the famous bronze sculpture of the *Dancing Girl* of Mohenjo-daro (*see below, left*). This signaled an increased sophistication of craftsmanship that would later combine with new Greek influences to produce the iconic Buddhist art of the Gupta era—the Golden Age of Indian arts and sciences—in the Gandhara and Kushan schools of art of the first millennium CE. Until this time, the Buddha had been represented by stupas (dome-shaped monuments), or symbols, such as a tree, an empty throne, or footprints, but during the Gupta era he was increasingly represented in human form, seated, standing or even lying, with lowered eyes and a serene expression. The Gupta era created the definitive forms and gestures in which the Buddha is still depicted today.

Sarnath (where the Buddha preached his first sermon) became an important center of art during the Gupta period. The style of this renowned school of art can be seen especially in the World Heritage Sites of the Ajanta caves (2nd to 7th centuries) and the Ellora caves (6th to 10th centuries), two sets of caves near Mumbai where monks painted and carved an extraordinary series of murals into volcanic rock. A total of 29 caves in Ajanta, and 34 caves at Ellora were created as beautifully decorated temples and prayer halls. Those at Ajanta depict Buddhist tales, while the Ellora caves celebrate Buddhism, Hinduism, and Jainism. The sites are illuminated with magnificent paintings of Buddhist tales, stories from Hindu mythology, and a multitude of scenes of kings, queens, merchants, beggars, lovers, musicians, elephants, and monkeys—all garlanded with lotus blossoms and curling vines.

The Gupta Empire adopted Hinduism as its official religion, resulting in a resurgence of images of Hindu gods and goddesses. The 6th-century roofs and walls of the Badami caves in Karnataka and the rock-hewn caves of Ranigumpha and Udaygiri in Orissa, created as early as the 2nd century, demonstrate this. Their painted murals and stone sculptures of gods and goddesses in amorous poses are early examples of the *shringar rasa*, the erotic mood, which would attain its peak with the creation of the famous 10th-century temple complex of Khajuraho (*see pp. 274–275 and pp. 352–355*).

THE CHOLA SCULPTURES

The highlight of the medieval age of Indian art (880–1279) is the outstanding school of Chola sculptures cast in bronze and *ashtadhatu*, a compound of eight metals. The Chola sculptures are a throwback to the Mohenjo-daro figurines, and the most famous example is the Chola *Nataraja*: Shiva, the cosmic dancer. This statue has become the supreme statement of Hindu art, embodying everything that is common to Indian art forms: myth, symbolism, movement, and mysticism.

The figure of the *Nataraja,* the Lord of the Dance, is the image used to profile Indian culture all over the world, and it is a perfect example of the deeply philosophical roots that lie at the heart of all of the Indian arts. The home of the dancing Shiva is the Nataraja Temple at Chidambaram, Tamil Nadu, where the sculpture rests in the Chitsabha, the Hall of Consciousness. In the *Nataraja*, Shiva is seen dancing the *Ananda Tandava*, the cosmic Dance of Bliss. His left leg, lifted across the body, with the foot pointing downward, represents "refuge for the devotee," which is reinforced in the protective gesture of the left hand, pointing toward the raised leg. The right leg is planted firmly on a demon, the personification of *maya* (illusion) and ignorance, who tries to lead humankind astray.

> Without the knowledge of dance, the knowledge of sculptural art cannot be known.
>
> The *Vishnudharmottara Purana*

The front right hand is held in the gesture of *abhaya*, signifying that the devotee should "be without fear," while the two upper hands, which frame the figure, carry fire and a *damaru* (an hourglass-shaped drum). The drum symbolizes the vibrating sound of creation—Om—while the fire represents Shiva's power of destruction, leaping from his hands to devour the whole wheel of the cosmos—the field within which Shiva dances.

The *Nataraja* Shiva balances the creative and the destructive powers of the universe, and promises that his devotees can be transported from a world of ignorance, to salvation and ultimately *moksha*—true liberation.

THE NATARAJA Shiva's dance symbolizes *pancha krityas*, the five divine acts: creation, sustenance, dissolution, concealment, and the bestowing of grace.

SYMBOLS AND ARTISTIC CONCEPTS

The *rasa* theory of aesthetics, whereby an emotion is recognized by the viewer and causes a corresponding feeling and state of mind, is evident in all Indian art forms (*see also pp.246–247*). Another unique Hindu concept called Ardhanareshwara—the unity of the male and female principle in every living thing—is also represented in many art forms, but particularly in sculpture. The giant Trimurti sculpture (810–1260) at Elephanta, near Mumbai, is one famous example. This three-headed sculpture shows Shiva on the right side, Parvati on his left, and a benign face in the center, symbolizing the harmonious state that results when the male and female principles are combined.

Indian philosophy also gave birth to a symbolic language that could be used to represent complex concepts. This includes, for instance, the *chakra*, or revolving wheel of time, which symbolizes both the circularity of time and the spiritual and psychic centers of energy in the human body (*see p.227*). The *padma* (lotus), is a symbol of purity and the universal creative force that springs from the earth, unmindful of the dirt from which it raises its beautiful head. Another frequently seen symbol, the *Ananta* (serpent), represents a life-giving force, and the infinite ocean from which all life emerged and will one day be resubmerged. Also known as *Shesha*, the serpent is the symbol of time, watchfulness, and wisdom.

Surya, the sun, represents light, birth, death, and the artist—the sun is said to "paint" the world as it controls the black of the night, the yellow of the moon, the blue of the sky, and the green of trees and plants. Other symbols within Indian art include the *swastika*—symbolizing the fourfold aspects of creation and motion, and the union of opposites; the *Purnakalasa* (overflowing pot)—which symbolizes creativity and prosperity; the wish-fulfilling creeper plant (*Kalpalata*) and tree (*Kalpavriksha*)—symbolizing imagination and creativity; and *lingam* and *yoni*—the male and female fertility symbols.

Birds and animals are also popular symbols of Indian art. The cow is the archetypal symbol of Indian culture, signifying motherhood and fertility. The deer is symbolic of erotic desire, while the elephant and peacock both signify wealth, prosperity, and good fortune. The horse represents male energy and bravery; the parrot and the turtle are symbols of love and fertility; while the fish—a particular favorite of folk art—is the definitive emblem of fertility.

◁ MUGHAL MINIATURE
The Mughal paintings were a brilliant synthesis of Persian ideas and Indian techniques, which focused mainly on courtly life and aristocratic pastimes.

MINIATURE PAINTINGS

Indian painting is often classified as belonging to court, temple, or folk forms of art. But such distinctions are arbitrary. Until Mughal rule in the early 16th century, the royal courts were not a closed society and the same painters would work for both the rulers and the elite, such as bankers, merchants, and landlords. The quality of their wares differed only in terms of the material used and the time allowed for their execution, both of which depended on the remuneration paid to the artist, who usually operated as a freelance.

The Mughals introduced the idea of exclusive court studios, which were then copied by the local governors and minor nobility, whose artists were also quick to integrate the new miniature styles. The energy, inventiveness, and lyricism found in the Mughal studios combined the aesthetics of Persian art with native Indian sensibilities and artistic talents—especially of artists

THE KALIGHAT SCHOOL
The bold, contemporary style of the 19th-century Kalighat paintings was a highly inventive aesthetic achievement by the artists of Bengal.

from the hereditary painter families of Gujarat, who were originally trained to work in a folk style for minor courts and others with modest means.

At first glance, a Mughal miniature painting can appear to be nothing more than a flat, perspective-less, cluttered pastoral setting, peopled by figures. Yet these scenes are not detached visions of artistic expression; most are *ragamalas*, or visual depictions of the *ragas*—the musical modes of Indian classical music (*see pp.248–249*) which are said to "color" and convey a mood and emotion. The six principal *ragas* are sung during the six seasons of the Indian year: summer, monsoon, fall, early winter, deep winter, and spring. These seasons are portrayed in the paintings, which also aim to convey the spirit of the melodic *raga* itself. The miniatures employ distinctive strong lines and bold colors, and often incorporate silver, gold, and gemstones among the mineral- and vegetable-colored paints, on a substrate of paper, wood, leather, marble or cloth.

Besides the Mughal school, the Pahari schools of miniatures such as Guler, Kulu, and Kangra, and the Rajasthani genre also provided artists with a wide scope for creative expression. The Rajasthani miniatures reflect the Jaipur school's fascination with the richness of life, portraying fierce battles, seductive women, and rich scenes from court life. The later 18th-century Kangra miniatures were also influenced by Mughal art, but they remain distinctive for their use of cool colors and naturalistic style, while the Tanjore paintings of southern India often feature Krishna and Shiva, reflecting the mythical source of music and the *ragas*.

FOLK ART

Folk art has always flourished in India, and is traditionally used for marking rituals and festivals in public and private spaces. Whereas classical art was largely created by men, folk art has always been the preserve of women. The school of Madhubani paintings, from Madhuban in the Mithila district of Bihar, is the home of women artists who have famously passed down the art and ritual of decorating the walls, floors, and objects of their houses through the generations. These paintings are used to celebrate festivals and rites of passage (*samskara*), to mark an occasion and to bring blessings. Female relatives may gather, for instance, to decorate a bridal chamber with images of divine couples, such as Shiva and Parvati, or Rama and Sita, alongside symbolic figures, such as parrots and turtles for love, fish for fertility, and the moon for long life.

> Painting cleanses the mind and curbs anxiety, augments future good, causes the greatest delight, kills the evils of bad dreams and pleases the household deity.
>
> The *Vishnudharmottara Purana*

Ordinary people, from antiquity and still today, paint their doorways and decorate their floors with the auspicious *rangoli* (*see pp.228–229*), creating a fresh design every morning. These designs use easily available vegetable dyes and common household materials such as the white of *atta* (ground wheat powder), the yellow of turmeric, the blue of the indigo plant, and the red of gulmohar or champak flowers. In working with these natural dyes, people are said to rely on the kindness of nature for their colors.

RAJA RAVI VARMA
The best-known Indian artist of the 19th century, Varma integrated European realism and Indian tradition in his famous portraits.

MADHUBANI STYLE
Women in the villages around Madhuban have been practicing their folk art for centuries, but they have only been recognized as "artists" in the last 30 years.

MADHUBANI FOLK ART

The Madhubani paintings of North India feature scenes from mythology and nature. They are characterized by simple lines and bright colors, in paints made from local plants and minerals.

From the Golden Age of the 5th century onward, there was a flowering of Indian literature. A succession of poets, dramatists, and prose writers produced a stream of outstanding works in the ancient Sanskrit language, which included religious writings, epic and lyric poetry, plays, novels, and a variety of books on the arts and sciences. Together, they add up to one of the great world literatures, flourishing especially in the 5th and 7th centuries, building on the foundations laid in much earlier, pre-Classical texts, most notably the Vedas and the great epics.

finding a language

Early works such as the scriptural texts of the Vedas (c.1500 BCE) were hugely influential within India and remain so to this day. They were written in Sanskrit, the language of the Aryans and the Brahmanical hierarchy that dominated Indian culture until the arrival of the Mughals in the 16th century.

The Vedas inspired a series of commentaries, including the Upanishads, which form the foundation of Hindu philosophy. These writings are valued for their influence on Hinduism, their lyrical language, and their subtle use of philosophical concepts. The two great Indian epics, the *Ramayana* (*see pp.272–273*) and the *Mahabharata* (*see pp.268–269*), date back to c.200 BCE, but their engaging characters and dramatic stories have ensured that they remain among the most popular of all Indian works.

Sanskrit was widely used as a literary language until the 11th century, when its use declined and writers turned to languages such as Hindi, Marathi, Tamil, Telugu, and—from the Mughal period onward—Urdu. But Sanskrit was still used by some writers, and there have been various attempts at reviving the language, notably following Indian independence in 1947.

Pali was the one other major language of early Indian literature. This was the tongue in which the Buddhist scriptures were set down from the 5th century BCE onward. The major Buddhist Pali texts are the scriptures of the Tripitaka, the Jataka stories (tales of creatures and humans who are earlier incarnations of the Buddha) and the Dhammapada. There were also Buddhist works in Sanskrit, including two epics by the 1st-century poet Asvaghosa: the *Buddhacarita*, describing the Buddha's life, and the *Saundaryananda*, which focuses on the conversion of the Buddha's half-brother, Nanda.

THE CLASSICAL AGE

The greatest writer of the classical period was Kalidasa, who was active around 400 CE (*see pp. 252–253*). As well as writing three successful plays, Kalidasa was the author of a large body of poetry. His epic, *Raghuvamsa*, tells the story of the dynasty of which Rama, the hero of the *Ramayana*, was a prominent member. His long poem *Meghaduta* (The Cloud Messenger) is loved for the its beauty of language, as are his collections of shorter lyrics, which are also models of clarity.

> Of what use is the poet's poem,
> Of what use is the bowman's dart,
> Unless another's senses reel
> When it sticks quivering in the heart?
>
> Anonymous Sanskrit poem

The Indian love of *katha* (story) surfaced spectacularly around this time in the *Panchatantra*, a collection of animal fables by the storyteller Vishnu Sharma. These simple but wise animal tales bear many resemblances to the

CLASSICAL LITERATURE
FICTION AND FABLE

◁ **THE PANCHATANTRA FABLES**
The moral lessons in the *Panchatantra* tales warn of the losing of gains, and the consequences of rash action.

later fables of Aesop. The original five books contained 84 stories, with others interwoven among them, connecting them in the traditional Indian style. The stories traveled all around the world; between the 6th and the 15th centuries the collection was translated into Persian (Pahalvi), Syrian, Arabic, Greek, Hebrew, Latin, and German, after which the tales spread rapidly throughout Europe.

There were several notable Sanskrit writers in the 7th century. Bhartrhari, for example, produced three collections of short poems on the subjects of love, justice, and *moksha* (liberation). His poems on love are especially prized for their tender descriptions of passion and their questioning of love's consequences and outcomes. Other writers of the period excelled in prose. Bana is known for two prose works, a novel called *Kadambari,* a highly complex love narrative, and a work of history called *Harsacarita*, which celebrates the life of Bana's royal patron, the Buddhist emperor, Harsadeva. Another major prose writer of the 7th century, Dandin, was the author of *Dasakumaracarita* (History of Ten Princes), which paints vivid pictures of both the upper and lower classes of urban Gupta India.

Early Indian writers produced a profusion of prose treatises on all kinds of subjects, and many of these texts date from the classical period of Sanskrit literature. These books were called *sutras*, from a word meaning "thread." However, the thread of their argument was sometimes hard to follow because of their compressed, aphoristic, often obscure language, and consequently they inspired many further works of commentary and explanation. Some of the *sutras*, such as the Brahma and yoga *sutras*, were on religious subjects. Others were on different topics; one of the most famous is the *Kamasutra* (*see pp.274–75*), which covers the subject of *kama*, or pleasure, particularly of a physical nature. Other *sutras* and treatises covered scientific subjects. The scholars of the Gupta period, for example, excelled at astronomy, and this science is documented in books known as *siddhantas*. There are also works on mathematics from this era.

Although the classical period came to a close with the decline in the use of Sanskrit in the 12th century, a number of later writers continued to use the language in their works. Two outstanding later exponents of the tongue were the poets Somadeva and Vidyapati. Somadeva lived in the 11th century and he is still remembered for the *Katha-saritsagara* (Ocean of Stories). This is a huge collection of poetic retellings of Indian folk tales, and the best known story collection in Sanskrit. Like the *Arabian Nights*, this vast work is a framed narrative in which an overarching story generates a multitude of shorter tales.

The literature of the 12th century was dominated by a lyrical epic called the *Gita Govinda*, a devotional Sanskrit poem by Jayadeva, a writer from Orissa. It celebrates the great love of Krishna and Radha, and the legend that accompanies it reflects the eternal mingling of God and humankind in Indian life. The poet is said to have suffered a form of writer's block when he reached a critical part of the poem, so he broke off from writing to bathe in the river; as he bathed, a divine power continued to write in his place.

▷ **THE GODDESS SARASWATI**
Saraswati, the goddess of learning and wisdom, is also identified with Vak, the Vedic goddess of speech. She is therefore considered to be the source of all literature, art, and music.

the vedas and the upanishads

In the beginning was the word. The people called it *Vak*, the heard sound. Its primordial symbol—*Om*—symbolizes the manifest and the unmanifest universe, the heard and the unheard; it is the vibration of life itself.

This idea, which arose around 4,000 years ago, was so powerful that it became embodied in a deity: Vak Devi, the goddess of speech and learning. Traditionally, the first word breathed into a newborn's ear is "*Vak,*" and at the end of each day's recitation of the Guru Granth Sahib, the Sikh scripture, the priest pulls out of it, randomly, a *Vak* or commandment for the congregation.

> All *devas* (gods) have their abode in me, and I look after each one of them. I am the efficient and the material cause of the very creation, and I am sustaining the same. I am Knowledge and Enlightenment.
>
> Vak Devi, from the *Rig Veda*, Book 5

The goddess Vak is sometimes identified with the goddess Saraswati, who is said to have revealed the ancient mystical scriptures known as the Vedas.

The four Vedas—the *Rig Veda*, *Yajur Veda*, *Atharva Veda*, and *Sama Veda*—are the oldest sacred texts in the world. Written in Sanskrit, they are a series of poems or hymns dating back to around 1500 BCE, which were used for the ritual worship of the Vedic gods. Their compilation was no miraculous revelation, at a fixed time but spanned a millennium, from the Bronze Age to the Iron Age. They are considered to be *sruti*, "that which is heard"; they were divine revelations, not texts composed by humankind. Later texts, such as the Puranas and the great epics, are *smrti*: "that which is remembered."

The word "veda" comes from the Sanskrit word *vid*, meaning "to know." The *Rig Veda*—"Knowledge of the Verses"—is the oldest Vedic text, containing about 1,000 hymns praising the various deities to whom they are addressed. The hymns were recited by the Brahmins (priests) during their sacrificial fire rituals. The *Yajur Veda*—"Knowledge of the Sacrifice"—contains verses and exact details of these rituals, while the *Sama Veda*—"Knowledge of the Chants"—is a selection of verses from the *Rig Veda* arranged in a particular order, with musical notation. The *Sama Veda* was hugely influential in the sound and styling of Indian classical music (*see pp.248–249*)

The *Atharva Veda*—"Knowledge of the Fire Priest"—is very different in tone and content from the other Vedas: it is a collection of verses and incantations for magical spells. Although it was eventually adopted by the *Brahmins*, it is thought to belong to the pre-Aryan Harappan culture of the indigenous people (*see pp.218–219*). While the *Rig Veda* was used mainly by the priestly class, the *Atharva Veda* featured more functional gods, who could be revered in simple, domestic settings, without priests or elaborate ritual.

SURYA, THE SUN GOD
The three most important gods of the Vedic period were the sons of Dyaus (Heaven) and Prithivi (Earth): Surya, Indra, and Agni—the gods of sun, storm, and fire.

VARUNA, GOD OF THE SKY
Varuna was the Vedic god of the sky and the guardian of the cosmic law. His rope symbolizes the transgressions with which humankind fetters and strangles itself.

THE VEDIC GODS

The Vedas feature a large number of deities who embody natural forces (*see pp.228–229*). The chief Vedic deity is Indra, who takes many forms and has many names, such as Meghavahana ("having clouds as a vehicle") and Puramdara ("destroyer of cities"). The *Rig Veda* describes his main attributes as strength and power, and, like the other Vedic gods, he intervenes in the affairs of the world when things go wrong. In the *Rig Veda*, for example, Indra saves the world when he kills Vritra, a serpent demon who has locked away all of the world's water in some mountain caves. As the water rushes out, Indra places Agni—the god of fire—in the sky to provide heat, and Varuna, god of the sky, in the heavens, to watch over and maintain the world. Varuna's eye then becomes Surya, the sun god. Other Vedic gods included the twin Asvins, handsome young heroes who represented the dawn and the dusk; Vayu, the god of air and wind; Maruti, the storm god; Shakti, the goddess of power; and Vak, the goddess of speech. Some of the Vedic gods, such as Agni and Yama, the god of death, outlast the Vedas to become Hindu gods. The mighty Vishnu is also mentioned about 100 times in the *Rig Veda*, but as a minor god—he had not yet acquired the supreme status he was to hold in the Hindu faith.

> Not even nothing existed then;
> No air yet, nor a heaven.
> Who encased and kept it where?
> Was water in the darkness there?
> Neither deathlessness, nor decay—
> No, nor the rhythm of night and day:
> The self-existent, with breath *sans* air:
> That, and that alone was there.
>
> Creation Hymn from the *Rig Veda*

THE UPANISHADS

The 108 Upanishads are part of a great wave of religious and philosophical texts produced in the centuries after the Vedas which comment on them and develop many of the concepts raised therein. They form an evolving body of texts written by many authors over hundreds of years, from the 7th century BCE to the 16th century CE, and include some of the most widely read of all Indian writings.

The Upanishads are philosophical treatises, written mostly in a question-and-answer form, which was a favored device of Indian writers. They are post-Vedic observations on the physical and nonphysical worlds, and the existence and governance of mind, matter, and spirit. These later texts include discussion on a number of concepts that would become cornerstones of the Hindu faith, such as the Absolute (*Brahman*), the true self (*atman*), illusion (*maya*), and the relationships between these concepts. As mystical and spiritual interpretations of the Vedas, the Upanishads have long been regarded as *Vedanta*, meaning "the end part of the Vedas." These later texts caused a quiet revolution in Indian thought, formulating a new set of ideas that gradually moved the culture away from the Vedic gods toward the ideas and deities of Hinduism. They suggest four goals of life—*purusharthas*—to which a Hindu should aspire. By living a life of *dharma* (righteous conduct), while also paying due attention to *artha* (the means of earning wealth), and *kama* (sensual fulfillment), the Hindu can finally expect to find *moksha* (liberation). This in turn is said to lead to a state of absolute bliss (*swarga*) and absolute enlightenment (*kaivalya*). These philosophical concepts, which developed through the exploratory nature of India's earliest texts, were to become the key tenets of Hinduism.

APAH, THE VEDIC WATERS
The *Rig Veda* identified "the Waters" as the first home of the Supreme Being and the birthplace of humankind, imbuing all water with the power of purification.

the mahabharata

The *Mahabharata* is one of the oldest and longest epics in world literature; some parts are believed to date back to the 7th century BCE, while the form in which it is now known was written in Sanskrit around 300 BCE. Its 90,000 two-line stanzas make it eight times as long as Homer's *Iliad* and *Odyssey* put together, and three times the length of the Bible.

The main story tells of a great war between two rival sets of princely cousins, the Pandavas and the Kauravas. Woven in an intricate design around this are hundreds of myths and stories about kings and queens, yogis and gurus, and gods and goddesses. The *Mahabharata* is an excellent example of Hinduism's eternal preoccupation with the battle between good and evil. In its search for the truth, the epic travels along a road that continually takes detours but returns always to the core message: the supremacy of *dharma*, or righteous living.

Traditionally, the *Mahabharata's* authorship is ascribed to the sage Vyasa, who also features in the epic. The opening stanzas recount the story of how Vyasa asked Ganesha, the elephant-headed god, to help him by transcribing his dictation. Ganesha agreed, on condition that Vyasa never pause in his recitation. In the rush of keeping pace with Vyasa, however, Ganesha's pen failed, and rather than break the flow of the transcription, he broke off a part of his tusk to serve as a replacement. This explains why some Hindus invoke Ganesha before beginning any major task or ceremony: he is the god who brooks no obstacles.

All manner of magical morphs feature in this story: men turn into women, animals, gods, and even hydra-headed demons. Each one engages in betrayal, love, revenge, or sorcery, while masking his or her true identity to pursue a personal agenda. There is an endless stream of blessings and curses, cast by people with magical powers, and of unfailing vows that bind people and events in an implacable way. The laws of *karma* play out their unbending course; all this and much more is wrapped up in moral and existential questions, making the *Mahabharata* a unique cornucopia of literary and philosophical material.

MORALITY TALES WITHIN THE TALE One of the tales within the *Mahabharata* tells the story of how the gods tricked the evil Sunda and Upasunda by creating the beautiful Apsara Tilottama (*center*).

The story begins with the death of King Bharata, head of the Kuru family and ruler of the kingdom of Hastinapur in North India. On his death, two strands of the Kuru family—the Pandavas and the Kauravas—begin a long struggle to seize control of the throne. On the king's death, his descendant Shantanu becomes king. He meets and marries Satyavati, the daughter of a lowly fisherman, who already has a son called Vyasa. King Shantanu promises her that if she marries him, any son she has in the future will become king. She agrees, but after the sons they have together die prematurely, Satyavati persuades her first-born, Vyasa the poet, to cohabit with their widows, in order to produce an heir. The widows' dislike of his unkempt appearance leads the first one to close her eyes in disgust as he approaches her, while the second turns pale. Consequently the two sons born to them, Dhritarashtra and Pandu, are born blind and yellow-skinned. The older son, blind Dhritarashtra, is unable to rule, and so his pale brother Pandu becomes king. But still there is no heir—Pandu is unable to have sons with his two wives, Kunti and Madari, because he was once cursed by a Brahmin to die if ever he made love with a woman. The problem of finding an heir is solved by Queen Kunti, who invokes her boon of being able to summon any god and instantly have a child with him. She already has one son, Karna, through testing this gift. She now summons the god Yama to father the noble Yudhishtara; then Agni, the god of fire, to sire the mighty Bhima; and the powerful Vayu, god of wind, to father

> Picking up his conch, Arjuna blew on it fiercely; the heavens echoed with the noise, and the chariot warriors stood petrified on the field. Their horses stood paralyzed, with eyes wide open…
>
> The *Mahabharata*, Book 7

THE MAHABHARATA IN DANCE The *Mahabharata* is often reenacted by the Kathakali dancers of Kerala, who depict the story through highly stylized hand gestures and facial expressions.

Arjuna. These brothers become known as the Pandavas. Pandu's brother, Dhritarashtra, meanwhile, has produced 100 sons—who are really demons—and they are known collectively by their family name, the Kauravas.

The Kauravas are led by the eldest son, Duryodhana, who is an incarnation of the goddess Kali. He usurps the throne, tricking the Pandavas out of their inheritance, and forces them into exile. The Great War becomes inevitable and finally takes place over 18 days. On the battlefield of Kurukshetra, at the center of an assemblage of grand characters, both godly and demonic, is the larger-than-life persona of the god Krishna.

THE BHAGAVAD GITA

Krishna helps the Pandavas by agreeing to be Arjuna's charioteer. However, at the start of the battle, Arjuna develops cold feet at seeing so many known faces on the opposite side. In order to help him, Krishna delivers the *Bhagavad Gita*, a sermon exhorting Arjuna—and all humankind—to fulfill his or her *dharma* and thereby achieve salvation *(see pp.270–271)*. This poem serves as the ultimate moral guide for all Hindus.

The *Mahabharata* ends with a moving message of the futility of war, showing how the victorious, too, in the end achieve only a costly victory. "War is evil in any form. To the dead, victory and defeat are the same," says the warrior Yudhishtara. The timeless themes of this tale, and its very modern conclusion, have kept the *Mahabharata* at the forefront of world literature for over 2,000 years.

◁ **HEROES AND GODS**
The *Mahabharata* is peopled by gods and superheroes, such as the warrior Bhishma, whose body hovers above the ground after he is felled by arrows.

△ **A RIGHTEOUS BATTLE**
The battlefield's symbolism is revealed in the poem's opening lines: *Dharmakshetre, Kurukshetre* ("On the field of *dharma*, on the field of the Kurus").

the bhagavad gita

Part of the *Mahabharata*, the *Bhagavad Gita* (Song of the Lord) is also an important text in its own right. It explains some of the key concepts of Hinduism, and it is one of the most popular of all Hindu writings.

The *Bhagavad Gita* takes the form of a conversation between Prince Arjuna, hero of the *Mahabharata*, and his charioteer, the god Krishna, before the battle of Kurukshetra. Although Arjuna is brave and skilled, he does not want to fight because he fears he will kill relatives who are fighting on the opposing side.

Thy tears are for those beyond tears; and are thy words
words of wisdom? The wise grieve not for those who live;
and they grieve not for those who die—for life and death
shall pass away.

Because we all have been for all time: I, and thou, and those
kings of men. And we shall all be for all time, we all for ever
and ever.

As the Spirit of our mortal body wanders on in childhood, and
youth and old age, the Spirit wanders on to a new body: of
this the sage has no doubts.

From the world of the senses, Arjuna, comes heat and comes
cold, and pleasure and pain. They come and they go: they are
transient. Arise above them, strong soul.

The man whom these cannot move, whose soul is one, beyond
pleasure and pain, is worthy of life in Eternity.

The unreal never is: the Real never is not. This truth indeed has
been seen by those who can see the true.

Interwoven in his creation, the Spirit is beyond destruction.
No one can bring to an end the Spirit which is everlasting.

For beyond time he dwells in these bodies, though these
bodies have an end in their time; but he remains
immeasurable, immortal. Therefore, great warrior, carry
on thy fight.

If any man thinks he slays, and if another thinks he is slain,
neither knows the ways of truth. The Eternal in man cannot
kill: the Eternal in man cannot die.

He is never born, and he never dies. He is in Eternity:
he is for evermore. Never-born and Eternal, beyond times
gone or to come, he does not die when the body dies.

When a man knows him as never-born, everlasting,
never-changing, beyond all destruction, how can that
man kill a man, or cause another to kill?

In exquisite language, Krishna explains that people should follow their *dharma*, or righteous path, while still pursuing salvation. It is Arjuna's *dharma* to be a warrior, so he should fight in the battle. He should not fear death, because the Eternal in man is never born and never dies. Krishna also explains key Hindu ideas such as devotion to the Absolute, and why deities—including himself—periodically come to Earth to correct imbalances between good and evil.

The excerpts given below come from Chapter 2 of the *Bhagavad Gita*. The god Krishna is addressing Arjuna and his reluctance to fight.

. . . Beyond the power of sword and fire, beyond the power of the water and winds, the Spirit is everlasting, omnipresent, never-changing, never-moving, ever One.

Invisible is he to mortal eyes, beyond thought and beyond change. Know that he is, and cease from sorrow.

But if he were born again and again, and again and again he were to die, even then, victorious man, cease thou from sorrow.

For all things born in truth must die, and out of death in truth comes life. Face to face with what must be, cease thou from sorrow.

Invisible before birth are all beings and after death invisible again. They are seen between two unseens. Why in this truth find sorrow?

. . . Think thou also of thy duty and do not waver. There is no greater good for a warrior than to fight in a righteous war.

There is a war that opens the doors of heaven, Arjuna! Happy the warriors whose fate is to fight such a war.

But to forgo this fight for righteousness is to forgo thy duty and honor: is to fall into transgression.

Men will tell of thy dishonor both now and in times to come. And to a man who is in honor, dishonor is worse than death.

The great warriors will say that thou hast run from the battle through fear; and those who thought great things of thee will speak of thee in scorn.

And thine enemies will speak of thee in contemptuous words of ill-will and derision, pouring scorn upon thy courage. Can there be for a warrior a more shameful fate?

In death thy glory in heaven, in victory thy glory on Earth. Arise, therefore, Arjuna, with thy soul ready to fight.

Krishna to Arjuna, in the *Bhagavad Gita*, Chapter 2

the *ramayana*

The second of the two major Hindu epics, the *Ramayana* tells the story of Rama, the seventh incarnation of Vishnu, and his adventures on Earth with his wife, Sita. Made up of around 96,000 verses in seven books, the epic is one of the world's longest poems, but it is shorter and more focused than the *Mahabharata* (see pp.268–269). Full of action and colorful characters, the *Ramayana* contains some of the most popular stories in Indian literature, encompassing some dramatic battles, supernatural events, the evil deeds of the demon Ravana, Rama and Sita's marriage, and the daring exploits of the much-loved monkey god, Hanuman. Popular narratives from the epic have often been retold in the form of plays, dance, and children's books. No one knows for sure when the *Ramayana* was first composed, but it was probably written down in Sanskrit in around 2000 BCE. It is traditionally said to be the work of the poet Valmiki, who gathered together various myths from the oral tradition, and stories from the Vedas and other sources, to create a continuous narrative. The one certain fact is that the work was not originally compiled as we know it today. The first and last books are later additions, and the main body of the poem also contains sections that were added after the majority of the epic had been assembled.

> Then Raghu's son, as if in sport,
> Before the thousands of the court,
> The weapon by the middle raised
> That all the crowd in wonder gazed.
> With steady arm the string he drew
> Till burst the mighty bow in two.
>
> The *Ramayana*, Book 1

RAMA AND SITA

Rama was the son of King Dasharatha of Ayodhya, which is one of the seven holy cities of Hinduism (now in Uttar Pradesh). He grew up in his father's court, but as a young man he traveled to the court of King Janaka. Many years previously, Janaka had been about to make a sacrifice to the gods to ask them to give him a child, when he came upon a baby girl in the earth. She was given the name Sita ("furrow") and was brought up as Janaka's daughter. When Rama arrived at Janaka's court many years later, he fell in love with the beautiful Sita. But King Janaka had vowed that only someone strong enough to bend Shiva's bow could marry his daughter, so he called for 5,000 men to bring in the mighty bow, which no man had been able to lift or bend. On seeing the bow, Rama effortlessly picked it up and bent it so far that it snapped in two; and he was duly given Sita's hand in marriage.

Rama's father, King Dasharatha, decided to make Rama his successor, but was thwarted by his third wife, Kaikeyi, who demanded that her son, Bharata, be appointed instead and that Rama be sent into exile for 14 years. The king was horrified, but he was forced to carry out her demands because of an earlier vow. Rama was sent into exile, where he was joined by Sita and his faithful brother, Lakshmana. The three were forced to live in the forest, where they conversed with ascetics and received wisdom.

One day, a female demon, Surpa-nakha, saw Rama and fell in love with him. When he spurned her, she attacked Sita, but Lakshmana fought her off. Injured and rejected, Surpa-nakha sought the help of her brother, the terrible demon Ravana, who vowed to abduct Sita and defeat Rama. Knowing that Rama was an avid hunter, Ravana lured him away from Sita with a magical deer, before projecting his voice to sound like Rama's, shouting for help in the forest, and so lured Lakshmana away from her, too. Left alone, Sita was kidnapped by Ravana, who flew her off in his chariot to his palace on the island of Lanka.

THE BATTLE BEGINS

When Rama discovered that Sita had been taken, he was distraught and vowed revenge. He sought help from Sugriva, king of the monkeys, who agreed to assist him in return for Rama's help in resecuring his own kingdom. The deal was struck; and when they had

RAMA—THE IDEAL HERO
Rama is also known as *Maryada Purushottam* (the supremely righteous man), because he never deviates from the virtuous path, or *dharma*.

STORMING THE CASTLE
Lakshmana was wounded during the long battle against Ravana, but his life was saved by the magical herb *sanjivini*, brought to him by Hanuman.

won back Sugriva's kingdom, the monkey king offered Rama the help of his armies under his general, Hanuman, the extraordinary monkey hero. Hanuman flew to where Sita was imprisoned, and built a bridge across the sea with the help of his monkey army. With Rama, Hanuman and his army engaged in a long battle against Ravana and his demons, finally defeating them. Rama and Sita were reunited, and Sita, Rama, and Lakshmana returned to Ayodhya triumphant.

THE FIRST DIWALI
Diwali, the festival of lights, celebrates Rama's triumphant return to Ayodhya, and the triumph of good over evil, in Rama's vanquishing of Ravana.

This is the end of the real epic, but a seventh, final book was later added to the tale. This states that after a while, rumors grew that Sita had been unfaithful to Rama while she was living in Ravana's palace. Rama became suspicious, and felt his position as a righteous king was untenable if Sita remained; so he ordered Lakshmana to take Sita back to the forest and abandon her there. Lakshmana reluctantly obeyed, but fortunately, Sita did not die; she was rescued by the poet Valmiki, who offered her sanctuary in his home, where she gave birth to Rama's twin sons, Kusha and Lava. Sita lived in Valmiki's house for 12 years, during which time he wrote the *Ramayana*. Rama then held a great festival, at which he recognized his sons, and yearned to see his beloved Sita. When summoned, Sita came, but her heart had been broken, and she called on Mother Earth to confirm that she had been faithful by "taking her home." So the Earth opened up and swallowed its daughter. After many years, Rama and Sita were finally reunited once more in heaven.

"If unstained in thought and action I have lived from day of birth,
Spare a daughter's shame and anguish and receive her, Mother Earth!"
Then the Earth was rent and parted, and a golden throne arose,
Held aloft by jeweled *Nagas* as the leaves enfold the rose,
And the Mother in embraces held her spotless sinless Child,
Saintly Janak's saintly daughter, pure and true and undefiled.

The *Ramayana*, Book 7

the kamashastras

Hindu philosophy pays particular attention to the science of *kama*—physical pleasure—and some of the best known works of Hindu thought cover this subject. They approach the subject frankly and with clarity, and aim to show how *kama* is an integral part of both the physical and spiritual life. A number of ancient texts from the 7th century BCE, known as the Kamashastras (Rules of Love), were written on this theme, but most were lost over time. However, one of the later works on *kama*, the *Kamasutra*, survived to become one of the most famous, but least understood, of all the Hindu texts.

> The territory of the text extends only so far as men have dull appetites; but when the wheel of sexual ecstasy is in motion, there is no textbook at all, and no order.
>
> The *Kamasutra*, Book 2

The Sanskrit and Pali word *kama* encompasses a wide range of meanings: the pleasure of the senses; sensual enjoyment; sexual fulfilment; love; and aesthetic pleasure. *Kama* is essential: it was embodied in the Vedic god of cosmic desire, also called Kama, who was once destroyed by an angry Shiva; without the driving forces of love and desire the world shriveled and died, and the other gods were forced to plead for his rebirth. In later texts, Kama the god is depicted as an eternally-young, handsome man who shoots flower-tipped, love-producing arrows. In many ways, he is like his Roman mythical counterpart, Cupid.

Hindus regard *kama* as one of the most important parts of life; it sits at the lowest level of a four-part hierarchy of *purusharthas* (life goals) that covers *kama, artha* (worldly status), *dharma* (the righteous path), and *moksha* (liberation from rebirth). Although ranked the lowest of these four aims, *kama* is still important within Hinduism because physical pleasure is seen as a vital part of life—it is essential in the begetting of children, for example.

The Kamashastras discuss the various aspects of *kama*, outlining the various reasons for sexual relations, including the begetting of children (enjoining a husband and wife); pure physical pleasure (when a man makes love to a courtesan or to an experienced woman); humiliating another man (through adulterous relations); and for occult purposes (as might occur among certain sects, including Tantrism).

The Kamashastras also cover such subjects as the progress of a physical relationship, from courtship to consummation, and the kinds of people who might act as go-betweens, taking messages between lovers. The texts discuss astrology (including ways of working out the best time for consummating a relationship), meeting places (encompassing subjects such as décor, ambience, and music), and etiquette (the best subjects for conversation with a loved one and the most polite way to bring a meeting to a close).

THE KAMASUTRA

The *Kamasutra* is the best known of the Kamashastras. The author of the book is said to be Vatsyayana, an Indian writer who lived during the Gupta period (4th to 6th centuries CE), who also wrote a commentary on the Nyayasutras, philosophical texts from c.300 BCE.

ANCIENT PLEASURES
Scenes of sensual pleasure can be found adorning the walls of the Ajanta caves, demonstrating the importance of *kama* as far back as the 2nd century BCE.

LAKSHMANA TEMPLE, KHAJURAHO
The walls of the 10th-century Lakshmana Temple are covered with erotic motifs, which may have acted as protective and auspicious symbols.

Tradition says that Vatsyayana was celibate, and compiled his treatise as a corrective, because many of the existing books on the subject were too specialized and obscure. Its instructions are aimed mainly at sophisticated urban men, but Vatsyayana hoped that women would also benefit from reading it.

Although it is most widely known in the West for its series of instructions on sexual intercourse, especially sexual positions, the *Kamasutra* in fact covers a much wider range of subjects. It is divided into seven parts. The first, introductory, part outlines the aims and priorities of life: how one gains knowledge; how a well-bred man (the target reader of the book) should behave; and how to identify the people who can help the lover in his pursuit of love. The second part covers acts of lovemaking, from embracing and kissing, to sexual intercourse in all its numerous varieties. Many different *asanas* (positions for lovemaking) are described, together with advice on the different stages of life or experience for which they are deemed appropriate.

The third part looks at marriage, from the process of acquiring a wife and putting a prospective marriage partner at her ease, to the marriage itself. In the fourth part, Vatsyayana examines the role of the wife and he advises her on how to behave in a polygamous marriage. Stepping outside marriage, the fifth part covers the seduction of "the wives of other people," while the sixth part looks at courtesans. The final part contains suggestions on how to attract others and how to restore weakened sexual energy with the use of various herbs and other medicines. The main interest of the *Kamasutra* lies beyond these details, however, as it also provides an extraordinary insight into life in India around 1,500 years ago, and particularly into the life of the cultivated townsman at whom the book was aimed. He is instructed in 64 arts, or skills, which he is told to acquire not just in order to achieve pleasure but also to form the foundation of a proper education. He is expected to have a deep interest in subjects from across the arts, such as poetry, music, and the visual arts, which themselves are sources of *kama*. He should also provide himself with good, well-seasoned food; make his surroundings elegant, and make himself attractive through the application of fine perfumes. In short, he is to live the life of an aesthete, putting his love of pleasure into a context of culture.

> In a woman who is of the same class, who is a virgin, and who has been taken in accordance with the texts, a man finds religion, power, sons, connections, the growth of his faction, and sexual pleasure.
>
> The *Kamasutra*, Book 3

THE PRINCE'S PRIVATE PLEASURE The beautiful miniature paintings from Rajasthan were often concerned with the aesthetic classification of *shringar rasa*, or erotic love.

ARCHITECTURE

BUILDING A NATION

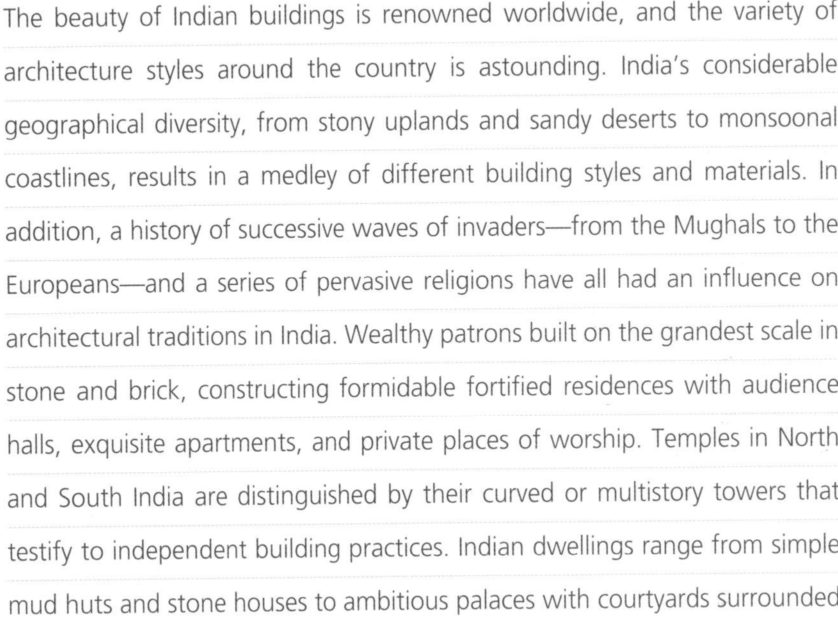

The beauty of Indian buildings is renowned worldwide, and the variety of architecture styles around the country is astounding. India's considerable geographical diversity, from stony uplands and sandy deserts to monsoonal coastlines, results in a medley of different building styles and materials. In addition, a history of successive waves of invaders—from the Mughals to the Europeans—and a series of pervasive religions have all had an influence on architectural traditions in India. Wealthy patrons built on the grandest scale in stone and brick, constructing formidable fortified residences with audience halls, exquisite apartments, and private places of worship. Temples in North and South India are distinguished by their curved or multistory towers that testify to independent building practices. Indian dwellings range from simple mud huts and stone houses to ambitious palaces with courtyards surrounded by colonnades. What links all these buildings is a love of decoration and a profusion of figural and floral imagery imbued with auspicious symbolism.

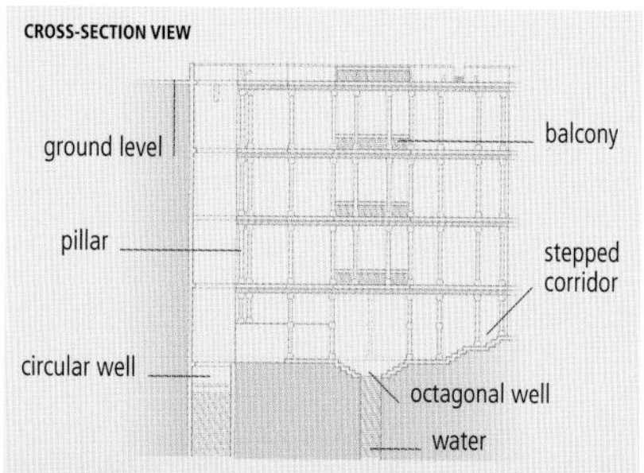

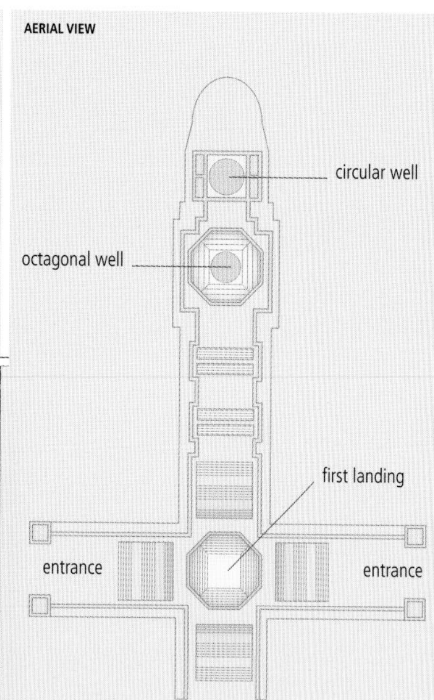

▽ **GROUND LEVEL**
Looking along the stepwell at ground level, the architectural complexity of the subterranean steps and landings of the well are largely hidden from view. Only the pillars of the first level are glimpsed.

▽ **LIGHT SHAFTS**
Openings in the roof at ground level admit light to the steps and connecting landings that descend to the wells below.

Water is a precious commodity in the arid regions of western India. Historically, considerable trouble was taken to dig deep wells to reach dependable, year-round sources of groundwater. Some of these wells are elaborate subterranean constructions. At the core of each one is the circular or octagonal well-shaft. There are brackets at ground level to secure the ropes needed to hoist buckets filled with water to the surface, either with the help of bullocks, or through human power alone. However, water is also gathered in pots brought by women from nearby villages. As a result, the wells often have steps descending to the water, arranged in such a fashion that the water can easily be gathered as its level rises and falls during the different seasons. These "stepwells" are known as *vavs* in Gujarat and *baolis* in Rajasthan.

Since the activity of collecting water by women is considered an important ritual, many stepwells are decorated with carved floral designs and even images of Hindu divinities. The carvings are believed to ensure the purity of the water and protection for the villagers who depend on it.

One of the most elaborate stepwells in western India is that at Adalaj, a short distance outside Ahmedabad, in Gujarat. Built in 1499 by Rudabai, the wife of a local Hindu chieftain, it is a rare example of female patronage of a utilitarian structure intended for the use of local women.

Adalaj Vav has two wells: the main well is circular, with a ramp at the top for bullocks to draw water; the secondary well is octagonal and overlooked by balconies at different levels. The flights of steps that lead down to the water are lined with columns and beams, giving the whole building the air of a temple hall. As the steps descend, the well complex becomes more and more intricate, growing into a labyrinth of pavilions, landings, and balconies, all concealed from view at ground level. Relief carvings of motifs derived from the auspicious lotus flower cover the walls, which are also studded with ornate niches. This intrusion of religious themes into the decoration of Adalaj Vav shows that the monument functioned as a spiritual sanctuary, as well as a reliable source of life-sustaining fresh water.

△ ▷ **SIDE CHAMBERS**
The landings between the flights of steps are flanked by side chambers. With their lotus-shaped thresholds, square columns, and ornate, overhanging eaves, they resemble the sanctuaries of Jain and Hindu temples.

ADALAJ VAV

STEPPED WELL, ADALAJ, GUJARAT

BEAM NICHES
Small niches framing lotus flowers emerging from stylized pots adorn the beams that run around the side walls and landing ceilings.

LOTUS-FLOWER CARVINGS
Derived from Hindu and Jain architecture, these symmetrical, eight-petaled blooms are ubiquitous in Adalaj Vav.

STAIRCASE LANDING
The landings that regularly interrupt the descending flights of steps are sheltered by roof slabs supported by stone columns and beams.

COLUMN BRACKETS
Temple-style brackets with curved ends, and column panels with lotus motifs emphasize the well's sacred nature.

LOOKING UP
The well, staircases, and landings are illuminated by the light shafts in the roof above. These roof openings are framed by decorated beams.

LANDING LIGHT SHAFTS
The light shafts penetrate the whole structure, plunging through the landing floors between sturdy stone columns. The access stairs to the well are visible through the opening on the far side.

NICHE DECORATION
The flowering-tree motif in the wall niches is derived from mosque and tomb architecture. Other niches have lotus blooms and hanging lamps.

RECESSED ARCH
This view across one of the balconies overlooking the main octagonal well shows a recessed arch in the wall of the circular well beyond.

LOOKING DOWN
The landing ceilings increase in height as the steps descend toward the water. In the lower center is the metal grille that covers the well itself.

COLUMN DESIGNS
Diamond-shaped lotus flowers and geometric patterns of square holes adorn the tops of the columns supporting the roof beams.

FIGHTING ANIMALS
Tucked away among the intricate carvings are animal scenes, such as this fight between an elephant and imaginary, lionlike beast.

LEAFY MOTIFS
As well as flowers, trees, and animals, leaflike designs are also incorporated into the rich decoration, as can be seen on this supporting bracket.

CIRCULAR WELL SHAFT
The main well is located at the bottom of a deep, circular shaft. The sides of the shaft are divided into "stories" by lotus friezes, interspersed with templelike niches.

WELL CHAMBER
At the lowest level of the octagonal well is a square chamber surrounded by double tiers of arched openings. It is here that local women would come to get water.

FLORAL FRIEZE
Lines of six- and eight-petaled blossoms, based on the aquatic lotus flower, have a sacred, protective quality that is believed to guarantee the purity of the water in the well.

SCULPTED FISH
Looking through an archway to the main well, one can see fish motifs sculpted onto the walls of the well-shaft. Like the octagonal well, this well is fed by the subterranean water table.

SHEKHAWATI HAVELI

MERCHANT MANSION, BISSAU, RAJASTHAN

PLAN VIEW—FIRST FLOOR

stairs to lower floor
storeroom
bedroom
gallery
stairs to lower floor

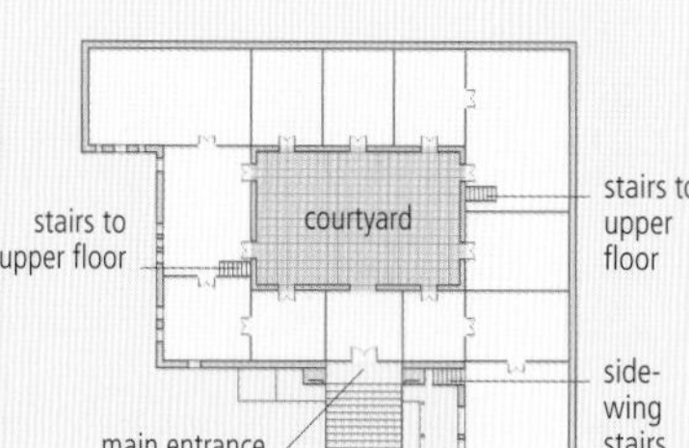

The landowners of the Shekhawati region in Rajasthan encouraged merchants to settle in their towns with the lure of the caravans that traversed the area trading in spices, silk, opium and other goods. But with the decline of this trade in the 19th century due to the development of the railroad network, many of these merchants were compelled to leave Shekhawati to seek their fortunes in the flourishing port cities of Calcutta (Kolkata) and Bombay (Mumbai). Even so, they continued to maintain their mansions, or *havelis*, in the Shekhawati towns from which they originated.

Intent on expressing their new-found wealth, these trading families did not hesitate to provide their ancestral homes with multistory, grand facades entered through lofty entrance gateways approached from the street by long flights of steps. The apartments within, generally arranged on two levels around one or more courtyards, were lavishly adorned with brightly toned murals and frescoes that illustrated popular Hindu legends as well scenes of contemporary life, including British military officers and the newly introduced trains.

The Didwaniya family home in the town of Bissau is a typical example of a Shekhawati painted *haveli*. The apartments of this dwelling are arranged on three sides of a single courtyard, screened from view from the street by the imposing arch above the entrance gate. The reception room and dining hall are at the lower level of the courtyard, while an additional side wing for visitors is provided just outside the gate. The family's private chambers, which include a lavishly decorated bedroom, are situated at the upper level of the mansion, where they are linked by a gallery that overlooks the courtyard below.

Remarkably preserved in their full splendor, the paintings of the Didwaniya *haveli*, especially those of the bedroom, express the religious sentiments of the family, as well as representing the architecture of various nearby towns. While the paintings are executed in the lively, somewhat folkish Rajasthan manner, there is evidence of Mughal artistic influence, such as in the beautifully executed, carpetlike motif that fills the central panel of the ceiling in the bedroom.

▷ **GATE AND SIDE WING**
A metal roof shelters the entrance to the side wing. Like the main facade, it is painted with scenes of daily life, as well as with floral designs, maidens, and warriors.

▽ **ENTRANCE GATE**
Steps rise to the *haveli's* entrance. The doors are framed by a carved wooden lintel and topped by a painted masonry arch.

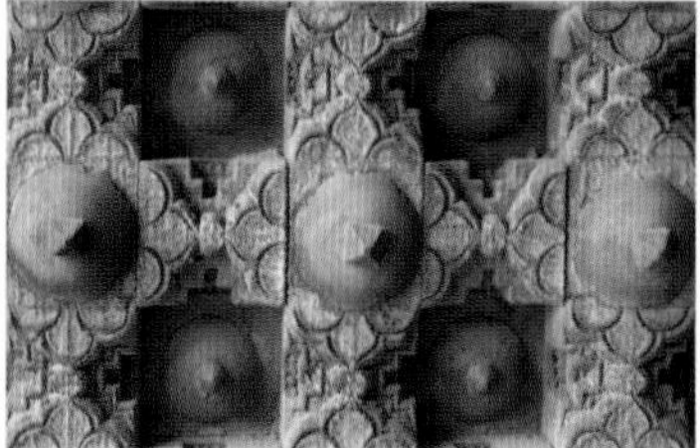

◁ △ **ENTRANCE DOORS**
Richly worked in wood, the doors are divided into multiple panels by crossbars. The crossbars are fixed by brass plugs fashioned as stylized lotus buds.

△ **ARCHED WINDOW**
Additional light reaches the reception room via a wooden-framed, shuttered window topped by a curved arch.

▽ **COURTYARD VIEW**
This view of the interior courtyard shows the open room at the far end. Above this, carried on brackets, can be seen the gallery that links the rooms on the upper floor.

▽ **RECEPTION ROOM ARCADE**
A line of three ornate, lobed arches serve as the entrance to the spacious side wing on the lower level of the interior courtyard.

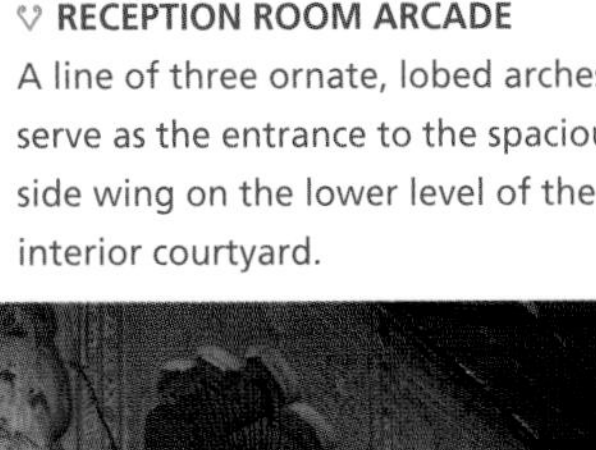

△ **SIDE PANELS**
The seating areas on either side of the main entrance are elevated on stone panels bearing relief carvings of leafy arabesque patterns.

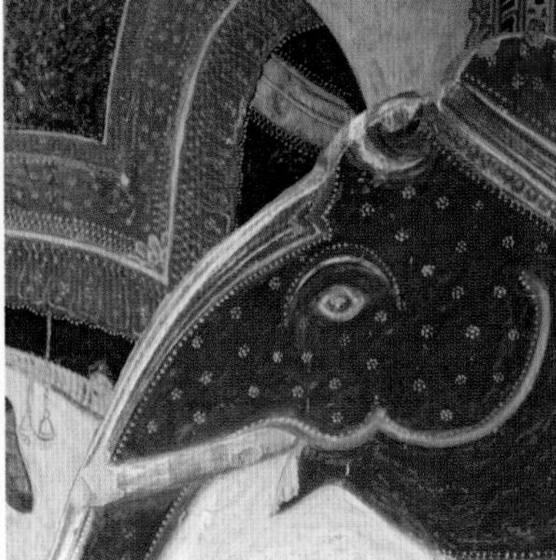

◁ △ **ELEPHANT BALUSTRADE**
A balustrade painted with an elephant displaying a curling trunk flanks the steps leading to the side wing of the *haveli*. A striding elephant adorns the wall beyond.

▷ **PAINTED BEDROOM**
The ornate bedroom, reached from the gallery that runs around three sides of the courtyard, consists of a central space with arcades on two sides and a doorway leading to a side chamber.

△ **FLORAL PATTERNS**
The plastered archway in the center of the bedroom adds character and is adorned with brightly colored patterns, including friezes of petals in red and blue, and similarly toned full blossoms. Such auspicious floral themes and motifs are considered appropriate for this most private of rooms.

▷ **PLASTER DETAIL ON COLUMN**
The floral theme of the bedroom's decoration runs throughout the entire room, even extending to the cut-plaster details of the columns supporting the arches.

◁ △ **NICHE DECORATION**
Niches in the bedroom walls are painted with designs showing flowering trees with peacocks and parrots. The niches are bordered by ornate mirrorwork.

▷ **CEILING FIGURES**
A fierce warrior and a benign-looking European are among the figures painted onto the bedroom ceiling.

▷ **MAIDEN AND SOLDIER**
This mural of an unusual warrior couple bearing sticks and swords shows Mughal artistic influences.

▽ **WALL PANELS**
Framed by an arch, the end wall of the bedroom has panels painted with flowering trees, above which can be seen the warrior couple.

◁ △ **WOODWORK**
Intricately carved floral ornamentation enlivens the wooden frames of this doorway, which leads from the bedroom to a side chamber.

◁ △ **PARCHESI BOARD**
A board for this popular dice game played by women and children is painted onto the plaster floor of the bedroom.

▽ **GENERAL VIEW**
The circular mud wall is broken only by a single doorway on one side and by four small windows.

▷ **GRASS ROOF**
The dried grasses of the thatch are secured by string that wraps around the conical roof.

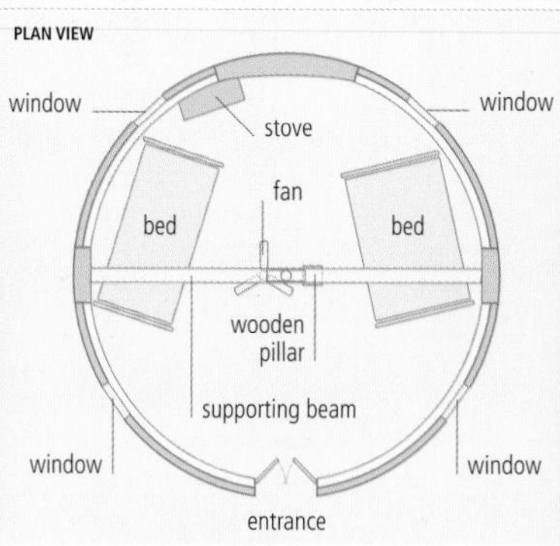

Many rural communities on the fringes of settlements in India live in simple, rudimentary structures. One example is this circular thatched hut in Dhordo, a tiny village in Kutch, in the extreme west of Gujarat. The people of Dhordo are breeders of buffalo and cows. Because they spend much of their time away from home with their cattle, they have little need for spacious or elaborate accommodations. Even so, these simple huts are well planned, imaginatively ornamented, and even climatically efficient.

Built of solid mud bricks and topped with conical roofs of wooden sticks covered with thick grass, the huts are well insulated against the intense summer heat. These circular structures, which can be more than 23 ft (7 m) in diameter, serve as a living space, sleeping zone, and cooking area for an entire family. Walls are coated with plaster and enlivened by painted patterns that outline doorways and windows. Similar patterns decorate the mud and plaster floors of the interior. In some huts, the walls inside are also decorated with minute pieces of mirror inserted into molded plasterwork to create gleaming effects, especially around shelves and stoves. This decoration is believed to have some magical protective power, and it is therefore employed in those parts of the houses where precious items are stored or food is prepared. Such mirror-work also adorns the brightly patterned textiles worn by the women of the village, and even the cloths that decorate their wheeled carts and their cattle. Larger textiles of this type are displayed at weddings and other festive occasions; they sometimes also hang from the roofs of the huts to create vividly toned ceilings.

Typical of circular dwellings dotted all over Kutch, this particular hut belongs to a Muslim cattle breeder and his family. Apart from the illustrations of various Muslim holy places stuck onto his cupboard, the construction and decoration of the interior is no different from the huts of his Hindu neighbors. The interior is fitted with shelves and recesses, all crammed with pots and other domestic utensils. Carved wooden furniture is restricted to a chest for storing clothes and blankets, and two beds.

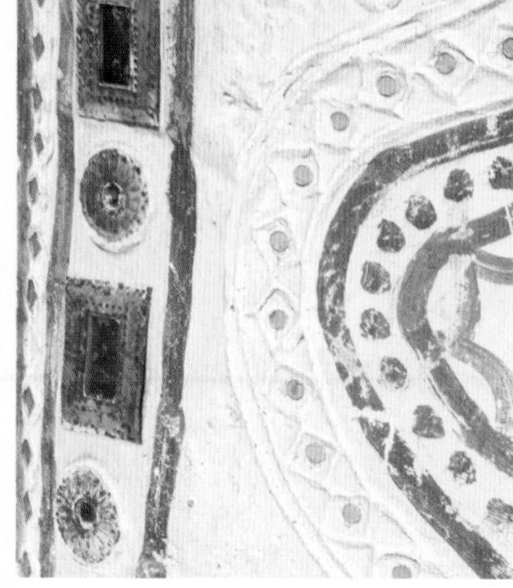

△ ▷ **PAINTED DESIGNS**
Window openings are emphasized by lobed patterns in ocher paint, as well as by relief plaster strips. These curvaceous motifs are imbued with a magical significance believed to keep evil influences at bay, thereby protecting the inhabitants of the hut.

▷ **WINDOW SHUTTERS**
The shutters of this window, partly concealed by a metal grille, are painted with brightly toned flowers that contrast with the more abstract designs on the walls and around the windows and door.

▷ **DOORWAY DECORATION**
Looped patterns around the door suggest an ornate archway hung with banners and textiles, echoing a grand house or palace.

THATCHED MUD HUT

CIRCULAR RURAL DWELLING, KUTCH, GUJARAT

ROOF OVERHANG
The dried-grass coating of the roof is carried on rough timbers. These project beyond the walls, creating an overhang that protects the exterior of the hut.

DOOR PANEL
The rings of painted dots are intended to represent full lotus flowers—an auspicious motif for the entrance to the hut.

ROOF INTERIOR
The roof frame supports a tightly knit web of timbers, shielding the interior from dust and rare rainstorms.

CEILING CLOTH
This locally embroidered cloth decorates the apex of the ceiling, in the hut's center, adding a touch of color to the interior.

BEAM AND FAN
Now that Dhordo has electricity, the house owner has installed a fan for the comfort of his family. It is attached to the hut's central beam.

SHUTTERS VIEWED FROM INSIDE
On the inner surfaces of these window shutters are lotus blossoms and leafy sprays that complement the door decoration. Closed by day to keep out the heat and dust, the shutters are generally opened at night.

ORNATE DOORS
The plaster-coated stove is built into the outer walls of the hut. Its doors are ornately treated, as are the surrounding wall surfaces.

BRASS POTS
Neatly stacked, the brass pots of the household rise in an impressive array on top of the stove—the center of all domestic activity.

INTERIOR FURNISHINGS
Living, cooking, and sleeping activities can only take place within the confined space of the hut because furniture is kept to an absolute minimum.

MIRRORED PLASTERWORK
Molded plaster punctuated by minute pieces of glass is used to create geometric patterns that adorn the frames around the wall panels and windows.

BED AND DOLLS
One of the beds in the hut has a metal frame and is covered by a blanket woven by the women of the household. Also made by the women are the two dolls embroidered in the local style.

◁ **DISPLAY OF UTENSILS**
The shelf beneath the conical roof makes an ideal spot for displaying the brass dishes, cups, and kettle used for formal entertainment.

▷ **HANGING MIRRORS**
Suspended from wall hooks, this collection of mirrors is embellished with colorful woven textile bands, thereby adding to the interior decor.

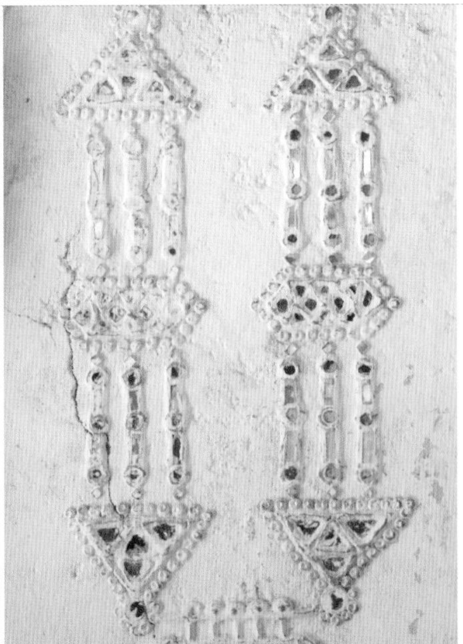

▷ **WALL DECORATION**
This plaster wall relief, enlivened with minute colored pieces of glass, resembles the woven ribbons and panels worn as decoration by the women of the household.

◁ **BED AND CHEST**
This bed has a typical Kutchi blanket, with woven geometric designs. The small wooden chest with camel-bone knobs at the head of the bed is for storing precious items.

△ **ORNATE CHEST**
Printed scenes of the Kaaba and other holy Muslim places stuck onto this wooden chest reveal the religious affiliations of the family; the outer frame is enhanced by gleaming metallic inserts.

PORTUGUESE MANSION

EUROPEAN-STYLE BUNGALOW, LOUTOLIM, GOA

ENTRANCE GATE
This view past the flanking gateposts shows the steps that ascend to the *balcao*—the formal entrance to the building that faces outward toward the street.

PLAN VIEW

kitchen
bathroom
bedroom
dining room
courtyard
music room
chapel
child's bedroom
dance hall
hall
study
bedroom
balcao
benches
roof overhang

BALCAO
Four massive columns and four smaller piers support the roof overhang of the *balcao*. This overhang shelters the benches lining the approach to the front door of the house, on which family members and visitors would sit.

Nowhere is the impact of Europe on domestic Indian architecture more evident than in Goa's "Portuguese" bungalows. Built for local aristocratic families and wealthy merchants who traded with the Portuguese, these mansions hosted a graceful and elegant way of life that was much influenced by Europe—hence the spacious reception areas, dining rooms, libraries, studies, and even private Catholic chapels.

Goan bungalows are constructed of laterite stone blocks coated with plaster, which is usually painted in bright colors that reflect Indian rather than European tastes. Roofs are steeply sloping and clad in terra-cotta tiles—a necessity in a region subject to severe monsoon rains. Facing outward toward the street or a private garden, most bungalows are fronted with extensive verandas, along which run cast-iron balconies sheltered by roof overhangs. Entrance porches, known as *balcao*s, with masonry benches are characteristic. The *balcao* was where the family members would converse with neighbors and receive guests, or survey events on the street. Windows are fashioned from translucent oyster shells, rather than glass. Inside, the bungalows have floors of polished wooden boards or gleaming glazed tiles, and ceilings are stuccoed or painted with ornate designs.

Many of these features can be seen in the Alvarez mansion in Loutolim. Until recently, this mid-19th-century, Portuguese-style bungalow was lived in by descendants of the original owner. Instead of a long veranda, the house is fronted by a line of eight arched openings, each with double glass-paneled doors. These admit light to the dance hall and study, which open off the entrance hall. Aligned with the *balcao* is a chapel reserved for family use, facing toward the entrance. Closed off by screens, the interior of the chapel is furnished with a crucifix and religious icons. The side wings of the house are arranged around an open courtyard: one has a formal dining room; the other has extra bedrooms and bathrooms. The kitchen and store are located at the rear of the courtyard. Throughout the house, there is a medley of influences; European musical instruments, gilded mirrors, and crystal chandeliers mingle with Chinese porcelains. The richly carved rosewood furniture is, however, locally made.

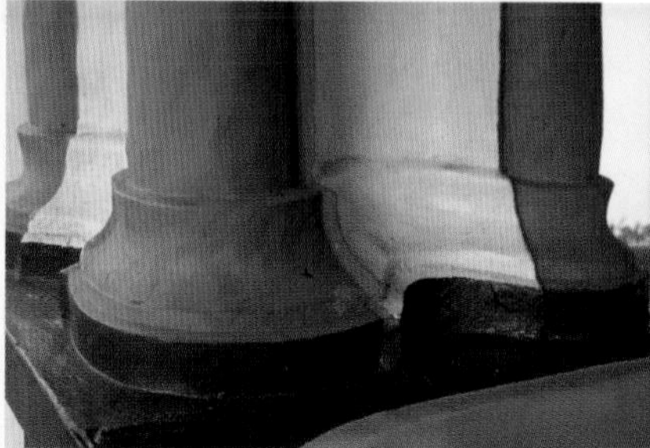

COLUMN BASES
Painted in contrasting colors, the plaster columns at the corners of the *balcao* are Neo-Classical in style, in keeping with the European character of the house itself.

WINDOW ARCHES
The arched openings along the main facade accommodate painted cast-iron balconies, as well as double doors with glass panels rather than traditional oystershell pieces.

HALL DOORS
These rosewood half-doors with "peep windows" separate the entrance hall from the corridor that runs around the house; the chapel can be seen beyond.

DOOR DETAIL
Swirls of cut-out foliation serve as a decorative fringe along the top of the half-doors between the public entrance hall and the private corridor.

HALL STAND
This piece of hallway furniture—complete with mirror, hat pegs, and cane storage—reflects the European lifestyle of the Alvarez family.

PRIVATE CORRIDOR
Lined with occasional furniture and old photographs, the corridor that runs around the courtyard links the entrance hall and chapel at the front of the house to the dining room and bedrooms on the sides, and to the kitchen and bathrooms at the rear.

CHAPEL ENTRYWAY
The view from the corridor through this elaborately carved wooden screen shows the altar of the family's private chapel. The molded band surrounding the arched entryway is faced in polished plasterwork, which is cleverly painted to resemble black-veined white marble.

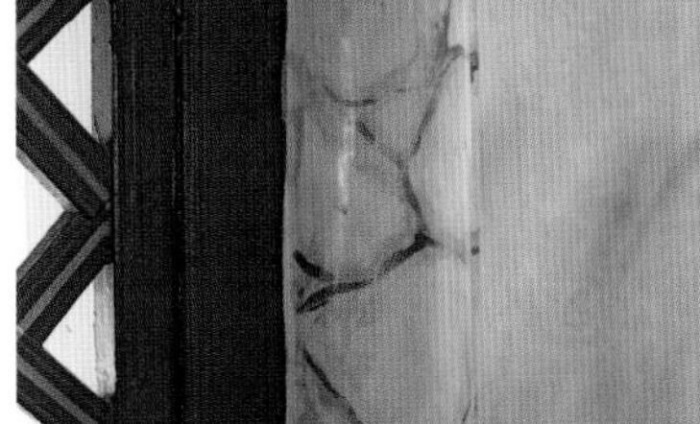

ALTAR
The altar is the chapel's focus. On its marble surface, at the foot of the crucifix's painted wooden surround, stand religious artifacts, candles, vases, and flowers.

PELMET
Over the door from the dance hall to the dining room is an ornate gilded pelmet in Neo-Classical style, from which hangs delicate lacework.

SIDE WINDOWS
A line of four windows illuminates the dining room—by far the longest room in the house. This room was often used for formal banquets.

DINING ROOM
Twenty-two chairs, each bearing the engraved "AA" monogram of the Alvarez family on its back, surround the long dining table. The doorways at the rear lead to the kitchen and service areas.

FLOOR DESIGN
The polished plaster floor with a diagonal pattern marked out in ocher, pink, and black enlivens the decor of the dining room.

DANCE HALL
Serving also as a formal sitting room, and displaying an array of costly furniture, mirrors, and chandeliers, the dance hall is the largest room at the front of the house.

▷ LACE DRAPES
Homespun lace drapes are hung across the principal doorways of the house, such as this one linking the study to the private corridor.

◁ DOORWAY
The view through the doorway in the study toward the dance hall shows how well lit the interior of the house is.

▽ STUDY
In this corner of the study, the doorway to the right leads to the master bedroom with its four-poster bed. The doorway to the left opens onto the main corridor.

△ PAINTED DADO
Around the base of the study walls runs an ornate dado decorated with a painted geometric pattern.

◁ MASTER BEDROOM
This marble-topped side-table with mirror is placed in the master bedroom. Beside the tall window is a traditional "planter's chair."

◁ WOODEN FLOOR
The dance hall is the only room in the house with an expensive wooden floor. The boards are laid in parquet fashion to create a patterned surface.

▽ **LATERITE WALLS**
While the street and garden facades of the house are coated with painted plaster, the walls of the inner courtyard, away from public view, are built of untreated laterite blocks.

▽ **INTERIOR COURTYARD**
The laterite walls of the attractively planted courtyard are punctuated by windows and screens. In its heyday, fruit and vegetables would have been grown in the courtyard for use in the kitchen.

▷ **ROOF VENT**
Smoke from the service area escapes via a terra-cotta vent set into the sloping tiled roof; the vent's curved contour helps to shed rain during the monsoon season.

△ **CONCRETE SCREEN**
Probably a replacement of an earlier timber screen, these concrete blocks keep out the elements but admit light and air to the service area between the kitchen and dining room.

▽ **SIDE CORRIDOR**
This passageway connects the bedrooms on the right with the bathrooms at the rear. The kitchen opens off to one side. Under the window is a stone basin for hand-washing.

▷ **STORAGE JARS**
Large earthenware jars for storing oil and wine are kept at the end of the side corridor. The room straight ahead is the women's bathroom.

△ **SERVICE AREA**
To one side of the house, immediately outside the corridor, is a lean-to that shelters an area used for storage. Wood is also burned here to heat water for the adjacent bathrooms.

▽ KITCHEN VIEW
The earthen-floored kitchen at the rear of the house is well stocked with cooking pots, utensils, and other items for food preparation, including a grinding stone. In the corner is a wash-up area.

▷ KITCHEN ROOF
The steep kitchen roof is covered with terra-cotta tiles manufactured in Mangalore. These are laid so that they overlap one another, to ensure protection against the torrential monsoon rains.

◁ KITCHEN ESSENTIALS
In one corner of the kitchen is a collection of vessels for storing kitchen staples such as wine, vinegar, and pickles. The brass water pot here is even equipped with its own tap.

△ ▷ WATER BASIN AND STOVE
The kitchen has a metal water basin on a stone base, and a wood-fueled clay stove. Waste water from the kitchen is used to irrigate the courtyard plants.

PLAN VIEW—FIRST FLOOR

bedroom
pillar
pillar
steps to roof
dividing wall
stone steps
window bench
main entrance

▷ **VIEW FROM THE STREET**
Painted brilliant white to distinguish it from adjacent dwellings and reflect the sun's rays, the stone house sits high above the street, overlooking the city's fortifications.

▽ **INNER DOOR**
The entrance to the lower level of the house is this painted door, which is accessed from the interior courtyard.

PLAN VIEW—GROUND FLOOR

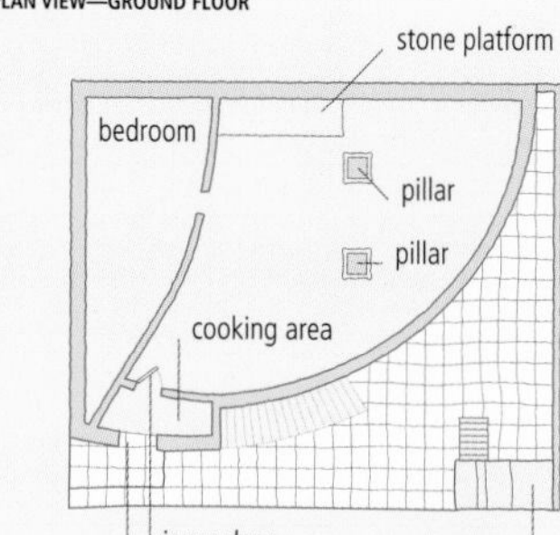

Overlooking the wastelands of the Thar Desert, in the far west of Rajasthan, Jaisalmer served as the fortified citadel of the Bhatis from the 15th century onward. This Rajput clan ruled over a kingdom that derived much of its wealth from the lucrative caravan trade that traversed the desert. As a result, Jaisalmer became home to numerous merchants and artisans, and the citadel was thronged with people. Because lumber is scarce in this waterless region, the local yellow sandstone became the primary building material. This stone was used for virtually every type of construction: from Jaisalmer's ramparts and the palace of the Bhatis that crowns the citadel, to the grand mansions of bankers, councilors, and merchants, and even the unpretentious but comfortable homes of the city's artisans and workers.

A representative example of Jaisalmer's domestic stone architecture is this modest dwelling. Built at the very edge of the citadel, with a view out over the parched landscape, the stone house presents a blank exterior to the eye, with doors and windows reduced to a minimum. Except for the brilliant green front door, the whole building is whitewashed to help ward off the intense heat of this desert region.

The interior is arranged on two levels, linked by a narrow, ladderlike staircase. The lower level is cooler, and therefore used by the family in the hot summer season. This is where the main living space is located, with provisions for grinding grain, cooking, and washing. For the winter months, when the heat abates, the family moves to the upper level, where they can enjoy the desert panorama from seats beneath the windows. From here, steps lead up to the flat roof of the house, where family members may socialize with neighbors, and even sleep outside on warmer nights.

While stone is used throughout the house, the floors are coated with painted cow dung and mud; painted mud also covers the precious timbers that support the intermediate floor. White paint is applied to interior stone surfaces, outlining individual stone flags and recessed wall shelves. Painted green doors add a welcome flourish of color to what otherwise would be a visually austere dwelling.

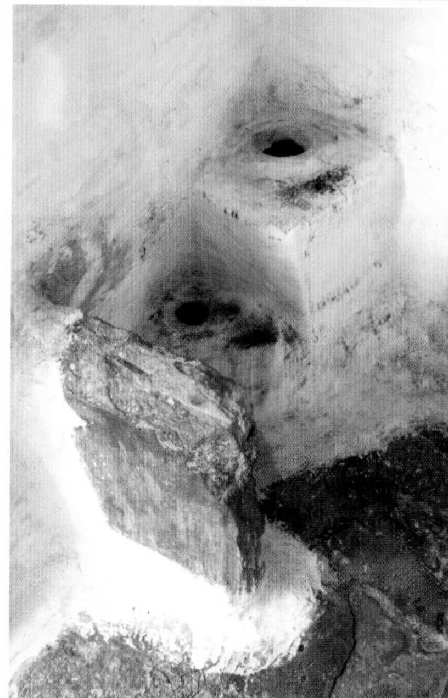

△ ▷ **HOLES FOR COOKING**
Carved out of stone blocks set into one corner of the interior courtyard, these holes are filled with hot coals onto which are set iron pans for cooking various types of bread.

STONE HOUSE

DESERT DWELLING, JAISALMER FORT, RAJASTHAN

◁ DOOR TO STREET
Bright green and now slightly crooked on its hinges, the external door at the top of the steps opens onto the small courtyard.

▷ WASHING AREA
This recessed stone slab in the courtyard floor is used for washing cooking vessels. Waste water flows along the channel to the street.

▷ OUTHOUSE STEPS
These steps up to the roof of the now-disused outhouse show how the house would have looked before it was whitewashed.

FOOD PREPARATION AREA
Many tasks associated with preparing meals take place in this recess on the lower level of the house. On the left is the doorway leading out to the small courtyard.

SKYLIGHT
This opening in the roof of the upper level of the house lets in light, aids ventilation, and gives a refreshing glimpse of the skies above.

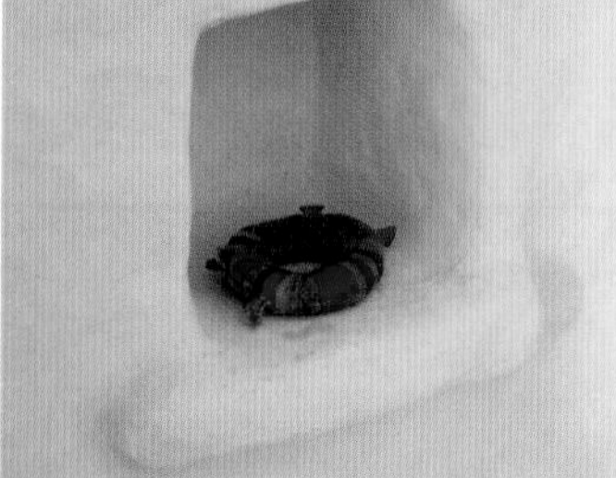

WALL NICHE
Even the smallest wall niche has a purpose. This one contains a cloth ring for supporting round-bottomed pots.

WATER POT
Propped up on bricks in the food preparation area, this former cooking pot is now used for storing water.

STORAGE CHEST
Clothing and other precious items are safely locked away in a wooden chest set on the lower level. A cloth cover transforms it into a usable surface.

WALL STEPS TO ROOF
Steps formed from projecting stones set into the wall lead up through the skylight to the roof, from where there are superb views over Jaisalmer.

GRINDING STONE
An essential part of food preparation is the hand-operated, circular stone mortar. This is used for grinding rice and other grains for everyday meals.

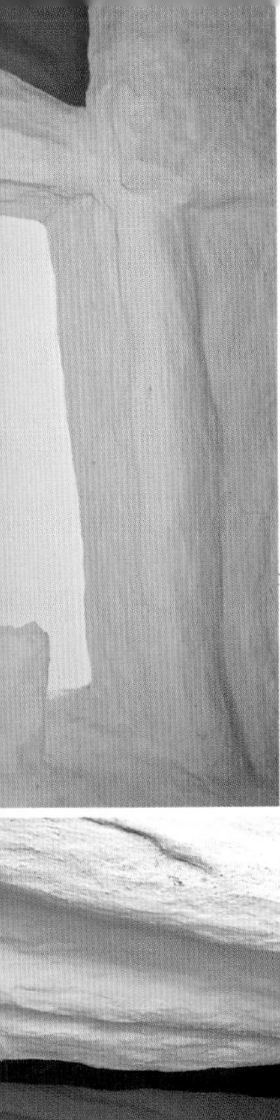

▷ **FOOD CONTAINERS**
Gleaming stainless steel pots and platters, as well as cups for cooking oils, are stored on high shelves and in niches set into the whitewashed walls.

▽ **WINDOW SEAT**
An outside view with an invigorating breeze can be enjoyed from this stone seat, which is placed below a window in the outer wall of the upper story.

▽ **UPPER LEVEL**
Used only during the cooler months, the upper level of the house is totally devoid of furniture. All necessary items are stacked on shelves on the walls.

△ **WALL CUPBOARD**
Small valuable items are locked away in this little wall cupboard. Its wooden shutter is painted the same color as the doors.

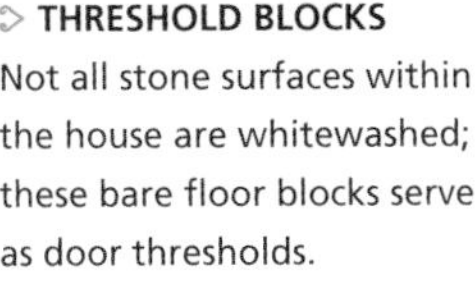

▷ **THRESHOLD BLOCKS**
Not all stone surfaces within the house are whitewashed; these bare floor blocks serve as door thresholds.

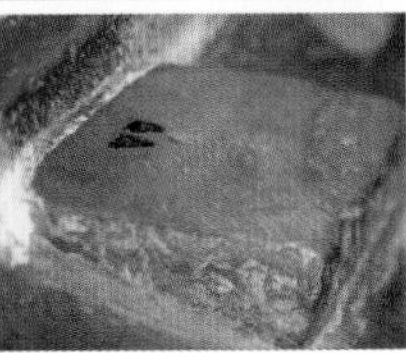

◁ ▷ **BEDROOM DOOR**
This door, with its bare stone step, leads to the upstairs bedroom, where the family sleeps during winter.

FATEHPUR SIKRI

MUGHAL PALACE COMPLEX, UTTAR PRADESH

▷ **NAUBAT KHANA**
The principal bazaar street leading through the city to Akbar's palace passes through this triple-arched gate, which has a chamber on top—the *naubat khana*—for musicians.

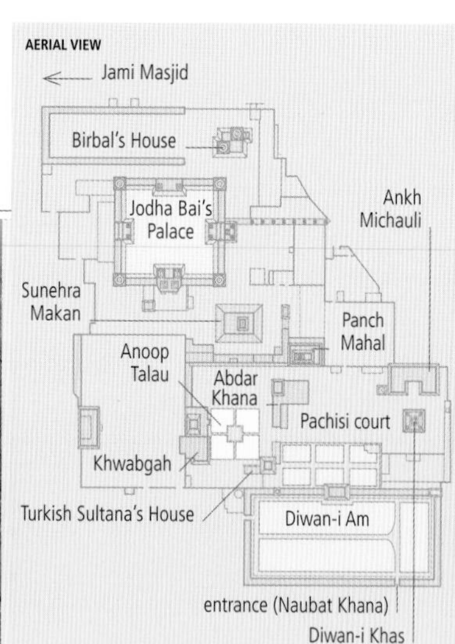

The palaces of the Mughals emperors were conceived as military encampments, but realized in masonry rather than canvas. The typical Mughal royal complex of the 16th and 17th centuries comprises open pavilions of different designs arranged around a sequence of courtyards, all shielded from view by high walls. Entrance to the complex is via well-guarded arched gateways.

Within the complex, there is a hierarchy of spaces: at Fatehpur Sikri it emphasizes the progression from the Diwan-i Am (Hall of Public Audience), to the Diwan-i Khas (Hall of Private Audience). Beyond are the residential apartments, pleasure pavilions, and gardens with ornamental pools and water channels intended for the emperor and his household. A small mosque for royal use is often incorporated as part of the royal complex, while kitchens, stores, bath-houses, workshops, stables, and other service buildings are generally located outside the palace walls.

Fatehpur Sikri lies a short distance from Agra, in Uttar Pradesh, and is the most completely preserved Mughal royal complex, probably because it was used for a mere 14 years before being abandoned in 1585 when its founder, Emperor Akbar, moved his court to Lahore. Construction work on the Sikri complex was initiated by Akbar in 1571 after one of his queens gave birth to a son, as predicted by the Sufi saint, Salim Chishti, who resided in the village of Sikri. The City of Victory—Fatehpur—that Akbar constructed at Sikri was intended as a showpiece of imperial Mughal magnificence.

Surrounded by walls and provided with a vast reservoir that guaranteed a continuous supply of water, Fatehpur Sikri consists of an extensive palace and a spacious mosque set atop a ridge that rises above the houses of the city. The royal complex is divided into three distinct zones: a public courtyard overlooked by the Diwan-i Am; a paved compound with buildings for the exclusive use of the emperor and his male courtiers; and a private compound with residential apartments for Akbar's various queens. Built to inventive designs out of locally available red sandstone, the halls, pavilions, and apartments of the palace zone testify to the creativity and skills of Akbar's architects and craftsmen.

△ **DIWAN-I AM**
The emperor held public audiences in the first courtyard, seated in the Diwan-i Am, which here takes the form of an open pavilion.

▷ **PUBLIC COURTYARD**
The courtyard of the Diwan-i Am is surrounded by colonnades where visitors could take shelter. (The lawn in the center is not an original feature.)

SECOND COURTYARD
The second courtyard, as seen from Akbar's bedchamber, is a vast paved area dominated by the Diwan-i Khas (*center rear*).

ROOFTOP CHHATRIS
Open, domed pavilions called *chhatris* mark the rooftop corners of the Diwan-i Khas.

DIWAN-I KHAS
Though called the Hall of Private Audience, this building more likely served as the emperor's private meditation chamber.

INTERIOR OF DIWAN-I KHAS
The double-height interior of the Diwan-i Khas has a central column bearing a small circular dais reached by walkways from each corner. Akbar may have sat here in meditation, or listened to religious discourses.

PACHISI COURT
The colored stones in the paving of the second courtyard define a *pachisi* game board. Courtiers would act as the playing pieces.

CONFERENCE CHAMBER
To one side of the Diwan-i Khas is the conference chamber (Ankh Michauli). It contains secret passageways for spies to observe discussions and negotiations.

ASTROLOGER'S SEAT
This small vaulted pavilion, with ornamental lintels springing from its corner columns, is where the court astrologer made predictions.

▷ **STONE SCREEN**
Light and air were admitted to the library via sandstone screens with complicated interlocking geometric patterns.

▽ **TURKISH SULTANA'S HOUSE**
This small, highly decorated sandstone pavilion in the second courtyard is named after one of Akbar's foreign queens, even though this area was reserved for men.

▽ **ARABESQUES**
Carvings of symmetrically arranged leafy stems and petals adorn the column capitals in the veranda of the Turkish Sultana's house.

▽ **SLEEPING CHAMBER**
The pavilion at the top of the Khwabgah, which has a gently sloping roof, was Akbar's private sleeping chamber. The room below may have been a library.

△ **STAR-SHAPED PATTERNS**
Geometric designs adorn the ceiling in the Turkish Sultana's house (*top*); recesses in the veranda walls (*above*) may have held oil lamps.

△ **KHWABGAH**
In the second courtyard, at the opposite end to the Diwan-i Am, is this two-story building housing Akbar's sleeping chamber and the library.

▷ **LIBRARY**
The lower portion of the Khwabgah is divided into two levels by colonnades that support a mezzanine floor; this may have housed the emperor's library.

△ **ARCADED CORRIDOR**
This corridor beneath the sleeping chamber led Akbar to a balcony, where he would appear before an assembled crowd each morning.

◁ **WATER WALKWAYS**
The second courtyard of the palace was used by Akbar himself and his nobles. Stone walkways lead across a pool to a balustraded platform.

ANOOP TALAU
The platform in the center of the second courtyard's ornamental pool, the Anoop Talau, was where the seated emperor and his guests would enjoy poetry readings and musical concerts.

BATTLEMENT FRIEZE
The second and third tiers of the five-story, pyramidal Panch Mahal are decorated with friezes of battlements.

PANCH MAHAL
The innermost private zone, reserved for Akbar's queens and members of his household, is dominated by the Panch Mahal, which is topped by a *chhatri*.

ARCHED NICHE
Probably intended to hold a small oil lamp, this wall niche in the Sunehra Makan still retains visible remnants of its original paintwork.

SUNEHRA MAKAN
Used by Akbar's wives, the Sunehra Makan ("Golden House") was named after its rich frescoes and gilding.

COLONNADES
The colonnades of the Panch Mahal were hung with awnings to conceal the women of the royal household who gathered here.

PILLAR DETAIL
The pillars of the colonnades bear a variety of carved designs, such as these stylized lotus-flower buds.

VAULTED INTERIOR
Chambers with ornamental fluted vaults in the Sunehra Makan accommodated Akbar's queens and their female retinue.

CHRISTIAN INFLUENCE
One of Akbar's wives converted to Christianity, and the fading wall paintings show influence of Christian art.

FARTHER AFIELD
Rooftop *chhatris* give a distant view of the impressive gateway to the Jami Masjid, the city's sacred mosque complex.

ENTRANCEWAY
The arched entrance to Jodha Bai's palace is framed by cut-out lotus buds, and flanked by vaulted balconies.

JODHA BAI'S PALACE
This palace-within-a palace, the largest residence in the private zone, is modeled on a typical Rajasthani palace; Akbar had several Hindu wives from Rajasthan.

COURTYARD OF JODHA BAI'S PALACE
A spacious, interior courtyard, overlooked by two-story apartments with rooftop *chhatris,* offered vantage points for the queens and their retainers.

COLUMN BASE
Stylized motifs decorate the interior of Jodha Bai's palace, such as this geometric pattern carved onto the base of a pillar.

PADMANABHAPURAM

WOODEN ROYAL PALACE, TAMIL NADU

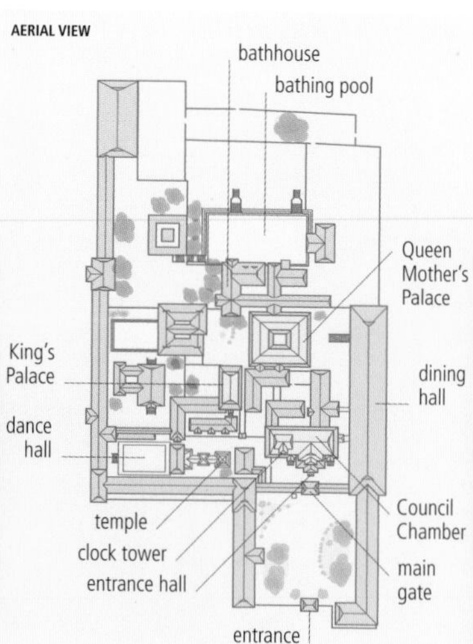

Little is left today of India's ancient and widespread tradition of wooden domestic architecture, an exception being the houses and palaces of Kerala. Subject to heavy monsoon rains, this verdant region of southern India is dotted with wooden buildings topped by sloping roofs clad in terra-cotta or copper tiles. The steeply gabled roofs of these buildings, sometimes rising in two or more superimposed tiers, are supported on elaborate timber structures. Light enters the buildings through wooden screens, and is reflected off polished plaster floors and gleaming bronze lamps and vessels. The plastered walls are typically covered with brightly toned murals that illustrate Hindu mythological themes; similar motifs adorn the woodwork that decorates the gabled ends of roofs.

All of these features are present in the palace at Padmanabhapuram—the most extensive and spectacularly adorned example of Kerala-style royal architecture, even though the complex is now actually situated in Tamil Nadu. It was established by King Martanda Varma (r. 1729–58) as the headquarters of the rulers of Travancore, in the southern part of Kerala. The palace takes its name from Padmanabha, the Lotus Born [God]—this is the form of Vishnu who served as the patron deity of this line of kings. After 1750, when the Travancore capital was shifted to present-day Thiruvananthapuram (Trivandrum), the Padmanabhapuram Palace was reduced to a minor residence, thereby ensuring its preservation into modern times.

The Padmanabhapuram complex consists of a number of freestanding, gable-roofed structures that serve as gateways, council chambers, audience halls, dance pavilions, residential apartments, dining halls, and bath-houses. These different elements are arranged around a sequence of courtyards that marks a transition from public to private spaces.

The complex is dominated by a lofty masonry tower known as the Upparika Malika. From bottom to top, the tower houses the treasury, the king's bed chamber, the royal meditation room, and the god's bedroom. All the rooms are linked by narrow flights of steps. To the rear of the complex is a private garden and bathing pool.

VIEW TOWARD THE ENTRANCE HALL
The double wooden doors in the main gate give access to the outer enclosure of the Padmanabhapuram Palace, onto which faces the palace's entrance hall.

ENTRANCE HALL ROOF
The entrance hall has double tiers of steeply sloping roofs clad in terra-cotta tiles. Each roof has a gable decorated with cut-out wooden screens.

WOODWORK ON MAIN GATE
Among the carvings that enhance the wooden architecture is this stylized lotus motif, which affords magical protection for the palace's main entrance.

CEILING DETAILS
This ceiling panel depicts the goddess Lakshmi (*center*) bathed by elephants with raised trunks. She is flanked by stylized flower designs.

ROOF STRUCTURE
A framework of angled rafters, horizontal beams, and vertical pillars supports the council chamber roof.

BRASS LAMP
Ornate metal lamps like this one, with circular trays for holding oil and wicks, once illuminated the corridors of the palace.

PILLAR BRACKET
The intricate wood carvings of the palace interior include this pillar bracket, which is fashioned as a warrior astride a leaping, richly bridled horse.

HANUMAN
One of the granite columns within the council chamber is carved with an image of Hanuman, the monkey hero who assisted Rama in the epic tale of the *Ramayana*.

STAINED-GLASS WINDOW
This stained-glass window in the council chamber filters strong sunlight, as do the angled wooden louvers.

COUNCIL CHAMBER
The upper story of the entrance hall was used as a council chamber. This was where the Travancore rulers would hold their private audiences.

QUEEN MOTHER'S PALACE
Within the Padmanabhapuram Palace's private zone is the residence of the queen mother, which has sleeping apartments arranged on four sides of a small interior courtyard.

KITCHEN
The preparation of the food for feeding the Brahmins priests took place at ground level, beneath the dining hall, where mortars and cisterns for grinding grains can still be seen.

CONSTRUCTION DETAILS
The palace's interior woodwork is a vehicle for intricate carving, such as this roof gable with cut-out bird and foliate motifs. The sloping, tiled roofs have preserved such details through the centuries.

COLUMN CARVINGS
The upper parts of the columns in the Queen Mother's Palace are embellished with carvings of tiny cobra hoods, as well as hanging brackets in the form of stylized lotus motifs.

VIEW TOWARD COURTYARD
Arched doorways in the walls of the Queen Mother's Palace look toward the interior courtyard, which has a pool for collecting water.

◁ **GARDEN COMPOUND**
The open spaces between the halls, apartments, dining rooms, kitchens, and stores form a private garden lined with rows of plants.

▷ **BED CHAMBER STAIRCASE**
The staircase in the tower of the King's Palace links the king's private bedroom with the sleeping chamber reserved for the god.

▽ **INTERIOR ROOF DETAIL**
The gable-ended roof that tops the King's Palace, as seen from the god's bedroom, has exposed, steeply angled beams that carry the terra-cotta roof tiles.

◁ **SHIVA AND PARVATI FRESCO**
Commissioned by Martanda Varma, a wall painting in the god's bedroom depicts Shiva seated with Parvati, surrounded by a crowd of gods.

△ **GOD'S BEDROOM**
The chamber at the top of the King's Palace contains a European-style canopied bed intended for the use of Padmanabha—the god to whom the entire palace is dedicated.

PRIVATE POOL
At the rear of the palace is a bathing pond that was reserved for the use of members of the royal family. The steps that descend to the water are concealed from view by a sloping tiled roof.

LOOKING DOWN INTO THE TEMPLE
A wooden screen at the upper level of the colonnade in the middle of the palace allowed a glimpse of the ceremonies that took place beneath.

TEMPLE AND UPPARIKA MALIKA
Rising above the granite colonnade and sanctuary of the temple, which lies at the heart of the palace, is the multistory Upparika Malika, a masonry tower with tiered roofs.

TEMPLE COMPOUND
The stone temple within the palace was used only by the royal family; here, the king and his family members, aided by priests, worshipped the goddess Saraswati.

STONE ELEPHANT
The granite elephant beside the steps leading up to the dance hall lends a royal theme to this otherwise sacred zone of the palace.

DANCE HALL
Used for celebrations of the Navratri festival, the dance hall attached to the temple is made entirely of granite, with a flat stone roof.

MAIDENS HOLDING LAMPS
These pillars in the dance hall are carved with maidens holding lamps, a mark of respect for the goddess worshipped in the temple beyond.

◁ **VIEWING SCREENS**
Wooden panels on the dance hall's upper level permitted ladies of the royal household to discreetly view the activities below.

▽ **INSIDE THE DANCE HALL**
Rows of elaborately carved granite pillars, seen here reflected in the polished, black-plaster floor of the dance hall, lead to the door of the temple sanctuary.

▷ **AUSPICIOUS GOOSE**
Animal and bird motifs borrowed from Hindu temple art, such as this goose with a fanciful foliate tail, are carved in shallow relief on a granite pillar in the dance hall.

△ **TEMPLE DOORS**
Opened only for private ceremonies at particular times of the day, the wooden temple doors are adorned with deeply cut panels bearing lotus-flower motifs.

AMBER FORT

FORTIFIED RAJPUT PALACE, RAJASTHAN

AERIAL VIEW

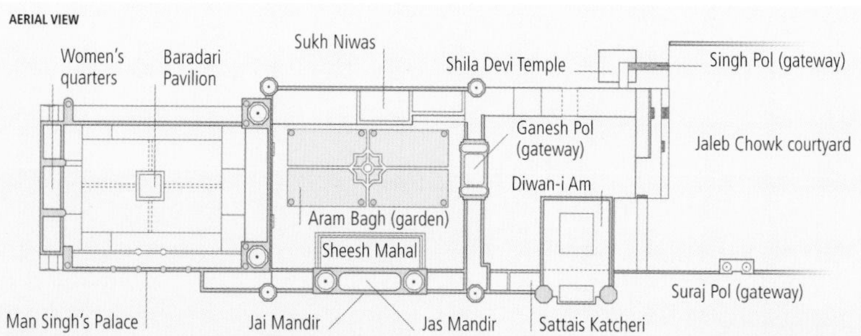

SURAJ POL
The main entrance is the east-facing Sun Gate (Suraj Pol). Its arch is high enough for elephants and their riders to pass through.

SINGH POL
Access to the first inner courtyard of the fort is via the Lion Gate (Singh Pol). This is reached by a steep flight of steps flanked by open pavilions, or *chhatris*.

Historically, Rajasthan was never unified as a single state. Instead, over the centuries, the region was divided into a number of kingdoms presided over by Rajput warrior families, who fought with each other for supremacy, but also united against such common enemies as the neighboring sultans of Delhi. This more or less continuous state of warfare—which continued into the Mughal era (1526–1757), despite marriage alliances between the Rajputs and Mughal emperors—explains why Rajput palaces were conceived as formidable citadels, elevated on hilltops that overlooked the cities below. Ringed by massive walls reinforced with bastions and towers, these fortified residences were entered through gateways with cunningly devised "bent" entrances to hamper the progress of attackers.

Such highly evolved military architecture provided excellent protection for the private headquarters of the different Rajput royal families. Within the walls, the palaces were generally laid out as a sequence of aligned courtyards, arranged at different levels. The courtyards marked a transition from the public outermost zones of the palaces, where the rulers held audience and conducted state business, to the private apartments of the royal families in the innermost parts of the palaces.

Among the most imposing of these fortified palaces in Rajasthan is that at Amber, headquarters of the Kachhwaha rulers from the beginning of the 16th century until their move in 1727 to the newly planned city of Jaipur, a short distance away. The Amber Fort is built as a series of courtyards ascending a steep hill that overlooks a strategic mountain pass, through which runs the highway to Delhi.

Developed by two Kachhwaha rulers, Man Singh (r. 1592–1615) and Mirza Jai Singh (r. 1621–67), into a showpiece of Rajput strength and magnificence, the Amber Fort has sumptuous halls, apartments, and pavilions facing onto paved courtyards and formal gardens with pools, water channels, and fountains. The carved marble panels, inlaid mirrorwork, and vivid murals imitate the decoration of contemporary Mughal palaces. This is hardly surprising, since Man Singh and Mirza Jai Singh served as commanders in the service of the Mughal emperors.

FIRST INNER COURTYARD
After passing through the Singh Pol, visitors to Amber arrive at a spacious courtyard bounded at one corner by the Diwan-i Am and the Sattais Katcheri.

VIEWING BALCONIES
The small arched openings in the projecting balconies at the upper level of the Sattais Katcheri were for surveying the activities that took place in the courtyard below.

MONSTER-HEAD BRACKETS
These brackets in the Diwan-i Am depict the heads of aquatic monsters, or *makaras*, with curling snouts.

DIWAN-I AM
The first inner courtyard is dominated by the Diwan-i Am (Hall of Public Audience), which imitates the pillared audience halls of Mughal palaces.

ELEPHANT BRACKET
The cut-out brackets that top the columns in the Diwan-i Am incorporate Hindu motifs, such as elephants and lotus buds.

RECEPTION ROOM
The interior of the Diwan-i Am has a spacious reception room roofed with a lofty vault. Here, the Kachhwaha rulers met with visitors and conferred with their commanders and nobles.

COLUMN BASES
Stylized arabesque designs like these are carved in shallow relief onto the bases of the polygonal columns that line the reception room of the Diwan-i Am.

SATTAIS KATCHERI
This two-story building next to the Diwan-i Am has Mughal-style lobed arcades. This is where scribes recorded revenue petitions presented to the Kachhwaha rulers.

▽ ▷ **STALACTITE VAULTS**
The arched vaults of the Ganesh Pol enhanced by plaster stalactite are painted with floral patterns; these imitate similar features in Mughal architecture.

▽ **GANESH POL**
Built in 1640, this intricately decorated gateway is the entrance to the private zone of the palace, which includes the sumptuous apartments where the Kachhwaha rulers and their families lived.

▷ **FLOOR DETAIL**
The floor of the Ganesh Pol's entrance porch is enlivened by designs formed from polished slabs of colored marble.

FLORAL DESIGNS
The walls of the Ganesh Pol are festooned with floral designs, including these flowers encircled by swirling foliage, which surround the arch of the entrance porch.

UPPER BALCONIES
The upper level of the Ganesh Pol has a screened balcony with an opening, from which women could look out unseen on the activities in the Diwan-i Am and the courtyard below.

ENTRANCE PORCH
Above the doorway within the entrance porch is a painting of a seated figure of Ganesha—the elephant-headed god after whom the Ganesh Pol is named.

FLOWERING PLANT
This floral carving on a stone panel is typical of the Mughal-style motifs that decorate the Ganesh Pol.

GEOMETRIC SCREENS
The balconies in the Ganesh Pol have stone screens bearing geometric patterns based on repeated interlocking stars and octagons.

PLEASURE GARDEN
The residential apartments of the palace's private zone look out onto a formal pleasure garden, the Aram Bagh, which is divided into geometric plots by walkways and water channels.

JAI MANDIR
The Jai Mandir consists of two vaulted halls: the lower one is surrounded by an arcaded veranda, and the upper one by a curved roof and a pair of *chhatris*.

FLORAL CEILING PANEL
The arabesque designs and motifs of flowers and foliage on the ceiling's central panels are inlaid with tiny pieces of glittering mirror.

PETAL-MOTIF CAPITAL
Stylized petal shapes arranged in tiers decorate the capitals of the double columns that support the lobed arches lining the veranda of the Jai Mandir.

JAI MANDIR VERANDA
Mughal-style marble arches resting on polygonal columns create an open veranda on three sides of the private pavilion known as the Jai Mandir, which faces onto the Aram Bagh garden.

◁ **CURVED CEILING**
Where the veranda's ceiling curves up toward the central panels, the plaster niches give way to geometric floral designs.

▷ **PANELS AND NICHES**
The veranda walls are divided into marble panels below, and arched niches with molded plaster and mirrorwork above. This niche sports a flowers-in-vase motif.

▽ **ENTRANCE TO SHEESH MAHAL**
This doorway leads to the mirrored hall, or Sheesh Mahal, which serves as the main reception room of the Jai Mandir.

◁ **RULER'S DWELLING**
The stately elegance of the Jai Mandir's veranda reflects the fact that this building was the personal apartment of the Kachhwaha ruler himself.

▷ **BARADARI PAVILION**
In this pavilion in the Zenana (women's quarters), the queens would enjoy performances of music and dance.

TAJ MAHAL

MONUMENTAL GARDEN TOMB, AGRA, UTTAR PRADESH

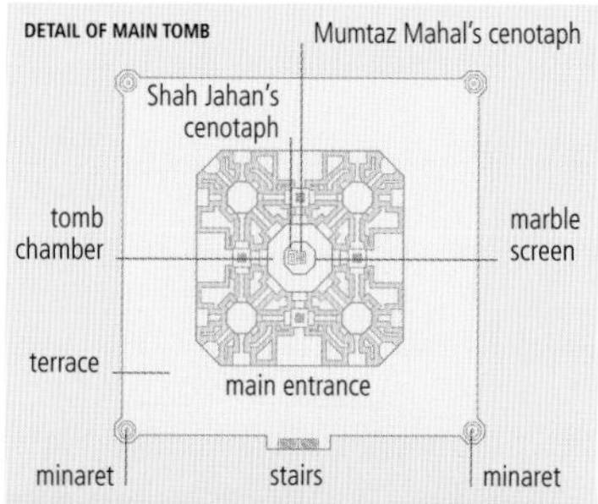

AERIAL VIEW

Masjid (mosque)
Mehmankhana (guesthouse)
pool
main tomb
pool
water channel
garden walkways
garden pavilions
water channel
chahar bagh (garden)
Lotus Pool
gateway
entrance
entrance
entrance

Celebrated as India's most famous building, the Taj Mahal belongs to a long tradition of monumental garden tombs that ultimately derives from the architecture of Iran and Central Asia. However, the combination of a domed tomb and *chahar bagh*, or four-square garden, within a symmetrically planned, walled complex is specifically a 16th-century Mughal invention. Here, the cenotaph of the deceased is raised above ground level and placed within an octagonal chamber surmounted by a lofty dome symbolizing the heavens. The *chahar bagh* in which the tomb stands, or which it overlooks from one side, as in the Taj, is imbued with a comparable significance: traversed by channels of constantly running water, the *chahar bagh* represents paradise. Koranic verses in Arabic script proclaiming the rewards of the faithful in God's heaven, reproduced in bands around the doorways to the tomb and on the cenotaphs inside the chamber, guarantee the deceased a permanent home in paradise.

Erected by the Mughal emperor, Shah Jahan, in memory of his beloved wife, Mumtaz Mahal, who died in 1631 and who gave the tomb its name, the Taj Mahal was completed in 1645 after 12 years of construction, employing many thousands of workers. The monument, which is situated on the right bank of the Yamuna River, on the outskirts of Agra, is unsurpassed in its grandiose planning and huge scale.

The Taj Mahal complex consists of a sandstone terrace raised above the river, from which rises a marble plinth with four towering minarets at its corners and a domed tomb at its center. To one side of the plinth is a mosque, and to the other a guesthouse for visitors. Completing the complex is a vast *chahar bagh* with water channels and a central pool; a monumental gateway overlooking the plaza outside the complex; and a commercial quarter with four caravanserais (inns) called Tajganj. Income from Tajganj contributed to the upkeep of the monument.

The white-marble tomb itself is remarkable for the perfection of its proportions and the refinement of its floral, geometric, and calligraphic decoration. As such, the Taj Mahal embodies the high point of Mughal architecture and decorative design.

CHHATRI CREST
The main gateway is topped by a crestlike line of ornamental domed open pavilions known as *chhatris*.

MAIN GATEWAY
The *chahar bagh* is entered from the south through a monumental gateway with a central arched portal and part-octagonal buttresses at the corners.

DISTANT VIEW
Looking through the arch of the main gate, one can appreciate the beautiful balance of the Taj Mahal's design.

FORMER FLOWER GARDEN
Marble strips set into the grass create geometric garden plots, where brightly colored flowerbeds originally created a brilliant, carpetlike effect.

◁ **SURROUNDING WALLS**
The Taj Mahal complex is enclosed within a high boundary wall constructed out of red sandstone.

▽ **GARDEN PAVILION**
The transverse walkway of the *chahar bagh* ends in two-story pavilions with rooftop *chhatris*, which give visitors an elevated view of the garden.

◁ **GARDEN TERRACE**
Immediately inside the gate, overlooking the *chahar bagh*, is a terrace paved with shaped sandstone and marble slabs.

▽ **PAVILION SCREENS**
Set into the lobed arches of the garden pavilions, and here framing a door, are carved red-sandstone screens decorated with repeated hexagonal designs.

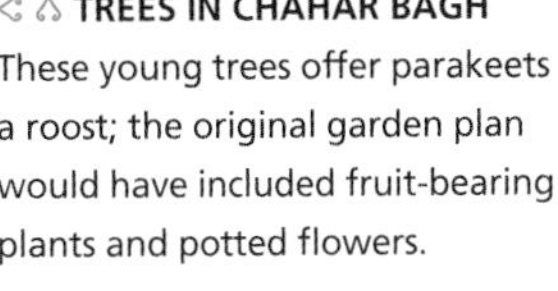

◁ △ **TREES IN CHAHAR BAGH**
These young trees offer parakeets a roost; the original garden plan would have included fruit-bearing plants and potted flowers.

◁ **STONE PATHS**
Planted with lawns shaded by trees, the square plots of the *chahar bagh* are outlined by raised stone paths, along which visitors can stroll.

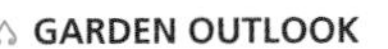

△ **GARDEN OUTLOOK**
This colonnade at the southern end of the Taj complex looks out over the *chahar bagh*. The domed tomb itself lies at the northern end, beyond the trees.

GUESTHOUSE AND POOL
The marble plinth on which the tomb stands lies between two identical red sandstone structures. The building to the west is a mosque, for visitors to the tomb; to the east is the Mehmankhana, which was used as a guesthouse. Each building has a pool in front of it, with sandstone corner seats.

CEILING DETAIL
The red sandstone ceilings in the guesthouse and mosque are decorated with delicate, painted floral designs.

GUESTHOUSE ARCHWAY
Looking through one of the guesthouse's smaller archways of sandstone and inlaid marble, one can see the garden beyond.

ARCADED GALLERIES
To the sides of the guesthouse are arcaded galleries that lead to flanking pavilions. Similar structures adjoin the mosque on the far side of the tomb.

TERRACE FLOOR
The main area of the terrace around the marble plinth is covered with lozenge- and star-shaped paving stones in contrasting sandstone hues.

◁ ▽ RIVERSIDE VIEW

At the very end of the Taj Mahal complex, the lofty sandstone terrace beneath the tomb's marble plinth drops sharply away to the bank of the Yamuna River.

◁ ▽ PAVING AND DRAINS

Beside the river, the terrace is paved with stars of red sandstone and diamonds of white marble. Drainage holes are cleverly disguised at the center of floral motifs.

△ LOTUS POOL

In the middle of the *chahar bagh* is the Lotus Pool, which reflects the perfect proportions of the domed tomb, and the changing skies above.

▷ CYPRESSES AND LOTUS SPRINKLER

Cypress trees (*far right*) line the central water channel. This white marble fountain (*right*) is shaped like a lotus, with flowing petals and a central bud.

▷ **TOMB BUILDING**
Recessed arches in the tomb's facade provide depth, while their inlaid panels reflect the changing light to give the tomb a mystical aura.

▽ **STAIRCASE TO TOMB**
The tomb stands on a huge marble plinth that is 22 ft (6.7 m) high and 313 ft (95 m) square. The only way to reach it from the garden level is via this covered staircase.

△ **MARBLE PARAPET**
At the edge of the plinth is a marble parapet set with black rectangular designs, seen here as it snakes around the base of a minaret.

▷ **FLORAL IMAGERY**
A profusion of friezes and panels depicting flowering plants, foliage, and vases are carved in relief throughout the complex, symbolizing the Taj Mahal's central theme of paradise.

◁ **PIETRA DURA**
Plain marble is embellished by inlays of precious and semiprecious stones using the technique of *pietra dura*, giving the tomb the look of a jeweled casket.

CROWNING CHHATRI
The octagonal *chhatris* crowning the quartet of 130-ft- (40-m-) high minarets at the corners of the plinth can be reached by staircases within the minarets' circular shafts.

PORTAL FINIALS
The slender, minaret-like finials that rise up the sides of the arched portals are adorned with chevron patterns and topped by curving petals.

ARCHED PORTAL
In the center of each side of the tomb is a monumental portal with a recessed arch framed by bands of calligraphy and spandrels filled with arabesque patterns.

KORANIC INSCRIPTIONS
Black marble calligraphic inlays, quoting excerpts from the Koran, run in bands around the arched portals of the tomb like banners.

ROOFTOP CHHATRI
The bulging marble dome on the roof of the tomb is flanked by four *chhatris*, which are similar in design to those on the minarets.

DOOR INTO TOMB CHAMBER
The tomb chamber is entered through wooden, brass-clad doors with bold geometric patterns. Just inside is a marble doorstop (*above*).

▷ **APEX OF THE DOME**
Black-marble inlays at the apex of the dome over the cenotaphs form a swirling design that is ringed by interlaced strapwork.

▽ **SCREENS**
An octagon of finely crafted *jali* (perforated stone) screens, augmented by floral designs in *pietra dura*, encases the cenotaphs of the emperor and his queen.

△ **TOMB CHAMBER**
Lit by windows on four sides, this chamber houses the cenotaphs of Shah Jahan and Mumtaz Mahal (the actual graves are at ground level).

▽ ▷ **LIFELIKE FLOWERS**
Pietra dura is widely employed in the Taj Mahal to give naturalistic renderings of flowers, with delicate tonal effects.

ABSTRACT TREE
The cut-out, treelike designs of the *jali* screens have central "trunks" from which leafy tendrils swirl.

QUEEN'S CENOTAPH
In the center of the tomb chamber lies the white marble cenotaph of Mumtaz Mahal, decorated by *pietra dura* and calligraphy.

STYLIZED FLOWERS
As well as naturalistic forms, *pietra dura* is used to create more abstract, stylized floral motifs on the *jali* screens and the queen's cenotaph.

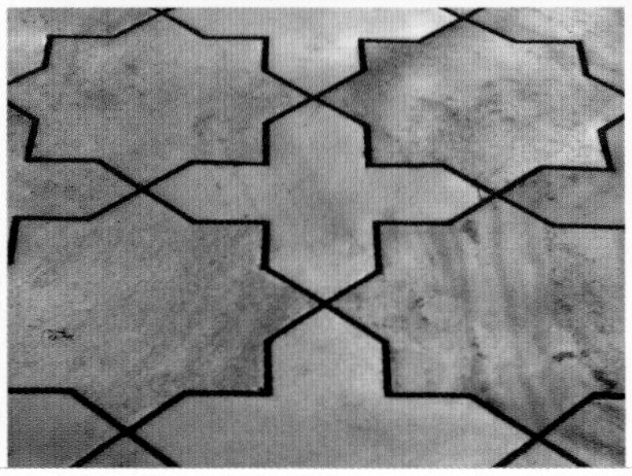

GEOMETRIC FLOOR PATTERN
The white marble floor of the tomb chamber has a geometric pattern of repeated eight-pointed stars outlined by thin, black stone strips.

EPITAPH
The black-marble calligraphy on the queen's cenotaph serves as an epitaph for Mumtaz Mahal; as well as giving the date of her death as 1631, it quotes excerpts from the Koran describing paradise.

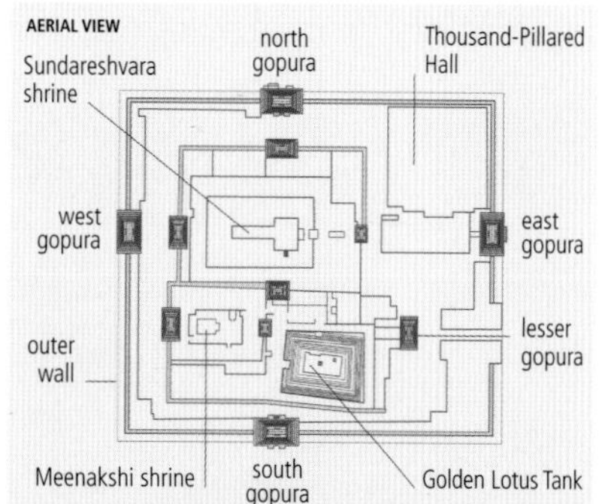

▷ **YALI HEAD**
A *yali* head with protruding eyes caps the ornate arched end of the barrel-vaulted roof of a *gopura* within the Meenakshi temple complex.

▷ **OUTER GOPURA**
As seen from the streets surrounding the temple complex, this *gopura* presents a steeply pyramidal tower encrusted with plaster figures.

▽ **INNER GOPURA**
This smaller towered gateway within the temple complex serves as the entrance to the inner enclosure of the Sundareshvara shrine.

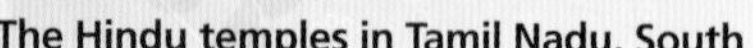

The Hindu temples in Tamil Nadu, South India, which were developed from the 16th century onwards, resemble urban complexes, their spacious interiors being crowded with shrines, pillared halls known as *mandapas*, kitchens and eating houses, and huge bathing tanks. The typical temple complex is divided into a number of concentric quadrangular enclosures contained by high masonry walls. It is entered from one or more sides via monumental gateways with steep, pyramid-like, brick-and-plaster towers. Known as *gopuras*, these gateways are an outstanding feature of the South Indian architectural style. They soar above the surrounding streets and houses, affirming the presence of the temple divinity at the core of the city or town. The hollow interiors of their brick-and-plaster towers are concealed from view by tiers of exuberant, multicolored sculptures depicting crowds of Hindu gods and goddesses with their consorts and attendants. Here, too, are found the auspicious but ferocious monsters known as *yalis*, with their vicious teeth and bulging eyes and horns. Carvings of *yalis* and other animals also adorn the granite piers of the *mandapas* that precede the temple's various shrines.

One of the largest Hindu temples in Tamil Nadu stands in the middle of Madurai. The temple complex contains a pair of shrines, one consecrated to Meenakshi, the protective goddess of the city and of the Nayaka rulers who made Madurai their capital between the 16th and 18th centuries, and the other to Sundareshvara (another name for Shiva), who is her divine lord. The monument's twin dedication is reflected in the layout of the temple, which consists of two matching shrines, each standing in its own quadrangular enclosure surrounded by colonnades, and approached through a succession of *mandapas* and courtyards.

The locations of the Meenakshi and Sundareshvara shrines can be identified from outside the complex by four lofty *gopuras*, more than 164 ft (50 m) high, which are aligned with the sanctuaries of the goddess and god within. Lesser *gopuras* inside the temple mark the transition from one enclosure to the next. Additional *mandapas*—and even an unfinished colossal *gopura*—lie outside the temple walls.

MEENAKSHI TEMPLE

HINDU HOUSE OF WORSHIP, MADURAI, TAMIL NADU

◁ **MARRIAGE SCENE**
This tableau shows the marriage of Meenakshi to Sundareshvara in the company of Vishnu (*center*).

▽ **DETAIL OF SHIVA**
Among the vivid sculptures on the *gopuras* is this terrifying figure of Shiva brandishing a full range of weapons in his 16 arms.

◁ ▽ **GOPURA PASSAGEWAY**
Even seemingly unimportant surfaces, such as the passageways between the *gopuras*, are decked with carvings.

△ **GANESHA SHRINE**
This colorful shrine is dedicated to the elephant-headed god who attends Meenakshi and Sundareshvara.

◁ **SHRINE TOWER**
The gleaming square domed tower that crowns the Meenakshi shrine is faced with gilded metal sheets.

△ **SAGES AND CONSORTS**
On the upper tier of one of the *gopuras* is this row of figures representing bearded sages and female consorts.

△ **KAMBATTADI MANDAPA**
Pillars with sculpted shafts, and attached small columns, define the central space of the hall preceding the Sundareshvara shrine.

▽ ▷ **LION CAPITALS**
The flat granite slabs that roof the temple's halls and corridors are carried on cut-out lion capitals, the animals being tripled at the corners.

▷ **DOORWAY TO SHRINE**
At those times of day and night when the god and goddess are not being worshipped, the doors to their sanctuaries are closed.

◁ **NANDI**
Sundareshvara's bull mount, Nandi, is an important image within the temple complex.

▽ **FRAME AND LAMP-COLUMN**
Deep within the Kambattadi Mandapa are this ornate brass frame and a lamp-column that extends up through the roof.

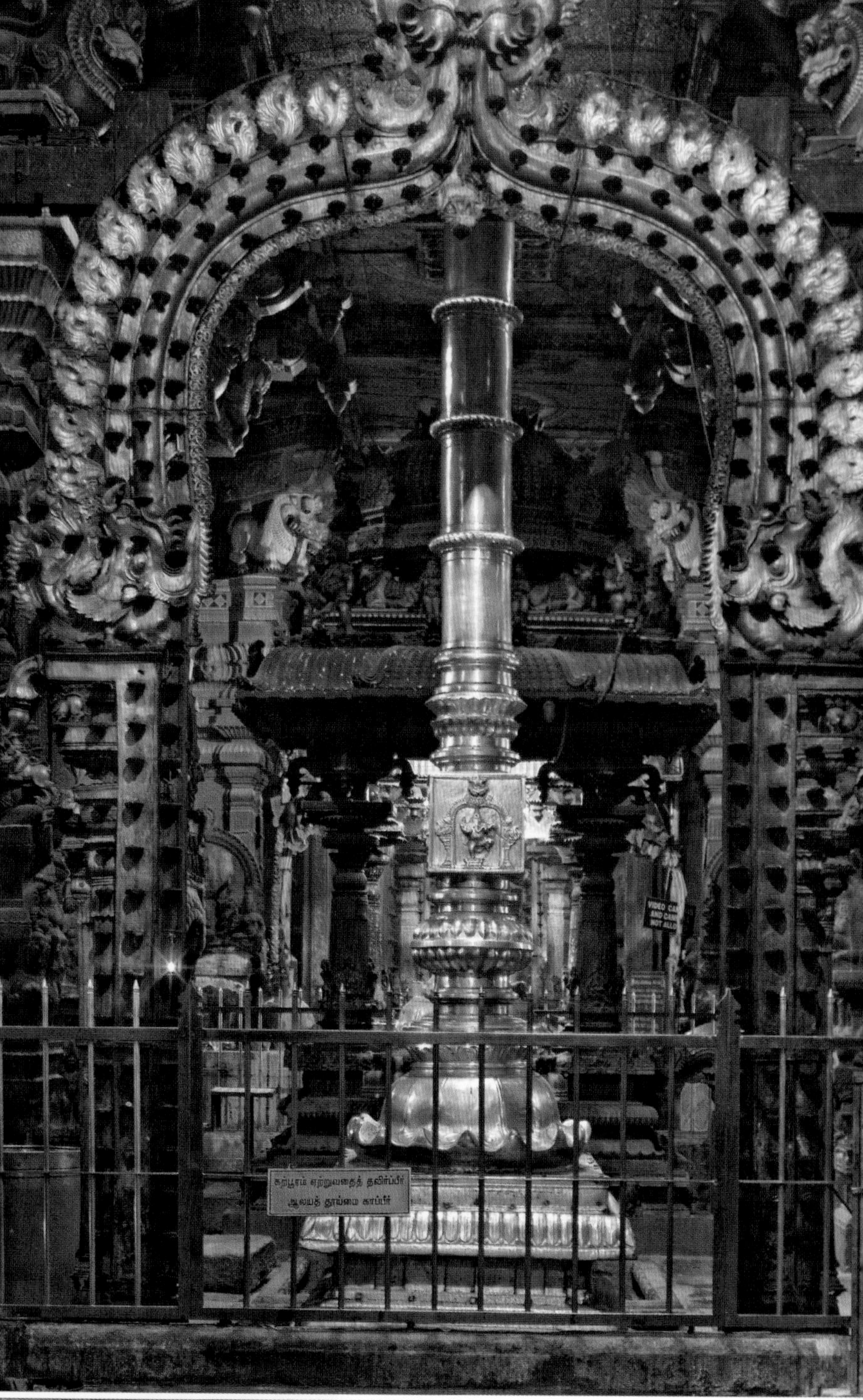

◁ **DANCING MAIDEN**
This miniature carving depicting an energetic female dancer graces a panel within the doors of the Sundareshvara shrine.

◁ STONE SCULPTURES
The sculptures in the Thousand-Pillared Hall include this dancing maiden and column brackets shaped like crouching *yalis*.

▽ THOUSAND-PILLARED HALL
During ceremonies, images of the gods and goddess were placed on this hall's podium. On either side of the aisle are pillars carved as leaping *yalis*.

▽ GANESHA COLUMN
This pillar is sculpted with a large, detailed statue of the elephant-headed god Ganesha, shown here cradling his consort on his knee.

◁ △ GODDESS RATI AND ELEPHANT
On the Thousand-Pillared Hall's porch is Rati, goddess of love, on a goose (*left*). An elephant (*above*) flanks the steps to the podium at the end of the *mandapa*.

▷ SEATED GANESHA
Placed on the floor beneath a wall niche is this small, sculpted image of Ganesha, who is generally considered the son of the god Shiva and goddess Parvati.

▷ **COMBINED ELEPHANT-AND-COW**
The ceiling of the pillared corridor is painted with lotus blossoms, as well as medallions filled with birds and animals, as seen here.

▽ **PILLARED CORRIDOR**
The stepped bathing tank known as the Potramarai Kulam is surrounded by a pillared corridor that gives access to Meenakshi's shrine at the heart of the temple complex.

△ ▷ **POTRAMARAI KULAM**
Filled with water, this stepped bathing tank is the largest open space in the temple. The brass-clad, wooden lamp-column in the middle gives the tank its name of Potramarai Kulam (Golden Lotus Pond). This gilded flower (*right*) appears to float on the water.

◁ **GOPURA ROOF**
Fierce monster images with protruding eyes, horns, and teeth mark the arched ends of the *gopuras'* barrel-vaulted roofs, with brass finials in between.

▽ **STUCCO WORK**
The brightly colored stucco figures of deities that decorate the outer walls of the *gopuras* are repainted and ritually reconsecrated every 12 years.

△ **EAST GOPURA**
One of the tallest *gopuras* is that which serves as the principal entrance to the temple from the east, aligned with the shrine of Sundareshvara.

▽ **KRISHNA AND MAIDENS**
Though dedicated to Meenakshi and Sundareshvara, other gods also appear on the temple, such as Krishna, who is accompanied here by maidens.

◁ **SHIVA FIGURES**
Among the figures that adorn the upper stories of the east *gopura* is Shiva who is depicted dancing within a circular frame, riding on his mount, Nandi, with Parvati, and with his bow.

ELEVATED CORRIDOR
The entrances open onto an elevated corridor that surrounds the prayer chamber. Light streaming through the glass panels reflects off polished marble, creating a bright interior.

REINFORCED GLASS
The glass panels between the arches of the domed vault are reinforced by narrow vertical fins of metal to achieve maximum lightness and strength.

SUPPORTING ARCHES
This view across the prayer chamber shows the massive interlocking arches that support the immense weight of the building's reinforced-concrete superstructure.

GLASS PANELS
The curved glazed openings beneath the supporting arches have doors to link the elevated corridor to the upper terrace, which looks down on the pools below.

LINKING STAIRS
Marble steps connect the elevated corridor to the prayer chamber. Air passing over the fountains enters the basement and passes through these step openings, cooling the audience in the hall.

FLOOR DETAIL
Like the marble facing of the concrete petals on the outside of the building, the floor of the prayer chamber is also covered with precisely cut, white-marble slabs.

◁ **SKYLIGHT AND LANTERN**
The supporting ribs of the soaring vault converge on a nine-pointed skylight high above the prayer chamber.

▽ **DOMED VAULT**
The domed vault of the central prayer chamber is carried on 18 intersecting, curved ribs that give an air of unbounded space and lightness.

▷ **SKYLIGHT INSCRIPTION**
In the center of the skylight is a gilded panel bearing Persian script. Delicate gilded ribs extend outward from the panel on all sides.

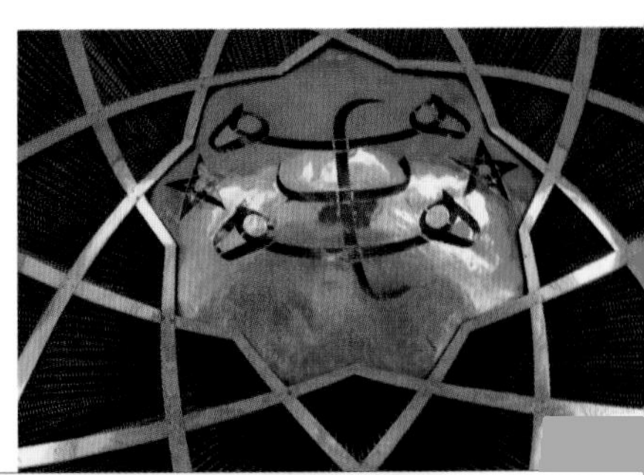

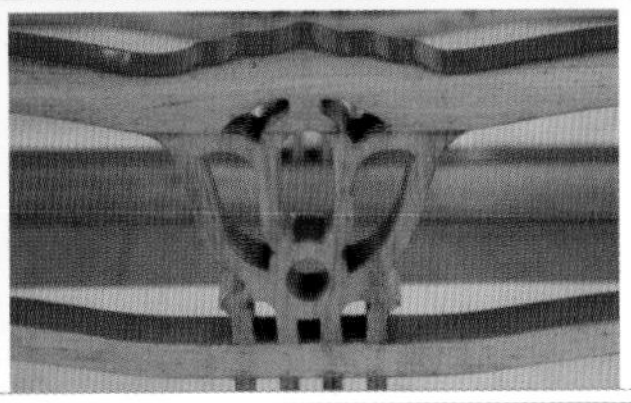

◁ **BACKRESTS**
The backrests of the custom-built wooden benches inside the prayer chamber are adorned with elegant carved motifs.

◁ **INTERIOR SEATING**
Rows of wooden benches arranged in concentric arcs face toward a podium where prayers are held several times each day.

▷ **FLORAL DISPLAY**
Each day fresh flowers are placed on the podium from where speakers lead the congregation in prayer.

◁ **SIDE SHRINE**
These stone columns are the remains of the Buddhist shrine to the south of the Great Stupa. They were once topped by a vaulted timber roof.

▷ **PATHWAY RAILINGS**
Sandstone posts and railings imitating wooden construction encircle the stupa mound itself.

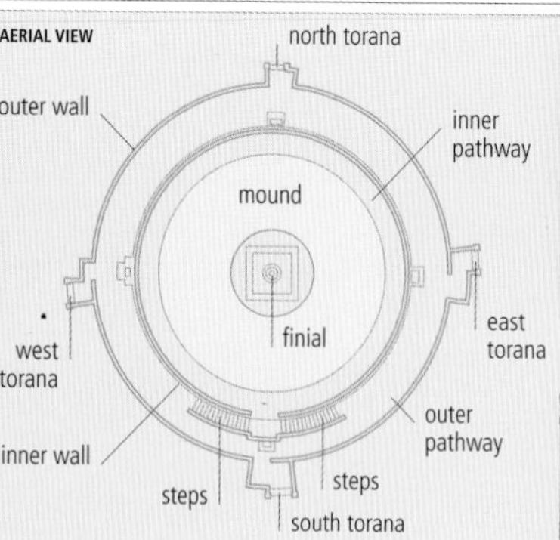

△ **LION CAPITAL**
Regal lions—emblems of royal authority—are carved with convincing naturalism onto the pillars of the *torana* on the south side of the Great Stupa.

▽ **HOMAGE TO THE DHARMA CHAKRA**
A relief carved on a pillar from the south *torana* portrays devotees paying homage to the *dharma chakra*, the Wheel of Law representing Buddha's teaching.

△ **MAIN ENTRANCE**
The south *torana* served as the principal entryway to the Great Stupa's circular inner pathway.

▷ **WORSHIP SCENE**
This pillar carving, from the south *torana*, depicts devotees worshipping Buddha's turban.

The Great Stupa at Sanchi, in the state of Madhya Pradesh, is the best preserved early example of monumental Buddhist architecture in India. Hemispherical solid mounds, called stupas, were erected as funerary monuments all over India, and even in Nepal and Sri Lanka, to contain a portion of the ashes of Buddha and his disciples. Over time, stupas came to represent the teachings and practices of the new religion.

Buddhist devotees who came to pay homage at the stupa would have proceeded around the structure in a clockwise direction, reciting prayers and worshipping sacred images placed against the base of the mound, in a ritual known as *pradakshina*. This act was imbued with cosmic significance, since the architectural form of the stupa was intended to be a replica of the hemispherical form of the universe. Such cosmic symbolism was reinforced by freestanding portals, known as *toranas*, which marked the axial points of the pathway around the structure, and also by umbrella-like finials that rose above the summit of the stupa mound itself, representing the three ascending levels of heaven.

Composed at first of bricks and packed earth, and surrounded by wooden railings, stupas were eventually clad in finely finished stone blocks, and provided with stone railings that were modeled on their wooden forebears. A stone pillar placed inside the stupa, not visible from the outside, served as a symbolic link between earth and heaven.

The Great Stupa at Sanchi dates back to the era of the Emperor Ashoka, who in the 3rd century BCE founded the monument to house relics of Buddha's closest followers. Two centuries later, the stupa was patronized by merchants from the nearby town of Vidisha, who added the sandstone railings and portals. That a flourishing Buddhist community based at Sanchi survived into later times is confirmed by the many shrines and monasteries around the site that were occupied until the 5th to 6th centuries CE.

By the 8th and 9th centuries, however, the site was abandoned, and for this reason it escaped the vandalism of Muslim invasion. In the 19th century, British explorers cleared the site of jungle and reerected two of the *toranas*, which had by then collapsed.

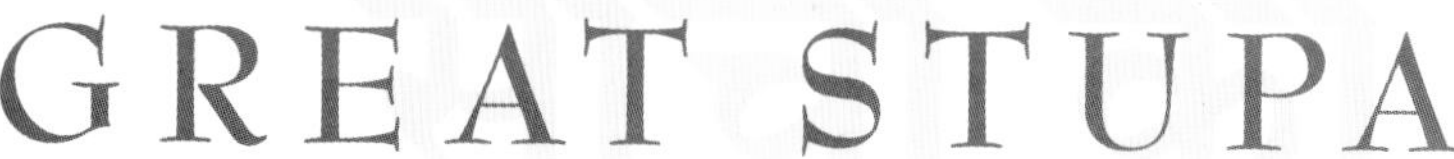

GREAT STUPA

BUDDHIST MONUMENT, SANCHI, MADHYA PRADESH

◁ **BALUSTRADED STAIRCASE**
Steps lead up the south side of the stupa to a pathway at the upper level that encircles the mound.

▷ **STONE FINIAL**
At the apex of the masonry mound is a pillared enclosure containing stone umbrellas that symbolize the triple tiers of heaven.

△ **POSTS AND RAILINGS**
Paths at the ground and upper levels are defined by posts and railings, which are also used to form the staircase balustrade.

▽ **POLISHED STONEWORK**
The finely finished railings and posts of the balustrade contrast with the crudely made, bricklike stone blocks of the stupa mound.

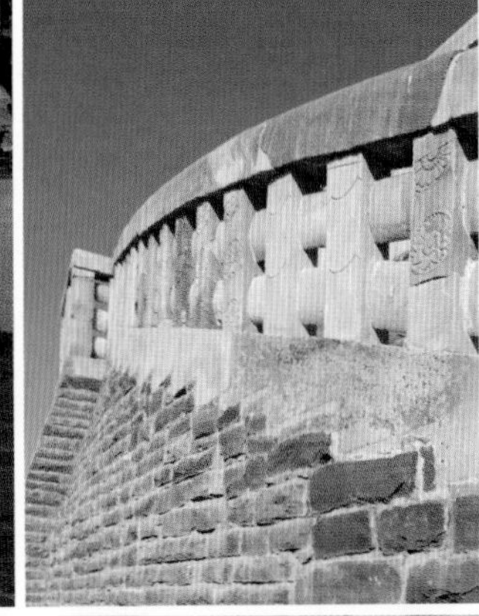

▷ **TORANA AND PILLAR**
To the right of the south *torana*, with its regal lion capitals, is the stump of a freestanding sandstone pillar. This was erected at an earlier date by the Emperor Ashoka.

◁ △ **BALUSTRADE CARVINGS**
The outer faces of the posts on the staircase balustrade are adorned with lotus flowers—an ancient motif that here suggests the perfection of Buddha and his teaching. These full blossoms are ringed by crisply carved petals.

◁ **WEST TORANA**
This gateway was discovered collapsed in the mid-19th century. Note the restored lower section of the pillar on the left.

▷ **UPPER PATHWAY**
Worshippers on the upper pathway performed the ritual *pradakshina* devotion in a propitious clockwise direction around the mound.

△ **KNEELING ELEPHANTS**
Carved onto the lintels above the dwarfs on the west *torana* is a line of palm trees, and elephants bedecked in richly ornamented coverings, and ridden by courtly figures holding parasols and garlands.

▷ **SEA MONSTER**
The west *torana* shows a half-fish/half-bird creature carrying a pavilion in which worshippers venerate an empty throne.

△ **DWARFS**
On the west *torana,* the capitals are supported by quartets of auspicious dwarfs. These pot-bellied figures with grimacing faces carry the lower lintel on their upraised hands. The pillar below shows scenes of village life and tree worship.

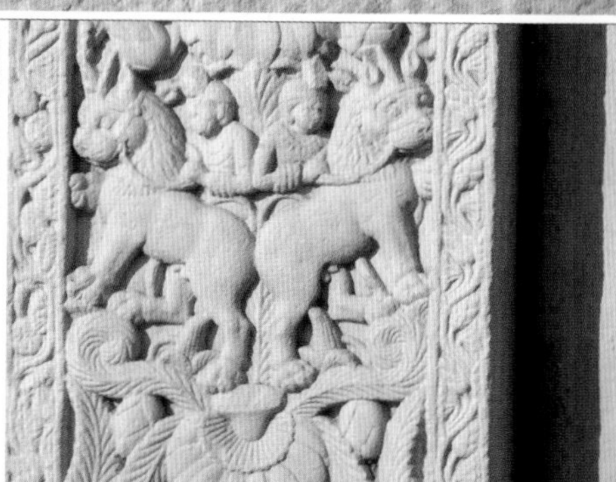

▷ **FLOWERS AND ANIMALS**
The side panels on the *torana* pillars often display formal compositions made up of animal and floral motifs.

HUNTING SCENE
This relief panel depicting a royal hunting party may illustrate one of the Buddhist Jataka tales.

NORTH TORANA
Many of the sculpted brackets on this gate are still in place. Even portions of the cut-out tridents and Wheel of Law on the topmost lintel survive.

MEDITATING BUDDHA
This figure on the lower pathway is from the 5th century CE, when it was acceptable to show Buddha in human form.

LION BRACKET
With a fierce expression and finely modeled mane and paws, this lion bracket guards the entrance to the pathway on the east.

EAST TORANA
This gateway's carvings range from the worship of the stupa and scenes from Buddhist legends, to striding elephants and auspicious maidens clutching trees.

ROYAL RIDERS
Despite the stupa's religious nature, many *torana* carvings show courtly figures and animals, such as these brackets fashioned in three dimensions as royal riders mounted on richly dressed horses.

ADINATHA TEMPLE

JAIN HOUSE OF WORSHIP, RANAKPUR, RAJASTHAN

TOWERS OF MINOR SHRINES
The walled compound consists of a line of minor shrines. Each shrine is topped by a curving clustered tower, above which rises a pole bearing a fluttering banner.

AERIAL VIEW

courtyard
main shrine
shrine door
courtyard
main entrance

Temple architecture in western India reached its climax under Jain patrons in the 15th century. In the many white-marble sanctuaries of this era dotted throughout Rajasthan and Gujarat, it is the clustered *shikhara* tower that forms the ritual and visual focus of the religious complex. This tower generally contains two or more chambers, one placed above the other. Each chamber is open on four sides, with quadruple images of the Jain saviors facing outward through doorways aligned with the cardinal points. The *mandapas* (pillared halls) that precede these multi-doored sanctuaries are conceived as lofty spaces, with double- or triple-height columns supporting stepped domes. The domes are virtuoso constructions of impressive dimensions and intricate designs, adorned with lotus motifs at the summits and ringed by intricately sculpted figural brackets.

The finest example of Jain architecture in Rajasthan is not found in any of the Rajput capitals, but instead is located at the comparatively remote site of Ranakpur, in the forested foothills of the Aravalli ranges. The monument is dedicated to Adinatha, the first of the Jain Tirthankaras, or saviors, but it is not a royal foundation. It was commissioned in 1439 by a Jain minister of Rana Kumbha, the reigning monarch of the Mewar kingdom based in far-off Chittor.

The Ranakpur Temple occupies a vast enclosure measuring over 165 ft (50 m) on each side. It is raised on a high terrace, with balconied entrances in the middle of each side that give access to an interior of immense spatial complexity. With strict symmetry of layout, it has double- and triple-story *mandapas* on four sides of the central Adinatha sanctuary. Galleried balconies at different levels look down on the *mandapas*, while a slender-proportioned, clustered *shikhara* tower rises over the sanctuary.

Crisp carvings decorate the marble columns and brackets of the *mandapas*, while the outer walls of the sanctuary are crowded with sculpted depictions of Jain saviors, as well as accessory divinities and guardians. The interior decor of the temple is further enhanced by fanciful swirls of scrollwork and geometric cosmological diagrams.

MAIN ENTRANCE
A flight of steps ascends to the multi-story gateway, which stands out from the row of minor shrines set into the walled compound of the temple complex.

ELEPHANT BRACKET
Projecting outward from the roof of the temple entrance is this three-dimensional carving of an elephant energetically grasping a pole with its trunk.

UPPER BALCONY
The upper stories of the main entrance to the temple have balconies decorated with shallow friezes of painted battlement motifs.

CEILING PANEL
Set on a decorative background on the ceiling within the main entrance is a relief carving of the fierce god Narasimha, the man-lion form of Vishnu, encircled by five interlocking bodies.

SHRINE DOORWAY
This doorway into one of the minor shrines built into the wall of the temple compound is surrounded by a wealth of minute carvings, including guardian figures and auspicious lotus motifs.

ARMED DEITY
This figure of a god bearing arms is sculpted onto the balcony slabs on the outside of the temple wall. He stands guard to protect the Jain saviors who are worshipped within.

EXTERIOR CORNER
The deeply molded walls of the minor shrines (*left*) contrast with the open projecting balconies of the main temple entrance (*right*).

UPPER GALLERY
The *mandapas* (pillared halls) are aligned with the central sanctuary of the Adinatha Temple. They are overlooked by balconies at the upper levels, each of which has a balustraded gallery.

HEAVENLY HIERARCHY
This triangular relief carving inside the Adinatha Temple shows successive tiers of seated figures. It suggests the hierarchy of heavenly abodes inhabited by the different Jain saviors.

LOTUS BUDS
Wherever one looks inside the temple, the eye is met by elaborate carving. Here, the undersides of the marble beams are adorned by fully sculpted lotus flowers with sharply pointed, hanging buds.

COSMIC DIAGRAM
In this carving, four clusters of tiny, sculpted shrines are symmetrically arranged within a circular frame. The design serves as a symbolic diagram of the Jain cosmos.

DONOR ON ELEPHANT
This sculpted elephant carries a *howdah* (carriage) occupied by a figure representing one of the donors who contributed toward the cost of erecting the temple.

SCULPTED COLUMNS
At the heart of the temple is Adinatha's sanctuary, which is approached through a sequence of *mandapas*, or halls. Lining the *mandapas* are ornate pillars covered with dense carvings of animals, flowers, deities, and guardians.

◁ **CORBELED DOME**
Rising high above the *mandapas* are intricately worked marble domes, with central lotuses supported by sculpted brackets.

▽ **COURTYARD**
Several colonnaded courtyards admit light to the *mandapas*; the lofty tower that rises over the central sanctuary is seen beyond.

▽ **STANDING DONOR**
This carved figure represents a donor, his hands held together in the act of venerating the temple savior, whom he faces.

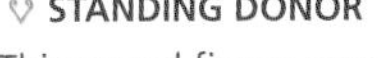

△ **BRONZE BELL AND SANCTUARY DOORWAY**
The four doorways into Adinatha's sanctuary are richly decorated. Before worshipping at the central sanctuary, devotees ring one of the bells that hang from the beams of the *mandapas*.

LAKSHMANA TEMPLE

HINDU PLACE OF WORSHIP, KHAJURAHO, MADHYA PRADESH

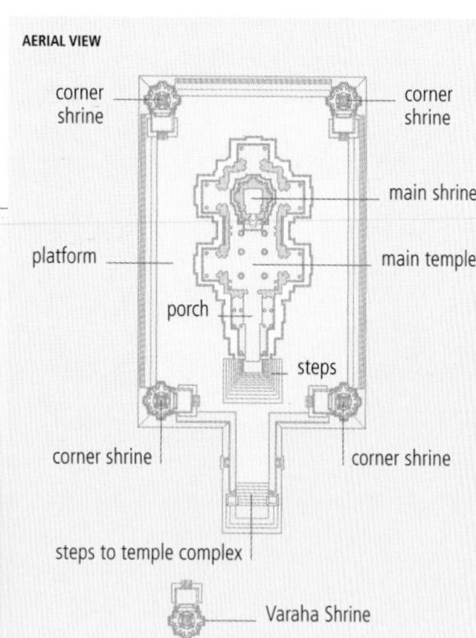

The yellow sandstone Lakshmana Temple at Khajuraho, in Madhya Pradesh, represents the culmination of the Nagara architectural style of northern India. The temple forms part of a group of Hindu monuments built in the 10th and 11th centuries by the rulers of the Chandella dynasty. Abandoned and ruined by the time of the Muslim invasions in the 13th and 14th centuries, the temples miraculously escaped destruction; they survive today as the best-preserved examples of Hindu religious architecture and art in Madhya Pradesh.

Erected in 954 by one of the Chandella kings, the Lakshmana Temple is topped by a soaring curved tower that is a characteristic feature of Nagara architecture. Known as a *shikhara*, or "peak," the tower suggests the mythological mountain homes of the Hindu gods. Like Khajuraho's other Hindu monuments, the Lakshmana Temple consists of a porch, columned hall, and towered sanctuary, all laid out on an east–west axis. This sequence is marked by a transition from open, well-lit spaces to confined, dark, claustrophobic ones—a progression that is imbued with increasing sanctity.

A passageway around the sanctuary within the temple allows devotees to make an auspicious walk around the Vishnu sanctuary; only priests may enter the sanctuary itself, where the stone image of the god to whom the temple is consecrated receives worship. In front of the temple is a small pavilion housing a sculpted representation of Varaha, the boar avatar of Vishnu.

Raised on a high plinth with moldings that cast deep shadows, the outer walls of the Lakshmana Temple are covered with tiers of carved images of Vishnu and other Hindu deities, accompanied by attendants and consorts. Some of the male and female figures are coupled in sexual union, a motif that is charged with a magical, protective significance. Balconies projecting outward from the frontal hall and the sanctuary's surrounding passageway permit light to enter the temple interior. The crescendo of towers over the porch and hall reaches a climax in the great *shikhara* that soars above the sanctuary. Its central shaft is surrounded by a cluster of lesser, half- and quarter-*shikhara* forms that create a complex towered mass.

VARAHA SHRINE
The small pavilion in front of the temple houses a sculpted image of Varaha, who rescued Bhumi, the earth goddess, from the clutches of a serpent demon.

MAIN TEMPLE
The temple is approached from the east via an open porch. The *shikhara* tower over the sanctuary rises behind; smaller towered shrines mark the platform's four corners.

BOAR'S HEAD
This boar's head represents Varaha, an avatar of Vishnu. Carved in naturalistic detail, it has a realistic snout and tusks. The raised head faces toward the image of Vishnu located within the temple.

EMBLEMATIC LION
Set beside the platform on which the temple stands is a sculpted lion, depicted with one paw suppressing a tiny human figure. The lion was a royal emblem of the Chandella dynasty.

TOWER SUMMIT
The *shikhara* is topped with two disk-like, ribbed elements called *amalakas*, as well as a stone finial that imitates an earthenware pot filled with sacred water.

CORNER SHRINE
The corner shrines are dedicated to subsidiary aspects of Vishnu, who is also worshipped in the main temple.

ACCESS STEPS
Devotees visiting the temple must climb a steep flight of steps to the entrance porch, sheltered by an angled overhang.

GANESHA
One of the most popular Hindu gods is Ganesha, who assures his worshippers of success. An icon of the god Ganesha is inserted into the roof over the entrance porch of the corner shrine.

FRIEZE SCENES
The sides of the temple platform have a continuous frieze, portions of which portray figures engaged in orgiastic activities, while others show warlike scenes with soldiers and elephants.

PORCH ENTRANCE
The temple's entrance porch is framed by an ornate lintel that rests on the heads of two aquatic monsters known as *makaras*. An image of Surya, the sun god, is set into a niche above the porch.

▷ **CEILING PANEL**
The porch and hall ceilings have ornate lotus flowers ringed by petaled lobes, and monster masks at the corners.

◁ **INSIDE THE PORCH**
High balcony seating and columns flank the passageway of the porch. An inscribed slab names the temple patron and gives the history of its construction.

▽ **FIGURAL BRACKETS**
The temple's column brackets depict corpulent figures, with legs kicked back as if flying, and arms upheld as if supporting the beams above.

△ **COLUMN DECORATION**
Auspicious motifs, such as lotus stalks and leaves, monster masks, and vases overflowing with foliage, are delicately carved onto the column shafts within the entrance porch.

△ ▷ **IN FRONT OF THE SANCTUARY**
The hall that precedes the Vishnu sanctuary—the temple's ritual focus—has a quartet of slender fluted or circular columns; the steps ascending to the sanctuary doorway are ornately treated.

SEQUENCE OF TOWERS
Rising over the porch, hall, and sanctuary is a sequence of stepped towers that culminates in the clustered *shikhara*—a dramatic climax to the whole building.

TEMPLE WALLS
Enriching the walls of the temple exterior are tiers of deeply sculpted panels; these are set between balconies that admit light to the hall and the inner passageway.

GANESHA NICHE
The niches set into the temple plinth are conceived as model buildings, complete with overhangs and ornamental roofs; this one is occupied by a dancing Ganesha.

ELEPHANT TORSOS
Among the courtly themes reserved for the temple plinth are these majestic royal elephants, shown frontally as torsos only, accompanied by attendants.

MONSTER MASKS
One the most popular themes in Hindu art is the fierce leonine monster with protruding eyes and curving horns, here reduced to a frieze of animal masks.

WALL SCULPTURES
The temple's outer walls are carved with tiers of images depicting the major Hindu deities, including Vishnu and his avatars, accompanied by attendants.

SHIVA
Though consecrated to Vishnu, images of Shiva also appear on the temple's exterior; here the god is shown bearing a trident and snake, flanked by seductive maidens.

TRAVEL

EXPLORING INDIA

For visitors to the country, India can be a powerful assault on the senses—noisy, frenetic, vibrant, and chaotic. It is a land of incredible contrasts and paradoxes, and yet, underlying the contrasts there are patterns of continuity, an indefinable essence that is quintessentially Indian. Overwhelming at first, this country of a billion people and "a million mutinies" can gradually reveal rare delights. You may find these in the centuries-old temples and forts; in the exquisite crafts still made in the traditional way; in the bustle and aromas of the bazaars; or in the glimpses of serene beauty that filter through the chaos. For visitors planning a trip to India, the choice of where to go and what to see is almost overwhelming—with impressive transportation links and a plethora of accommodations, much of the country is accessible. From buzzing metropolises, imposing forts and palaces, and ancient architectural sites, to desert landscapes, mountain vistas, and tropical beaches, a trip to India is sure to leave a lasting impression.

As rich in natural beauty as in historical sites, North India is a much visited region. A wide variety of landscapes can be enjoyed here, from the snowcapped peaks, alpine valleys, and pine forests of Ladakh and Himachal Pradesh, to the flat plains of Haryana and the Punjab, dappled with fields of golden mustard and wheat. In sharp contrast is the urban sprawl of Delhi, a bustling metropolis and the nation's capital. Ladakh's dramatically sited clifftop monasteries and pristine trekking trails are major attractions for visitors, as are Shimla's Raj-era ambience and Dharamsala's distinctive Tibetan flavor. Amritsar's great Sikh shrine, the Golden Temple, and Delhi's magnificent Mughal monuments are other popular destinations.

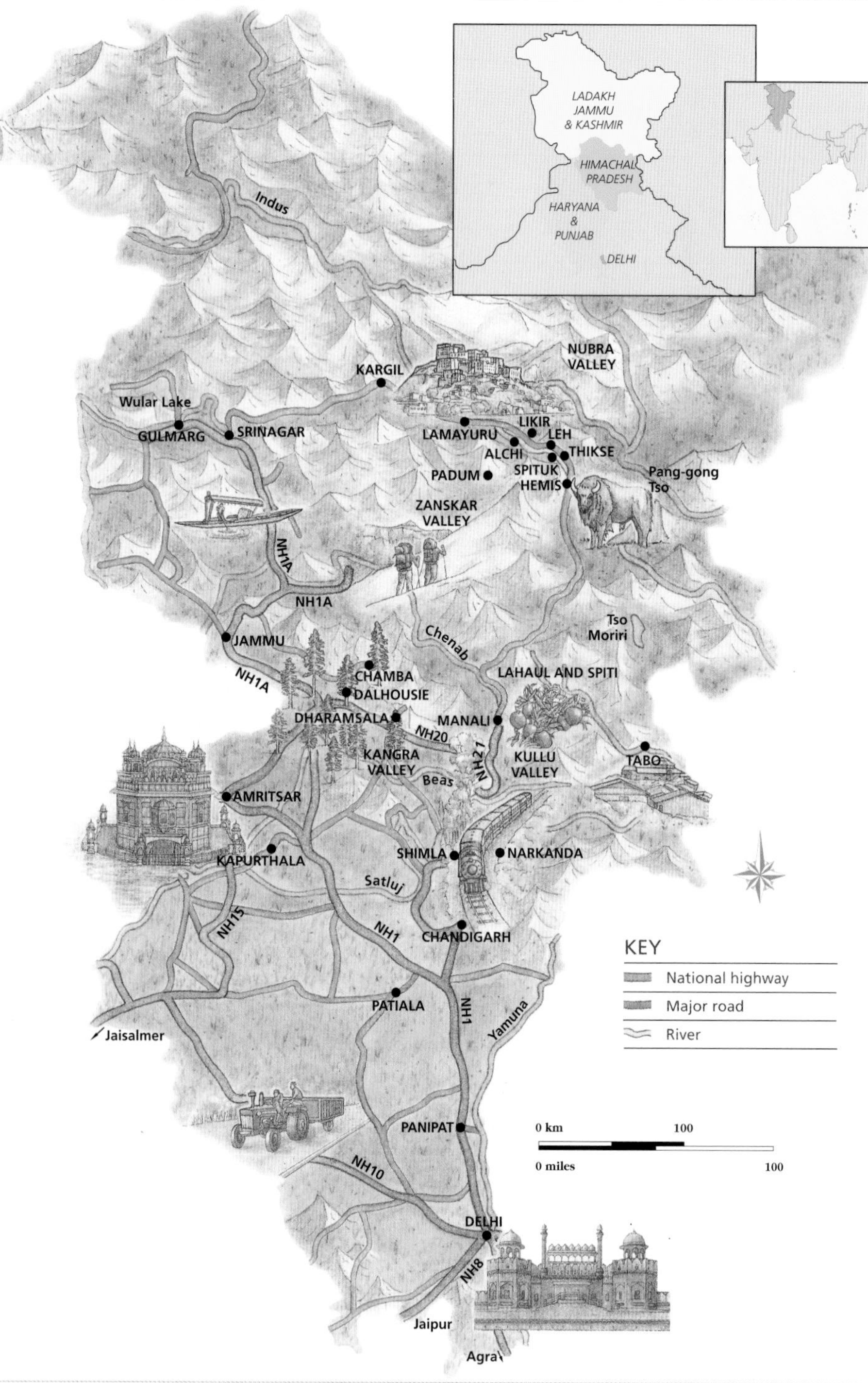

1 Delhi

Most visitors to North India start out from Delhi, the country's capital and a city that is a blend of several historical eras. Its grand Mughal past is evident in its many superb monuments and tombs. The elegant tree-lined avenues and bungalows of New Delhi evoke the period of British rule. Yet both coexist with the modern world of Internet cafés, shopping arcades, and multiplex cinemas.

VIJAY CHOWK

Vijay Chowk, or "Victory Square," is the vantage point for the grand sweep of Raj buildings grouped on Raisina Hill. The impressive Rashtrapati Bhawan, situated on the crest of the hill, is now the official residence of the President of India. Running east of Vijay Chowk is Rajpath, a 2-mile (3-km) long tree-lined avenue used for parades, with ornamental fountains, canals, and lawns on either side. At Rajpath's eastern end is the India Gate, a massive red sandstone arch, which was built to commemorate the Indian and British soldiers who died in World War I.

QUTB MINAR

India's highest single tower, the Qutb Minar (Arabic for "pole"), marks the site of the first Muslim kingdom in North India, established in 1193.

HUMAYUN'S TOMB

The first great example of a Mughal garden tomb, the perfectly symmetrical Humayun's Tomb was an inspiration for later monuments such as the Taj Mahal.

OLD DELHI

The vast urban sprawl of contemporary Delhi is, in fact, a conglomeration of several distinct enclaves, chief among which is Old Delhi. The Chandni Chowk area is still the heart of Old Delhi, where religious

DELHI & THE NORTH

HIMALAYAS, MUGHAL MONUMENTS, AND INDIA'S CAPITAL

THE GOLDEN TEMPLE, AMRITSAR
The temple shows a superb synthesis of Islamic and Hindu styles of architecture. Its dome is covered in gold and its interiors exhibit lavish decoration.

and commercial activity mix easily. India's largest mosque, Jami Masjid, is situated here. To its east lies the Red Fort—an imposing structure that was once an imperial citadel.

2 The Golden Temple, Amritsar

Founded by the Sikh guru Ram Das, Amritsar is home to the Golden Temple, the Sikh community's holiest shrine. It is surrounded by a maze of lanes and 18 fortified gateways. The temple complex is actually a city within a city and the main entrance is through its northern gateway, known as the Darshani Darwaza, which also houses the Central Sikh Museum.

3 Hill Stations

The state of Himachal Pradesh extends to the trans-Himalayan heights of the Zanskar range and has many picturesque hill stations that serve as a welcome summer getaway.

JAMI MASJID, DELHI
India's largest mosque, Jami Masjid, with its soaring minarets and vast marble domes, is grandly positioned on top of a mound overlooking Old Delhi.

SHIMLA
The capital of Himachal Pradesh, Shimla attracts countless visitors with its spectacular location, thickly forested slopes, and invigorating climate.

KULLU AND MANALI
The Kullu Valley, watered by the Beas River, is famous for its apple orchards and Dusshera, a Hindu festival that is celebrated with great pomp and show. Nearby, picturesque Manali offers a variety of scenic walks and treks through dense forests.

LAHAUL AND SPITI
Unlike the lush meadows of the Kullu Valley, barren rocky massifs and hanging glaciers comprise the scenic beauty of Lahaul and Spiti. The beautiful Tabo Monastery, Spiti's pride, is a product of the resurgence of Tibetan Buddhism in India.

NARKANDA
At a height of 9,022 ft (2,750 m), the towering Himalayan peaks seem remarkably close to Narkanda. Walks through the dense temperate forests here provide spectacular views.

DALHOUSIE
Sprawling over five hills, Dalhousie still retains its colonial-era ambience, with spacious, gable-roofed bungalows and churches flanking its leafy lanes.

4 Dharamsala, or "Little Tibet"

The hill station of Dharamsala is today the home of the Dalai Lama and the Tibetan Government-in-Exile. The town consists of two sections—the lower town with its bustling bazaar and the upper town, which is primarily a Tibetan settlement. Its many monasteries, craft centers, and the Dalai Lama's residence attract Buddhists from around the world.

5 Monasteries along the Indus

The Ladakh region of Jammu and Kashmir has several ancient, world-famous Buddhist monasteries situated in the Indus river valley.

LIKIR
Founded in the 12th century, this monastery houses a fine collection of Buddhist images framed in beautifully carved wood.

THIKSE
A 15th-century architectural gem, Thikse Monastery also has a temple consecrated by the Dalai Lama.

ALCHI
The jewel among Ladakh's monasteries, Alchi's simple whitewashed buildings with bands of deep red trim stand out against the backdrop of barren mountains.

6 Kashmir Valley

The predominantly Muslim Kashmir Valley is a mosaic of forests, rice fields, lakes, and waterways. Despite armed insurgency in the valley, its breathtaking beauty still attracts a fair share of tourists each year.

SRINAGAR
The summer capital of Jammu and Kashmir, Srinagar is a city of lakes and waterways, gardens, and picturesque wooden architecture. Houseboats that remain moored in one place on lakes have become the favored accommodation for most visitors. *Shikaras*, skiffs propelled by boatmen with paddles, ferry tourists from the shore to the houseboat.

GULMARG
At an altitude of 8,950 ft (2,730 m), Gulmarg, or the "Meadow of Flowers," was developed by the British on the Pir Panjal range. Gulmarg, together with Khilanmarg, is among India's few ski resorts. Its facilities cater to all levels of proficiency, including beginner courses.

7 Trekking Trail from Ladakh and Zanskar

Trekking in the arid, extremely cold trans-Himalayan desert of Ladakh and Zanskar can be a uniquely exhilarating experience. The terrain, as starkly beautiful as any highland setting in the world, has a number of trails, many of which trace ancient trading routes from India into Central Asia.

HATU PEAK, NARKANDA
A small wooden temple on the slopes of Hatu Peak, a day's hike from the Himalayan town of Narkanda.

LIKIR TO TINGMOSGANG
At a height of 13,100 ft (4,000 m), this is an easy, two-day, 14-mile (22-km) trek, past several villages.

SPITUK TO HEMIS
Ladakh's most popular trek, this 65-mile (105-km) path runs along the Indus River through the Markha Valley, finishing at the Hemis Monastery.

PADUM TO LAMAYURU
This 100-mile (160-km) path follows the Zanskar River via Karsha, past the impressive Lingshet Monastery and through the Singe-la ("Lion Pass").

GETTING AROUND Delhi is very well connected by air, rail, and road links to the rest of the region. There are daily flights to Leh, Srinagar, Amritsar, and Chandigarh. Amritsar and Chandigarh are also connected to Delhi by fast, well-serviced trains and a national highway. From Chandigarh, there are air services to Shimla and Manali as well as road links with frequent bus services. A particularly charming journey is on the Toy Train, "Shivalik Queen," which travels from Kalka, near Chandigarh, to Shimla. Other great journeys, with spectacular mountain scenery en route, include the trip by road from Manali to Leh, and the journey along the old Hindustan-Tibet Road (National Highway 22), which runs from Shimla to the India–China border near Shipkila.

CENTRAL INDIA

THE GANGES, HOLY CITIES, AND MEDIEVAL FORTS

The densely populated region of Central India is the country's Hindi-speaking belt (often called the "cow belt"). The presence of the sacred Ganges River has shaped much of the history of the area, which is remarkable as much for its rich past and religious and cultural diversity as for its mineral wealth. Some of India's most visited destinations are to be found in this vast and varied region, which covers the flat Gangetic Plains, several Himalayan ranges, and the lush, verdant forests of the Central Indian heartland. These include the Taj Mahal at Agra, the holy city of Varanasi, the exquisitely sculpted temples of Khajuraho, the great Buddhist sites of Sanchi and Bodh Gaya, and the medieval forts and palaces of Gwalior and Orchha.

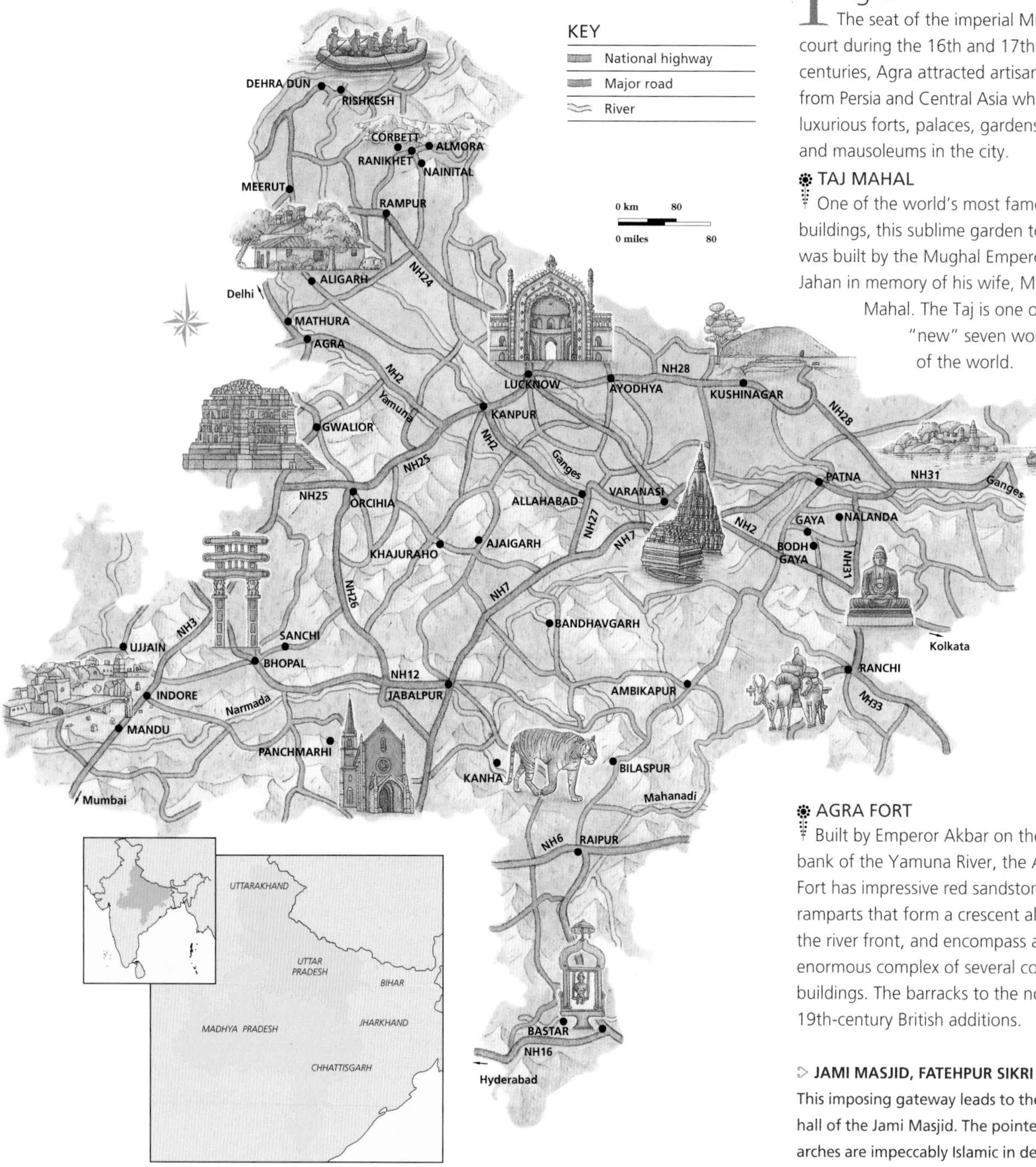

1 Agra

The seat of the imperial Mughal court during the 16th and 17th centuries, Agra attracted artisans from Persia and Central Asia who built luxurious forts, palaces, gardens, and mausoleums in the city.

TAJ MAHAL

One of the world's most famous buildings, this sublime garden tomb was built by the Mughal Emperor Shah Jahan in memory of his wife, Mumtaz Mahal. The Taj is one of the "new" seven wonders of the world.

AGRA FORT

Built by Emperor Akbar on the west bank of the Yamuna River, the Agra Fort has impressive red sandstone ramparts that form a crescent along the river front, and encompass an enormous complex of several courtly buildings. The barracks to the north are 19th-century British additions.

2 Fatehpur Sikri

A fine example of a Mughal walled city, with well-defined public and private areas, Fatehpur Sikri was built in the Agra district by Emperor Akbar, and is a harmonious blend of Islamic and Hindu architectural styles. The grand open mosque of Jami Masjid, with its majestic entrance—the Buland Darwaza—towers over Fatehpur Sikri. Flanked by arched cloisters, its vast congregational area houses the tomb of the Sufi mystic, Salim Chisti.

3 Varanasi

Also known as Benaras, Kashi, or "the City of Light," Varanasi is the holiest city of the Hindu faith. Situated on the west bank of the Ganges River—sacred to the Hindus—Varanasi has around 90 ghats (steps along the river banks leading down to the water) and several temples and shrines that stay busy with the endless cycle of Hindu religious practice.

4 Bastar

Bastar district in the newly-created state of Chhattisgarh, near Madhya Pradesh, is home to numerous small tribes and communities of craftsmen. Animal, bird, and plant motifs embellish many of the

▷ **JAMI MASJID, FATEHPUR SIKRI**
This imposing gateway leads to the prayer hall of the Jami Masjid. The pointed exterior arches are impeccably Islamic in design.

utilitarian, decorative objects that the craftsmen fashion out of materials such as clay, wood, metal, and cotton yarn.

5 Buddhist Pilgrimage Sites

All places associated with the life and teachings of Buddha now form part of a well-traveled pilgrimage circuit that Buddhist pilgrims from all over the world undertake.

BODH GAYA
The holiest site for Buddhists, the town of Bodh Gaya is where Buddha attained enlightenment. The focal point of the town is the Mahabodhi Temple, and the Bodhi Tree in its enclosure, under which Buddha sat and attained enlightenment.

SANCHI
The tranquil hill of Sanchi has one of India's best preserved and most extensive Buddhist sites. From the 3rd century BCE to the 7th century CE, this was a thriving Buddhist establishment of stupas and monasteries.

6 Hill Stations

Nainital, Ranikhet, and Almora form a picturesque triangle of hill stations that are a popular summer retreat for those seeking relief from the intense heat of the plains.

NAINITAL
Described as India's Lake District, Nainital's environs have a number of serene lakes, surrounded by thick forests.

RANIKHET
The true allure of Ranikhet lies in its impressive views; on a clear day it is possible to see nearly 220 miles (350 km) of the Greater Himalayan Range.

ALMORA
The distinctive bazaar of this scenic hill station sells locally crafted copper and brass products, as well as the town's trademark confectionery, *bal mithai*, which is a dark brown milk candy.

7 Trekking Trail from Garhwal to Kumaon

Garhwal and Kumaon are a wonderful introduction to the Himalayas. A single walk can lead through forests, valleys bursting with wild flowers, and panoramic views of glacial rock and ice.

THE GAUMUKH TRAIL
This 16-mile (26-km) path traces the infant Ganges River along an ancient pilgrim trail, from Gangotri to its glacial source at Gaumukh.

VALLEY OF FLOWERS
Around 12 miles (20 km) from the town of Govindghat, this national park is best visited between the months of June and September, when a profusion of beautiful wild flowers bloom.

DODITAL
One of Garhwal's popular treks, the 14-mile (23-km) path from Kalyani follows the Asi Ganga river valley, past Agoda to the lake of Dodital.

8 Medieval Forts and Palaces

Gwalior and the adjoining region of Bundelkhand (named after the Bundela Rajputs), make up a culturally distinctive area in Central India. The region's glorious history and refined artistic traditions are reflected in countless forts, palaces, and temples.

GWALIOR
The main attraction in Gwalior is the Gwalior Fort that stands atop a 328-ft (100-m) high sandstone and basalt hill. Its formidable bastioned walls enclose exquisite temples and palaces.

BUNDELKHAND
The beautiful boulder-strewn landscape of the Bundelkhand region is dotted with countless forts and monuments. Dramatically positioned on a rocky island, the medieval city of Orchha has temples, cenotaphs, and tiered palaces that are perfect examples of Bundelkhand architecture.

9 Khajuraho

The magnificent group of temples in Khajuraho is a UNESCO World Heritage Site. The most impressive of the temples is the Kandariya Mahadev, which has 800 sculptures depicting gods and goddesses, beasts and warriors, dancers, musicians, and, of course, erotic scenes for which the Khajuraho temples are famous.

THE BUDDHA, BODH GAYA
The gilded stone image of Buddha in the main sanctum of the Mahabodhi Temple has an aura of great serenity.

KUMBH MELA, ALLAHABAD
Pilgrims congregate at Allahabad's Kumbh Mela, a Hindu festival that takes place by the Ganges River every three years.

10 Wildlife Safaris

Central India is home to three of the country's finest wildlife sanctuaries: the Corbett, Kanha, and Bandhavgarh national parks.

CORBETT NATIONAL PARK
This national park has a remarkable variety of wildlife, notably tigers, elephants, four-horned antelopes, and an astonishing 600 species of birds.

KANHA NATIONAL PARK
India's finest game sanctuary and a model for wildlife conservation, Kanha is a prominent tiger reserve where wildlife abounds in its forests.

BANDHAVGARH NATIONAL PARK
One of India's most important tiger reserves, the Bandhavgarh national park has rocky hills, lush deciduous forests, marshes, and meadows.

11 River Tours along the Ganges

From September to April, when the Ganges is swollen by the monsoon rains, a few stretches of breathtaking rapids become a favorite circuit for enthusiasts of white-water rafting.

KAUDIYALA
The most popular starting point of the river tour, Kaudiyala has a number of camp sites situated on the river bank.

SHIVPURI
A truly scenic spot, Shivpuri is favored by both rafting enthusiasts and those looking for a quiet retreat.

GETTING AROUND Major destinations and state capitals in this region, such as Agra, Varanasi, Dehra Dun, Khajuraho, Bhopal, Raipur, and Patna, are well connected by domestic airlines. There is also a good network of fast intercity trains between these cities. A special train service, the air-conditioned Taj Express, makes a comfortable day trip from Delhi to Agra possible. An extensive road network connects most of the towns in this region: National Highway 2 connects Agra, Allahabad, Varanasi, and Bodh Gaya, while several state highways branch off from National Highway 24 to the hills of Nainital and Mussoorie.

EASTERN INDIA

MANGROVES, TEA PLANTATIONS, AND TEMPLE CITIES

The best-known destination for visitors to Eastern India, Kolkata is India's second-largest city. Apart from this endlessly fascinating metropolis, the region offers an astonishing diversity of landscapes, peoples, and cultures. These include the steamy mangrove forests along the Bay of Bengal—habitat of the royal Bengal tiger, the spectacular mountain vistas of Darjeeling and Sikkim, and Orissa's magnificent temples and beaches. Farther east are Assam and the northeastern states, home to many different tribal communities, whose distinct cultures flourish in areas of pristine natural beauty. The tea plant is indigenous to Northeast India, and lush tea gardens enhance the glorious landscape of Assam, northern Bengal, and Darjeeling.

1 Kolkata

The vibrant city of Kolkata lies in a long strip, with the river to its west and the wetlands to its east. Along the river front, the Strand, is the city center and Maidan—a huge park where Kolkata's residents play football, hold political rallies, or enjoy the cool evenings. On the other side of the park is the city's main thoroughfare, the Chowringhee, or Jawaharlal Nehru Road, with shops, hotels, and residential buildings. The southern part of the city is relatively new, while north Kolkata is the older part of the city with its maze of narrow lanes crowded with houses and shops.

VICTORIA MEMORIAL
The city's most celebrated landmark, this domed Classical structure is constructed entirely from marble. Now a museum, its 25 galleries are spread over the ground and first floors. The collection, which covers a fascinating selection of Raj memorabilia, includes the Calcutta Gallery, with oil paintings and watercolors of the city's history.

KUMARTULI
Literally, the "Area of the Potters," Kumartuli is a maze of alleys, where images of various Hindu gods and goddesses are made. The best time to visit is late August and early September, when potters create the idols for the ten-day-long Durga Puja festival.

INDIAN MUSEUM
The oldest and largest museum in India, the Indian Museum was founded in 1814. The museum's impressive exhibits include artifacts from the Indus Valley Civilization and a fine collection of 5th-century Gupta coins.

◁ **SHIKHARA, BISHNUPUR**
One of the five *shikharas* (spires) of the Shyama Raya Temple. Their design is inspired by the temple architecture of nearby Orissa.

2 Bishnupur

Bishnupur is renowned for its elaborately adorned terra-cotta temples, made of the local red clay. The most imposing of these is the Shyama Raya Temple, built in 1643. It is richly decorated with scenes from Lord Krishna's life, as well as episodes taken from *The Ramayana*.

3 Sunderbans

The vast Ganges-Brahmaputra delta has the world's largest tropical mangrove forest. The Sunderbans Reserve, a UNESCO World Heritage Site created within the delta, was declared a tiger reserve in 1973 to protect the endangered royal Bengal tiger. The intricate network of waterways, creeks, and islands abounds in a variety of marine life. Boat tours take visitors for leisurely rides through the mangroves.

4 Hill Stations

Hill stations in this region offer superb views of emerald-green tea gardens, tranquil valleys, and the snow-clad range of the eastern Himalayan peaks.

DARJEELING
The presence of Kanchenjunga, India's highest peak, dominates the town of Darjeeling. Some of the best views of the Eastern Himalayan range can be enjoyed from the windy, prayer-flag-lined Observatory Hill. The best way to travel to Darjeeling from Siliguri is by the "Toy Train," officially known as the Darjeeling Himalayan Railway (DHR).

KALIMPONG
Memories of the Raj era are recalled by the charming stone cottages in the town of Kalimpong. The Thongsa Monastery is its oldest monastery. The town's many nurseries produce a large number of exotic orchids, gladioli, amaryllis, and cacti. A good one to visit is the Uda Mani Pradhan Nursery.

GANGTOK
The capital of Sikkim, Gangtok is set in beautiful alpine environs. The splendid Rumtek Monastery can be found 15 miles (24 km) southwest of Gangtok. It is an impressive complex, its flat-roofed buildings topped with golden finials, and filled with treasures brought from the monastery at Tsurphu in Tibet.

▷ **VICTORIA MEMORIAL, KOLKATA**
A statue of the young Queen Victoria, sculpted by Thomas Brock in 1921, stands in the central hall of Victoria Memorial.

GETTING AROUND Kolkata, Guwahati, and Bhubaneshwar, the three major cities in this region, are well connected by air and rail to most parts of India. From Kolkata and Guwahati, there are regular flights to all the northeastern states. The hill station of Darjeeling and Sikkim's capital Gangtok are accessible by air or rail up to Bagdogra-Siliguri, from where buses and taxis complete the journey up to the hills on National Highway 31. Kolkata has a good network of trams and a reliable metro service. From Kolkata, most destinations in West Bengal are reached on National Highway 34. In Orissa, the major sights are connected by National Highway 5. The gateway to the northeast, Guwahati in Assam, has good road links to the other six states. Visitors require travel permits for some destinations in the northeast.

5 From Shillong to Cherrapunji

The road from Shillong to Cherrapunji through the East Khasi Hills winds through dense pine and oak forests, full of ferns and orchids. En route are dramatic gorges and ravines, waterfalls, and limestone caves. This road trip takes about 6–7 hours. Shillong, with its mist-shrouded hills, pine forests, lakes, and waterfalls, is a popular hill station. Cherrapunji is one of the wettest places on earth, and is surrounded by groves of orange and banana trees.

6 Wildlife Sites

A number of wildlife sanctuaries protecting a many species of wildlife are supported by the wetlands of the east.

CHILIKA LAKE

Believed to be the largest brackish water lake in Asia, Chilika is recognized as one of the most important wetlands in the world because of the phenomenal variety of aquatic and birdlife it supports.

KAZIRANGA NATIONAL PARK

Situated on the banks of the Brahmaputra, Assam's magnificent Kaziranga National Park is home to a rich variety of plant and animal life, including the Indian one-horned rhinoceros, 80 tigers, Asiatic wild buffalo, herds of wild elephants, and 300 species of birds.

7 Loktak Lake, Imphal

Imphal lies in a valley enclosed by forested hills, and its star attraction, Loktak Lake, is one of the most enchanting places in northeast India. Almost two-thirds of this huge expanse of freshwater is covered by unique floating saucer-shaped islands of reed and humus, locally called *phumdi*, which are home to a community of fishermen.

8 Temple Cities

Orissa's most famous sites are clustered together on the eastern coast, in the fertile delta of the Mahanadi River. These include the cities of Puri, the capital Bhubaneswar, and Konark, all of which have exquisitely sculpted temples.

BHUBANESWAR

More than 400 temples remain of the 7,000 that are said to have once embellished Bhubaneswar, earning it the title of "City of Temples."

PURI

Puri is dominated by the Jagannath Temple. During the spectacular Rath Yatra (chariot festival) in June–July, the idols of deities are taken out in a procession of huge wooden chariots, pulled by thousands of devotees.

KONARK

One of India's great architectural marvels, the Sun Temple in Konark was conceived as a gigantic chariot. The temple is also remarkable for its superb sculptures. Gods and demons, kings and peasants, and elephants and horses jostle for space on its walls with dozens of erotic couples. Konark is now a UNESCO World Heritage Site.

KEY
National highway
Major road
River

9 Brahmaputra River Cities

The majestic Brahmaputra River dominates life in Assam and much of Arunachal Pradesh.

GUWAHATI

The city of Guwahati, the capital of Assam, stretches along both sides of the river. An ancient seat of Hinduism, it has several temples in its environs.

TEZPUR

Situated on the north bank of the river and covered by tea gardens, Tezpur is a convenient stop and a take-off point for trips to Arunachal Pradesh.

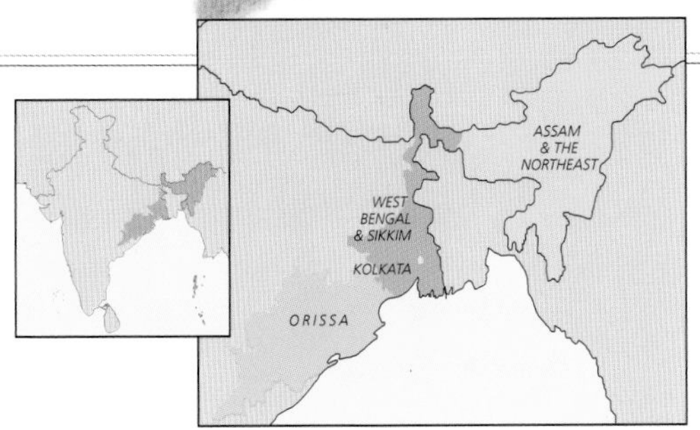

TEA PICKING, DARJEELING Women picking tea leaves on a plantation in Darjeeling, West Bengal. The tea leaves are stored in a cloth bundle that hangs from their heads.

WESTERN INDIA

DESERT FORTS, REGAL PALACES, AND TEMPLES

This region has some of India's most popular destinations. In Rajasthan, the desert forts of Jaisalmer and Jodhpur, the palaces and lakes of Udaipur, and the Ranthambhore National Park evoke all the splendor of the state's princely past. Many palaces and feudal castles have been converted into delightful hotels. Fairs and festivals offer visitors a memorable encounter with the people and culture of rural Rajasthan. Gujarat's Jain temples and intricately designed stepwells are architectural marvels, while its natural wonders can be enjoyed on the beaches of Diu and at the lion sanctuary at Gir. The landscapes in this region range from the sand dunes of Rajasthan to the vast salt flats of Kutch, to the urban bustle of the two state capitals, Jaipur and Ahmedabad.

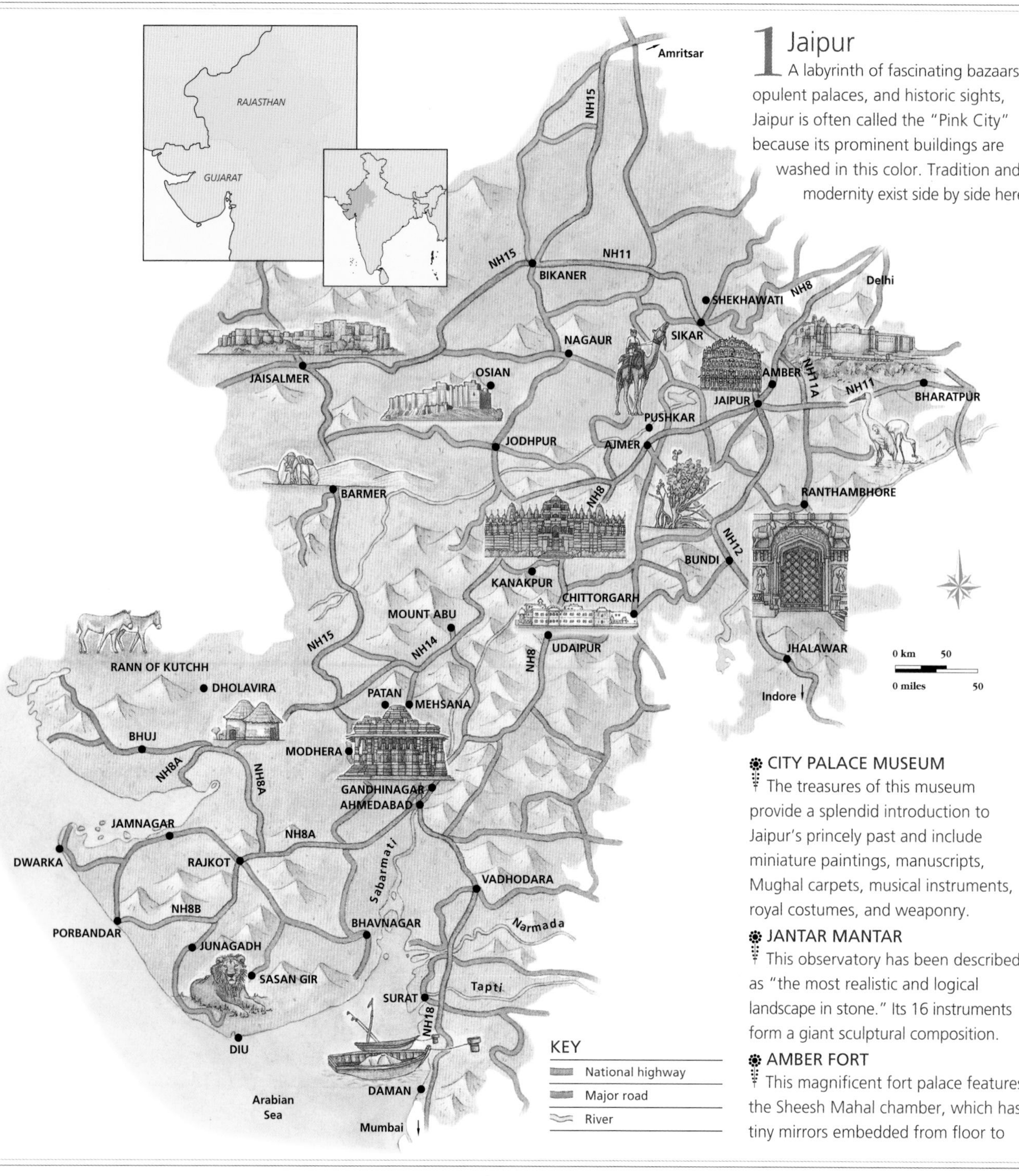

1 Jaipur

A labyrinth of fascinating bazaars, opulent palaces, and historic sights, Jaipur is often called the "Pink City" because its prominent buildings are washed in this color. Tradition and modernity exist side by side here.

CITY PALACE MUSEUM
The treasures of this museum provide a splendid introduction to Jaipur's princely past and include miniature paintings, manuscripts, Mughal carpets, musical instruments, royal costumes, and weaponry.

JANTAR MANTAR
This observatory has been described as "the most realistic and logical landscape in stone." Its 16 instruments form a giant sculptural composition.

AMBER FORT
This magnificent fort palace features the Sheesh Mahal chamber, which has tiny mirrors embedded from floor to ceiling, Ganesh Pol, which is a shimmering three-story gateway, and the elegant Jas Mandir hall and Shila Devi Temple.

HAWA MAHAL
The fanciful Hawa Mahal, or "Palace of Winds," was erected in 1799. This tiered Baroque-like composition of projecting windows and balconies with perforated screens is five stories high but just one room deep.

2 Shekhawati Havelis

These sprawling old *haveli* mansions, with their exuberantly frescoed walls, were built between the late 18th and early 20th centuries by local merchants. Modern urban trends are reflected in later frescoes that depict cars, airplanes, and telephones.

3 Jodhpur

With the Mehrangarh Fort towering over palaces, bazaars, and the sands of the Thar Desert, Jodhpur epitomizes all the romance and feudal splendor of Rajasthan.

MEHRANGARH FORT
Rising sheer out of a 410-ft- (125-m-) high rock, Mehrangarh is perhaps the most majestic of Rajasthan's forts. Its

VILLAGERS AT PUSHKAR
Two camel owners at the Puskhar Fair, which attracts thousands of buyers, sellers, and tourists every year.

◁ **KEALADEO GHANA NATIONAL PARK** The male Sarus crane dances to attract his mate. This park draws over 375 bird species.

▷ **ELEPHANT RIDE, AMBER FORT** Tourists can enjoy a ride on a decorated elephant on the pathway to the Amber Fort.

forbidding ramparts are in sharp contrast to the ornate palaces within. The royal apartments in the fort now form part of an outstanding museum.

UMAID BHAWAN PALACE
Built of creamy-pink sandstone and marble, the Umaid Bhawan Palace is a prime example of princely India's opulence. Its 347 rooms include eight dining halls, two theaters, a ballroom, and lavishly decorated reception halls.

4 Jaisalmer

Splendid palaces and *havelis* stud the austere desert surroundings of Jaisalmer. Made of the local golden-yellow sandstone, they are the most spectacular examples of the Rajasthani stonemason's art.

JAISALMER FORT
Jaisalmer Fort rises like a fabulous mirage out of the sands of the Thar Desert, the awesome contours of its 99 bastions softened by the golden hue of the stone. Thousands of people reside here, making it India's only living fort.

HAVELIS
Built in the 19th century by the town's merchants and ministers, these mansions dominate the city's labyrinthine lanes. Their golden stone facades are so finely carved that they could be made of lace.

CAMEL SAFARI
The desertscape around Jaisalmer is best explored on a camel safari. Overnight stays in tents offer magical dawns and sunsets amid the dunes.

5 Udaipur

The fairy-tale city of Udaipur is dominated by the massive City Palace overlooking Lake Pichola. Charming *havelis*, ghats, and temples line the lake front, with colorful bazaars stretching behind them.

CITY PALACE
The largest palace in Rajasthan, the City Palace is actually a complex of several palaces. Much of it is now a museum, and parts of it house luxury hotels. It is a fascinating combination of Rajput military architecture and Mughal-style decorative techniques.

JAG NIWAS, OR LAKE PALACE
Built between 1734 and 1751, Jag Niwas was once a royal summer retreat and is now one of the world's finest hotels. Both palaces can be seen from a boat tour of Lake Pichola.

6 Wildlife Sanctuaries

Western India has a number of wildlife sanctuaries that are home to a rich variety of fauna, including some rare species. The more prominent ones are the Keoladeo and Ranthambhore National Parks in Rajasthan, and the Sasan Gir National park in Gujarat.

KEOLADEO GHANA NATIONAL PARK
A UNESCO World Heritage Site, this national park is regarded as one of the world's most important bird sanctuaries. Expert boatmen navigate the wetlands and identify bird colonies. Bicycles and cycle rickshaws are also available for touring the forest paths.

SASAN GIR NATIONAL PARK
The Sasan Gir National Park in Gujarat is the only habitat of the lion left outside Africa. A number of rivers wind through Gir, making it a haven for a range of wildlife, including a substantial leopard population.

RANTHAMBHORE NATIONAL PARK
The razor-sharp ridges, deep boulder-filled gorges, lakes, and jungles of this park are the habitat of carnivores such as the caracal, panther, jackal, and hyena, numerous species of deer, and a rich variety of resident and migratory birds. Its most famous resident, however, is the endangered Indian tiger.

7 Dilwara Jain Temples

Rajasthan's only hill station, Mount Abu, has one of India's most spectacular sights—the Dilwara Jain Temples. This group of five marble temples is situated on a hill 2 miles (3 km) northeast of the town. These temples have intricate and delicate carvings, the marble worked so finely that in places it is almost translucent.

8 Pushkar Fair

The famed Pushkar Fair of Rajasthan, which takes place in October or November, is now one of Asia's largest cattle fairs. Numerous camel, horse, and donkey races and contests take place in a specially built amphitheater on the outskirts of the town. A festive, carnival atmosphere prevails in Pushkar during the fair's two-week duration. At dusk, hundreds of clay lamps on leaf boats are lit and set afloat in a magical tableau on the Pushkar Lake.

9 Modhera Sun Temple

The Sun Temple at Modhera in Gujarat is so precisely laid out in an east–west direction that the sun's rays course through its chambers and strike the center of the inner sanctum at high noon every day. The highly detailed carvings depict Hindu deities, as well as scenes from everyday life.

10 Craft Villages of Kutch

Kutch is home to several communities that are skilled in a variety of crafts. Among them are the Rabaris, whose round houses with conical roofs (*bhoongas*) are a distinctive feature of the Kutch landscape. *Rogan* is a unique technique by which cloth is decorated with embossed lacquer-work patterns. Other crafts include pottery, silverwork, and embroidered leather.

GETTING AROUND Jaipur, Jodhpur, Udaipur, and Ahmedabad are well connected by air to Delhi and Mumbai as well as to each other. Trains travel between all the major cities, with fast trains connecting Delhi and Jaipur. Two luxury trains, the Palace on Wheels and the Royal Orient, offer a more romantic way to explore Rajasthan and Gujarat. Within Rajasthan, a network of national highways links most major destinations by road, while national highways 8, 14, and 15 continue on to Gujarat. Local transit within these states includes buses, taxis, jeeps, auto rickshaws, and cycle rickshaws that are cheap and convenient.

SOUTHERN INDIA

IDYLLIC BEACHES, ANCIENT RUINS, AND MODERN CITIES

The south is a region of many varied splendors. The area's key attractions include cosmopolitan Mumbai, Goa's idyllic beaches and Portuguese churches, the ancient caves and temples of Ajanta and Ellora, and the magnificent ruins of Hampi. Farther south are Bangalore—often described as Asia's Silicon Valley—the former princely state of Mysore, and the great Hoysala temples of Belur and Halebid. South of the Vindhya range, India's Dravidian heartland has all that a visitor could wish for. Tamil Nadu has some of India's most magnificent ancient temples. Its capital, Chennai (formerly Madras), is a vibrant commercial and political center. Kerala is rich in beautiful scenery as well as in cultural heritage, while Andhra Pradesh is full of fascinating historic sites.

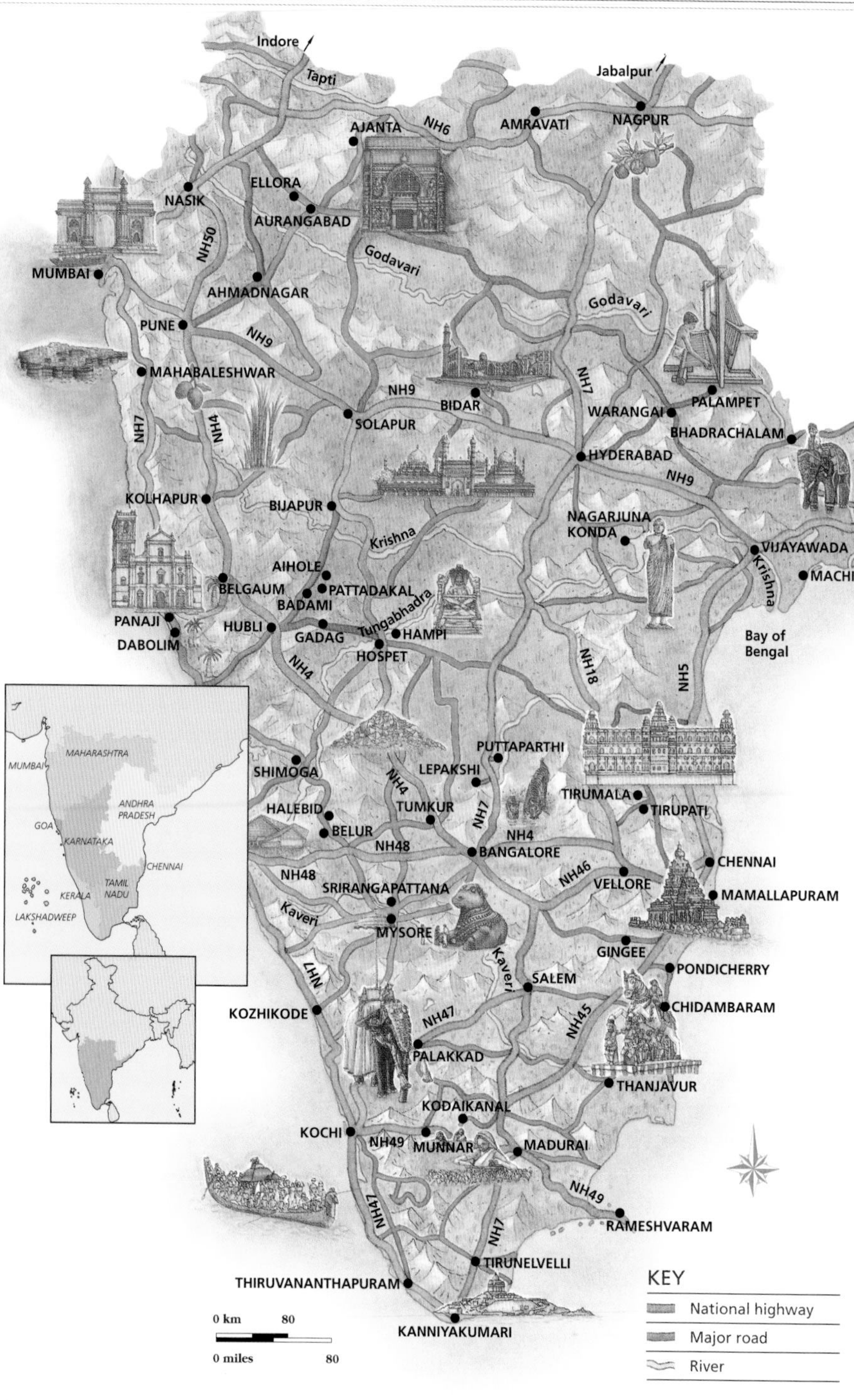

Indore
Tapti
Jabalpur
AJANTA
NH6
AMRAVATI
NAGPUR
NASIK
ELLORA
AURANGABAD
NH50
Godavari
MUMBAI
AHMADNAGAR
Godavari
Bhubaneswar
PUNE
NH9
MAHABALESHWAR
NH7
NH9
BIDAR
PALAMPET
NH7
NH4
SOLAPUR
WARANGAL
BHADRACHALAM
VISAKHAPATNAM
HYDERABAD
NH5
NH9
KOLHAPUR
BIJAPUR
RAJAHMUNDRY
Krishna
NAGARJUNA KONDA
VIJAYAWADA
AIHOLE
Krishna
MACHILIPATNAM
BELGAUM
PATTADAKAL
BADAMI
Tungabhadra
PANAJI
HUBLI
GADAG
HAMPI
DABOLIM
HOSPET
Bay of Bengal
NH4
NH18
NH5
PUTTAPARTHI
SHIMOGA
LEPAKSHI
NH4
TIRUMALA
HALEBID
TUMKUR
NH7
TIRUPATI
BELUR
NH4
NH48
BANGALORE
CHENNAI
NH48
NH46
VELLORE
SRIRANGAPATTANA
MAMALLAPURAM
Kaveri
MYSORE
Kaveri
GINGEE
PONDICHERRY
NH7
SALEM
KOZHIKODE
NH47
NH45
CHIDAMBARAM
PALAKKAD
THANJAVUR
KODAIKANAL
KOCHI
NH49
MUNNAR
MADURAI
NH49
NH47
RAMESHVARAM
NH7
TIRUNELVELLI
THIRUVANANTHAPURAM
KANNIYAKUMARI
0 km 80
0 miles 80
KEY
National highway
Major road
River
MAHARASHTRA
MUMBAI
ANDHRA PRADESH
GOA
KARNATAKA
CHENNAI
TAMIL NADU
KERALA
LAKSHADWEEP

1 Mumbai

The capital of Maharashtra, Mumbai is indisputably India's most dynamic and crowded city. The country's financial center and its busiest port, the city is also home to the country's film industry, popularly known as Bollywood.

GATEWAY OF INDIA
Mumbai's most famous landmark, the Gateway of India, is at the heart of Mumbai's tourist district. Boats and barges moored here provide regular services across the bay and to nearby islands such as Elephanta. Around the Gateway are some majestic buildings dating from the colonial era.

VICTORIA TERMINUS
The most impressive example of Victorian Gothic architecture in India, the Victoria Terminus Railway Station (now renamed Chhatrapati Shivaji Terminus) is a rich extravaganza of domes, spires, and arches.

PRINCE OF WALES MUSEUM
Renowned for its superb sculptures and miniature paintings, the Prince of Wales Museum houses its exhibits in a grand Indo-Saracenic building that has galleries on three floors.

ELEPHANTA ISLAND
A UNESCO World Heritage Site, the Elephanta cave temples contain some great masterpieces of Indian sculpture. Located on an island off Mumbai's eastern shore, it can be visited on a day trip by boat from the city.

2 Goan Beach Vacation

Goa is one of India's most popular vacation destinations, with its idyllic beaches, coconut plantations, and white-washed churches. Its splendid beaches stretch over 66 miles (106 km). Each beach has its own distinct character, though in general, south Goa's beaches are more peaceful than the lively shores of north and central Goa. Many beaches now have shacks serving beer, snacks, and seafood, lively flea markets, and vendors offering a variety of services from head massages to dolphin-watching boat trips.

GATEWAY OF INDIA, MUMBAI Built to commemorate the visit of King George V, the Gateway was the first sight to greet travelers to Indian shores during the heyday of the British Raj.

GETTING AROUND This region has international airports at Mumbai, Bangalore, Dabolim in Goa, Chennai, Thiruvananthapuram, and Hyderabad. With domestic airports at other smaller cities, the region is well connected by air. The Indian Railways also cover the region extensively. Fast trains run between the large cities, and air-conditioned trains also connect most medium-sized cities and townships. The hinterland is crisscrossed with national highways, and both major and minor roads. The region is also well connected by bus; private operators run luxury tour buses on the more popular routes, including the Mumbai–Pune and Mumbai–Goa–Hampi stretch. Cruises to Lakshadweep are available from Kochi, and to the Andamans from Chennai, Kolkata, and Visakhapatnam.

3 Old Goa

A magnificent complex of cathedrals, churches, and monasteries, spread along a 1-mile (1.5-km) stretch, marks the quaint site of Old Goa, the capital of Portuguese territories in India until the mid-18th century.

BASILICA DE BOM JESUS
The Basilica de Bom Jesus is revered by Roman Catholics all over the world, as it houses the sacred remains of Goa's patron saint, Francis Xavier. This Baroque structure blends Corinthian, Doric, Ionic, and composite styles in its magnificent three-tiered facade.

BRAGANZA HOUSE
The awesome scale of Braganza House and the magnificence of its interior make this Goa's grandest colonial mansion. The top floors of the private apartments contain a splendid ballroom, library, and chapel, as well as fine collections of 18th-century furniture and exquisite Chinese porcelain.

4 The Caves of Ajanta and Ellora

A UNESCO World Heritage Site, the 30 extraordinary rock-cut caves at Ajanta lie within a horseshoe-shaped escarpment. The earliest and finest examples of Buddhist painting in India can be seen in these caves. The Ellora group consists of 34 rock-cut caves, the finest of which is the magnificent Kailasanatha Temple.

5 Mysore

An important cultural center, Mysore is renowned for its ivory work, silk weaving, sandalwood incense, and carvings. In the heart of the city is the Amba Vilas Palace, a treasure house of exquisite carvings and works of art from all over the world. The main block of the palace features domes, turrets, arches, and colonnades in the Indo-Saracenic style. During weekends and festivals, thousands of light bulbs enliven the palace's stern gray exterior.

6 Hyderabad

Located in the heart of the Deccan plateau, Hyderabad was once the seat of the powerful and wealthy Nizams. The city's sights include the grand palaces of its erstwhile rulers, as well as the colorful bazaars and mosques of the old city.

CHARMINAR
Charminar ("Four Towers") is Hyderabad's signature landmark, with grand arches framing its four sides. Today, Charminar is a busy commercial area, where the grand mosques and palaces are surrounded by lively bazaars.

FALAKNUMA PALACE
The most opulent of the Nizams' many palaces, the facade of the Falaknuma Palace is in the Palladian style, while the rear is a jumble of Indo-Saracenic domes and cupolas. The tooled leather ceilings were created by Florentine craftsmen, and furniture and tapestries were ordered from France.

GOLCONDA FORT
Just outside Hyderabad city, the colossal Golconda "Shepherd's Hill" Fort was the citadel of the Qutb Shahi dynasty, which ruled from 1507 to 1687.

7 Chennai

Formerly known as Madras, Chennai is the state capital of Tamil Nadu and the gateway to the rich and varied culture of the south Indian peninsula. It is the region's commercial and cultural capital, and the fourth-largest metropolis in India.

ST. ANDREWS KIRK
A magnificent example of Neo-Classical architecture, St. Andrew's Kirk was consecrated in 1821. The body of the church is a circle, with rectangular compartments to the east and west. It is crowned by a shallow dome and is supported by 16 fluted pillars with Corinthian capitals.

A WALK ALONG THE MARINA
Chennai's seashore hosts one of India's largest urban beaches, the Marina, which stretches for 8 miles (13 km). This marine promenade is a favorite place for Chennai's citizens to escape the humid heat.

8 Pondicherry

Often described as a sleepy French provincial town, this former French colony retains a distinct Gallic flavor. Pondicherry's main promenade, the 2-mile- (3-km-) long Goubert Salai, running along the Bay of Bengal, formed part of the French Quarter, with its elegant colonial mansions, tree-lined boulevards, and bars and cafés.

9 Ruins of Hampi

Located on the south bank of the Tungabhadra River in Karnataka, Hampi is a UNESCO World Heritage Site where the evocative ruins of Vijayanagar, or the "City of Victory," lie. The key sites to visit here include the Virupaksha Temple, the Vitthala Temple, the Narasimha Monolith, and the Lotus Mahal.

ELEPHANTA ISLAND, MUMBAI
The 18-ft- (5.5-m-) high Mahesamurti, the three-headed statue of Lord Shiva, dominates the Hindu cave temple.

10 Kerala

Kerala is an enchanting mosaic of coconut groves and paddy fields, wide beaches, labyrinthine waterways (the backwaters), verdant hills, and rainforests. Its outstanding natural beauty has earned it the title "God's own country."

BACKWATERS CRUISE
A cruise along the backwaters is one of the most enchanting experiences that Kerala offers. The network of waterways weave through villages set amid lush vegetation, offering glimpses of Kerala's rural lifestyle.

AYURVEDA THERAPY
Ayurvedic treatment using special herbal oils is widely practiced in Kerala. Two well-known centers are the Kairali Ayurvedic Health Resort at Palakkad and Arya Vaidyasala in Kottakal.

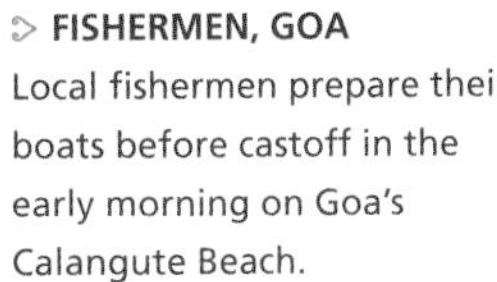

FISHERMEN, GOA
Local fishermen prepare their boats before castoff in the early morning on Goa's Calangute Beach.

Tourist destinations throughout India offer a wide range of accommodations to suit every taste and budget. Visitors can choose from modern Western-style deluxe hotels and grand old palaces or simple hotels, bungalows, and dormitory lodgings. Restaurants offer anything from local snacks to pizzas and pasta to sophisticated multicourse meals accompanied by local and imported wines. International restaurant chains now have outlets in most big towns. For those wishing to purchase local goods, India's superb tradition of textiles, arts, and crafts makes shopping in this country a tremendous experience. Traditional bazaars and markets coexist with the convenient multistory department stores and shopping malls of urban India.

ROHET GARH, JODHPUR
A 17th-century palace near Jodhpur, Rohet Garh is now a classified heritage hotel.

CAFÉ MONDEGAR, MUMBAI
Visitors can savor a meal at Café Mondegar, one of bustling Mumbai's many restaurants.

CIDADE DE GOA, GOA
This luxurious beach resort is situated on the serene Vainguinim beach.

Where to Stay

A wide choice of accommodation is offered to the rising number of visitors to India. Prices vary accordingly, depending on the quality of services offered, and the location. The hotel bill includes taxes levied by the federal and state governments, as well as local taxes such as sales tax and service tax.

LUXURY HOTELS
India's luxury hotels are comparable with the best found anywhere in the world. They offer spacious suites and rooms, excellent service, and a host of amenities. Staff are polite and attentive and can often help plan itineraries.

HERITAGE HOTELS
Several palaces, forts, and *havelis*, particularly in Rajasthan, Madhya Pradesh, Himachal Pradesh, and Gujarat, have been restored, modernized, and converted into plush luxury hotels. These establishments have an old-world charm, and many are still run by former princely families, who treat visitors like honored guests. Classified as Grand, Classic, and Ordinary under the umbrella of the Heritage Hotels Association of India (HHAI), these hotels can be booked through private agencies or well-known travel agents.

MIDDLE-RANGE HOTELS
Three- and four-star hotels offer a scaled-down version of five-star luxury and are less expensive. Levels of comfort, cleanliness, and professional services offered are, however, high. Rooms are air-conditioned and have private bathrooms.

BUDGET HOTELS AND TOURIST LODGES
Budget hotels are often found around bus stands and train stations. They are inexpensive, with simple decor, Indian or Western-style toilets, ceiling fans, and basic food options usually served in a dining hall. The tariff in major cities is higher than in the smaller towns. An excellent option, particularly in lesser-known tourist destinations, is the countrywide network of tourist bungalows and lodges run by the state tourism departments. Moderately priced, they offer both private rooms and dormitory accommodations.

DAK BUNGALOWS
Government-run *dak* bungalows (inns with very basic facilities) are cheap, clean, and conveniently located. Although not easily available for public use, visitors can contact the local or district authorities for help in making reservations. Visitors should book in advance as priority usually goes to visiting officials.

YOUTH HOSTELS
India has an excellent network of youth hostels. Although these are available at very low rates, they also tend to fill up quickly. Members of the Youth Hostel Association of India and Youth Hostel International get priority bookings, but nonmembers can reserve a room for a higher fee. Both room and dorm-style accommodations are available. The YMCA is better equipped, though more expensive, and located in fewer towns.

Where to Eat

Indian cuisine is as rich in variety as the country itself. The flavors of classical cuisine that developed in the imperial courts of Delhi, Kashmir, Hyderabad, and Lucknow are complemented by a vast range of regional specialties. From the arid deserts of Rajasthan come chilli-hot robust curries, whereas fish dominates the cuisine of the lush coastal areas of West Bengal, Goa, and Kerala. The cuisine of Gujarat and Tamil Nadu is mostly vegetarian.

TRAVELERS' NEEDS

HOTELS, SHOPS, AND PLACES TO EAT

RAJASTHANI PUPPETS
Brightly colored puppets wearing traditional dresses can be bought in Sireh Deori Bazaar in Jaipur.

RESTAURANTS
Most urban restaurants are air-conditioned, and the more expensive ones offer decor and service that is comparable with international standards. Traditional eating places are usually large, noisy halls catering to a local clientele. Simple and wholesome (mainly vegetarian) meals are served here. The growing appreciation for international cuisine has led to a rise in upscale specialty restaurants in most major cities.

ROADSIDE AND MARKET FOOD STANDS
Improvised stands, vans, or carts, equipped with stoves and other cooking appliances, dish out tasty meals with speed and efficiency. The choice ranges from vegetarian snacks, to tandoori chicken, kebabs, "fish fry," and Indian-style Chinese chow mein and spring rolls. Unpretentious eateries also serve good fast food. These include the North Indian *dhabas* (which serve both nonvegetarian and vegetarian food), the Goan beach shacks (which specialize in fish curries with rice), and the South Indian Udipi restaurants (which serve only vegetarian meals).

Shops and Markets

Shopping in India is a fascinating experience, since the bazaars and boutiques showcase a wide range of the country's decorative arts and crafts. The quality can vary, but the choice is enormous.

DEPARTMENT STORES AND BOUTIQUES
Plush, air-conditioned department stores, malls, and plazas, as well as upscale boutiques, are now a regular feature in most large towns. International brands of cosmetics, perfume, fashion accessories, home appliances, glassware, and more are also available here. Boutiques specialize in popular Indian designer labels, including high-fashion Western-style and traditional Indian apparel.

GOVERNMENT EMPORIA
All state governments have special outlets, with fixed prices, selling textiles and handicrafts from the region. These emporia have large premises in all state capitals, and although the range and quality of the items vary, they are ideal places to shop for gifts and souvenirs.

CRAFT CENTERS AND BAZAARS
The diversity of traditional Indian crafts is one of the attractions of traveling in this country. In some smaller villages, it is possible to observe artisans at work and buy directly from them. Shopping in local bazaars, with their noise and color, is a unique experience. Located in the heart of the old quarters, bazaars are typically a maze of tiny shops and sidewalk stands, selling a variety of merchandise, from flowers, vegetables, and other fresh produce, to cooking utensils, textiles, and jewelry.

SPECIALTY STORES
Specialty stores have built their reputation on the quality of the merchandise they sell. The passion for antiques has led to a proliferation of shops selling bronzes, stone sculpture, and metal artifacts. Jaipur, Udaipur, and Jodhpur specialize in high-quality miniatures, folk paintings, jewelry, and religious *pichhwais* on cloth. India's renowned textile tradition ranges from South India's glorious silk saris and Varanasi's brocades to fine handwoven cottons, in a wide range of designs and colors. Tea, spices, herbal products, and incense are also popular items.

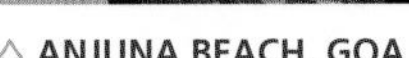

ANJUNA BEACH, GOA
A woman sells sarongs at the Anjuna flea market. Silver jewelry, richly dyed fabrics, and trinkets are also sold there.

CHOR BAZAAR, MUMBAI
Mumbai's Chor Bazaar is a treasure trove of antiques, including old clocks and gramophones.

BRASS WATER POT
An essential household item in villages, these pots are now available in antique shops.

GARLANDS, KOLKATA
This flower-seller displays garlands on a pavement in Kolkata. Garlands are used during auspicious ceremonies.

TRAVELERS' TIPS

- It is worth negotiating for a good discount on accommodations, as flexible prices dominate the market during the off-peak season (April–September).
- Book well in advance during the peak tourist season (October–March). Getting a reservation confirmed in writing is a sensible precaution.
- Indians eat with their fingers, and there is usually a washbasin on the premises for washing hands before and after a meal. Restaurants also often provide finger bowls with warm water and lemon for this purpose.
- Credit cards are usually accepted in upscale restaurants. However, always keep cash on hand to pay for meals at eateries in small towns and cafés.
- Most shops in the principal shopping areas in urban India are open from about 10 am to 7:30 pm. Government emporia have fixed shopping hours, from 10 am to 6 pm, with a lunch break between 1 pm and 2 pm.
- A good way to get the best results when bargaining is to check out costs and quality at a number of outlets to make sure you are getting a good deal.

India receives over 2.2 million visitors each year. The peak season is in winter (October–March), and it is wise to book your trip ahead during this time. English is widely spoken in most parts of the country, so communication is rarely a problem. Tourist infrastructure is of international standards in the larger cities; the remoter areas offer fairly basic accommodations, and some areas are still not equipped to cater to the international tourist, who may seek banking services or prefer to pay by credit card. The Department of Tourism has offices across the country that provide brochures, itineraries, and guided tours. There are many travel agencies in India, but it is wise to approach an established one for accommodations, tickets, and tours.

Indian Etiquette

India is still a traditional society, governed by strong family values. Respect for elders is deeply ingrained, so it is important to treat older people with special courtesy.

GREETING PEOPLE

The traditional greeting in India is *namaskar* or *namaste* (pronounced "nah-MAH-stay") when meeting or parting. The palms are pressed together, raised toward the face, and the head is bent slightly forward.

BODY LANGUAGE

The feet are considered to be the lowliest part of the body, and shoes are treated as unclean. Putting your feet up on the furniture is considered bad manners, as is touching someone inadvertently with your feet. If you are sitting on the floor, as is often the case, try to keep your feet tucked underneath rather than stretched out.

AT A PLACE OF WORSHIP

Whether you are visiting a Hindu temple, Buddhist monastery, Islamic mosque, or Sikh *gurdwara*, make sure that you behave and dress appropriately. Women should wear dresses that cover the upper arms, and are at least mid-calf in length, and should take a scarf along to cover the head.

Banking and Local Currency

The Indian rupee (Rs) is divided into 100 paisas. The most commonly used coins are 50-paisa and 1-, 2-, and 5-rupee coins. Currency notes are available in denominations of Rs5, 10, 20, 50, 100, 500, and 1,000. Foreign nationals are not permitted to bring or take Indian currency into or out of the country.

BANKING FACILITIES

India provides a range of accessible banking facilities and money exchange services, with English-speaking staff at the counters. These facilities are available in all the larger cities, at international airports, major banks and hotels, travel agencies, and registered exchange bureaus. Touts might offer enticing exchange rates, but they are illegal operators and should be avoided. Traveler's checks are the safest way to carry money, but always try to keep some cash for telephones, tips, transportation, and purchases, especially when traveling in smaller towns. Most foreign, and many Indian, banks in large cities have 24-hour ATMs; instructions are displayed in English, and cash is dispensed in rupees. Check with your bank at home which Indian banks will accept your ATM card, as not all machines are compatible.

SACHIYA MATA TEMPLE, RAJASTHAN Veiled women descend the temple steps. It is respectful to cover the head with a scarf when visiting places of worship in India.

Communications

The Indian postal system is fairly efficient, with a wide variety of options offered by post offices countrywide. All major hotels have business centers, and most markets, even in smaller towns, have shops or booths from where international calls can be made, emails sent, and the Internet accessed. A range of English-language newspapers and magazines are available, and foreign newspapers and magazines are sold in bookstores. Courier services are available across the country. While it is better to ship larger items such as furniture by regular land, sea, or air cargo, letters, documents, or smaller packages are best sent by courier.

SURVIVAL GUIDE

TRAVEL AND COMMUNICATIONS

▷ **OVERPASS, DELHI**
A man rides an elephant over a Delhi overpass, alongside traffic of camels, bicycles, auto rickshaws, and cars.

Traveling by Air

Most international visitors to India arrive by air, though road and ferry links also connect India and her neighboring countries. Air fares vary according to the airline and the season.

ARRIVING BY AIR
The country's four main international airports are at Delhi, Mumbai, Kolkata, and Chennai. Air India is the country's international carrier, and all major international airlines fly to India, usually as stopovers on routes between the East and West.

DOMESTIC AIR TRAVEL
The state-run Indian Airlines offers the widest choice of routes and the most frequent services. Private airlines also cover a number of cities and offer excellent services. There are a few low-cost airlines that connect even smaller cities. The fares are cheap, but be prepared for delays and cancellations.

Traveling by Train

For most visitors, train journeys add a fascinating new dimension to their experience of India—there are few better ways of getting to know the people and seeing the countryside. Trains are always crowded, so try to book your tickets in advance.

TRAINS AND TIMETABLES
Of the three kinds of trains (passenger, express, and mail), it is best to take the air-conditioned express trains, as they have fewer stops and offer better facilities. A printed schedule is available in most station bookstores, and train times can be checked on the official website: www.indianrail.gov.in.

TICKET RESERVATIONS
It is important to make train bookings well in advance for a confirmed reservation. Most railroad stations now have computerized ticket counters, though hotel travel counters or travel agents can also arrange them for a fee.

Traveling by Road

India has an extensive network of major and minor roads, as well as a number of well-maintained national highways, linking all the major cities. Driving is on the left, with right-hand-drive cars. Indian traffic, particularly in the cities, is very chaotic, so visitors are strongly advised to hire a driver along with a rental car, rather than try to negotiate the roads themselves.

CAR RENTAL
A number of international car rental companies, hotels, and taxi stands provide excellent car rental services.

BUSES
India has an extensive bus network, offering excellent connections to most cities as well as to the remotest parts of the country. Tour buses are usually much more comfortable, with air conditioning.

LOCAL TRANSPORTATION
Transit options vary from city to city. Many large cities have reliable bus, taxi, and auto rickshaw services. The main cities also have suburban trains and metro rails that provide speedy connections to areas within the city limits. In the smaller towns and in the old quarters of cities, it is better to opt for a small, light vehicle to cut through narrow, congested lanes.

Traveling by Ferry

A busy network of passenger ferries serves places along India's east and west coasts, and luxury cruises link the mainland to the Lakshadweep Islands as well as to the Andamans.

△ **PASSENGER TRAIN**
A typical multiclass passenger train linking towns in the Bikaner district of Rajasthan, western India.

◁ **THE MAHARAJA**
The Maharaja is the mascot of Air India, the country's international airline.

▷ **RICKSHAW**
A cycle rickshaw touts for customers at Delhi's Shivaji Stadium Terminal.

TRAVELERS' TIPS

- If you have booked internal flights before leaving for India, make sure you reconfirm on arrival. Flight cancellations and delays due to bad weather conditions in winter are common, so remember to reconfirm your ticket and departure times.
- If you need assistance with your luggage at railway stations, look for the licensed porters, or "coolies", who wear a red shirt, and an armband with a metal tag bearing a licence number on it. These official railway porters are well informed about delays and platform changes, which might not always be announced. Note your porter's armband number because you could lose sight of him in the crowds. His tariff will vary according to the weight of the luggage.
- Indian bus and railway stations can often be crowded and confusing. Keep your cool, make sure your valuables are stowed safely, and keep an eye out for pickpockets who take advantage of the chaos.
- Often taxi and auto rickshaw meters are not updated. You should ask for a tariff chart when in doubt or negotiate the price at the start of the journey.

INDEX

Page numbers in **bold** indicate main references

ACKNOWLEDGMENTS

The publisher would like to thank the following for their kind permission to reproduce their photographs:

(Key: a–above; b–below/bottom; c–center; f–far; l–left; r–right; t–top)

2 Corbis: Milepost 92 1/2 (b/Train). **3 Christopher Pillitz:** (t, cl).**6-7 Pradeep Bhatia:** Courtesy of Mrs Superna Bhatia. **8-9 Amit Pasricha. 10-11 Photolibrary:** Michele Falzone. **12-13 Photolibrary:** Hemis. **14-15 Photolibrary:** Anne Montfort. **16-17 Corbis:** Robert Harding World Imagery / Jochen Schlenker. **18-19 Mountain Images:** Ian Evans. **20-21 Getty Images:** Macduff Everton. **22-23 Axiom Photographic Agency:** Timothy Allen. **24-25 Axiom Photographic Agency:** Timothy Allen. **26-27 Corbis:** Lindsay Hebberd. **28-29 Corbis:** epa. **30-31 Corbis:** Amit Bhargava. **32-33 Lonely Planet Images:** Keren Su. **34-35 Photolibrary:** Walter Bibikow. **36-37 Getty Images:** Panoramic Images. **38-39 Fredrik Arvidsson. 40-41 Alfred Molon Photo Galleries. 42-43 Corbis:** Milepost 92 1/2. **44-45 Photolibrary:** Dinodia Photo. **46-47 Axiom Photographic Agency:** Karoki Lewis Phot41. **48-49 Getty Images:** Macduff Everton. **50-51 FLPA:** Sierra Madre / Patricio Robles Gil. **52-53 Amit Pasricha. 54-55 SuperStock:** V. Muthuraman. **56-57 Getty Images:** Panoramic Images. **58-59 Amit Pasricha. 60-61 Getty Images:** AFP / Deshakayan Chowdhury. **62-63 Corbis:** Stapleton Collection. **64 The Art Archive:** National Museum, Karachi (bl). **The Bridgeman Art Library:** National Museum of India, New Delhi (tc). **DK Images:** National Museum of India, New Delhi (br). **65 akg-images:** François Guénet (tr). **Alamy Images:** Richard Wareham Fotografie (bl). **The Bridgeman Art Library:** National Museum of India, New Delhi (cb). **Corbis:** Angelo Hornak (tl/Inset). **DK Images:** National Museum of India, New Delhi (tl). **66 The Art Archive:** (bl). **Corbis:** The Art Archive (tl). **66-67 akg-images:** Gérard Degeorge. **67 akg-images:** Gérard Degeorge (br). **68 akg-images:** Jean-Louis Nou (cla). **DK Images:** Dinesh Khanna (clb). **69 Alamy Images:** Visual Arts Library (London) (bl). **The Trustees of the British Museum:** (tl, cb). **Wellcome Library, London:** (cra). **Wikipedia, The Free Encyclopedia:** (br). **70 akg-images:** British Museum, London / Erich Lessing (bc). **Alamy Images:** World Religions Photo Library (tl). **71 Wikipedia, The Free Encyclopedia. 72 akg-images:** Musée du Louvre, Paris / Erich Lessing (bc). **British Library:** Add. 16624, whole manuscript (l). **DK Images:** National Museum of India, New Delhi (crb). Courtesy of **The Oriental Research Institute, University of Mysore:** National Mission for Manuscripts, New Delhi (tr). **73 akg-images:** Archaeological Museum, Sarnath / Jean-Louis Nou (bc). **Alamy Images:** Mary Evans Picture Library (t). **74 The Art Archive:** Musée Guimet, Paris / Dagli Orti (tl). **Wikipedia, The Free Encyclopedia:** (c, bc, clb). **75 Corbis:** Lindsay Hebberd (tr); Charles & Josette Lenars (b). **76 DK Images:** Archaeological Museum, Amravati / M. Balan; Judith Miller / Cooper Owen (tr). **Réunion des Musées Nationaux Agence Photographique:** Thierry Ollivier (bc). **77 The Trustees of the British Museum:** (tl). **Corbis:** Richard Cummins (bl); Macduff Everton (tr). **78 Werner Forman Archive:** Private Collection (cr). **Wikipedia, The Free Encyclopedia:** (cl). **79 akg-images:** British Library, London (tc); Jean-Louis Nou (cra). **Alamy Images:** Steve Allen Travel Photography (bl). **Wikipedia, The Free Encyclopedia:** (bc). **80 Alamy Images:** Dinodia Images (cla). **The Bridgeman Art Library:** (bl). **Corbis:** Lindsay Hebberd (tc). **Wikipedia, The Free Encyclopedia:** (tr). **81 The Bridgeman Art Library:** National Museum of India, New Delhi (t). **The Trustees of the British Museum:** (bc). **82 Alamy Images:** David Noble Photography (tl). **Wikipedia, The Free Encyclopedia:** (bc). **83 Alamy Images:** Travelib Asia. **84 Alamy Images:** James Burger (br); INTERFOTO Pressebildagentur (bl); Simon Reddy (tr). **Wikipedia, The Free Encyclopedia:** (tl). **85 Alamy Images:** Visual Arts Library (London) (tr). **The Bridgeman Art Library:** National Museum of India, New Delhi (cb). **Corbis:** Reuters / Sherwin Crasto (br). **86 akg-images:** Bogd-Khan-Museum, Ulan Bator (bl). **The Trustees of the British Museum:** (tl). **87 Alamy Images:** Wolfgang Kaehler. **88 The Bridgeman Art Library:** Edinburgh University Library, Scotland, With kind permission of the University of Edinburgh (bl). **DK Images:** National Museum of India, New Delhi (c); Ram Rahman (br). **89 Alamy Images:** Jon Arnold Images Ltd (tl); **Getty Images:** National Geographic (tr, b). **90 Alamy Images:** ArkReligion.com (bl). **The Bridgeman Art Library:** The Stapleton Collection (bc). **DK Images:** Fredrik and Laurence Arvidsson (tr). **Photolibrary:** Japan Travel Bureau (cl). **91 Alamy Images:** Trip (tl). **The Art Archive:** Atelier Hocquet Musée de L'Eventail, Paris / Dagli Orti (bl). **The Bridgeman Art Library:** British Library, London (c). **DK Images:** Judith Miller / Lyon and Turnbull Ltd (bc); National Museum of India, New Delhi (tr). **92 Alamy Images:** Dinodia Images (br). **The Art Archive:** British Library, London (tl). **The Bridgeman Art Library:** Victoria & Albert Museum, London (bl). **Getty Images:** Photofina / Gavin Gough (tr). **93 Alamy Images:** The Print Collector (br); Visual Arts Library (London) (tr). **The Bridgeman Art Library:** Royal Asiatic Society, London (bl). **The Trustees of the British Museum:** (c). **94 The Art Archive:** Bodleian Library, Oxford (tl). **The Trustees of the British Museum:** (bc/Inset). **DK Images:** National Museum of India, New Delhi (bc). **95 Alamy Images:** Arco Images. **Corbis:** Martin Harvey (br). **96 akg-images:** Taj Mahal Museum, Agra / Jean-Louis Nou (bl). **Alamy Images:** Dinodia Images (tr). **The Bridgeman Art Library:** Phoenix Art Museum, Arizona, Gift of George P. Bickford (br); Victoria & Albert Museum, London (tl). **97 Alamy Images:** Robert Harding Picture Library Ltd (tc); Joan Swinnerton (bc). **V&A Images:** (tl). **98 Alamy Images:** Mary Evans Picture Library (tr); Visual Arts Library (London) (bl). **The Bridgeman Art Library:** British Library, London (cl). **The Trustees of the British Museum:** (tc). **V&A Images:** (br). **99 The Bridgeman Art Library:** British Library, London (crb); Royal Geographical Society, London (bl); Victoria & Albert Museum, London (tr). **100 Alamy Images:** David Hosking (tr/Background). **The Art Archive:** (tl). **The Bridgeman Art Library:** National Army Museum, London, Courtesy of the Council (br). **British Library:** Add. 41300, f.73 (bl). **DK Images:** Courtesy of the National Railway Museum, New Delhi (tr). **101 Alamy Images:** Classic Image (tr). **DK Images:** (cla); Bobby Kohli (b). **102 Alamy Images:** Dinodia Images (tl). **103 Alamy Images:** Dinodia Images(br). **104 Alamy Images:** Mary Evans Picture Library (cb). **Corbis:** Angelo Hornak (t). **Getty Images:** Hulton Archive / Stringer (bl); IPC Magazines / Picture Post (br). **105 Alamy Images:** Mary Evans Picture Library (tr). **Corbis:** Bettmann (b). **106 Alamy Images:** Tim Graham (bc). **Getty Images:** AFP / Raveendran (c). **107 www.dinodia.com:** (tr, bc, bl). **Getty Images:** Adrian Murrell (crb); Popperfoto (tc). **108 DK Images:** Bharath Ramamrutham (tl). **Getty Images:** AFP / Douglas E. Curran (b); AFP / Romeo Gacad (c). **109 www.dinodia.com:** (br). **The Kobal Collection:** DAMFX (tl). **Wikipedia, The Free Encyclopedia:** (cr). **110 Alamy Images:** PCL (clb). **Corbis:** Reuters / Dave Amit (ca). **Nick Dean:** (cla). **110-111 Panos Pictures:** Atul Loke (b). **111 Getty Images:** AFP / Raveendran (tl). **Indian Space Research Organisation:** (tc). **112-113 Getty Images:** The Image Bank / Peter Adams. **190 Alamy:** Danita Delimont (tc). **216-217 British Library:** Add. 15295, f.2. **218 DK Images:** Courtesy of the Archaeological Museum, Alampur / M. Balan (l). **219 Alamy Images:** V&A Images (br). **The Bridgeman Art Library:** India Office Library, London / Ann & Bury Peerless Picture Library (tl). **220 Alamy Images:** Martin Broeze. **221 The Bridgeman Art Library:** The Stapleton Collection. **222 DK Images:** National Museum of India, New Delhi. **223 DK Images:** St Mungo, Glasgow Museums / Ellen Howdon. **224 The Bridgeman Art Library:** The Stapleton Collection (bl). **Corbis:** Lindsay Hebberd (tr). **225 DK Images:** National Museum of India, New Delhi. **226 Alamy Images:** Dinodia Images. **227 Alamy Images:** Dariusz Klemens (br). **British Library:** Add. 24099, f.118 (tl). **228 DK Images:** Barnabas Kindersley (tr). **Getty Images:** AFP / Noah Seelam (bl). **229 Alamy Images:** ArkReligion.com. **230-231 DK Images:** Bharath Ramamrutham (c). **232-233 Corbis:** Peter Adams. **235 Alamy Images:** Tribaleye Images / J. Marshall (tr). **Getty Images:** Panoramic Images (b). **236 Alamy Images:** World Religions Photo Library. **237 Getty Images:** AFP / Prakash Singh. **238 Getty Images:** AFP / Dibyangshu Sarkar. **239 The Bridgeman Art Library:** Musée Guimet, Paris / Giraudon (br). **240 Getty Images:** AFP / Douglas E. Curran. **241 British Library:** Mss.Panj.B.40, f.184v. **243 Corbis:** Reuters / Kishore Kamal. **244 Alamy Images:** Dinodia Images. **245 Alamy Images:** Dinodia Images. **246 The Art Archive:** Marco Polo Gallery, Paris / Dagli Orti. **247 Alamy Images:** Hornbil Images (br). **The Bridgeman Art Library:** Victoria & Albert Museum, London (tl). **248 Alamy Images:** Dinodia Images. **249 British Library:** J.35,29. **250 Alamy Images:** Dinodia Images (tl, tr). **Corbis:** Hemis / Paule Seux (tc). **250-251 Corbis:** Martin Harvey (c). **252 www.dinodia.com. 253 www. dinodia.com. 254 Alamy Images:** Tom Allwood (bl); Fredrik Renander (tr). **255 Werner Forman Archive:** Private Collection. **256 Alamy Images:** Photos 12. **257 Getty Images:** Taxi / DreamPictures. **258 akg-images:** National Museum of India, New Delhi / Jean-Louis Nou (bl). **Corbis:** Lindsay Hebberd (tc). **259 DK Images:** St Mungo, Glasgow Museums / Ellen Howdon. **260 DK Images:** Aditya Patankar. **261 Alamy Images:** Dinodia Images (br); Visual Arts Library (London) (bc). **Corbis:** Brooklyn Museum (tl). **262-263 DK Images:** Akhil Bahkshi. **264 Corbis:** Angelo Hornak. **265 Alamy Images:** Tim Gainey (br). **Wikipedia, The Free Encyclopedia:** (tl). **266 The Bridgeman Art Library:** Bibliothèque Nationale, Paris / Archives Charmet (tr). **267 Alamy Images:** Steve Bloom Images. **268 Corbis:** Baldev (bl); Michael Freeman (tr). **269 British Library:** Add. 5639, xcix. **270-271 akg-images:** Bharat Kala Bhawan Museum, Benares / François Guénet. **272 DK Images:** Courtesy of the Crafts Museum, New Delhi. **273 Alamy Images:** Tim Gainey (l). **DK Images:** Courtesy of the Crafts Museum, New Delhi / Akhil Bakshi (tr). **274 The Bridgeman Art Library:** (bl). **275 The Bridgeman Art Library:** Fitzwilliam Museum, University of Cambridge. **276-277 Alamy Images:** Philip Bigg. **298 Alamy Images:** Photofrenetic (tl). **302 Corbis:** Yann Arthus-Bertrand (tl). **324 Corbis:** Yann Arthus-Bertrand (tl). **331 DK Images:** Dinesh Khanna (c). **332 Getty Images:** Panoramic Images (tl). **336-337 Alamy Images:** Hornbil Images (c). **339 Corbis:** Peter Adams (t). **342 SuperStock:** Hidekazu Nishibata (tl). **358 Fotomedia:** Manu Bahuguna (br). **365 Still Pictures:** A. Liedmann (tl).

Jacket Images: Pictures Colour Library: Adrian Pope (Front). **Corbis:** Milepost 92 1/2 (Back tr). **Christopher Pillitz:** (Back t, cl).**SuperStock:** Michele Burgess (Spine).

All other images © DK. For further information see: www.dkimages.com

18 Extracts from *Collected Poems 1970–2005* by Keki N. Daruwalla, and **39** *St. Cyril Road and other Poems* by Amit Chaudhuri both reproduced by permission of Penguin Books India; **36** extract from "Jaisalmer I" by Gulam Mohammed Sheikh from *The Oxford Anthology of Modern Indian Poetry*, reproduced by permission of Oxford University Press India, New Delhi; **270–71** extract from *The Bhagavad Gita* translated by Juan Mascaró (Penguin Classics, 1962) reproduced by permission of Penguin Books Ltd.

DK would like to thank Dr. Premlata Puri, Shanta Serbjeet Singh, and Philip Wilkinson for writing the Culture chapter; Guy Naronha; Ted Kinsey; Phil Hunt; Leila Samson; Bhavna and Shatrunjai Singh; Cherry Cherian and the CGH group; Col. Adil Mahmood; Bejoy and Bina George; Umrao Jewels (*see pp.160–61*); Shri Madhup Mudgal, principal Gandharva Mahavidyalaya (*see pp.190–91*); Rakesh Thakur (*see pp.128–29*); Mr. Raja, Meenakshi Temple; Ms. Jayashree, Padmanabhapuram Palace; Sri Mohammed K.K, ASI Bhopal Circle; Mr. Mahendra Alvarez of The Bigfoot in Loutulim; Dr. Adelia Costa of Quadros de Costa Mansion, Loutulim; Mr. Rajendra Sharma; all of DK General Books, Delhi, including Aparna Sharma, Kingshuk Ghoshal, Neha Ahuja, Pallavi Narain, Saloni Talwar, Shefali Upadhyay, Arunesh Talapatra, Romi Chakraborty, Neerja Rawat, Alicia Ingty, Dipali Singh, Aditi Ray, Pankaj Sharma, Dheeraj Arora, Harish Aggarwal, Preetam Singh, Jagtar Singh; Caroline Hunt for proofreading; and Hilary Bird for the index.

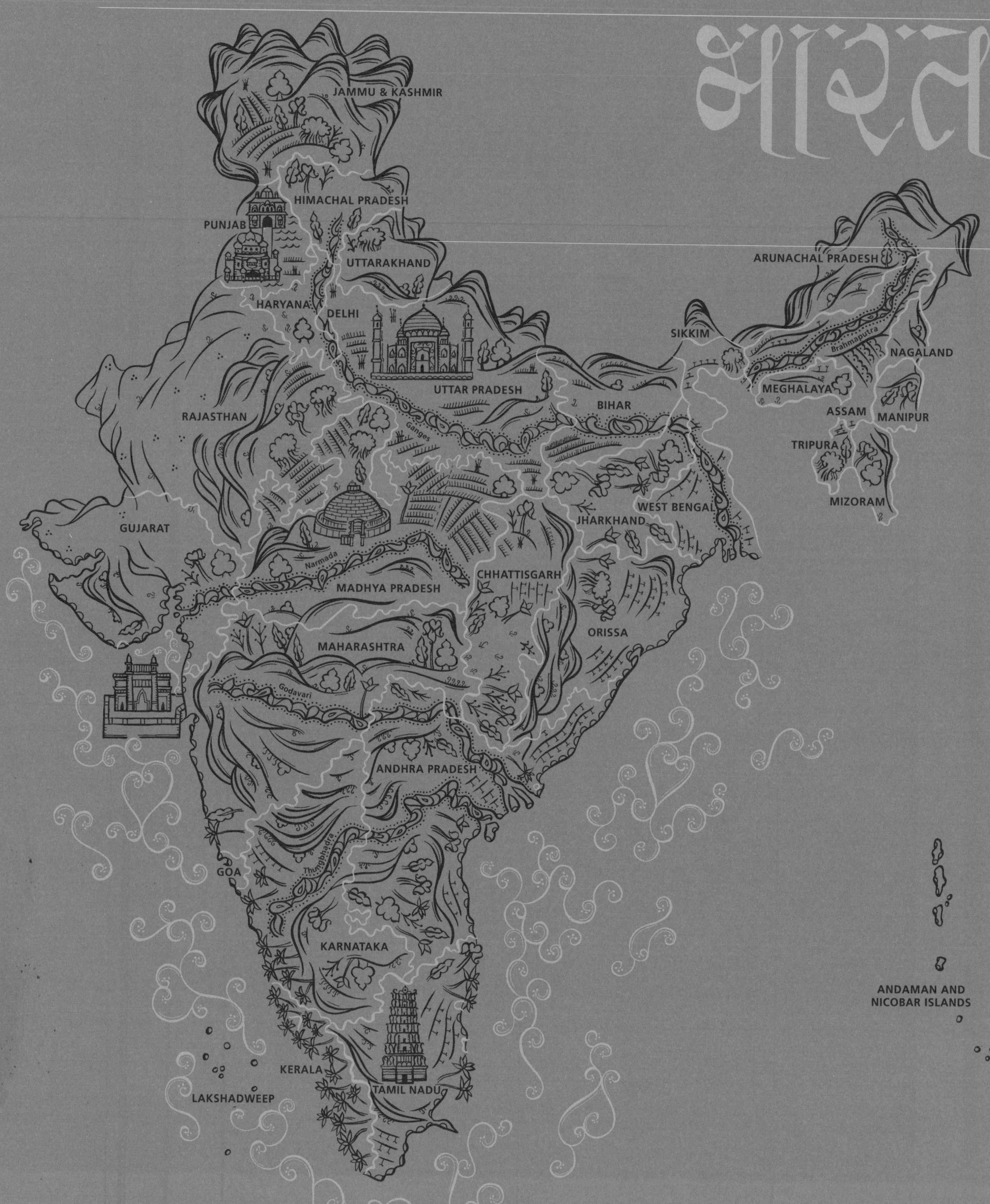
भारत
JAMMU & KASHMIR
HIMACHAL PRADESH
PUNJAB
UTTARAKHAND
HARYANA
DELHI
UTTAR PRADESH
RAJASTHAN
Ganges
SIKKIM
ARUNACHAL PRADESH
Brahmaputra
NAGALAND
MEGHALAYA
ASSAM
MANIPUR
BIHAR
TRIPURA
MIZORAM
WEST BENGAL
JHARKHAND
GUJARAT
Narmada
MADHYA PRADESH
CHHATTISGARH
ORISSA
MAHARASHTRA
Godavari
ANDHRA PRADESH
Thungbhadra
GOA
KARNATAKA
KERALA
TAMIL NADU
LAKSHADWEEP
ANDAMAN AND
NICOBAR ISLANDS